Decentralized Finance and Blockchain

Scrivener Publishing
100 Cummings Center, Suite 541J
Beverly, MA 01915-6106

Publishers at Scrivener
Martin Scrivener (martin@scrivenerpublishing.com)
Phillip Carmical (pcarmical@scrivenerpublishing.com)

Decentralized Finance and Blockchain

A Game Changing Duo

Edited by

Renuka Sharma
Chitkara Business School, Chitkara University, Punjab, India

Kiran Mehta
Chitkara Business School, Chitkara University, Punjab, India

Vishal Vyas
ABV-IIITM, Gwalior, Madhya Pradesh, India

and

Vinod Kumar Shukla
School of Engineering, Architecture & Interior Design, Amity University Dubai, UAE

Scrivener Publishing

WILEY

This edition first published 2025 by John Wiley & Sons, Inc., 111 River Street, Hoboken, NJ 07030, USA and Scrivener Publishing LLC, 100 Cummings Center, Suite 541J, Beverly, MA 01915, USA

For more information about Scrivener publications please visit www.scrivenerpublishing.com.

Wiley Global Headquarters
111 River Street, Hoboken, NJ 07030, USA

For details of our global editorial offices, customer services, and more information about Wiley products visit us at www.wiley.com.

The manufacturer's authorized representative according to the EU General Product Safety Regulation is Wiley-VCH GmbH, Boschstr. 12, 69469 Weinheim, Germany, e-mail: Product_Safety@wiley.com.

Library of Congress Cataloging-in-Publication Data

ISBN 978-1-394-24265-8

Cover image: Generated with AI using Adobe Firefly
Cover design by Russell Richardson

Set in size of 11pt and Minion Pro by Manila Typesetting Company, Makati, Philippines

Printed in the USA

10 9 8 7 6 5 4 3 2 1

Contents

Preface

In today's digital age, the convergence of blockchain technology and decentralized finance (DeFi) stands at the forefront of innovation, ushering in a new era of financial possibility. Few technological advancements have sparked as much excitement or shown such transformative potential. Together, these forces form a powerful synergy that is reshaping traditional financial systems and democratizing access to financial services on a global scale—breaking down barriers that have long excluded underserved populations from the financial mainstream.

Blockchain, with its inherent transparency, immutability, and decentralization, forms the backbone of the DeFi ecosystem. Unlike traditional centralized systems that rely on intermediaries to facilitate transactions, DeFi uses blockchain to create trustless environments where users can transact directly. This paradigm shift is revolutionizing how people engage with financial services, making them more accessible, cost-effective, and inclusive. By removing traditional gatekeepers, DeFi is opening new doors for individuals and businesses worldwide, especially in regions with limited access to conventional banking infrastructure.

The significance of researching the synergy between DeFi and blockchain lies in its potential to address critical challenges and uncover new opportunities within the evolving financial landscape. As these technologies advance, they are poised to redefine global financial norms—offering solutions that go far beyond mere convenience. DeFi applications such as decentralized exchanges, lending platforms, and smart contracts have the potential to greatly enhance financial inclusion, allowing individuals to save, invest, and transact securely without being limited by geography or institutional barriers.

However, these benefits come with challenges that demand thoughtful analysis and innovation. One of the most pressing concerns is scalability. As adoption of blockchain and DeFi continues to grow, so does the need for faster and more efficient transaction processing. Research into scalability solutions—such as layer-2 technologies and sharding—is essential to ensure the ecosystem can support its expanding user base. Security is another critical area, as the decentralized nature of DeFi can leave systems vulnerable to exploits and attacks. By advancing cryptographic techniques and developing robust security protocols, researchers can play a key role in building trust and resilience within the DeFi ecosystem.

Regulatory compliance remains a complex yet essential component in ensuring the sustainable growth of DeFi. Balancing the decentralized ethos of blockchain with the requirements of legal frameworks presents an ongoing challenge. Research in this area can offer valuable insights into how policymakers and industry leaders might collaborate to foster innovation while protecting users. Ultimately, examining the technological advancements, economic impacts, and potential risks associated with blockchain and DeFi contributes to a deeper understanding of their transformative potential. This research is vital not only for promoting economic empowerment and resilience but also for paving the way toward a more inclusive, efficient, and equitable financial future.

The chapter titles in this book reflect the multifaceted nature of this rapidly evolving field. Each chapter offers a distinct perspective, expanding our understanding of DeFi and blockchain technology. Chapter 1 focuses on cross-chain interoperability—a critical element for integrating blockchain networks and enabling seamless data and asset exchange across platforms. Chapter 2 explores the integration of artificial intelligence with DeFi, emphasizing how AI can enhance decision-making, improve user experiences, and strengthen security within decentralized ecosystems. In Chapter 3, the synergy between fintech and green finance is examined, highlighting how these technologies can drive sustainable development in response to global environmental challenges. Chapter 4 introduces the "money Lego" concept, illustrating the modular nature of DeFi and its capacity to create innovative, composable financial solutions. Chapter 5 offers a foundational overview of blockchain and cryptocurrency, providing newcomers with essential context for understanding the origins and mechanics of DeFi.

Chapter 6 provides a detailed analysis of the economic impact of cryptocurrencies through the lens of the PESTLE framework, offering insights into their implications for the Indian economy. Chapter 7 explores how blockchain technology is disrupting traditional banking systems, highlighting DeFi's potential to foster more inclusive and transparent financial models. In Chapter 8, the focus turns to safe-haven assets, illustrating how DeFi and blockchain enable individuals to protect and grow their wealth amid market volatility.

Chapter 9 explores DeFi-powered marketing, demonstrating how these technologies are revolutionizing customer engagement and reshaping marketing strategies. Chapter 10 offers a comparison between decentralized finance (DeFi) and centralized finance (CeFi), presenting a balanced analysis of their respective strengths, limitations, and the potential for coexistence within the broader financial ecosystem. Chapter 11 takes an empirical approach to green foreign direct investment, linking environmental efficiency with sustainable economic development and further reinforcing the book's sustainability focus. Finally, Chapter 12 examines the intersection of AI and blockchain in healthcare using network analysis, highlighting their combined potential to transform medical systems.

Together, these chapters weave a comprehensive narrative that addresses critical themes such as interoperability, sustainability, healthcare, marketing, and economic impact. They underscore the transformative potential of blockchain and DeFi across industries while fostering a deeper understanding of the challenges and opportunities ahead. This structure ensures the book remains relevant, insightful, and impactful for a wide-ranging audience—including academics, technologists, policymakers, and financial professionals.

In closing, we offer special thanks to Martin Scrivener and Scrivener Publishing for their support, guidance, and commitment to advancing scholarly work in this rapidly evolving field.

Editors
Renuka Sharma
Chitkara Business School, Chitkara University, Punjab, India
Kiran Mehta
Chitkara Business School, Chitkara University, Punjab, India
Vishal Vyas
ABV-IIITM, Gwalior, M.P., India
Vinod Kumar Shukla
School of Engineering, Architecture & Interior Design, Amity University Dubai, UAE
June 2025

1

A Comprehensive Analysis on Cross-Chain Interoperability in Blockchain

Cyriac Philip Alexander* **and Tabitha Durai**

Department of Commerce, Madras Christian College, University of Madras, Tambaram East, Tamil Nadu, India

Abstract

Blockchain interoperability is becoming increasingly important in the field of blockchain technology. Nonetheless, the required knowledge for attaining it is still scattered and incomplete. This reality presents a significant obstacle for the industry and academics in their efforts to establish seamless interoperability among blockchains. The proliferation of varied and specialized blockchains is a significant obstacle in cross-chain interoperability. This article rigorously evaluates the current methods for facilitating communication and transferring value between separate blockchain systems. We analyze the communication protocols, cross-chain procedures, and the challenges associated with achieving cross-chain interoperability in blockchain technology. Our primary recommendations emphasize the implications for investors, as well as the authorities and government. Finally, we explored the prospects and advancements in promoting smooth cross-chain interoperability within the ever-changing blockchain industry.

Keywords: Cross-chain interoperability, communication protocol, cross-chain mechanisms, blockchain, decentralized finance

1.1 Introduction

The blockchain underpins decentralized finance (DeFi) and secures transactions. The blockchain's consensus assures DeFi transaction integrity. The consensus method chooses blockchain ledger nodes. Nodes having

**Corresponding author*: cpalexander72@gmail.com

Renuka Sharma, Kiran Mehta, Vishal Vyas and Vinod Kumar Shukla (eds.) Decentralized Finance and Blockchain: A Game Changing Duo, (1–22) © 2025 Scrivener Publishing LLC

accounting permissions add DeFi application transactions to a block. DeFi's financial logic requires smart contracts [1]. Once launched on the blockchain, the smart contract is inaccessible. DeFi presents the oracle [2] to deliver trustworthy real-world financial asset pricing information. Cross-chain refers to the seamless transfer of assets and data between two distinct and independent blockchain ledgers. This could potentially include the movement of assets or the exchange of information between the two systems. When it comes to information, interoperability is all about being able to share and use information between different systems or modules. Cross-chain technology promotes trust and connectivity across chains, reducing blockchain isolation. It can benefit everyone by promoting asset interoperability between chains.

1.1.1 Decentralized Finance (DeFi)

The rapid expansion of the DeFi industry shows that digital currencies and decentralized platforms may challenge traditional finance, which has stifled innovation and disregarded financial inclusiveness. DeFi is laying the groundwork for unlimited, blockchain-driven financial services in the digital economy [3]. The financial environment is exposed to various types of risks [4–8]. DeFi offers several apps. Stablecoins, tied to the U.S. dollar, may be bought on decentralized exchanges. Money can be earned by transferring assets to a decentralized lending platform. These interest-bearing securities can then be placed in a decentralized liquidity pool or on-chain investment fund. The rapid growth of these assets and the launch of innovative protocols suggest that DeFi might be important in more domains [9].

DeFi has many benefits, but its creative character, quick expansion, unique technological aspects, and unpredictable social impact make it hard to explain. Less intermediaries mean DeFi users have greater accountability, which is vital to consider [10]. This includes securely storing their fund-accessing private keys. DeFi users may find banking services less convenient due to the extra obligation. The researchers have examined the cryptocurrency behavior as there is an increased interest of the investors in this digital financial instrument [8, 11]. End-users must understand DeFi to avoid mistakes and hazards when using the app. Conventional financial institutions such as asset management businesses and FinTechs, including crypto-asset exchanges, are adopting this ecosystem. In addition to offering DeFi-based services and products [12, 13]. Several techniques can be used to investigate the price movement of various financial instruments [14–16].

Customers worldwide use cellphones or PCs to access a 'DeX' or decentralized money exchange. A digital asset or 'token' is ordered there. Smart contracts automatically execute purchase orders with matching criteria. The token is transferred straight from the seller's wallet to the buyer's wallet since the user protects the assets. The token is held by the individual during the procedure. The seller and buyer become proud owners and custodians of the item after the exchange. Additionally, this commercial transaction guarantees anonymity [17]. The DeFi space is fast-evolving and becoming more sophisticated. In 2020, several fascinating new procedures emerged. Most protocols adopted new ideas like sophisticated staking strategies. Staking, especially staking incentives, drives DeFi space development. The rise may not be sustainable [18].

1.1.2 Blockchain

Ethereum, Bitcoin, as well as the Metaverse, are blockchain applications that depend on the blockchain. The market value of Bitcoin fell below 50% for the first time in May 2017, while Ethereum's transaction volume overtook Bitcoin's in August 2017. Private chains, public chains, as well as consortium chains are growing. Blockchain application scenarios are expanding, and the industry needs for cross-chain is clear. Social networks and 3D virtual environments have embraced the metaverse since Facebook rebranded itself as Metaverse in October 2021 [19].

According to research and industry efforts, cross-chain technology began with Ripple's 'Interledger Protocol' (ILP) in 2012. It allows cross-ledger transfer utilizing the notary method and offers a blockchain industry-first interoperability framework. Schwartz E., Hope-Bailie A., and Thomas S. presented an atomic swap in May 2013. This novel concept allows cross-chain asset exchange while ensuring transaction integrity [20, 21]. Interoperable chains enable asset transfers between platforms and payment-versus-payment and payment-versus-delivery methods. Retrieving data from 'identity chains' and payment systems is also possible. Third parties can integrate this without burdening base blockchain protocol operators. Chain interoperability has primarily been studied in theory until now. The major reason is that chain interoperability requires two stable blockchains. However, improvement is evident [22].

Biswas and Pillai [23] claim that "cross-communication is not intended to directly modify the state of another blockchain system. As an alternative, cross-communication must activate a certain set of features on the other system that is intended to operate in its network." Thus, the exchange procedure must match the system's goal. This divides interoperability into centralized and decentralized techniques. Personal cross-communication is initiated by a single entity and works directly between the sender and receiver blockchains. This allows information sharing in a constrained space. Smart contracts in a distributed context enable protocol-level cross-communication in a decentralized method [24–26].

1.1.3 Cross-Chain Interoperability in Blockchain

This study explores the importance of blockchain interoperability, as well as the significance of communication protocols and upcoming advancements and solutions. Exploring the potential interactions among numerous blockchains is an area that has yet to be fully explored. At present, a single blockchain can be used for various functions, such as transferring tokens between participants, implementing smart contracts written in a blockchain, and verifying the integrity of data stored in a blockchain [27].

Cross-chain interoperability helps shape blockchain functionalities by solving the limits of isolated and segregated blockchain networks. Interconnected blockchain ecosystem components increase efficiency, scalability, and functionality. A more linked and adaptive financial ecosystem is created by improving asset transfers and data interchange between blockchains. Cross-chain interoperability lets developers use unique features of multiple blockchains to create powerful and diverse decentralized apps. Cross-chain interoperability makes blockchain technology more accessible and popular. It enables isolated networks to overcome their restrictions and creates interesting cooperation and integration opportunities.

1.2 Communication Protocol

Cross-chain communication is driven by the requirement for data access and functionality in widely utilized and dispersed systems. The consensus approaches' atomicity, liveness, and safety are examined. The protocols are also thoroughly examined to determine their suitability for permission, permission, or blockchains. Finally, protocols are categorized by whether they require blockchain software updates to function as a blockchain application [28].

A blockchain network communications protocol is allocated as follows. Initial cross-chain communication requests must be encoded as transactions and logged onto the sub-chain. The connector then assembles sub-chain blocks and recognizes cross-chain communication requests. Connectors send cross-chain communication transactions and accompanying proof to validators. Finally, validators verify the transaction and record the result on their block. The target sub-chain connections receive blocks from the blockchain router and provide the information and proof [29].

By implementing cross-chain communications, various applications can be facilitated, including cross-chain decentralized exchanges, cross-chain asset trading, cross-chain private chain as a key manager, decentralized asset transformation, cross-chain backup, information syndication, national data sovereignty, logistics and finance blockchain collaboration, as well as blockchain oracles. The various usages are built upon fundamental features, such as atomic swaps, cross-chain communications, and pinning [30].

1.2.1 Atomic Swap

Users often have assets on one blockchain that they want to transfer to another blockchain. Atomic swaps are a commonly used method for transferring value. As an example, X and Y have accounts on both Blockchain A & B. Blockchain A supports three different currencies that are used by X. Y owns two coins on Blockchain B. X is open to swapping the coins they hold on Blockchain A with the coins owned by Y on Blockchain B. An atomic swap is a process that allows for the seamless exchange of coins between two parties, X and Y. It ensures a smooth and efficient transaction without any delays or complications. Importantly, in the event of a failure on either Blockchain A or B, the transfer on the other blockchain will also be unsuccessful.

Another form of currency that can be used on a blockchain, like Ethereum for the Ethereum main network or Bitcoins for the Bitcoin blockchain, is called Atomics. In the case where tokens are signified as allocations within Ethereum smart contracts, the value transfer could be for fungible tokens like ERC20 [31, 32] or non-fungible tokens like ERC721 tokens [33].

1.2.2 Cross-Chain Communication

Users can create messages on one blockchain and then receive them on another, making the process more user-friendly and accessible. This innovation makes it possible for values to be stored and transferred between blockchains seamlessly. Nodes on the source chain have to persuade nodes on the destination chain that messages coming from the source chain are reliable. Atomic cross-chain transactions ensure that modifications across blockchains happen simultaneously, making the process more streamlined and efficient.

Simply put, the state changes linked with transactions are either accepted across all blockchains or rejected across all blockchains. This guarantees that the information remains in a uniform state across blockchains [34].

1.2.3 State Pinning

A state or dataset is securely anchored or 'pinned' in a blockchain to serve as a reference point for other blockchains *via* 'state pinning'. Including one blockchain's state in another is state pinning [35]. State pinning lets minority players show government authorities and others that the chain's state has changed by comparing the right state to the pinned block hash. While pinned, a private blockchain must maintain 'block transaction rate privacy' and 'participant privacy' for transaction rates and participants. Hackers can use a private blockchain's transaction rate to identify activity, so keep it hidden. "Anonymous State Pinning" hides the transaction rate of the pinned private blockchain, as well as the participants' identities, save in certain cases. Anchoring provides a persistent reference for cross-chain communication, improving its reliability and honesty. Timestamping, cryptographic proofs, and consensus mechanisms may authenticate and protect the state pinning [36].

1.2.4 Cross-Chain Mechanisms

In complex commercial applications, chains lack a coherent linking mechanism. This defect severely limits growth. Connecting comparable or dissimilar blockchain networks is necessary to create a genuine and useful blockchain network. Data transport, as well as transaction access between blockchains, is addressed *via* notary methods, sidechain/relay systems, distributed private key control, and hash-locking. They enable asset transfers across blockchains to varying degrees of cross-chain interoperability [19].

1.2.5 Notary Mechanism

The notary system verifies and forwards cross-chain transactions like traditional exchanges. A trustworthy middleman makes messages more personal and relevant. One or more entities are designated as notaries to oversee blockchain events when assets are traded and transferred. They do this automatically or upon request and assess if the event uses a consensus mechanism. These incidents should be addressed quickly [37].

The single signature notary mechanism, also known as the centralized notary mechanism, is a simple cross-chain notary technique. A specialized notary node or organization is the main notion. This notary collects, verifies, and confirms cross-chain transactions. It mediates disputes and substitutes technical repute with a trustworthy third party. The paragraph emphasizes the one signature notary mechanism's compatibility and quickness. Though confined to cross-chain asset exchange, its use is noted [38].

Randomly picking notaries improves transaction verification with the multi-signature notary technique. Together, these notaries sign using cryptography, reducing notary authentication needs. A set of independent nodes or institutions acts as the multi-signature notary. Every node has a key. To authorize cross-chain transactions, a minimum number of notaries must sign on their ledgers and agree [37, 39].

Continuously running cross-chain distributed signature notary provides better security and reliability and optimizes with the multi-signature notary. The distributed signature notary technique uses multiparty computation (MPC) to secure and protect the key, unlike the multi-signature notary process. The distributed signature notary method divides the cryptography-generated unique key into various pieces and randomly distributes them among notaries. All notaries try to assemble the shards, but the key is unachievable. The whole key may only be constructed when a certain number of notaries are permitted to sign. This allows cross-chain contacts to be more diffused [39, 40].

The ILP is an open protocol for secure payments across payment networks. The W3C Interledger Community Group is developing it. The ILP's use of web technologies, a simplified protocol for joining payment networks like cryptocurrencies and banks, and the ability to instantly find the best payment method for each recipient make it unique [41]. The ILP prioritizes push-based payments by default, giving customers maximum flexibility and allowing merchants to take payments without collecting hackable user data. Internet protocols transmit and route information, whereas the ILP manages monetary transactions. The ILP should be adopted by present and future payment systems, retailers, websites, as well as browsers [20].

The ILP protocol facilitates interledger payments, enabling individuals with accounts on separate ledgers to establish connections between them. This document presents a method for implementing a two-phase commit protocol for financial transactions across a distributed collection of ledgers on the internet. The ILP plays an essential role in enhancing the reliability of the two-phase commit protocol by providing a secure mechanism for ledgers to securely process and complete transfers. This is achieved by using an escrow and ensuring that transactions are only completed once a predetermined condition has been met and confirmed through cryptographically signed proof. By implementing this feature, it becomes possible to securely process payments even when using untrusted connections. It is simple to incorporate the ILP into any ledger by allowing escrowed transfers. Unlike previous methods, the ILP does not depend on a centralized system or ledger to process payments [38, 42, 43].

PalletOne employs a jury consensus mechanism, where multiple verifiers can execute a single contract. The group of verifiers is commonly known as the Jury, which comprises individual verifiers called Jurors. PalletOne enables interchain connection by decoupling smart contracts from the blockchains. The Mediator plays an essential role in ensuring the safety and reliability of PalletOne, making it an essential part of the system. This technology serves as the foundation for building and running contracts that can be executed. PalletOne enables developers to choose the programming language they are skilled in and the platform they require. The token abstract layer aims to create a more user-friendly and relatable paragraph by establishing a comprehensive set of definitions and operations for tokens. This will greatly enhance the security of token definitions within smart contracts, making them more accessible and understandable for everyone.

Deploying templates in PalletOne – many services are created using smart contracts and templates are used to build contracts. PalletOne provides contract templates for typical cases to simplify the procedure. Users may easily build and deploy new contract templates to PalletOne. The mediator decides on a contract template deployment. Mediation involves examining contract template syntax, requirements, and other factors. The contract template must meet certain conditions to be executed. PalletOne's distributed storage will securely store a successful deployment contract template to simplify contract deployment [44, 45].

Contract deployment PalletOne is more user-friendly and accessible since every contract instance is based on templates. Deploying a template if PalletOne does not have the contract template you require. PalletOne follows these steps when a contract issuer deploys the contract: **Step I:** The mediator receives the template hash and initial contract parameters from the contract issuer. **Step II:** The mediator will randomly choose jurors from a 'juror pool' according to contract requirements. **Step III:** This jury will communicate, as well as receive basic guidelines from the mediator. A distributed storage system will provide the jurors with a template code. **Step IV:** The jury will establish a contract utilizing initial parameters and a template code. It will be validated and executed. The state data, contract ID, as well as the juror list will be distributed by the jury after validation and execution. Lock jury mode along with unlock juror mode can be used to bind a contract. Users can pick numerous jury kinds when constructing a contract template.

Contract invocation – **Step I:** Using the contract ID, the contract invoker queries distributed storage. Then, the store will offer the contract program and a list of locked jurors to execute the contract. In "unlock juror mode, the mediator can choose a new jury. After collecting all the data, the contract will be neatly wrapped with its specifications and delivered to the jury *via* a request object. **Step II:** After receiving the request, the jurors carry out the contract using the most recent contract state and invocation parameters. If all goes well, the jurors' results will match, and the contract state will easily transfer. **Step III:** Interchain transactions are signed on the relevant blockchain with multi-signature transactions.

Contract Termination – After the contract is completed, or the criteria are satisfied, the issuer can seek termination. **Step I:** The contract issuer first contacts the mediator to terminate the contract. **Step II:** In lock juror mode, the mediator carefully selects contract ID-based jurors from the dispersed storage. In unlock juror mode, the mediator can choose a new jury. **Step III:** The" mediator informs the jury of termination. **Step IV:** The jury obtains the contract program and state data from the distributed storage using a contract ID. **Step V:** If termination requirements are satisfied, the jury conducts the termination function [45].

1.2.6 Sidechain

When addressing cross-chain transferable digital assets, 'sidechain' is sometimes used. However, this phrase can be deceptive and confusing. First, Blockstream defines a "sidechain" as a blockchain that validates other blockchains. However, the phrase is wide. Since BTC Relay (explained below) makes Ethereum a sidechain to Bitcoin, this definition applies. Daily talks refer to Blockstream's 'pegged sidechain' as a 'sidechain.' This sidechain uses blockchains to access data from other blockchains, allowing asset transfers between chains. This phase is more sophisticated and requires either sidechains or a trustworthy federation (see notary schemes). To transfer assets between chains, a scheme must be added to the cross-chain communication mechanism [46].

Second, the phrase 'chain A is a sidechain of chain B' implies subservience that, in many cases, does not exist. For instance, Ethereum is a technically 'a sidechain to' Bitcoin, but it is not subservient to Bitcoin. A chain with a pegged token was naturally called a 'pegged sidechain' since the terms 'sidechain' and 'pegged sidechain' originated in a blockchain with a single dominating asset. In actuality, 'pegged sidechaining' is more a trait of particular assets on top of blockchains than of blockchains themselves [19, 47].

1.2.7 Hash Lock

A hash lock mechanism is utilized to make payments routable across multiple payment channels, and it is also suitable for cross-chain atomic swaps. If Alice and Bob want to exchange assets on different chains, here is how the mechanism works:

1. Alice generates, hashes, and transmits Bob a secret key.
2. Alice has secured her assets in a contract that Bob can redeem within a certain term. If Bob fails, Alice gets her money back. Bob seals his assets within a contract that Alice can redeem within a defined timeframe. The requested time range must be longer than the first one or Bob will receive the cash.
3. Bob gives Alice time to redeem currency. Bob then realizes he can trade coins with Alice.

Alice and Bob have an endless window to regain assets, depending on the chain. In this atomic transaction, Bob should have enough time to redeem currency after Alice's action. Alice might also refuse to reveal the money, receiving their full refund. Alice shines when the currency rate swings. Alice may patiently await a beneficial exchange rate during the timeframe. State channels are sometimes used to speed transactions and reduce the rewards of the initiator to remedy this imbalance. Hash locking can only assist atomic swaps between chains, but asset mobility and cross-chain oracle are issues [48].

1.2.8 Distributed Private Key

Assets are securely moved to the chain's decentralized system. The original blockchain assets are linked to the cross-chain, allowing asset circulation and value transfer between blockchain systems. Using a blockchain asset template, distributed private key control is implemented. Cross-chain transaction data is used to install new smart contracts to create cryptocurrency assets. Cross-chain nodes create equal tokens in the current contract for users when the original blockchain transfers an asset to the cross-chain. The original blockchain assets can be traded and circulated on the cross-chain [49, 50].

1.3 Challenges of Cross-Chain Interoperability in Blockchain

In this section, we delve into the challenges surrounding blockchain interoperability and the wider adoption of blockchain technology. According to a study conducted by Liu *et al.*, it is highlighted that the absence of a trusted authority to oversee executions on separate blockchains poses significant challenges in ensuring accurate and trustworthy transactions. Interoperability remains a theoretical concept with very little practical application, notwithstanding recent major advances that have moved interoperability closer to reality. Currently, a large portion of the work being done is primarily conceptual [51].

Given the wide range of blockchain platforms available, there is a notable level of fragmentation when it comes to solutions and how they work together. This becomes especially clear on the Internet of Things (IoT) scenarios. A combination of various platforms created for certain purposes, whether they are public, private, or consortia, adds an extra challenge in handling processes [52]. This issue becomes more pronounced when numerous blockchains are utilized for a certain application. When it comes to the scalability of blockchains, there is a possibility of achieving an internet of blockchains by improving the current performance of both public and private blockchains. By incorporating methods like implicit consensus and data-sharing, we can significantly improve transaction performance and storage capacity. Resolving the challenges of cross-blockchain transaction routing, retrieval, and asset reference, commonly known as the discoverability problem, is a crucial aspect of humanizing the blockchain-sharing process [53, 54].

1.3.1 Cross-Chain Interaction Protocol

Users must obtain data from other systems for blockchain's cross-chain technology to progress. However, a single blockchain system is closed, limiting access to outside information and causing the "data island" effect. Cross-chain technology addresses the "data island" effect caused by single chains by securely sending data from chain A to chain B, allowing for queries, storage, and updates. On-chain assets (tokens) from the data storage layer are encrypted and tamper-resistant. Traditional centralized ledgers allow administrators to modify and query data, but blockchains require precise bookkeeping for cross-chain data interaction. A cross-chain protocol is necessary to ensure consistency, atomicity, as well as data security, are in every blockchain system [55].

1.3.2 Consortium Chain Extensibility

Consortium chains can determine public access based on application scenarios, with member institutions collectively maintaining the network. The gateway nodes of member institutions provide access to nodes. It is ideal for storing, managing, authorizing, monitoring, as well as auditing dynamic data across several member institutions [56]. Practical applications involve access and authorization activities for users, resources, services, and terminals. Significant variations in consensus, authority control, chain code architecture, and node control of coalition chains have hindered the development of blockchain technology. To address scalability issues, consortium chains should be established using a uniform cross-chain protocol and blockchain-as-a-service architectural platform (BaaS) [57].

1.3.3 Privacy Leaking in Cross-Chain

Privacy leaking is overlooked in most cross-chain systems. While some studies provide some privacy protection, none satisfy all requirements. Data privacy and identity protection are challenged when linked blockchains run without authorization or employ unencrypted transmission in cross-chain interactions. An attacker with cross-chain data or identities might harm involved participants. Tamper attacks can fool message recipients. Additionally, privacy-related criteria might be difficult to meet. These include conditional traceability, unlikability, and indistinguishability. These criteria are harder to humanize than data and identity privacy [58–60].

1.3.4 Fairness in Cross-Chain Technologies

Achieving fairness can often be more challenging than other criteria. For example, the concept of atomicity is achieved through the adoption of consensus protocols with a Practical Byzantine Fault Tolerance. However, fairness is not guaranteed because of the potential loss of freshness as mentioned by Rui, Jiang, and Yi in 2021 [61]. When one party engages in dishonest behavior, it can have a negative impact on the other party who is acting honestly. This lack of fairness can be detrimental to the overall utility. Therefore, achieving fairness in cross-chain technologies poses a significant challenge [62].

1.3.5 Wormhole Attack

In the wormhole attack scenario, two adversaries manage to infiltrate the network and establish a covert communication tunnel. They then proceed to inform other nodes about their abbreviated transaction path. This will ensure that other nodes are unable to participate in the transaction, which could result in the unauthorized acquisition of fees from honest actors. Wormholes take advantage of the fact that the hashed timelock contract (HTLC) only requires two communication rounds [63].

1.3.6 Timing Attack

Side chains are distinct blockchains that use their own block configurations and consensus mechanisms to speed up transactions. In addition, they promote compatibility and seamless communication between different systems. Loom is a fantastic Ethereum sidechain that opens a world of possibilities for decentralized app development. Amritraj Singh *et al.* highlight the problem of Loom's transaction history being consistently updated on the mainchain and stored on the sidechain. Timing attacks between updates can pose a risk to sidechains if they are not kept up to date [64].

1.3.7 Fraud-Proof Attack

There have been some recent developments in the creation of Ethereum scaling solutions that are based on proof. PLASMA, a blockchain built on top of Ethereum's sidechain, is currently facing a challenge. When exit proof is provided, PLASMA does not address security concerns. However, if a malicious actor presents proof of fraud, and the honest actor stays offline for a week, it can pose a challenge. There is a possibility that someone with ill intentions could seize the tokens [34].

1.4 Implication to Investors

Investors now experience a transformative shift in digital asset investing with the advent of blockchain cross-chain interoperability. Investors always look for various investment strategies to earn abnormal returns [65]. By promoting interoperability, investors can broaden their investment options and gain access to a wider range of assets. This is made possible through seamless communication and transaction capabilities that are facilitated between different blockchain networks. Investors can spread their investments across multiple chains, which helps to reduce the risk associated with any one network. Interoperability brings together different liquidity pools and enables arbitrage opportunities. Investors are interested in cross-chain interoperability because it demonstrates a strong potential for long-term success and the ability to adapt to changing circumstances. To minimize interoperability risks, investors must address regulatory concerns and conduct thorough due diligence. At its core, cross-chain interoperability enhances blockchain innovation and efficiency, providing investors with more opportunities for growth and portfolio optimization.

1.5 Implication to Regulators and Government

Blockchain cross-chain interoperability poses financial monitoring and technology governance issues and opportunities for regulators and governments. Interoperability may boost digital asset efficiency and creativity, but authorities must manage a decentralized ecosystem across jurisdictions. Harmonized regulatory regimes across countries are needed to prevent regulatory arbitrage and safeguard investors. By enabling cross-chain interoperability, regulators and industry players can collaborate to establish robust standards, as well as protocols that promote transparency, security, and market integrity. Regulators can find a way to strike a balance between fostering innovation, safeguarding consumer interests, and ensuring the stability of the system. This can be achieved by engaging with the blockchain community and leveraging emerging technologies, such as decentralized identifiers and zero-knowledge proofs.

1.6 Trends and Future Development in Cross-Chain Interoperability

The creation of blockchain interoperability standards may present a means of improving backward compatibility flexibility. Considering the current study and the challenges that have been identified, we suggest research directions based on certain sections of our survey: supporting technologies and standards, hybrid connectors, governance and supervision, data model innovation, and relationship with IT technologies.

1.6.1 Hybrid Connectors

Improve the credibility of reliable intermediaries by effortlessly incorporating them into public blockchains. This may be accomplished by regularly transmitting the current state to a publicly accessible blockchain. Examine how blockchain-agnostic protocols may effortlessly incorporate themselves into existing ledgers. Explore the groundbreaking concept of a blockchain of blockchains, which represents a major leap forward in the growth of dependable applications based on blockchain technology [66]. Improve the level of atomicity and consistency assurances for decentralized apps that operate across several blockchains. Explore the transfer of blockchain technology from public to permissioned ledgers. Migration plans can be decentralized and customized to meet the functional and non-functional criteria set by stakeholders. Consider investigating the possibility of migrating to the blockchain *via* non-trusted relays, such as employing a group of public escrow nodes that follow a specified protocol [67]. Create frameworks to effectively oversee and control various blockchains. Frameworks of this kind should be specifically developed to cater to the requirements of many stakeholders and distribute trust in a decentralized fashion. The purpose of our model integration abstraction layers is to simplify the process of creating universally related contracts. Investigating the display of cryptocurrency transaction data [68].

1.6.2 Supporting Technologies and Standards

Working with authorities and standardizers to standardize blockchain interoperability across sectors. Blockchain interoperability programming languages, tools, as well as standards research are essential for smooth blockchain network communication. Cross-blockchain programming languages, decentralized IDs, frameworks, and verified credentials are explored. For industry collaboration and interoperability, enterprise blockchain interoperability standards are needed. Multiple blockchains and 'value-level' interoperability unlock new use cases [69]. Research cryptocurrency-based interoperability, blockchain of blockchains, and hybrid connector synergies. Examine blockchain interoperability security. Understand value, semantic, organizational, and other interoperability levels. Explore these layers' consequences and relevance in many circumstances [70].

1.6.3 Governance and Supervision

Designing a "cross-chain transaction processing mechanism that eliminates single-point dependence is crucial. This mechanism aims to create a protocol for cross-chain data (asset) circulation and contract invocation, ensuring the atomicity of data (asset) circulation and contract invocation even in abnormal conditions [71]. Explore the cross-chain governance mechanism, develop the system access mechanism" for cross-chain transactions, establish an authority system, implement a reward and punishment system, and create a mechanism for audit and supervision. The cross-chain governance encompasses various aspects such as controlling the authority of the underlying chain, handling illegal transactions, managing network exceptions, conducting supervision and audits, and governing network upgrades [19, 72].

1.6.4 Data Model Innovation

Most commonly, blockchain systems utilize a data storage mechanism based on chains. A block contains multiple transactions, organized in a sequence based on their timestamps, which serve as the primary data. Handling just one block of data at a time poses challenges when it comes to managing complex state operations, as well as dynamic data storage. Blockchain systems currently utilize consensus algorithms like proof of stake and proof of work to ensure data consistency. However, these algorithms can lead to higher computer overhead, resource consumption, and slower processing speed. The system's performance, as well as scalability, are affected by the high number of users accessing it simultaneously. To address the problem of slow processing performance for large-scale commercial usage, a topologically ordered DAG structure with fine-grained transactions replaces blocks in the traditional chain-based blockchain [19]. The DAG-based blockchain brings a significant improvement in concurrent processing efficiency and reduces the computational burden for verification, unlike the traditional chain-based structure that relies on serialized verification processing [73].

1.6.5 Relationship with IT Technologies

Blockchain is increasingly interwoven with IoT and cloud computing, which underpin many revolutionary applications. These advances emphasize technical development and pressure to move quickly. This paragraph attracts government officials, entrepreneurs, and developers who want to benefit from digital transformation's merger of critical technologies. These include blockchain, AI, edge computing, as well as IoT. Consider BaaS, which blends blockchain with cloud computing. This platform provides blockchain services for economic financial organizations [73].

Blockchain has maintained its appeal in recent years. Many nations have made blockchain a strategic priority, racing to lead blockchain research and development. Countries throughout the world have adopted blockchain as part of their new information architecture due to rising demand for blockchain applications and official backing. Step by step, it will overcome the technological challenges of a new generation of credibility, interconnection, as well as efficacy. It will provide support for applications across different scenarios and regions, enabling cross-chain interoperability and collaboration. This will pave the way for a more dynamic and promising business model, ushering in a period of multi-chain interconnection.

1.7 Conclusion

In the past, it was completely impossible to transfer tokens or any other data from one network to another. Today, we have illustrated *via* our knowledge that it is both feasible and essential to create practical and highly secure solutions. Our goal is to empower users with maximum freedom and eliminate any potential limitations in the utilization of blockchain technology. We have discussed the mechanisms and the communication protocols of cross-chain interoperability in the blockchain. In addition, there is a lack of extensive research exploring the concept of cross-chain interoperability in blockchain technology.

Ultimately, we view the current application of blockchain as a developing financial system that possesses certain characteristics that both contribute to and define its value propositions. It seems that to address its challenges, cross-chain interoperability may need to embrace collaboration with traditional financial institutions, relinquishing some of its emphasis on complete decentralization and independence. This study has shed light on implications for investors and government and suggested future directions and development. It seems unlikely that DeFi will completely substitute traditional finance along with its institutions. As an alternative, it is anticipated that both financial systems will need to come together to prioritize the well-being of users.

References

1. Jensen, J.R., von Wachter, V., Ross, O., An introduction to decentralized finance (defi). *Complex Syst. Inform. Model. Q.*, 1, 26, 46–54, 2021.
2. Werner, S., Perez, D., Gudgeon, L., Klages-Mundt, A., Harz, D., Knottenbelt, W., Sok: Decentralized finance (defi), in: *Proceedings of the 4th ACM Conference on Advances in Financial Technologies*, pp. 30–46, 2022, September.
3. Behrens, A., The Growth of DeFi. Retrieved from Circle website, 2022, https://www.circle.com/blog/the-growth-of-defi.
4. Mehta, K., Sharma, R., Vyas, V., A quantile regression approach to study the impact of aluminium prices on manufacturing sector of India during COVID era. *Mater. Today: Proc.*, 65, 7, 3506–3511, 2022.
5. Sharma, R. and Mehta, K., Credit risk and bank specific factors: An empirical study using panel GMM. *Int. J. Econ. Bus. Res.*, 27, 2, 294–309, 2024.
6. Sharma, R. and Mehta, K., *Deep Learning Tools for Predicting Stock Market Movements*, John Wiley & Sons, New Jersey, USA, 2024.
7. Sharma, R., Mehta, K., Chugh, A., Using Analytic Hierarchy Process to determine forex risk hedging strategies of SMEs. *AIP Conf. Proc.*, 2916, 1, 120008, 2023.
8. Sharma, R., Mehta, K., Rana, R., Cryptocurrency adoption behaviour of millennial investors in India, in: *Perspectives on Blockchain Technology and Responsible Investing*, pp. 135–158, 2023.
9. Schär, F., Decentralized fnance: On blockchain- and smart contract-based fnancial markets. Federal Reserve Bank of St.Louis. *Review*, Second Quarter, 103, 2, 153–174, 2021, https://doi.org/10.20955/r.103.153-74.
10. Gramlich, V., Principato, M., Schellinger, B., Sedlmeir, J., Amend, J., Stramm, J., Zwede, T., Strüker, J., Urbach, N., Decentralized Finance (DeFi) foundations, applications, potentials, and challenges. 2022, Retrieved from https://www.researchgate.net/publication/362058434_Decentralized_Finance_DeFi_Foundations_Applications_Potentials_and_Challenges.
11. Vyas, V., Mehta, K., Sharma, R., Are bitcoin prices isolated or co-integrated? *Int. J. Bus. Glob.*, 35, 1–2, 5–19, 2023.
12. Gramlich, V., Guggenberger, T., Principato, M., Schellinger, B., Urbach, N., A multivocal literature review of decentralized finance: Current knowledge and future research avenues. *Electron. Mark.*, *33*, 1, 11, 2023.
13. Lockl, J. and Stoetzer, J.-C., Trust-free banking missed the point: The efect of distrust in banks on the adoption of decentralized finance. *European Conference on Information Systems*, AIS, 2021, Retrieved from https://aisel.aisnet.org/ecis2021_rp/138/.
14. Mehta, K. and Sharma, R., Unraveling quantum complexity: A fuzzy AHP approach to understanding software industry challenges, in: *Deep Learning Tools for Predicting Stock Market Movements*, pp. 39–60, 2024.

15. Vyas, V., Mehta, K., Sharma, R., Investigating socially responsible investing behaviour of Indian investors using structural equation modelling. *J. Sustain. Financ. Invest.*, 12, 1, 1–23, 2020.
16. Mehta, K., Sharma, R., Vyas, V., Kuckreja, J.S., Exit strategy decision by venture capital firms in India using fuzzy AHP. *J. Entrep. Emerg. Econ.*, 14, 4, 643–669, 2022.
17. Schueffel, P., DeFi: Decentralized Finance-An Introduction and Overview. *J. Innov. Manag.*, 9, 3, I–XI, 2021.
18. Nadler, M. and Schär, F., Decentralized finance, centralized ownership? an iterative mapping process to measure protocol token distribution. *J. Blockchain Res.*, 1, 29–36, 2020, arXiv preprint arXiv:2012.09306.
19. Ou, W., Huang, S., Zheng, J., Zhang, Q., Zeng, G., Han, W., An overview on cross-chain: Mechanism, platforms, challenges, and advances. *Comput. Netw.*, *218*, 109378, 2022.
20. Hope-Bailie, A. and Thomas, S., Interledger: Creating a standard for payments, in: *Proceedings of the 25th International Conference Companion on World Wide Web*, 2016, April, pp. 281–282.
21. Schwartz, E., A payment protocol of the web, for the web: Or, finally enabling web micropayments with the interledger protocol, in: *Proceedings of the 25th International Conference Companion on World Wide Web*, 2016, April, pp. 279–280.
22. Buterin, V., Chain interoperability. *R3 Res. Pap.*, *9*, 1–25, 2016.
23. Pillai, B., Biswas, K., Muthukkumarasamy, V., Blockchain interoperable digital objects, in: *Blockchain–ICBC 2019: Second International Conference, Held as Part of the Services Conference Federation, SCF 2019, San Diego, CA, USA, June 25–30, 2019, Proceedings 2*, pp. 80–94, Springer International Publishing, 2019.
24. Jin, H., Dai, X., Xiao, J., Towards a novel architecture for enabling interoperability amongst multiple blockchains, in: *2018 IEEE 38th International Conference on Distributed Computing Systems (ICDCS)*, 2018, July, IEEE, pp. 1203–1211.
25. Alipour-Hafezi, M., Horri, A., Shiri, A., Ghaebi, A., Interoperability models in digital libraries: an overview. *Electron. Libr.*, *28*, 3, 438–452, 2010.
26. Chen, D., Doumeingts, G., Vernadat, F., Architectures for enterprise integration and interoperability: Past, present and future. *Comput. Ind.*, *59*, 7, 647–659, 2008.
27. Schulte, S., Sigwart, M., Frauenthaler, P., Borkowski, M., Towards blockchain interoperability, in: *Business Process Management: Blockchain and Central and Eastern Europe Forum: BPM 2019 Blockchain and CEE Forum, Vienna, Austria, September 1–6, 2019, Proceedings 17*, Springer International Publishing, pp. 3–10, 2019.
28. Robinson, P., Survey of cross-chain communications protocols. *Comput. Netw.*, *200*, 108488, 2021.

29. Wang, H., Cen, Y., Li, X., Blockchain router: A cross-chain communication protocol, in: *Proceedings of the 6th International Conference on Informatics, Environment, Energy and Applications*, 2017, March, pp. 94–97.
30. Zhang, W., Feenan, S., Robinson, P., Enterprise Ethereum alliance cross-chain interoperability use cases, 2020, URL https://entethalliance.org/wp-content/uploads/2020/08/CIFT_Use_Case.pdf.
31. Vogelsteller, F. and Buterin, V., EIP20: ERC-20 token standard, 2015, URL HTTPs: //github.com/ethereum/EIPs/blob/master/EIPS/eip-20.md.
32. Ethereum Foundation, ERC20 token standard, 2018, URLhttps://theethereum. wiki/w/index.php/ERC20_Token_Standard.
33. Shirley, D., EIPS/eip-721.md at master. ethereum/EIPs, 2018, URL https://github.com/ethereum/EIPs/blob/master/EIPS/eip-721.md.
34. Robinson, P., Consensus for crosschain communications, 2020, arXiv preprint arXiv:2004.09494.
35. Robinson, P. and Brainard, J., Anonymous state pinning for private blockchains, in: *2019 18th IEEE International Conference On Trust, Security And Privacy In Computing And Communications/13th IEEE International Conference On Big Data Science And Engineering (TrustCom/BigDataSE)*, 2019, August, IEEE, pp. 827–834.
36. Ahmed, A. and Zhang, J., Enhanced immutability of permissioned blockchain networks by tethering provenance with a public blockchain network, 2018.
37. Gu, X., Current research progress and development prospects of blockchain technology. *Inf. Comput.*, 16, 106–107, 2018, (Theoretical Edition).
38. Nakamoto, S. and Bitcoin, A., A peer-to-peer electronic cash system. Bitcoin. *4*, 2, 15, 2008, URL: https://bitcoin. org/bitcoin. pdf.
39. Zhang, S., Qin, B., Zhang, H., Research on the protocol of multiple cross-chains based on the hash-locking. *Cybersp. Secur.*, 9, 11, 57–62, 2018.
40. Mark, F., Compact SPV proofs *via* block header commitments [online], 2019, URL http://sourceforge.net/p/bitcoin/mailman/message/32111357/.
41. Siris, V.A., Nikander, P., Voulgaris, S., Fotiou, N., Lagutin, D., Polyzos, G.C., Interledger approaches. *IEEE Access*, *7*, 89948–89966, 2019.
42. Davies, D.W. and Price, W.L., *Security for computer networks: an introduction to data security in teleprocessing and electronic funds transfer*, John Wiley & Sons, Inc., New York, USA, 1984.
43. Schwartz, D., Youngs, N., Britto, A., The ripple protocol consensus algorithm. Ripple Labs Inc White Paper, vol. 5, 8, p. 151, 2014.
44. Fan, Y., A study on solutions of cross-ledger intercommunication: Classification, analysis and comparison of crosschain projects, 2020.
45. Ren, Y., Lv, Z., Xiong, N.N., Wang, J., HCNCT: A cross-chain interaction scheme for the blockchain-based metaverse. *ACM Trans. Multimed. Comput. Commun. Appl.*, *20*, 7, 1–23, 2024.
46. Chen, W. and Zheng, Z., Blockchain data analysis: current situation, trends and challenges. *Comput. Res. Dev.*, 55, 9, 1853–1870, 2018.

47. Dilley, J., Poelstra, A., Wilkins, J., Piekarska, M., Gorlick, B., Friedenbach, M., Strong federations: an interoperable blockchain solution to centralized third-party risks, 2016, arXiv preprint.
48. Qin, K. and Gervais, A., An overview of blockchain scalability, interoperability and sustainability, in: *Hochschule Luzern Imperial College London Liquidity Network*, pp. 1–15, 2018.
49. Wang, H.W. and Wang, J.W., How cryo-electron microscopy and X-ray crystallography complement each other. *Protein Sci.*, *26*, 1, 32–39, 2017.
50. Zhao, T. and Liu, Z., Analysis of one-person households who is young's characteristics in combination with social experience from the perspectives of interaction process in product use, social situation and public space, in: *Design, User Experience, and Usability. Design Philosophy and Theory: 8th International Conference, DUXU 2019, Held as Part of the 21st HCI International Conference, HCII 2019, Orlando, FL, USA, July 26–31, 2019, Proceedings, Part I 21*, pp. 557–576, Springer International Publishing, 2019.
51. Besançon, L., Da Silva, C.F., Ghodous, P., Towards blockchain interoperability: Improving video games data exchange, in: *2019 IEEE International Conference on Blockchain and Cryptocurrency (ICBC)*, 2019, May, IEEE, pp. 81–85.
52. Kokoris-Kogias, E., Jovanovic, P., Gasser, L., Gailly, N., Syta, E., Ford, B., Omniledger: A secure, scale-out, decentralized ledger *via* sharding, in: *2018 IEEE symposium on security and privacy (SP)*, 2018, May, IEEE, pp. 583–598.
53. Zhu, Q., Loke, S.W., Trujillo-Rasua, R., Jiang, F., Xiang, Y., Applications of distributed ledger technologies to the internet of things: A survey. *ACM Comput. Surv. (CSUR)*, *52*, 6, 1–34, 2019.
54. Liu, Z., Xiang, Y.X., Shi, J., Gao, P., Wang, H., Xiao, X., Wen, B., Hu, Y.-C., Hyper service: Interoperability and programmability across heerogeneous blockchains, in: *ACMSIGSAC Conference on Computer and Communications*, 2019.
55. Mao, H., Nie, T., Sun, H., Shen, D., Yu, G., A survey on cross-chain technology: Challenges, development, and prospect. *IEEE Access*, 10, 491–510, 2022.
56. Qiao, R., Cao, Y., Wang, Q., Traceability mechanism of dynamic data in Internet of Things based on consortium blockchain. *J. Softw.*, 6, 30, 1614–1631, 2019.
57. Mao, H., Nie, T., Shen, D., Yu, G., Xu, S., He, G., Survey on key techniques and development of blockchain as a service platform. *Comput. Sci.*, 11, 2, 4–11, 2021.
58. Baldimtsi, F., Miers, I., Zhang, X., Anonymous Sidechains, in: *Data Privacy Management, Cryptocurrencies and Blockchain Technology*, pp. 262–277, Springer, Berlin & Heidelberg, Germany, 2021.
59. Ghosh, B.C., Bhartia, T., Addya, S.K., Chakraborty, S., Leveraging public-private blockchain interoperability for closed consortium interfacing, in: *IEEE INFOCOM 2021-IEEE Conference on Computer Communications*, 2021, May, IEEE, pp. 1–10.

60. He, Y., Zhang, C., Wu, B., Yang, Y., Xiao, K., Li, H., Cross-chain trusted service quality computing scheme for multi-chain model-based 5g network slicing sla. *IEEE Internet Things J.*, 10, 126–139, 2021.
61. Han, R., Xiao, J., Dai, X., Zhang, S., Sun, Y., Li, B., HaiJin, Vassago: Efficient and Authenticated Provenance Query on Multiple Blockchains, in: *2021 40th International Symposium on Reliable Distributed Systems (SRDS)*, IEEE, pp. 132–142, 2021.
62. Han, P., Yan, Z., Ding, W., Fei, S., Wan, Z., A survey on cross-chain technologies. *Distributed Ledger Technol.: Res. Pract.*, *2*, 2, 1–30, 2023.
63. Malavolta, G., Moreno-Sanchez, P., Schneidewind, C., Kate, A., Maffei, M., Anonymous multi-hop locks for blockchain scalability and interoperability. *Cryptology ePrint Archive*, 2018.
64. Singh, A., Click, K., Parizi, R.M., Zhang, Q., Dehghantanha, A., Choo, K.K.R., Sidechain technologies in blockchain networks: An examination and state-of-the-art review. *J. Netw. Comput. Appl.*, *149*, 102471, 2020.
65. Mehta, K. and Sharma, R., Contrarian and momentum investment strategies: Evidence from Indian stock market. *Int. J. Appl. Bus. Econ. Res.*, 15, 2, 87–98, 2017.
66. Grone, S., Facilitating cross-chain cryptocurrency exchanges: An inquiry into blockchain technology and interoperability with an emphasis on cryptocurrency arbitrage, 2020.
67. Pang, Y., A new consensus protocol for blockchain interoperability architecture. *IEEE Access*, *8*, 153719–153730, 2020.
68. Belchior, R., Vasconcelos, A., Guerreiro, S., Correia, M., A survey on blockchain interoperability: Past, present, and future trends. *ACM Comput. Surv. (CSUR)*, *54*, 8, 1–41, 2021.
69. Hart, M., Hugo, B.P., Jonathan, H., Mic, B., Peter, S., Shingo, F., Rafael, B., Hyperledger cactus whitepaper, 2020.
70. Konashevych, O., Cross-blockchain protocol for public registries. *Int. J. Web Inf. Syst.*, *16*, 5, 571–610, 2020.
71. Mohanty, D., Anand, D., Aljahdali, H.M., Villar, S.G., Blockchain interoperability: Towards a sustainable payment system. *Sustainability*, *14*, 2, 913, 2022.
72. Madine, M., Salah, K., Jayaraman, R., Al-Hammadi, Y., Arshad, J., Yaqoob, I., appxchain: Application-level interoperability for blockchain networks. *IEEE Access*, *9*, 87777–87791, 2021.
73. Jin, H. and Xiao, J., Towards trustworthy blockchain systems in the era of "Internet of value": development, challenges, and future trends. *Sci. China Inf. Sci.*, *65*, 1–11, 2022.

2

Artificial Intelligence and Decentralized Finance

Asheetu Bhatia Sarin

Vivekananda Institute of Professional Studies – Technical Campus, Guru Gobind Singh Indraprastha University, New Delhi, India

Abstract

Artificial intelligence (AI) and decentralized finance (DeFi) are two of the most exciting and rapidly evolving fields in technology and finance. The intersection of these two areas could bring about significant changes to the cryptocurrency market, making it more efficient, transparent, and accessible. However, the full impact of AI in DeFi is yet to be determined, and it is essential to manage our expectations and carefully identify its potential applications. This chapter will help researchers, scholars, academicians, and policymakers understand the concept of DeFi and how its intersection with AI can bring changes in the Crypto market.

***Keywords*:** DeFi, decentralized finance, artificial intelligence, cryptocurrency, smart contracts, blockchain, decision-making

2.1 Introduction

The finance sector is currently experiencing a profound shift thanks to the rise of decentralized finance (DeFi). Grounded in the fundamentals of blockchain technology, DeFi seeks to overhaul conventional financial systems, providing individuals worldwide with transparent, inclusive, and self-governing solutions. The financial environment is exposed to various types of risks (Sharma and Mehta, 2023, 2024; Sharma *et al.*, 2023; Mehta *et al.*, 2022) [1–4]. In this swiftly changing environment, the fusion

Email: asheetu.bhatia@vips.edu

Renuka Sharma, Kiran Mehta, Vishal Vyas and Vinod Kumar Shukla (eds.) Decentralized Finance and Blockchain: A Game Changing Duo, (23–46) © 2025 Scrivener Publishing LLC

of artificial intelligence (AI) holds the promise of unveiling unparalleled prospects and reshaping the trajectory of DeFi in the future.

Decentralized finance comprises a network of blockchain-based applications facilitating various financial services. Within the DeFi ecosystem, products encompass crypto loans, liquidity provision, and decentralized exchanges (DEXs), all built on blockchain networks (Binanace.com). Unlike traditional financial systems relying on intermediaries like banks or brokers for transaction validation, DeFi services operate with smart contracts, ensuring decentralized and automated execution.

Artificial intelligence refers to the capability of computers or machines to imitate intelligent behavior. In the context of finance or trading, AI finds applications in diverse areas. Common uses involve the deployment of fraud detection software to identify and prevent fraudulent activities, employing trading bots for automated trading strategies based on predefined rules or learning from historical data, and implementing customer support chatbots to offer instant and personalized assistance. The integration of AI in finance and trading aims to enhance efficiency, accuracy, and automation within these domains.

Leveraging its capability to process extensive data, AI recognizes patterns, makes informed forecasts, can empower DeFi platforms in streamlining their operations, fortifies security protocols, and delivers tailored services to their users. The spectrum of AI applications in DeFi is wide and full of potential, spanning from automated trading algorithms and risk evaluation models to fraud detection systems and smart contract audits. This chapter will help in understanding the concept of DeFi and how its intersection with AI can bring changes in the crypto market.

2.2 Background

2.2.1 Evolution of Blockchain

Haber and Stornetta (1990) [5] incorporated Merkle Trees into their system, enhancing efficiency to accommodate more documents per block, as documented in their work in 1993. However, the tangible emergence of blockchain technology, exemplified by Bitcoin, began to take form around 2008, as referenced by Narayanan *et al.* (2016) [6]. Satoshi Nakamoto, credited as the innovative mind behind Bitcoin and blockchain, envisioned the first blockchain in 2008, a technology that has since expanded into various applications beyond cryptocurrencies. Nakamoto, notably, did not retain sole control over Bitcoin's development but rather entrusted it to other core developers to explore potential enhancements and diversification of applications. Consequently, the progression of digital ledger technology (DLT) has catalyzed the emergence of diverse applications, significantly influencing the historical narrative of blockchain technology. The evolution of blockchain can be understood through several key phases:

1. **Genesis (2008–2009)**: The concept of blockchain emerged with the creation of Bitcoin by an anonymous person or group known as Satoshi Nakamoto. The primary focus was on developing a decentralized, immutable ledger for peer-to-peer transactions, establishing the first successful application of blockchain.
2. **Blockchain 1.0 (2010–2013)**: The initial phase witnessed the proliferation of alternative cryptocurrencies and the expansion of blockchain applications beyond Bitcoin. Litecoin, Namecoin, and others emerged, each with its unique value propositions and variations in blockchain technology.
3. **Blockchain 2.0 (2014–2016)**: This phase introduced the concept of smart contracts and decentralized applications (DApps). The following phase witnessed the emergence of "smart contracts" within a second-generation blockchain system, as delineated by the Smart Contracts Alliance in 2016. Among the pioneers contributing to the Bitcoin database was Vitalik Buterin, who envisioned a blockchain with multifaceted capabilities beyond its conventional role as a peer-to-peer network (Abdulhakeem and Hu, 2021) [43]. Buterin (2023) [7] commenced the development of Ethereum, an adaptable blockchain framework designed to execute various functions, marking a significant departure from traditional blockchain concepts. Ethereum represents a natural progression from the functionalities pioneered by Bitcoin (Sarin, 2023) [8], offering an expanded capability through the introduction of smart contracts. These smart contracts, residing on a blockchain, possess the ability to manage assets and data while dictating interactions among network participants. Ethereum's designation as a smart contract platform stems from this unique capacity for executing smart contracts (Harvey *et al.*, 2021) [9]. Ethereum, a major milestone in blockchain evolution, provided a platform for developers to build and deploy smart contracts and DApps, enabling various use cases beyond simple value transfer.

4. **Enterprise blockchain (2017–2019)**: Industries recognized the potential of blockchain beyond cryptocurrencies. Enterprises began exploring permissioned, private blockchains to improve efficiency, transparency, and security in various sectors, such as supply chain management, finance, and healthcare.
5. **Interoperability and scalability (2020–Present)**: Recent developments focus on enhancing interoperability between different blockchain networks and addressing scalability issues. Projects are underway to create bridges that enable communication and data exchange among disparate blockchains. Additionally, efforts to enhance scalability aim to increase transaction throughput without compromising security or decentralization.

2.2.2 Decentralized Finance

Andreev *et al.* (2018) [10] explored different types of blockchain architectures, such as public, private, and consortium blockchains, discussing their respective features and use cases. Public blockchains, like Bitcoin and Ethereum, allow anyone to participate and validate transactions, while private blockchains restrict access to authorized participants. Consortium blockchains, on the other hand, are governed by a group of organizations, enabling shared control over transactions. Furthermore, the authors delved into the diverse applications of blockchain technology across various industries. The paper also discussed emerging trends such as tokenization, smart contracts, and DeFi, which leverage blockchain technology to innovate traditional processes and systems.

Decentralized finance represents an innovative and experimental financial model that operates independently of central authorities or intermediaries such as exchanges, brokerages, or traditional banks. Instead, DeFi relies on smart contracts executed on blockchain networks to facilitate financial transactions and operations. It also encompasses financial applications and services constructed on blockchain networks, predominantly employing smart contracts, which are automated agreements encoded in software. The fundamental goal of DeFi is to decentralize and democratize conventional financial systems by removing intermediaries and facilitating unrestricted, permissionless entry to financial services.

Decentralized finance draws its inspiration from financial technology (fintech), which encompasses any technology facilitating financial services through software. Additionally, Ethereum is shaped by the practical utility of blockchain technology, which provides a decentralized and transparent infrastructure for financial operations, eliminating the need for intermediaries, as noted by Zetzsche (2020) [11]. Lee *et al.* (2018) [12] defined fintech as the digital evolution of customer-oriented financial services, highlighting contemporary challenges, such as offering attractive customer packages and streamlining payment processes.

Decentralized finance embodies the utilization of blockchain technology in financial services, proposing that financial operations should not depend on centralized intermediaries like banks, brokers, or governments. Instead, it suggests a direct exchange between end users facilitated by peer-to-peer software built on blockchain technology (Schär, 2021) [13]. To ensure its secure and efficient operation, DeFi heavily relies on blockchain technology—a digital ledger characterized by decentralization, transparency, immutability, and public accessibility (IBM, 2022) [14]. The inherent decentralized ledger technology (DLT) within blockchain records, transactions and oversees assets, allows users to track the inception and culmination of each transaction without intermediaries. This digital ledger resides on PCs, referred to as nodes, provided by end-users who participate in the blockchain network is seen in Figure 2.2 below. The publications by Chen and Bellavitis (2020) [15], Schär (2021) [13], Jensen *et al.* (2021) [16], Bartoletti *et al.* (2020b) [17], Cousaert *et al.* (2021) [18] and Werner *et al.* (2021) [44] offer various viewpoints DeFi, discussing its structure, advantages, challenges, and specific applications. Researchers have shared their perspectives on DeFi based on personal experiences, lacking a structured, literature-guided approach. Conversely, Bartoletti *et al.* (2020b) [17] and Cousaert *et al.* (2021) [18] present 'Systemizations of Knowledge (SoKs)' focusing on distinct areas within DeFi, such as lending protocols and yield aggregators, amalgamating academic literature review with their independent analyses. Werner *et al.*, [44] meanwhile, conducted an SoK concentrated on security challenges within the wider DeFi realm, dissecting technical and economic aspects. However, despite these contributions, a comprehensive systematic review solely dedicated to surveying academic works within the rapidly expanding field of DeFi, discerning it from finance blockchain applications involving intermediaries, remains conspicuously absent. The outcomes of Meyer *et al.* (2022) [19], derived from the examination and synthesis of 83 peer-reviewed publications related to DeFi, contributed significantly in several ways that is adding to academic literature, Ethereum being the primary blockchain platform within the DeFi sphere and focusing on key research avenues only. These research priorities are poised to significantly advance and shape the future trajectory of DeFi-related academic investigations. Teng *et al.* (2022) [20]

provided an overview of the fundamental concepts of DeFi, emphasizing its decentralized nature and its reliance on smart contracts deployed on the Ethereum blockchain. They discussed how DeFi protocols facilitate various financial services such as lending, borrowing, trading, and yield farming without intermediaries. Moreover, the paper delved into specific use cases and applications of DeFi within the Ethereum network, highlighting real-world examples of DEXs, liquidity pools, decentralized lending platforms, and automated market-making protocols. Additionally, the authors provided insights into prospects and developments of DeFi on Ethereum, considering technological advancements, regulatory changes, and evolving market trends. The researchers have examined the cryptocurrency behavior as there is an increased interest of the investors in this digital financial instrument (Vyas *et al.*, 2023; Sharma *et al.*, 2023) [21, 22].

Decentralized finance stands apart from traditional banking applications (see Figure 2.1) through its distinct characteristics, notably transparency, global accessibility, and user empowerment. Its hallmark feature lies in transparency, where the open visibility of the code governing DeFi applications allows for audits by anyone. This transparency fosters trust as users can comprehensively understand the underlying functionalities. In contrast, traditional finance relies on intermediaries, limiting direct insight and potentially raising concerns about asset control and security. Geographically, traditional financial systems operate within specific boundaries, restricting access based on location, whereas DeFi's universal nature allows users worldwide to engage in its networks without geographical constraints. Furthermore, DeFi's accessibility and user control set it apart; there are no gatekeepers or intermediaries, enabling direct interaction with protocols using specialized crypto wallets. This decentralized model redefines financial access, placing control directly into users' hands and presenting a paradigm shift from conventional banking systems as

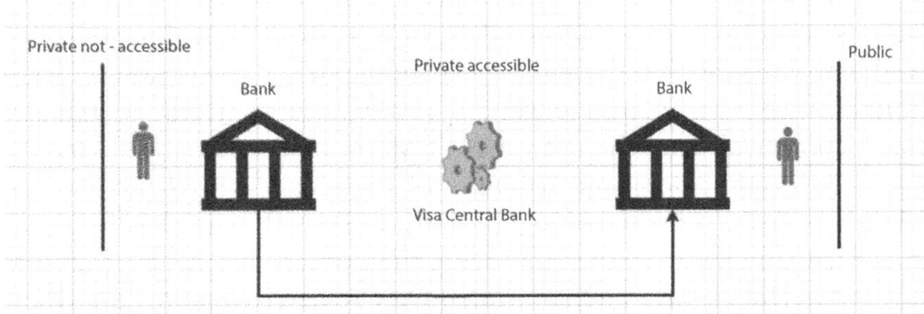

Figure 2.1 Information structure in the traditional digital payments.

seen in Figure 2.2. Decentralized finance operates on a blockchain infrastructure, distributing its encrypted records across multiple nodes globally (Pilkington, 2016) [23]. Notably, this technology often operates in an unregulated environment due to the anonymity prevalent in certain blockchain models, wherein no central entity governs participation eligibility. However, it is feasible to establish a permissioned blockchain framework, enabling a single entity or a select few to control and authorize access for others (IBM, 2022) [14].

Decentralized finance presents an alternative approach to conventional financial services by circumventing the expenses associated with third-party intermediaries (Roose, 2022) [24]. It fosters a decentralized innovation process that facilitates the controlled exchange of information among users (Chesbrough, Vanhaverbeke, and West, 2014) [25]. Several techniques can be used to investigate the price movement of various financial instruments (Mehta and Sharma, 2024; Vyas *et al.*, 2020; Mehta *et al.*, 2022) [26–28]. The core aim of DeFi is to empower individual users to engage directly in activities like lending, borrowing, asset management, and insurance without relying on intermediaries (Chohan, 2021) [29]. This study holds relevance in the contemporary context as it seeks to organize the ongoing public discussion surrounding the disruptive fintech rooted in blockchain. The primary objective and academic contribution of this paper revolve around providing evidence-based public policy suggestions to regulate the domain of DeFi effectively (Chohan, 2021) [29].

Certainly, the impact of DeFi on the traditional financial structure is evident in the process of purchasing a security, like a stock, providing a clear illustration of the contrasts between the two systems. In traditional finance, acquiring a stock involves a multi-step process. Initially, a client establishes a bank account and puts money into that account. Subsequently, the client requests the bank to execute a purchase order, prompting the bank to

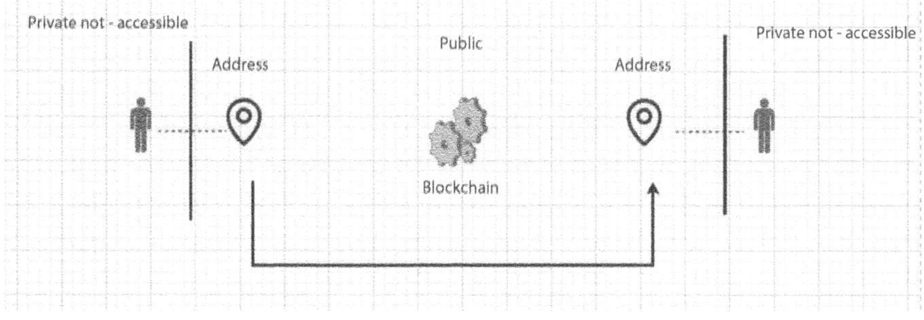

Figure 2.2 Information structure in the Bitcoin payment.

engage an intermediary to fulfill the order. The intermediary then proceeds to the stock exchange to purchase the stock on behalf of the client. The ownership information is relayed backward: from the stock exchange to the intermediary, then to the bank, and lastly to the client. This successive procedure in conventional methods necessitates the involvement of these mediators—the bank, intermediary, and stock exchange. Consequently, this extended buying process incurs substantial outlays and time insufficiencies and introduces potential sources of error at each stage, impacting both investors and companies (Schueffel, 2021) [45].

Various innovations like digital banking, m-commerce, P2P lending, smart contracts, and open banking APIs have expanded customer choices within the fintech landscape. However, the susceptibility of fintech to cyber-attacks and security breaches remains a concern. Consequently, a decentralized system can help alleviate some of the longstanding issues associated with traditional financial technology. The decentralized approach is known as DeFi.

In the realm of traditional finance, intermediaries like banks, exchanges, and lending institutions serve as central actors, facilitating transactions and overseeing funds. In contrast, DeFi harnesses the decentralized nature of blockchain technology to establish a trustless and transparent financial ecosystem, characterized by secure, transparent, and immutable transactions.

Decentralized finance has the potential to extend financial services to the unbanked and under-banked populations worldwide, who often lack access to conventional banking services. Given that DeFi platforms operate on blockchain networks, they are accessible to anyone with a smartphone, thereby opening efficient financial opportunities for individuals, including decentralized lending and borrowing, decentralized trading, and yield farming. Lending and borrowing platforms, that are DeFi lending platforms, enable users to lend or borrow digital assets without intermediaries. Users can earn interest by collateralizing their crypto holdings or borrowing assets against collateral. Decentralized exchanges facilitate direct peer-to-peer cryptocurrency trading without central entities. They enhance liquidity and eliminate the dependence on centralized exchanges. Yield farming and liquidity provision involve users, providing liquidity to DeFi platforms and receiving rewards or tokens in return. Liquidity providers earn additional tokens by contributing assets to decentralized liquidity pools. Governance and decentralized autonomous organizations (DAOs) that are DeFi projects often introduce governance tokens enabling user participation in protocol decisions as seen in the Figure 2.3. The DAOs empower token holders to propose and vote on protocol

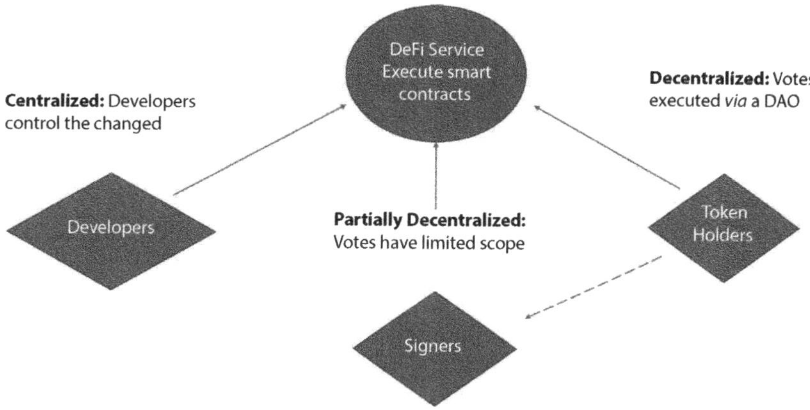

Figure 2.3 DeFi governance mechanisms.

changes. Decentralized finance aims to establish a fully automated, censorship-resistant, and decentralized substitute for traditional financial systems. Applications within DeFi operate on open-source principles, striving to grant users unrestricted access to their services (Carapella and Swem, 2022) [30]. Additionally, these applications are structured to prevent any singular entity from monopolizing decision-making authority within the system. The goal is to create an inclusive and DeFi ecosystem where users have the autonomy to access financial services without dependence on centralized entities (Carapella and Swem, 2022) [30].

These applications illustrate the transformative potential of DeFi, offering users increased financial independence, global market access, and opportunities for earning yields and contributing to decentralized governance.

2.3 Evolution of Artificial Intelligence

The domain of AI encompasses more than mere comprehension; it involves crafting intelligent entities—machines capable of computing effective and secure actions across diverse and unfamiliar scenarios (Russell and Norvig, 2023) [31]. Artificial intelligence has different meanings in different disciplines.

Artificial intelligence refers to the simulation of human intelligence processes by machines, typically computer systems, to perform tasks that usually require human intelligence. This field involves the development of algorithms and models that enable machines to perceive, reason, learn from data, and make decisions. As per Suman (2021) [32], AI entails computers' emulating cognitive processes, transitioning from a concept confined to science fiction to a pervasive reality within modern technology. Indeed, AI systems encompass a broad range of machine-based systems designed to perform tasks that typically require human intelligence. These systems can range from simple rule-based algorithms to more complex ones that exhibit advanced capabilities, often utilizing varying degrees of autonomy.

Artificial intelligence systems are developed to achieve specific human-defined objectives, whether it is making predictions, offering recommendations, or making decisions. One of the fundamental components driving the advancements in AI is the utilization of vast amounts of data, often referred to as 'big data.' This data is sourced from diverse and extensive datasets, including structured, unstructured, and semi-structured information.

Machine learning is a key subset of AI that heavily relies on big data to train models. Its algorithms learn patterns and insights from these datasets without explicit programming. Instead, they use the information to adjust their parameters and improve performance automatically through experience and exposure to new data. Machine learning is the process where machines learn patterns and make predictions or decisions based on data without being explicitly programmed to perform the task. Machine learning algorithms enable systems to improve their performance over time by learning from experience or patterns in the provided data. The process involves feeding these ML models with large datasets, allowing them to analyze, identify patterns, and make predictions or decisions based on the learned patterns. As more data is processed, these models continuously adapt and refine their predictive capabilities, often improving their performance over time.

The combination of AI techniques, big data, and ML plays a pivotal role in various applications across industries, including healthcare, finance, autonomous vehicles, recommendation systems, and natural language processing. The ability to process vast amounts of data and derive meaningful insights has significantly contributed to the advancement and efficacy of AI systems in addressing complex real-world problems.

The evolution of AI traces a remarkable journey from its conceptual origins to its current state as a transformative force across industries. The genesis of AI can be traced back to ancient myths and philosophical musings envisioning intelligent machines. However, formal inception occurred in the mid-20th century, marked by the coining of the term "artificial intelligence" in 1956 at the Dartmouth Conference (Russell and Norvig, 2023) [31]. The early AI projects laid the groundwork for subsequent advancements. The field experienced periods of success and setbacks, witnessing significant progress in expert systems, natural language processing, and neural networks in the latter part of the 20th century as seen in Figure 2.4 (Russell and Norvig, 2023, p.45) [31]. Advances in computing power, ML algorithms, and big data sparked a renaissance in the 21st century, propelling breakthroughs in deep learning, computer vision, and language understanding. This resurgence led to the integration of AI into diverse applications, revolutionizing sectors such as healthcare, finance, autonomous vehicles, and personalized services. Artificial intelligence continues to evolve, propelled by ongoing research, technological innovations, and its pervasive integration into various aspects of modern life, promising further transformative potential in the future. The timeline of AI is shown in the figure below.

The emergence of AI in recent years has marked a profound shift in various industries, notably within financial services, signifying the potential to revolutionize traditional practices. The rapid advancements in AI technologies, encompassing ML, natural language processing, and predictive analytics, have enabled financial institutions to leverage data-driven insights, automation, and intelligent decision-making processes (Sarin and Sharma, 2023) [33]. These advancements empower institutions to enhance customer experiences through personalized services, optimize risk management strategies, streamline operations, and develop sophisticated algorithms for trading and investment purposes. Furthermore, AI's ability to process vast volumes of data at high speeds facilitates more accurate predictions and pattern recognition, providing a competitive edge and unlocking new opportunities for innovation within the financial sector (Sarin and Sharma, 2023) [33]. As AI continues to evolve and integrate further into financial services, it holds the promise of reshaping industry standards, driving efficiency, and fostering a more inclusive and dynamic financial ecosystem.

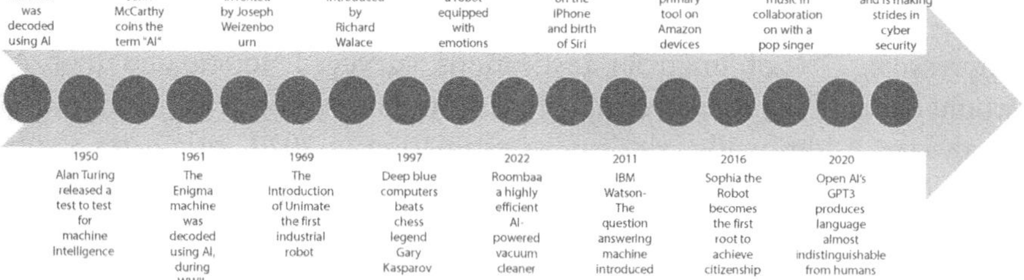

Figure 2.4 A timeline on artificial intelligence (AI). Source: Russell and Norvig, 2023 [31].

The review of literature by Rzpeka and Berger (2018) [34] concentrated on 91 primary studies sourced from conferences and journals, centering specifically on individual user interactions with AI systems in the realm of information systems (IS). Additionally, Hofmann *et al.*'s review (2019) [35] was predominantly related to the impact of AI and ML in the radiology value chain, focusing on its timeframe from 2012 to 2018, aligning with its scope. Borges *et al.*'s review (2021) [36] emphasized AI interactions with organizational strategy, potentially overlooking the contextual definition and value creation aspects. Furthermore, Karger's review (2020) [37] had a narrow focus solely on the interrelations between AI and blockchain, excluding broader contexts. In contrast, Collin *et al.* (2021) [38] encompasses a comprehensive analysis of relevant research spanning 15 years, encompassing various high-quality journals and conferences. In a recent study, researchers employed bibliometric-coupling review to delineate the thematic arrangement of ML and AI study within the finance domain, encompassing the period from 1986 to April 2021 (Ahmed *et al.*, 2022) [39]. Through these analyses, the researchers aimed to infer the interconnected thematic patterns prevalent in AI and ML research within the finance domain. Additionally, they utilized co-occurrence and confluence analyses to spotlight emerging trends and delineate evolving research directions about AI and ML in the realm of financial research. These methodological approaches enabled them to uncover underlying themes, track the evolution of scholarly connections, and identify pivotal trends shaping the landscape of AI and ML research in finance over the specified timeframe.

The financial sector, notably driven by the rise of financial technology enterprises, has witnessed a rapid and escalating integration of AI/ML systems. This surge in adoption is largely attributed to the financial industry's assimilation of advancements in technology, such as big data and cloud computing, alongside the expansive growth of the digital economy (Boukherouaa *et al.*, 2020; Sarin and Sharma, 2023) [33, 40]. These advancements have notably facilitated the effective implementation and deployment of AI/ML systems within financial operations. In 2020, a survey commissioned by the World Economic Forum revealed that an impressive 77% of financial institutions surveyed anticipated that AI would become significantly important for their operations in the following two years. Additionally, McKinsey's estimation in 2020 anticipates a substantial potential value, projecting that AI's impact in the banking sector could reach a staggering $1 trillion (Boukherouaa *et al.* 2020) [40]. Ahmed *et al.* (2022) [39] conducted a thorough review of literature concerning

AI and ML applications within the finance domain. It utilized a bibliometric approach, examining 348 articles published between 2011 and 2021 from journals indexed in the Scopus database. The study delineated diverse applications of AI and ML in finance, encompassing areas like liquidation prophecy, forecasting of stock prices, diversification strategies, forecasting of oil prices, counter-money laundering strategies, behavioral finance, and blockchain technology and big data analytics. The study's outcomes offer practical insights, especially for market participants such as fintech and financial companies, elucidating the potential of AI and ML methodologies in enhancing decision-making processes within the finance sector.

Artificial intelligence has emerged as a transformative force within traditional finance, revolutionizing critical aspects including risk assessment, algorithmic trading, and fraud detection. As can be seen from the work authored by Yawised *et al.* (2022) [41], it provided valuable insights into the evolving business landscape of the metaverse era. By examining both the opportunities and challenges presented by this transformative shift, the authors contributed to the understanding of how businesses can adapt and thrive in the increasingly digital and interconnected world of the metaverse. In the realm of risk assessment, AI-powered algorithms leverage extensive datasets to evaluate creditworthiness more accurately than conventional methods, considering diverse parameters such as credit history, income, spending patterns, and alternative data sources. This aids financial institutions in making more informed lending decisions. Furthermore, AI models facilitate risk prediction and management by analyzing market trends, historical data, and macroeconomic indicators, enabling proactive measures to mitigate potential risks. Within algorithmic trading, AI-driven strategies execute trades based on predefined rules or learning from historical data, optimizing portfolio management with enhanced efficiency and speed. Additionally, AI facilitates quantitative analysis, identifying intricate patterns and correlations within financial data for informed investment decisions. In the domain of fraud detection and prevention, AI-powered systems detect anomalies and patterns indicative of potentially fraudulent activities, bolstering security measures and mitigating risks in real-time. Moreover, AI contributes to personalized customer service through chatbots, delivering tailored assistance and recommendations based on individual preferences and behaviors. While AI applications in traditional finance have vastly improved accuracy and efficiency, challenges related to fairness in algorithms, data privacy, and regulatory compliance persist, necessitating ongoing ethical considerations and refinements in the deployment of AI within the financial sector.

2.4 The Intersection of DeFi and AI

The fusion of DeFi and AI brings together the best of worlds, offering innovative financial solutions and fostering greater efficiency and personalization. Key areas where DeFi and AI intersect include the following: firstly, algorithmic trading, i.e. AI-powered algorithms can analyze vast amounts of data to identify market trends and execute trades on DeFi platforms; secondly credit scoring and risk assessment, i.e. AI can enhance DeFi lending platforms by providing more accurate credit scoring and risk assessment, leading to better-informed lending decisions; thirdly fraud detection and prevention, i.e. by leveraging AI's pattern recognition capabilities; DeFi platforms can strengthen their security measures and detect fraudulent activities more effectively. The potential of AI to reshape the future of DeFi is profound and multifaceted, presenting a spectrum of transformative possibilities across various facets of the financial landscape. Artificial intelligence, when integrated into DeFi ecosystems, holds the promise of revolutionizing traditional financial processes and services. Through sophisticated algorithms and ML capabilities, AI brings forth several pivotal changes. Firstly, AI-driven automation streamlines and optimizes a myriad of financial operations, significantly enhancing the efficiency and speed of transactions within DeFi platforms. Moreover, AI augments risk assessment and management by swiftly analyzing extensive datasets in real time, leading to more accurate risk profiling and decision-making in lending, borrowing, and investment activities.

Another profound implication lies in the realm of personalized financial services. Artificial intelligence enables tailored offerings based on individual user behaviors, preferences, and risk profiles, thereby ensuring more customized and user-centric financial experiences. Additionally, AI-powered algorithms drive advanced predictive analytics, allowing for more accurate market trend forecasts and informed investment strategies, thereby reshaping how financial decisions are made in DeFi.

Furthermore, AI-driven algorithmic trading and liquidity provision mechanisms bring increased market efficiency, liquidity, and reduced volatility within decentralized financial markets. The seamless integration of AI technology in DeFi also fosters greater transparency, accountability, and auditability, bolstering user trust and confidence in the decentralized ecosystem.

However, challenges such as ethical considerations, data privacy, regulatory compliance, and ensuring the interpretability of AI-driven decisions remain significant hurdles to overcome. As the synergy between AI and

DeFi evolves, stakeholders must tread carefully, balancing innovation with responsible governance to unlock the full potential of AI and ensure the sustainable and inclusive growth of decentralized finance.

In 2021, the total value of blockchain technology enabling DeFi and the AI market amounted to $230.10 million. Anticipated growth by 2030 is projected to surpass $980 million. This promising data highlights the swift evolution of these interconnected technologies, poised to deliver increased security, inclusivity, and autonomous solutions to people worldwide, particularly in the financial sector.

The decentralization and transparency offered by blockchain technology have disrupted the DeFi space, as evidenced by Chen and Bellaviti (2020) [15]. Nevertheless, the concept of decentralized finance faces skepticism from governments due to its history of scams and thefts.

However, while AI in DeFi holds much promise, several delusions must be lectured. Hence, as the domain progresses, it will be essential for the cryptocurrency community to maintain vigilance in implementing AI, acknowledging its capabilities while exercising caution to prevent unintended repercussions. Additionally, the complete interpretability of AI remains a challenge for the public, further complicating the adoption of ground-breaking technologies. These factors create barriers to entry for revolutionary technologies.

Certainly, the opportunities for AI in DeFi (Decentralized Finance) are vast and multifaceted. Initially, AI can scrutinize real-time data from diverse origins, such as market predictions and tendencies, news articles, and on digital platform, to evaluate and forecast potential risks within DeFi protocols. This includes identifying vulnerabilities to flash loan attacks, smart contract vulnerabilities, and market volatility. Investors always look for various investment strategies to earn abnormal returns (Mehta and Sharma, 2017) [42]. Artificial intelligence-powered risk models can provide early warnings and allow DeFi platforms to take preventive measures, enhancing overall security. Secondly, AI algorithms can execute trades based on predefined criteria, market signals, and user preferences. This automation not only increases the efficiency of trading but also enables users to make better-informed decisions. Artificial intelligence-powered trading bots can respond quickly to market changes, execute complex strategies, and optimize trading strategies for higher returns. Thirdly, AI can analyze market data to identify liquidity imbalances and provide liquidity to DEXs and liquidity pools. Automated market makers powered by AI can efficiently manage liquidity, ensuring stable prices and reduced slippage for traders. Fourthly, AI can detect fraudulent activities such as rug pulls, pump-and-dump schemes, and phishing attacks by analyzing transaction patterns and network behavior. This enhances the security of DeFi platforms and helps protect users from financial fraud. Artificial intelligence-based tools can review and audit smart contracts for vulnerabilities and bugs. These tools can analyze contract code, detect potential security flaws, and suggest improvements before deployment, reducing the risk of exploitation. Artificial intelligence-driven credit scoring models can assess the creditworthiness of DeFi users by analyzing their transaction history and other relevant data. This enables more accurate lending decisions and expands access to decentralized lending platforms. The DeFi platforms must comply with regulatory requirements, such as anti-money laundering (AML) and Know Your Customer (KYC). Artificial intelligence can streamline the compliance process by automating identity verification, transaction monitoring, and reporting, reducing operational overhead and ensuring regulatory compliance can provide users with personalized investment recommendations, savings strategies, and portfolio management advice based on their financial goals and risk tolerance. This tailored approach can improve the user experience and help users achieve their financial objectives and can process and analyze vast amounts of data generated by DeFi platforms, offering valuable insights into market trends, user behavior, and performance metrics. These insights can inform strategic decisions and product development. Lastly, AI can facilitate interoperability between different blockchain networks, allowing DeFi applications to access a broader range of assets and liquidity pools. This can lead to increased efficiency and liquidity in the DeFi ecosystem. Artificial intelligence has the potential to enhance security, efficiency, and user experience in DeFi while opening new possibilities for innovation and risk management in the rapidly evolving DeFi landscape.

2.5 DeFi Real Life Examples

There were limited examples of fully AI-enhanced decentralized autonomous organizations (DAOs). However, AI was starting to play a role in enhancing the decision-making processes within some DAOs. Below are two case studies that illustrate how AI was being integrated into DAOs at that time:

2.5.1 Nectar DAO – Token Weighted Voting with AI Analysis

Nectar DAO is associated with the decentralized crypto exchange project, Ethfinex (now part of Deversifi). Nectar DAO manages the Nectar token

(NEC), and its primary function is to decide on changes and upgrades to the Deversifi exchange and the token itself. Nectar DAO introduced a novel concept where AI was used to assist token-weight voting decisions. The AI system analyzed discussions and proposals within the DAO, assessing sentiment, identifying key arguments, and offering insights to token holders before voting. When a proposal was submitted, the AI analyzed forum discussions, social media sentiment, and historical voting trends to provide a summary to token holders. This allowed participants to make informed decisions based on the collective wisdom of the community and AI-driven insights. The integration of AI-enhanced decision-making aimed to improve the efficiency and quality of governance decisions within the DAO. While it was a novel approach, it raised questions about the extent of AI's influence in decentralized governance and the need for transparency in the AI's decision-making process.

2.5.2 PieDAO – AI-Managed Index Funds

PieDAO is a DAO that manages tokenized portfolios, effectively creating decentralized index funds. Token holders in PieDAO can participate in the governance of these index funds and the DAO itself. PieDAO integrated AI to manage its token portfolios. Artificial intelligence algorithms analyzed market data, token performance, and economic indicators to make decisions about fund rebalancing. The AI autonomously proposed changes to the token portfolios, and the community could vote on these proposals. The AI continuously monitored the performance of the underlying assets and calculated the optimal asset allocation to maintain the fund's target. When a rebalancing event was deemed necessary, the AI submitted a proposal to the DAO. Token holders could then vote on whether to accept or reject the AI's proposal. This integration of AI in PieDAO aimed to create more efficient, low-cost, and automated index fund management. The decentralized governance allowed the community to validate or challenge the AI's decisions, ensuring transparency and control over the fund management process.

These case studies demonstrate early attempts to integrate AI into DAOs to enhance decision-making processes. They reflect the potential for AI to streamline operations and improve governance within decentralized organizations. However, as AI's role in DAOs expands, it raises important questions about transparency, governance, and the balance between automated decision-making and human control.

2.6 Future Trends and Possibilities

2.6.1 Forecasting the Future of AI-DeFi Integration

2.6.1.1 Potential Areas of Growth and Innovation

In the intersection of AI and DeFi, there exists a significant potential for reshaping the future of financial systems. Forecasts about the integration of AI within DeFi suggest several prospective developments poised to impact the financial landscape profoundly. Foremost among these is the enhancement of risk management within DeFi platforms through AI-driven risk assessment models, enabling more precise risk profiling, fraud detection, and continuous monitoring mechanisms. Furthermore, the integration of AI is anticipated to revolutionize the provision of personalized financial services within DeFi, allowing for tailored lending and investment options based on individual risk profiles and preferences. The automation of decision-making processes through AI algorithms is expected to optimize various financial activities within DeFi, facilitating the autonomous execution of transactions and management of portfolios. A pronounced focus on ethical AI governance to mitigate biases, ensure transparency in decision-making processes, and comply with regulatory standards is anticipated. Additionally, AI-driven cybersecurity solutions are envisaged to play a pivotal role in fortifying the security posture of DeFi platforms against potential cyber threats and vulnerabilities. This integration foresees the emergence of sophisticated AI-powered oracle systems, facilitating seamless integration of validated external data into DeFi platforms. It is expected that regulatory frameworks will adapt to encompass the complexities arising from the amalgamation of AI and DeFi, emphasizing aspects such as consumer protection, data privacy, and algorithmic transparency. Collaborations between the AI and DeFi sectors are poised to burgeon, fostering innovation and cross-industry synergies that drive novel advancements at the intersection of finance and AI. Nonetheless, the realization of these transformative potentials necessitates addressing challenges encompassing regulatory compliance, ethical governance, data privacy, and technological risks to ensure the responsible and sustainable integration of AI within DeFi.

2.6.1.2 Regulatory and Legal Considerations

The convergence of AI with DeFi presents a complex landscape of regulatory and legal considerations that demand scrutiny and adaptation.

As AI technologies become increasingly integrated into DeFi platforms, regulatory frameworks must evolve to address the intricate interplay between these domains. Regulatory considerations encompass diverse facets, including data privacy, algorithmic transparency, consumer protection, and compliance adherence. The decentralized nature of DeFi challenges traditional regulatory oversight, raising concerns about the application of existing financial regulations to this evolving ecosystem. Striking a balance between fostering innovation and safeguarding against potential risks, such as algorithmic biases or systemic vulnerabilities, remains a pivotal concern for policymakers. Additionally, legal frameworks governing smart contracts, liability, intellectual property rights, and cross-border transactions require refinement to accommodate the novel complexities arising from AI-driven DeFi applications. Collaborative efforts between regulatory bodies, industry stakeholders, and legal experts are essential to crafting adaptive frameworks that foster responsible innovation while ensuring consumer protection, financial stability, and legal compliance within the evolving landscape of AI-integrated DeFi.

2.7 Conclusion

2.7.1 Key Findings

Decentralized finance stands as the forthcoming disruptor in the financial ecosystem, leveraging blockchain technology to pioneer novel methods of transferring value across borders. It embodies an initial foray into innovative avenues that prioritize interoperability, accessibility, open-source frameworks, financial inclusivity, and transparency. By offering retail users access to services that are currently deficient within the conventional financial framework, DeFi presents a significant opportunity. Furthermore, institutions stand to benefit by migrating tangible assets onto the blockchain, thereby reducing costs and enhancing operational efficiencies. Importantly, the advent of blockchain technology does not necessitate an overthrow of the existing traditional financial system; rather, it holds the potential to complement it. This collaborative coexistence could foster a symbiotic relationship, leveraging the strengths of both DeFi and traditional finance to establish a more comprehensive and efficient financial landscape.

This chapter talks about the integration of AI within the realm of DeFi showcases a transformative potential that could redefine the landscape of financial services. As evidenced by numerous scholarly works and research papers, the fusion of AI technologies with DeFi applications offers multifaceted advantages across various domains of finance. Artificial intelligence's predictive analytics, ML algorithms, and automation capabilities enhance risk assessment, optimize trading strategies, enable personalized customer services, and fortify fraud detection within the DeFi ecosystem. This chapter looks into the amalgamation, which presents opportunities to expand financial inclusion and improve efficiency, transparency, and accessibility while reshaping traditional financial paradigms. However, challenges such as regulatory concerns, data privacy, algorithmic biases, and security risks necessitate thorough consideration and continuous refinement. Nevertheless, the promising synergy between AI and DeFi stands as a catalyst poised to revolutionize the financial sector, offering novel solutions and shaping a more inclusive, efficient, and technologically advanced financial future.

2.7.2 Recommendation and Implications

For DeFi developers, meticulous attention to security measures remains paramount in navigating the evolving landscape of DeFi. Emphasizing stringent smart contract auditing, rigorous testing, and transparent documentation are essential practices. Moreover, fostering user education and community engagement on risks associated with DeFi offerings is crucial. Diversification of investments, thorough due diligence, and staying informed about market trends is key for investors to navigate the DeFi landscape prudently. Additionally, policymakers should strive to establish clear and adaptive regulatory frameworks that foster innovation while ensuring consumer protection and compliance with evolving standards. Engaging with industry experts and staying abreast of technological advancements will enable policymakers to craft regulations that strike a balance between fostering innovation and maintaining market integrity in the dynamic realm of DeFi.

In the convergence of AI and DeFi, the financial sector witnesses a transformative landscape with profound implications. The integration of AI into DeFi brings forth a spectrum of opportunities and challenges, shaping the sector's trajectory in multifaceted ways. Artificial intelligence–DeFi integration augments efficiency by automating operations, enhancing risk management through real-time assessment, and offering personalized financial services tailored to individual needs. Moreover, it drives algorithmic trading, improving market liquidity and efficiency. However, these advancements pose challenges concerning job displacement due to automation, potential biases in AI-driven decision-making, and the necessity for robust regulatory frameworks to address new complexities in decentralized financial ecosystems. The symbiotic relationship between AI and DeFi presents a paradigm shift, promising innovation while demanding cautious navigation of ethical, regulatory, and security considerations to ensure sustainable growth and inclusive financial ecosystems.

References

1. Sharma, R. and Mehta, K., Credit risk and bank specific factors: An empirical study using panel GMM. *Int. J. Econ. Bus. Res.*, 27, 2, 294–309, 2024.
2. Sharma, R. and Mehta, K., *Deep Learning Tools for Predicting Stock Market Movements*, John Wiley & Sons, USA, 2024.
3. Sharma, R., Mehta, K., Chugh, A., Using Analytic Hierarchy Process to determine forex risk hedging strategies of SMEs. *AIP Conf. Proc.*, 2916, 1, 120008, 2023.
4. Mehta, K., Sharma, R., Vyas, V., Kuckreja, J.S., Exit strategy decision by venture capital firms in India using fuzzy AHP. *J. Entrep. Emerg. Econ.*, 14, 4, 643–669, 2022.
5. Haber, S. and Stornetta, W.S., How to time-stamp a digital document. *J. Cryptol.*, 3, 99–111, 1991, https://doi.org/10.1007/BF00196791.
6. Narayanan, A., Bonneau, J., Felten, E., Miller, A., Goldfeder, S., Clark, J., *Bitcoin and Cryptocurrency Technologies Introduction to the Book*, Princeton University Press, Princeton, NJ, 2016.
7. Buterin, V., Ethereum white paper, 2013, Retrieved from https://github.com/ethereum/wiki/wiki/WhitePAPER.
8. Sarin, A.B., Behavioral Finance and Cryptocurrency Market, in: *Revolutionizing Financial Services and Markets Through FinTech and Blockchain*, K. Mehta, R. Sharma, P. Yu (Eds.), pp. 217–236, IGI Global, USA, 2023, https://doi.org/10.4018/978-1-6684-8624-5.ch014.
9. Harvey, C.R., Ramachandran, A., Santoro, J., *DeFi and the future of finance*, John Wiley & Sons, USA, 2021, Retrieved from ssrn.com/abstract=3711777. Accessed October 1, 2023.
10. Andreev, R., Andreeva, P., Krotov, L., *et al.*, Review of blockchain technology: types of blockchain and their application. *Intellekt. Sist. Proizv.*, 16, 11–14, 2018, https://doi.org/10.22213/2410-9304-2018-1-11-14.
11. Zetzsche, D.A., Arner, D.W., Buckley, R.P., Decentralized finance. *J. Financ. Regul.*, 6, 172–203, 2020.
12. Lee, M.R., Yen, D.C., Hurlburt, G.F., Financial technologies and applications. *IT Prof.*, 20, 27–33, 2018.
13. Schär, F., Decentralized Finance: On Blockchain- and Smart Contract-Based Financial Markets. *Fed. Reserve Bank St. Louis Rev.*, 103, 2, 153–174, 2021.

14. https://www.ibm.com/annualreport/assets/downloads/IBM_Annual_Report_2022.pdf.
15. Chen, Y. and Bellavitis, C., Blockchain disruption and decentralized finance: The rise of decentralized business models. *J. Bus. Ventur. Insights*, 13, 1–22, 2020.
16. Jensen, J.R., von Wachter, V., Ross, O., An Introduction to Decentralized Finance (DeFi). *Complex Syst. Inform. Model. Q.*, 26, 46–54, 2021.
17. Bartoletti, M., Chiang, J.H.Y., Lluch-Lafuente, A., *SoK: Lending Pools in Decentralized Finance*, 2020b, arXiv preprint arXiv:2012.13230v1. arXiv.org. <https://ideas.repec.org/p/arx/papers/2012.13230.html>.
18. Cousaert, S., Xu, J., Matsui, T., SoK: Yield Aggregators in DeFi, 2021, https://ieeexplore.ieee.org/abstract/document/9805523.
19. Meyer, E., Isabell, W., Philipp, S., Decentralized finance—A systematic literature review and research directions. *ECIS 2022 Research Papers*, 2022, https://aisel.aisnet.org/ecis2022_rp/25.
20. Teng, H., Tian, W., Wang, H., *et al.*, Applications of decentralized finance (DeFi) on Ethereum, in: *Proceedings of IEEE Asia-Pacific Conference on Image Processing, Electronics and Computers (IPEC)*, IEEE, pp. 573–578, 2022.
21. Vyas, V., Mehta, K., Sharma, R., Are bitcoin prices isolated or co-integrated? *Int. J. Bus. Glob.*, 35, 1–2, 5–19, 2023.
22. Sharma, R., Mehta, K., Rana, R., Cryptocurrency adoption behaviour of millennial investors in India, in: *Perspectives on Blockchain Technology and Responsible Investing*, pp. 135–158, 2023.
23. Pilkington, M., Blockchain technology: principles and applications, in: Chapter 11 on *Research handbook on digital transformations*, Elgar Publishing, UK, 2016, ISBN: 9781784717759.
24. Roose, K., What Is DeFi?, The New York Times, 2022, https://www.nytimes.com/interactive/2022/03/18/technology/what-is-defi-cryptocurrency.html.
25. Chesbrough, H., Vanhaverbeke, W., West, J., *New frontiers in open innovation*, Oxford University Press, New York, 2014.
26. Mehta, K. and Sharma, R., Unraveling quantum complexity: A fuzzy AHP approach to understanding software industry challenges, in: *Deep Learning Tools for Predicting Stock Market Movements*, pp. 39–60, 2024.
27. Vyas, V., Mehta, K., Sharma, R., Investigating socially responsible investing behaviour of Indian investors using structural equation modelling. *J. Sustain. Financ. Invest.*, 12, 1, 1–23, 2020.
28. Mehta, K., Sharma, R., Vyas, V., A quantile regression approach to study the impact of aluminium prices on manufacturing sector of India during COVID era. *Mater. Today: Proc.*, 65, 7, 3506–3511, 2022.
29. Chohan, U., Decentralized Finance (DeFi): An Emergent Alternative Financial Architecture. *Critical Blockchain Research Initiative Working Papers SSRN*, 2021, http://dx.doi.org/10.2139/ssrn.3791921.
30. Carapella, F. and Swem, N., Decentralized Finance (Defi): Transformative Potential & Associated Risks. *Financ. Econ. Discuss. Ser.*, 57, 1–33, 2022, https://doi.org/10.17016/feds.2022.057.

31. Russell, S. and Norvig, P., *Artificial Intelligence: A modern approach*, 4th ed., Pearson, UK, 2023.
32. Suman, S., Artificial intelligence in nuclear industry: chimera or solution. *J. Clean. Prod.*, 278, 124022, 2021, https://doi.org/10.1016/j.jclepro.2020.124022.
33. Sarin, A.B. and Sharma, S., Artificial Intelligence in Behavioral Finance for Investment Decision-making, in: *AI and Emotional Intelligence for Modern Business Management*, B. Bhardwaj, D. Sharma, M. Dhiman (Eds.), pp. 194–212, IGI Global, USA, 2023, https://doi.org/10.4018/979-8-3693-0418-1.ch013.
34. Rzpeka, C. and Berger, B., User interaction with AI-enabled systems: A systematic review of IS research, San Francisco, 2018.
35. Hofmann, P., Oesterle, S., Rust, P., Urbach, N., Machine learning approaches along the radiology value chain – Rethinking value propositions. *ECIS 2019 Proceedings*, Stockholm, 2019.
36. Borges, A.F.S., Laurindo, F.J.B., Spínola, M.M., Gonçalves, R.F., Mattos, C.A., The strategic use of artificial intelligence in the digital era: Systematic literature review and future research directions. *Int. J. Inf. Manag.*, 57, 102225, 2021, https://doi.org/10.1016/j.ijinfomgt.2020.102225.
37. Karger, E., Combining Blockchain and Artificial Intelligence – Literature Review and State of the Art. *ICIS 2020 Proceedings*, 2020.
38. Collins, C., Dennehy, D., Conboy, K., Mikalef, P., Artificial intelligence in information systems research: A systematic literature review and research agenda. *Int. J. Inf. Manag.*, Elsevier, 60, C, 102383, 2021, DOI: 10.1016/j.ijinfomgt.2021.102383.
39. Ahmed, S., Alshater, M.M., El Ammari, A., Hammami, H., Artificial intelligence and machine learning in finance: A bibliometric review. *Res. Int. Bus. Financ.*, 61, 101646, 2022, https://doi.org/10.1016/j.ribaf.2022.101646.
40. Boukherouaa, E.B., AlAjmi, K., Deodoro, J., Farias, A., Ravikumar, R., *Powering the Digital Economy: Opportunities and Risks of Artificial Intelligence in Finance*, Departmental Papers, International Monetary Fund, USA, 024, p. A001, 2021, Retrieved Jan 1, 2024, from https://doi.org/10.5089/9781589063952.087.A001.
41. Yawised, K., Apasrawirote, D., Boonparn, C., From traditional business shifted towards transformation: the emerging business opportunities and challenges in 'metaverse' era. *INCBAA*, 162, 175, 2022.
42. Mehta, K. and Sharma, R., Contrarian and momentum investment strategies: Evidence from Indian stock market. *Int. J. Appl. Bus. Econ. Res.*, 15, 2, 87–98, 2017.
43. Abdulhakeem, S.A. and Hu, Powered by Blockchain Technology, DeFi (Decentralized Finance) Strives to Increase Financial Inclusion of the Unbanked by Reshaping the World Financial System. *Mod. Econ.*, 12, 01, 1–16, 2021.

44. Werner, S., Perez, D., Gudgeon, L., Klages-Mundt, A., Harz, D., Knottenbelt, W., *SoK: Decentralized Finance (DeFi)*, 2021, 10.48550/arXiv.2101.08778.
45. Schueffel, P., DeFi: Decentralized Finance - An Introduction and Overview. *J. Innov. Manag.*, 9, 3, i.2021. 10.24840/2183-0606_009.003_0001

3

Exploring the Synergy Between Fintech and Green Finance: A Catalyst for Sustainable Development

Renuka Sharma*, Kiran Mehta and Yashica

Department of Finance, Chitkara Business School, Chitkara University, Punjab, India

Abstract

This paper explores the dynamic intersection of financial technology (fintech) and green finance, elucidating their combined potential to drive sustainability and financial inclusion. Fintech innovations offer a unique opportunity to integrate green finance principles, promoting environmentally responsible investments, responsible consumption, and transparent reporting. However, several challenges, including regulatory complexities, data privacy concerns, competition from big tech, and interest rate volatility must be addressed to unlock fintech's full potential for green finance. Collaborative solutions involving regulators, fintech firms, traditional financial institutions, and investors are essential to create an enabling environment for innovation and sustainability. Regulatory harmonization, industry partnerships, investor engagement, and strategies to mitigate big tech competition and interest rate fluctuations are key recommendations. By navigating these challenges and embracing these recommendations, the fintech industry can catalyse the adoption of green finance, contributing to a more sustainable and inclusive global financial ecosystem.

Keywords: Fintech, green finance, sustainable development, literature review, environmental impact, climate finance, sustainable investment, financial innovation

**Corresponding author*: bhavyarenuka@gmail.com

Renuka Sharma, Kiran Mehta, Vishal Vyas and Vinod Kumar Shukla (eds.) Decentralized Finance and Blockchain: A Game Changing Duo, (47–76) © 2025 Scrivener Publishing LLC

3.1 Introduction

3.1.1 Climate Change and Sustainable Development

Human activities, particularly the emission of greenhouse gases, have unequivocally led to global warming, with a 1.1°C increase in global surface temperatures since 1850–1900. These emissions persist due to unsustainable energy use, land changes, and consumption patterns, causing rapid environmental changes. These human-induced climate changes have already triggered extreme weather events worldwide, substantially harming both nature and people. Vulnerable communities bear minimal responsibility for the crisis and are the hardest hit (Climate Change Synthesis Report, 2023) [1]. This underscores the urgent relevance of sustainable development in addressing these climate challenges. At the heart of sustainable development, as articulated in the Brundtland Report, lies the imperative to address present-day needs while ensuring the well-being of future generations, transcending developmental disparities and economic models (Udeagha and Ngepah, 2023; Holden *et al.*, 2014) [2, 3]. This fundamental principle serves as the cornerstone of our investigation into the mutually reinforcing dynamics of fintech and green finance (GFN), and their pivotal role in advancing sustainable economic growth. The United Nations (UN) has established a set of interconnected objectives and benchmarks referred to as the Sustainable Development Goals (SDGs), officially adopted in 2015. Within this framework, SDG 7 centers on the promotion of accessible and clean energy, SDG 12 emphasizes responsible methods of production and consumption, and SDG 13 underscores the imperative of acting on climate change (Awais *et al.*, 2023; Mehta and Sharma, 2024) [4, 5]. The Paris Agreement, instituted in 2015, was created to confront the threats posed by climate change to both our environment and society. Numerous nations across the globe are now under a legal obligation to execute strategies aimed at curtailing greenhouse gas emissions. The primary objective is to cap global temperature increases at levels below 2°C, with a preference for limiting the increase to 1.5°C, as compared to pre-industrial levels (Udeagha and Ngepah, 2023) [2]. As we approach the midway point to 2030, the progress on SDGs remains insufficient, with only 12% of the targets on track for achievement. This sobering reality underscores the urgency for collaborative action and innovation in the realms of finance and technology to accelerate progress toward a more sustainable future. One notable commitment in this regard is the G20's resolve to fully implement the 2030 Agenda, emphasizing digital transformation, data utilization, and financial mobilization. Additionally, the G20 recognizes the vital role of tourism, culture, and sustainable finance as drivers of socio-economic development and prosperity. These commitments reaffirm the importance of exploring the synergy between fintech and GFN, as it offers a promising pathway toward realizing the sustainable economic growth imperative for our world (*G20 New Delhi Leaders Declaration*, 2023) [6]. In the pursuit of sustainable development, it is imperative to acknowledge the intricate relationships among different facets of our society and environment. Given the intricacy and interrelated nature of these challenges, there are no simple remedies. Rather, embracing a "comprehensive systems" approach becomes paramount. This approach entails the cooperation of all stakeholders, including individuals, corporations, governmental bodies, and civil society, to catalyze substantial and transformative shifts (Rao & Kumar, 2023; Mehta *et al.*, 2019) [7, 8]. Several techniques can be used to investigate the price movement of various financial instruments (Mehta and Sharma, 2024; Vyas *et al.*, 2020; Mehta *et al.*, 2022) [9–11]. Technology, encompassing data management and financial operations, significantly impacts business performance and economic development (Afzal *et al.*, 2022) [12]. Its role extends to addressing environmental concerns by aiding in the achievement of SDGs and promoting green economic development. Technological innovation is a powerful tool for transitioning traditional economies into more environmentally sustainable models (Abid *et al.*, 2022) [13]. Overall, technology plays a crucial role in driving both business success and sustainability initiatives.

3.1.2 Fintech and Green Finance

In the ever-evolving landscape of finance, technological advancements have brought about profound transformations in the financial industry and the dynamics of financial markets. This backdrop has given rise to a burgeoning discourse that delves into the intricate relationship between fintech development and its environmental consequences. On one end of the spectrum, optimism abounds concerning the potential of fintech to combat climate change by fostering clean energy trade, improving carbon emission trading, and bolstering the flow of climate finance. However, this optimism finds itself counterbalanced by concerns surrounding the environmental footprint of fintech, including its increased electricity consumption and the hastened depletion of already scarce natural resources. Consequently, governmental bodies, regulators, and policymakers are continually engaged in deliberations, meticulously weighing the costs and benefits of the fintech ecosystem in the context of both economic growth and environmental preservation (Tao *et al.*, 2022) [14]. The financial environment is exposed to various types of risks (Sharma and Mehta, 2024; Sharma *et al.*, 2023; Mehta *et al.*, 2022) [15–17]. Fintech, a product of financial innovation driven by technology, is a vital topic in the technological landscape. It encompasses various technologies like mobile devices, wireless networks, blockchain, artificial intelligence (AI), security, Internet of Things (IoT), and cloud computing. Fintech's impact is profound, revolutionizing financial services, institutions, and markets (Awais *et al.*, 2023) [4]. Fintech encompasses a wide spectrum of financial activities, including payments, financial advice, project financing, deposits, loans, insurance, and regulatory compliance. Notable fintech examples are peer-to-peer lending, crowdfunding, big data credit assessments, robo-advisors, blockchain, and virtual currencies. These innovations are characterized by their asset-light nature, scalability, rapid development, and cost-effectiveness. Crucially, big data plays a pivotal role in fintech, enabling precise customer profiling and targeted financial solutions. Fintech serves as a bridge between traditional finance and information technology, reducing information asymmetry and trade costs while connecting surplus and deficit funds. It enhances affordability, inclusivity, and transparency, making investing accessible to smaller investors and addressing their financial needs. Importantly, fintech has also contributed to green financing and sustainable development by facilitating the availability of GFN, reducing costs and information gaps, enhancing efficiency, recognizing the value of natural assets, and promoting practical sustainable lifestyles. As a result, fintech emerges as a vital solution for sustainable financing needs. Research indicates the financial sector's significant role in an economy, and financial development contributes to achieving green growth and sustainable economic progress. Moreover, technology, including fintech, plays a central role in the transition to Industry 4.0, aligning with the goals of a circular economy that seeks economic progress while preserving the environment (Awais *et al.*, 2023) [4]. The researchers have examined the cryptocurrency behavior as there is an increased interest of the investors in this digital financial instrument (Vyas *et al.*, 2023; Sharma *et al.*, 2023) [18, 19]. Importantly, fintech has also contributed to green financing and sustainable development by facilitating the availability of GFN, reducing costs and information gaps, enhancing efficiency, recognizing the value of natural assets, and promoting practical sustainable lifestyles. As a result, fintech emerges as a vital solution for sustainable financing. The key to this circular economy is cleaner operations and sustainability. Fintech can enhance circular economy practices by facilitating the adoption of Industry 4.0 technologies in organizations. These technologies streamline processes, automate tasks, and ultimately contribute to increased sustainability. In summary, fintech's integration with Industry 4.0 holds promise for improving sustainability and aligning economic growth with environmental preservation (Awais *et al.*, 2023) [4].

3.1.3 Green Financing Strategies

Green financing is a multifaceted strategy aimed at augmenting the flow of financial resources from diverse sectors, including banking, micro-credit, insurance, and investments, toward sustainable development priorities. This comprehensive approach entails not only the provision of capital but also the adept management of environmental and social risks, the identification and exploitation of opportunities that yield both favorable financial returns and ecological benefits, and the establishment of mechanisms for heightened accountability. The promotion of green financing encompasses a spectrum of measures, including alterations in countries' regulatory frameworks, the harmonization of public financial incentives, increased investments in green financing across sectors, alignment of public sector financing decisions with the environmental facets of the SDGs, a surge in funding for clean and green technologies, support for sustainable natural resource-based green economies and climate-smart blue economies, and the amplification in the usage of green bonds. At the heart of this endeavor is the alignment with the 2030 sustainable development agenda, wherein the UN Environment Programme collaborates closely with countries, financial regulators, and the finance sector to steer financial flows toward advancing the SDGs (Nenavath and Mishra, 2023; Udeagha and Ngepah, 2023; Sharma *et al.*, 2020) [2, 20]. The globalized economy of today is intrinsically linked to financial markets, serving as conduits where banks and investors allocate capital to diverse sectors. Investors always look for various investment strategies to earn abnormal returns (Mehta and Sharma, 2017) [28]. Notably, the capital allocated in the present day will fundamentally shape ecosystems and mold the patterns of production and consumption in the future. Within the realm of green financing, several critical areas have taken precedence in ongoing efforts. Firstly, the UN Environment Programme is committed to assisting the public sector in creating an enabling environment conducive to green financing initiatives. Regulatory frameworks at the national level necessitate modifications to accommodate the evolving landscape of sustainable finance. As part of its resource efficiency program, the UN Environment Programme extends support to countries by conducting comprehensive reviews of their policies and regulatory landscapes concerning financing systems. The objective is to formulate sustainable finance roadmaps that resonate with the SDGs, a vital step in achieving long-term sustainability and aligning financial systems with global sustainability targets. Secondly, the promotion of public–private partnerships is a fundamental element in the pursuit of green financing. These collaborative initiatives facilitate the scaling up of green financing by leveraging the expertise and resources of both the public and private sectors. Of particular significance are mechanisms such as green bonds, which serve as critical instruments in mobilizing capital for environmentally sustainable projects. Public–private partnerships play an indispensable role in fostering cross-sectoral collaboration, thereby accelerating progress toward common sustainability objectives. Thirdly, the capacity building of community enterprises in the realm of micro-credit is of paramount importance. Community enterprises operating at the grassroots level often serve as the catalysts for sustainable development. The UN Environment Programme recognizes the pivotal role of micro-credit entities in providing financial resources to these enterprises. Therefore, it has initiated capacity-building programs aimed at empowering these community-based enterprises, enabling them to access micro-credit for the realization of sustainable development projects. In conjunction with these areas of focus, the enhancement of regulatory frameworks for domestic financial markets remains a critical endeavor. The UN Environment extends its support to central banks and regulatory bodies to facilitate the refinement of these frameworks. The goal is to ensure that they reflect the imperatives of sustainability and align with the SDGs, thereby fostering a financial ecosystem that prioritizes environmentally sound investments. Lastly, the UN Environment is deeply committed to catalyzing policy actions that inspire and inform both public and private investors. This catalytic role is essential in steering investments toward sustainable development. By connecting with green economy initiatives, the UN Environment fosters an environment that encourages responsible investment and stimulates the deployment of capital in projects that advance sustainability goals. The success of green financing initiatives hinges on the promotion of multi-stakeholder partnerships that encompass major actors in financial markets, including banks, investors, micro-credit entities, and insurance companies, in addition to the public sector. These partnerships create a collaborative ecosystem where financial resources are mobilized effectively to address global sustainability challenges, marking a significant step toward realizing the shared vision of sustainable development. Green financing is a multifaceted strategy that seeks to channel financial resources from diverse sectors toward sustainable development priorities. Through a combination of regulatory adjustments, public–private partnerships, capacity building, regulatory framework enhancements, and policy advocacy, the UN Environment Programme endeavors to align financial systems with the SDGs and inspire investments that promote sustainable and equitable futures (Nenavath and Mishra, 2023; Udeagha and Ngepah, 2023) [2, 20].

The convergence of fintech and sustainable development presents a significant opportunity to tackle environmental challenges while promoting economic sustainability. Recent research underscores the favorable impact of fintech on environmental objectives. In this context, blockchain technology, a fundamental component of fintech, emerges as a potent instrument for advancing business sustainability and ethical practices. Research has highlighted blockchain's ability to enhance transparency and address issues such as information opacity, security, and traceability, thus fostering improved information sharing across supply chains. This heightened transparency contributes to supply chain reliability and safety, effectively addressing these concerns. Moreover, blockchain's transparency acts as a deterrent to data manipulation by organizations seeking to obscure their environmental impact. This transparency also aids in identifying inefficiencies within business processes, subsequently reducing production costs and enhancing sustainability. Additionally, blockchain aids in the detection and prevention of unsustainable business practices within supply chains. Blockchain adoption also aligns with the objective of achieving low-carbon performance and analyzing carbon footprints, supporting global efforts to reduce carbon emissions. Furthermore, it facilitates the development of renewable energy sources, contributing to the reduction of carbon emissions. Artificial intelligence, an integral part of fintech, offers a wide array of applications that support sustainable development. Machine learning, a subset of AI, leverages data-driven algorithms to address complex issues in line with the SDGs. Artificial intelligence's data analysis capabilities empower decision-makers to tackle unique challenges within sustainable economic development. It excels in solving intricate problems and executing tasks beyond human capabilities, making it indispensable in modern high-tech societies. Fintech components, such as security and the IoT, further reinforce sustainable development endeavors. Fintech places a strong emphasis on secure data management. For instance, blockchain technology is renowned for its robust security measures. The IoT, when integrated with fintech, monitors real-time energy consumption, allowing organizations to effectively manage their environmental footprint. It plays a pivotal role in advancing sustainability, particularly in monitoring and controlling energy consumption. Cloud computing, another facet of fintech, offers opportunities for sustainable business operations while boosting profitability. Its eco-friendly advantages encompass resource efficiency, streamlined systems, and carbon neutrality, thus contributing to the development of environmentally responsible supply chains. In summary, the integration of fintech with technologies like blockchain, AI, IoT, and cloud-computing facilitates sustainability efforts by addressing environmental concerns, enhancing transparency, and supporting the pursuit of the SDGs. This convergence paves the way for a more sustainable and prosperous future (Awais *et al.*, 2023) [4]. Fintech, characterized by advanced financial solutions, has emerged as a transformative force in the banking, financial services, and insurance sectors. In India, it ranks as the third-largest fintech market globally, poised for substantial annual growth. Notably, fintech innovation aligns with green credit, investment, and initiatives that drive environmental sustainability. It encompasses technologies like mobile payments, money transfers, and asset management, with well-developed economies having an advantage in fostering fintech growth. Additionally, fintech democratizes access to financial resources, positively impacting economic growth. However, it raises concerns about resource demands and environmental impact. Despite these challenges, fintech's innovative potential, driven by technologies like blockchain and AI, can contribute to GFN and a sustainable economy.

3.2 Understanding the Fintech Landscape Today: Paving the Path for Sustainable Development

The global fintech revolution is currently in full force. While technology has been a component of the financial services sector dating back to the 1850s, it is only in the last two decades that the term "fintech" has gained prominence. It now commonly signifies technological innovations with the potential to revolutionize the delivery of financial services, spur the development of innovative business models, applications, processes, and products, and ultimately benefit consumers (Arner *et al.*, 2015; Sironi, 2016; Sharma and Mehta, 2024) [21, 22, 25].

3.3 Fintech's Evolution: Phases of Transformation and Future Horizons

3.3.1 Phase One: Digital Disruption (1998–2008)

From 1998 to 2008, a digital revolution swept through the financial services industry. The widespread adoption of internet-enabled devices marked a significant shift. Traditional financial institutions, both national and regional, faced disruption as they grappled with the advent of digital technologies. This era witnessed a fundamental change, offering consumers greater convenience and accessibility. Online banking, lending, and e-commerce took center stage, with platforms like Amazon and eBay becoming household names. Online payments, spearheaded by industry leaders like PayPal, reshaped transaction banking. Notably, digital lenders such as Capital One pioneered innovative lending practices powered by data and analytics (Global Fintech 2023: Reimagining the Future of Finance, 2023) [23].

3.3.2 Phase Two: Mobile and Social Adoption (2009–2014)

The aftermath of the 2008 financial crisis, coupled with evolving consumer behaviors and intensified regulatory scrutiny, opened doors for fintech startups during the period from 2009 to 2014. This phase saw a credit boom and rapid advancements in mobile and cloud technologies. Consumers gained real-time access to financial services, driving the meteoric rise of disruptive fintech entities. The emphasis on enhancing user experience/user interface (UX/UI) and the introduction of application programming interfaces (APIs) reduced friction in onboarding and digital customer journeys. Social media and data analytics played pivotal roles, enabling companies to gather granular data and offer highly personalized financial solutions (Global Fintech 2023: Reimagining the Future of Finance, 2023) [23].

3.3.3 Phase Three: Relevance and Scale (2015–2021)

Spanning from 2015 to 2021, the fintech industry experienced explosive growth. This growth was propelled by the widespread adoption of smartphones and further accelerated by the COVID-19 pandemic. Consumer expectations shifted towards round-the-clock online availability for all financial services. Fintech giants like Ant Financial, Nubank, PayTM, Square, and Stripe became synonymous with financial innovation, expanding access to financial services, harnessing new demand-generation channels, enhancing UX/UI, and driving cost efficiencies. Fintech funding surged to remarkable heights, reaching $440 billion between 2014 and 2022. In an environment characterized by low-interest rates and ample capital availability, valuations soared, attracting more talent and companies to the sector. Intense competition for market share and a flurry of mergers and acquisitions (M&A) defined this phase.

3.3.4 Phase Four: The Path Ahead (2022 and beyond)

In the current phase and beyond, the fintech landscape anticipates a proactive regulatory environment that will support infrastructure investments, including digital public goods, and foster innovation in regions aspiring to enhance financial inclusion. The horizon also promises the advent of new technological disruptions, such as generative AI and distributed ledger technology (DLT), which are already leaving their mark. Despite facing formidable challenges, fintech CEOs remain steadfast in their optimism about the industry's long-term potential and prospects.

In the realm of financial intermediation, banking has long been a cornerstone of progressive societies, symbolizing not just economic and financial strength but also societal and cultural progress. The evolution of banking has been shaped by the recognition of market imperfections in capital markets and trade, leading to increased transaction costs and asymmetric information. These imperfections have, in turn, underscored the pivotal role of financial institutions in addressing such market deficiencies.

A concise framework helps illuminate the transformation of traditional banking in recent times. Financial intermediaries have historically driven economic growth through two key functions: transforming the "nature of claims" by converting deposits into mortgages and loans and providing transactional services that bring together economic agents with complementary needs. This transformation is exemplified by banks, which efficiently manage disparities between liquidity demand and supply, while concurrently addressing credit risk through diversification and deposit insurance.

In the modern landscape, fintech firms have emerged as significant disruptors. While they excel in mobilizing funds and matching counterparties, their role in providing liquidity services directly challenges the traditional banking model. This disruption arises from various factors, including the absence of strict regulatory requirements, technological advancements, and lower operational costs. Notably, fintech firms often operate as brokers in an agency model, transferring credit risk to investors, leading to less diversified portfolios compared to banks.

As fintech reshapes the financial sector, the question arises: should banks perceive fintech as a threat or an opportunity for extending their reach and enhancing liquidity provision? The dynamics are multifaceted, with the extent of fintech's influence on banking varying by sector. For instance, fintech solutions have a significant impact on transactional-based functions, particularly in developing countries with limited financial infrastructure. Additionally, technologies like blockchain and smart contracts are reducing the need for intermediary banks in certain transactions.

In this evolving landscape, banks' unique positions as information processors and risk calculators become increasingly vital. They capitalize on economies of scale and scope by collecting and interpreting cross-sectional and intertemporal information, thus reducing information asymmetries. The advent of digitalization and information and communication technologies has revolutionized data storage and processing, further impacting the industry. Moreover, fintech firms, relying primarily on hard standardized information, big data, and machine learning, have enhanced the customizability and pricing of services, albeit with privacy and fraud-related risks.

In conclusion, the financial sector's landscape is witnessing a significant transformation driven by the disruptive force of fintech (see Figure 3.1). This transformation spans various functions, from liquidity provision to data utilization, resulting in a shift from soft to hard data. The impact of fintech on traditional banking practices is undeniable, making it crucial for banks to adapt and collaborate to thrive in this evolving ecosystem (Murinde *et al.*, 2022) [24].

3.4 Global Fintech Adoption Trends

Global fintech adoption trends reflect the profound impact of technology on financial services. In our extensive survey encompassing 27 markets and over 27,000 consumers, several key findings have emerged:

Figure 3.1 Fintech evolution: phases of transformation. The transformative impact of fintech on information and banking: from soft to hard data.

- Consumer adoption: the survey reveals a significant global fintech adoption rate, with 64% of consumers worldwide embracing fintech solutions. This adoption extends to various financial services, with 75% of consumers utilizing money transfer and payment fintech services. Additionally, 48% of consumers are engaging with insurance fintech services, underlining the diverse range of offerings in this sector.
- Drivers of adoption: consumers are drawn to fintech challengers primarily due to attractive rates and fees, signifying the importance of cost-effective solutions in this sector. Moreover, 33% of consumer adopters turn to entities other than their primary banks, showcasing the growing competition faced by traditional financial institutions. Furthermore, a noteworthy 68% of consumers are open to considering non-financial services companies for their financial needs.
- SME adoption: small and medium-sized enterprises (SMEs) are also actively participating in the fintech landscape, with 25% of them utilizing financing fintech services and 56% engaging with banking and payment fintech solutions. The SME adopters demonstrate a willingness to embrace technology, with 93% preferring technological solutions where possible. Additionally, 89% of SME adopters are open to sharing data with fintech companies.

These findings collectively depict a global financial landscape where consumers and SMEs are increasingly integrating fintech into their financial activities. The key drivers of this adoption include competitive pricing, convenience, and an openness to exploring innovative solutions beyond traditional banking institutions. As technology continues to advance, the fintech sector is poised for further growth and transformation in the years ahead (Global Fintech Adoption Index, 2019) [27].

3.5 Trends and Insights Across Diverse Sectors

3.5.1 Banking and Payments

The fintech revolution is reshaping the financial sector on a global scale, with digital payments at the forefront of this transformation. Over the past two decades, fintech has emerged as a powerful driver of change, revolutionizing the provision of financial services and creating novel business models, applications, and products. Amid this evolution, the payments sector has witnessed a remarkable shift, driven by innovations in instant payments and the rising adoption of digital wallets.

3.5.1.1 *Digital Payments: A Global Phenomenon*

Digital payments have witnessed exponential growth worldwide, outpacing traditional payments in recent years. According to global data, electronic payments transaction volumes have consistently outpaced payments revenue growth (17% versus 6%) over the past five years. This trend reflects the continuing evolution in payments preferences, a general migration toward lower-fee instruments, and the gradual decline in profit margins associated with scale.

3.5.1.2 *The Decline of Cash Usage*

The decline in cash usage is not merely a shift in payment preferences; it has broader implications for sustainable development. Globally, cash usage declined by nearly 4% in 2022. This trend indicates a global move toward more sustainable payment methods and an ongoing shift away from cash.

3.5.1.3 *Regional Variances*

The impact of instant payments and digital wallets on revenue growth varies across regions. In some countries, instant payments are perceived as premium options, offering significant potential for revenue growth. For instance, in Brazil, almost half of the transactional revenue growth through 2027 is expected to come from instant payments. Conversely, in countries like India, instant payments are expected to contribute less than 10% of future revenue growth due to the absence of fees for the Unified Payments Interface (UPI).

3.5.1.4 *India's Unique Case*

India serves as a compelling case study of payments evolution and its role in a rapidly growing economy. The adoption of digital payments, particularly through UPI, has grown exponentially. Despite generating minimal transaction fees, UPI adoption has significantly reduced cash reliance, offering economic and environmental benefits. In 2022, India's payments revenues reached $64 billion, making it the fourth-largest payments-revenue-generating country globally, ahead of mature economies (McKinsey Global Payments Report, 2023) [32].

3.5.2 Lending and Credit

3.5.2.1 Global Momentum in Fintech Lending

The fintech lending landscape is undergoing a global transformation. According to the Bank for International Settlements (BIS) and the Cambridge Centre for Alternative Finance (CCAF), the world witnessed fintech lending surge to around US$125 billion in 2020 (Fintech and the Future of Finance, 2023) [26].

3.5.2.2 India's Remarkable Fintech Lending Growth

On home turf, India's fintech lending sector has witnessed remarkable expansion. Over the past five years, the volume of digital payments within the country has multiplied tenfold, reaching an astounding 7.10 Crore loans disbursed worth Rs. 92,267 Crore in the fiscal year 2022–2023. A noteworthy transformation has occurred, with the majority of these digital transactions migrating directly to instant payments through the UPI network. In a matter of five years, UPI's share of digital transactions has soared from a modest 8% in 2017 to an impressive 75% in 2022 (FinTech Lending Trends, 2023) [29].

- Youthful enthusiasm: fintech lending has struck a chord with the youth. Younger customers, aged below 40 years, constitute a dominating force, contributing to a staggering 80% of the loans disbursed in India's digital lending.
- Geographic hotspots: across the globe and within India, fintech lending exhibits geographic concentrations. In the Indian context, five states stand out prominently, accounting for a significant 50% of total disbursements. Among these, Maharashtra, Karnataka, Uttar Pradesh, Telangana, and Tamil Nadu emerge as fintech lending hubs, each contributing uniquely to this dynamic landscape. Notably, Maharashtra and Tamil Nadu have seen substantial growth, reflecting the diversification and dynamism within India's fintech lending ecosystem.
- Personal loans take center stage: among the diverse array of loan products, personal loans stand tall as the undisputed leaders in fintech lending, commanding a lion's share in both disbursement volume, approximately 6 Crores, and value, nearly Rs. 66,432 Crores.

- Shift in loan size preference: despite the industry's exponential growth, the average ticket size of fintech loans has shown a consistent downward trend, indicating a preference for smaller, more accessible loans. In the fiscal year 2022–2023, the average ticket size for fintech loans reached Rs. 12,989, reflecting a 19% decline from the previous fiscal year.

In a nutshell, the fintech lending arena is witnessing an unprecedented global surge, while India stands at the forefront of this transformation. Youthful enthusiasm, geographic hotspots, and a preference for personal loans characterize this dynamic landscape. These trends underscore the immense impact of fintech lending on the modern financial landscape.

3.5.3 Wealth Management (Robo-Advisor)

In the current fintech landscape, robo-advisors have emerged as a transformative force, with significant implications for the wealth and investment management sector. The proliferation of robo-advisors is evident from the substantial number of these platforms, nearly 100, operating in 15 countries worldwide. This reflects the growing appetite for automated investment advisory services and signifies the sector's dynamism.

The potential for growth in the robo-advisory sector is immense. Leading institutions' estimates indicate that assets managed with the assistance of robo-advisory services reached a range between $2.2 trillion and $3.7 trillion in 2020. Looking ahead, projections suggest that this figure is set to skyrocket to over $16.0 trillion in assets under management (AUM) by 2025. To put this in perspective, this projected AUM surpasses the assets managed by BlackRock, the world's largest asset manager, by nearly threefold.

Robo-advisors are characterized by their automated, algorithm-driven approach to providing investment advice. They harness mathematical algorithms to facilitate investment decisions, utilizing online and mobile channels to deliver wealth management services. These platforms empower individuals to take control of their financial portfolios, eliminating the need for an extensive financial background. Robo-advisors translate client preferences, including risk tolerance and liquidity needs, into investment strategies. They often employ managed exchange-traded fund portfolios customized to individual preferences.

The evolution of robo-advisors in the market has witnessed a progression characterized by increasing sophistication and enhanced capabilities. These platforms have evolved to offer tailored investment solutions, cater to specific client needs, and provide a broader range of investment products. These advancements are driven by data-driven assessments of the robo-advisory landscape, with a strong emphasis on enhancing features and services to meet the evolving demands of clients.

In summary, the robo-advisory sector within the fintech industry is experiencing exponential growth and is poised to play a pivotal role in shaping the future of wealth and investment management. The transformative potential of these automated platforms is underpinned by their ability to democratize access to sophisticated financial advice, making it relevant to our research paper's exploration of fintech's impact on diverse sectors (Future of Robo-Advisors in Investment and Wealth Management, Report by Wipro) [30].

3.5.4 Real Estate (Proptech)

3.5.4.1 Proptech's Disruptive Potential

Proptech, a fusion of "property" and "technology," is a burgeoning field that leverages technology to revolutionize various aspects of the real estate industry. This innovative sector is characterized by businesses striving to enhance and streamline the way we buy, rent, sell, design, construct, and manage both residential and commercial properties. Despite being relatively young, proptech has already made a significant impact, with startups globally securing over $43 billion in funding since 2012. The pace of growth in proptech funding is remarkable, exemplified by an 82% increase in 2018 compared to the previous year.

3.5.4.2 Proptech's Financial Trajectory

Proptech's financial momentum is reminiscent of fintech's trajectory in its early stages. To emphasize the scale of proptech's potential, it is worth noting that its current funding size is on par with what fintech possessed in 2013. Given fintech's compound annual growth rate (CAGR) of 44.8% since then, proptech's prospects appear robust.

3.5.4.3 Rental Revolution

A pivotal driver of the proptech trend is the evolving preference from property ownership to renting, a shift often referred to as the "rent generation." Today, tenants are inclined toward better, updated living spaces that offer "digital occupant experience." This experience includes the ability to control lighting, temperature, access, and other features *via* digital channels, such as mobile apps. Proptech fulfils these demands by not only delivering the digital occupant experience but also using technologies like augmented and virtual reality to elevate the overall customer experience.

3.5.4.4 *Smart Buildings as the Foundation*

The foundation of many proptech solutions lies in the concept of smart buildings. These buildings serve as platforms for collecting and analyzing data, enabling integrated systems that provide deeper insights into end-user preferences and behaviors. Advanced technologies, such as those supporting smart buildings, have matured to a stage where they can be practically implemented.

3.5.4.5 *Proptech's Flourishing Ecosystem in Israel*

Israel, known for its innovation prowess, provides a glimpse into the future of the proptech sector. With over 400 multinational R&D centres and innovation hubs, Israel is at the forefront of disruptive technologies. The country boasts more than 100 proptech startups, marking an 80% CAGR in the number of proptech startups over the last five years. Notably, these startups often have strong fintech connections, underscoring the synergy between the two industries. Israel's proptech success is particularly evident in the area of managing and operating properties, which involves digitalizing tenant management, payments, and communication among stakeholders.

3.5.4.6 *The Promise of Proptech*

Proptech presents a rare opportunity to disrupt the real estate market, which has seen limited change for decades. Entrepreneurs, investors, and industry leaders recognize the transformative potential of proptech. This sector challenges conventional thinking and introduces new business models and technologies that are reshaping the real estate landscape. With innovation hubs like Israel embracing proptech, the trend is set to evolve further, cementing its place in the ever-changing world of real estate (Deloitte Real Estate Predictions, 2020) [31].

3.5.5 Green Finance and Sustainability

Green finance, also known as GFN, is a financial approach aimed at fostering sustainable development by connecting economic growth with environmental preservation. Unlike traditional finance, GFN places a strong emphasis on environmental benefits. Its primary goal is to channel financial resources into eco-friendly enterprises while reducing support for businesses contributing to environmental harm. Research on GFN focuses on its impacts on both the environment and the broader economy.

Sustainability is at the intersection of innovation, economic growth, and environmental well-being. It is important to note that while technological advancements drive economic progress, they can also harm the environment. Innovations can boost economic growth by improving production processes, cutting operational costs, and increasing efficiency. However, they may also increase the demand for finite natural resources, posing a challenge to sustainable development.

3.5.5.1 Sustainable Economic Growth through Green Finance and Fintech

Achieving sustainable economic growth requires the harmonious coexistence of GFN and fintech. Green finance is a potent instrument for steering economies towards environmental stewardship. It directs financial resources toward projects that promote ecological well-being, laying the groundwork for sustainable development. Simultaneously, fintech, with its innovative digital tools and financial services, enhances the efficiency of GFN initiatives.

Research has explored the combined impact of GFN and fintech on environmental quality in the BRICS economies from 1990 to 2020. Analytical methods such as the cross-sectional autoregressive distributed lag have revealed key insights. These findings underscore GFN's role in reducing per capita carbon emissions in both the short and long terms. Additionally, fintech is seen as a positive contributor to environmental quality. Research suggests that initial improvements in environmental quality may temporarily impact GDP, but in the long run, the positive effect of GDP squared aligns with the environmental Kuznets curve (EKC) hypothesis.

Understanding the intricate relationship between financial systems, technology-driven innovation, and the environment can provide valuable insights for policymakers, financial institutions, and businesses aiming to foster economic growth while protecting the planet.

3.5.5.2 *Unlocking Sustainable Development: Harnessing Fintech Opportunities*

In today's rapidly evolving financial landscape, the world of fintech presents a myriad of opportunities that are integral to exploring the synergy between fintech and GFN. Fintech, which refers to innovative solutions in financial services, is a dynamic sector with the potential to drive sustainable development (On the Cusp of the next Payments Era Future Opportunities for Banks, 2023) [32].

3.5.5.2.1 Opportunity 1: Accelerated Partnerships

The ongoing COVID-19 pandemic has forced fintech companies to adapt and innovate swiftly, resulting in the creation of new products and digital solutions. This environment is conducive to forging new partnerships, a space where traditional financial institutions often lack expertise. Fintech firms are well-positioned to establish collaborations with other fintechs, tech giants, and non-financial services companies.

These partnerships can yield innovative solutions that benefit both fintech companies and consumers. For example, collaborations between fintech firms and established tech companies can result in the development of advanced payment technologies, such as biometric authentication methods and contactless payment solutions. These innovations enhance the security and convenience of financial transactions, aligning with the fintech sector's commitment to improving user experiences.

Furthermore, partnerships with non-financial services companies can lead to the creation of integrated platforms that offer a wide range of services beyond traditional banking. These platforms can incorporate sustainable practices by providing users with information on eco-friendly products, services, and investments (Murinde *et al.*, 2022) [24].

3.5.5.2.2 Opportunity 2: Advancing Financial Inclusion

The economic disruptions caused by the pandemic have underscored the importance of financial inclusion, both in developed and developing economies. Governments worldwide have initiated programs to support low-income households, potentially leading to enhanced financial inclusion. Fintech companies, with their innovative solutions, can play a pivotal role in facilitating the efficient disbursement of government relief funds, particularly to individuals without traditional bank accounts.

Digital payment systems and mobile wallets can provide a means for governments to directly transfer funds to citizens, ensuring quick access to financial support during crises. This not only promotes financial inclusion but also reduces the reliance on physical cash, which is often associated with high transaction costs and security risks.

Moreover, fintech solutions such as peer-to-peer lending platforms and microfinance apps can empower individuals and small businesses by providing them with access to credit and investment opportunities. These platforms can assess creditworthiness based on alternative data sources, such as transaction histories and social media activity, expanding access to financial services to those previously excluded.

3.5.5.2.3 Opportunity 3: Accelerating Economic Relief Efforts

In response to the economic challenges posed by the pandemic, fintech companies can contribute to the acceleration of economic relief efforts. This includes aiding in the distribution of financial aid and support to individuals and businesses affected by the crisis.

One notable example is the use of blockchain technology to streamline relief fund distribution. Blockchain's transparency and immutability make it a secure platform for tracking the flow of funds from donors to beneficiaries. This technology can help reduce fraud and ensure that relief funds reach their intended recipients promptly.

Furthermore, fintech solutions can provide real-time financial insights to governments and relief agencies. Data analytics tools can assess the economic impact of relief measures, helping policymakers make informed decisions about the allocation of resources. By accelerating economic relief efforts, fintech contributes to stability and resilience in times of.

3.5.5.2.4 Opportunity 4: Empowering Gig Workers

Fintech firms can target gig economy workers, a segment often underserved by traditional banks due to their irregular income patterns. These workers have distinct financial, insurance, and tax needs, making them a growing opportunity for fintech companies.

Fintech solutions can address the financial challenges faced by gig workers by offering digital banking services tailored to their needs. These services may include income tracking tools, tax optimization algorithms, and flexible insurance options. By providing gig workers with access to financial resources and guidance, fintech enhances their financial stability and security.

Moreover, the adoption of IoT-enabled contactless payments, such as those enabled by connected cars, could further empower gig workers and enhance financial accessibility. Gig workers can seamlessly receive payments for their services through IoT-enabled devices, reducing the friction associated with traditional payment methods.

3.5.5.2.5 Opportunity 5: Green Finance Integration

The integration of GFN principles into fintech initiatives represents a crucial opportunity. Fintech can drive sustainable development by aligning with GFN goals and supporting environmentally responsible investments and initiatives.

Fintech platforms can facilitate investments in renewable energy projects, sustainable agriculture, and carbon offset initiatives. These platforms provide users with transparent information about the environmental impact of their investments, allowing them to make choices that align with their sustainability goals.

Additionally, fintech companies can leverage blockchain technology to create transparent supply chain finance solutions that incentivize sustainable practices. By tracking the origin and environmental footprint of products, blockchain-based systems can offer lower-cost financing options to businesses committed to reducing their carbon footprint.

3.5.5.2.6 Opportunity 6: Data-Driven Sustainability

Data-oriented technologies, as discussed in Murinde *et al.*, 2022 [24], present opportunities for fintech to advance sustainability efforts. By harnessing big data, AI, and predictive analytics, fintech firms can offer solutions that help individuals and businesses make environmentally conscious financial decisions.

For instance, fintech apps can analyze users' spending patterns and provide recommendations for eco-friendly purchases. These apps can suggest sustainable products and services, promote energy-efficient choices, and calculate the carbon footprint associated with different consumption habits. By leveraging data-driven insights, fintech encourages responsible consumption and investment.

Moreover, predictive analytics can enable fintech platforms to assess the environmental risks and opportunities associated with various investments. By providing users with comprehensive information on the sustainability performance of companies and projects, fintech contributes to informed decision-making in alignment with green finance principles.

3.5.5.2.7 Opportunity 7: Sustainable Investment Platforms

Murinde *et al.*, 2022 further highlight the rise of sustainable investment platforms within the fintech sector. These platforms cater to investors seeking to align their portfolios with environmental, social, and governance (ESG) criteria. Fintech firms can leverage these platforms to offer users a range of sustainable investment options, from green bonds to socially responsible mutual funds [24].

The opportunity here lies in providing user-friendly interfaces that simplify the process of assessing the sustainability of investment choices. By incorporating ESG data and impact metrics into their platforms, fintech companies empower investors to make informed decisions that support environmentally and socially responsible projects. Moreover, these platforms can use smart contracts and blockchain technology to enhance transparency and traceability in sustainable investments, thus building trust among investors.

3.5.5.2.8 Opportunity 8: Regulatory Technology (Regtech) for Sustainability Compliance

Another opportunity discussed in On the Cusp of the Next Payments Era Future Opportunities for Banks, 2023 and Murinde *et al.*, 2022, is the application of regtech in ensuring sustainability compliance. As governments and regulatory bodies worldwide introduce more stringent environmental regulations, businesses are under increased pressure to meet sustainability targets. Fintech firms specializing in regtech solutions can develop tools to help businesses track and report on their sustainability efforts.

These regtech solutions can automate data collection and reporting processes, reducing the administrative burden on companies while ensuring accurate and transparent sustainability reporting. They can also utilize blockchain and secure data storage to maintain a tamper-proof record of sustainability-related data, which can be crucial for regulatory.

In conclusion, the opportunities within the fintech sector not only drive economic growth and financial inclusion but also have the potential to significantly impact sustainability and GFN. Fintech's adaptability, innovative spirit, and capacity to form strategic partnerships position it as a powerful force for positive change in the financial industry. As fintech continues to evolve, researchers, policymakers, and practitioners must harness these opportunities to unlock sustainable development and create a more inclusive and environmentally responsible financial ecosystem.

3.5.6 Challenges in Fintech Adoption for Green Finance: A Catalyst for Sustainable Development

3.5.6.1 Regulatory and Oversight Challenges

The adoption of fintech solutions in GFN faces significant regulatory and oversight challenges. These challenges arise from the need to strike a delicate balance between fostering innovation and ensuring consumer protection. While fintech thrives on innovation and disruption, it must also adhere to regulatory frameworks that guarantee the security and stability of financial markets (The winds of change Trends shaping India's Fintech Sector: edition II, 2022) [33].

3.5.6.2 Incorporating Green Finance into Regulatory Frameworks

Green finance introduces a new dimension to financial services, emphasizing sustainability and environmental responsibility. Regulators need to adapt existing frameworks or create new ones to accommodate the unique features of GFN products and services. This process requires careful consideration to avoid stifling innovation while maintaining the integrity of GFN initiatives.

3.5.6.3 Data Privacy and Sustainability Reporting

Green finance often relies on extensive data collection and reporting to assess environmental impacts and compliance with sustainability goals. Ensuring the privacy and security of this data is paramount. Fintech firms operating in this space must implement robust data protection measures and adhere to evolving data privacy regulations.

3.5.7 Data Privacy and Security Concerns

The fintech sector, including GFN applications, handles sensitive data related to financial transactions, sustainability metrics, and user. Data breaches and mishandling of this data pose significant risks, including reputational damage and legal consequences.

Data breach risks: Fintech firms that collect, process, and store large amounts of data related to GFN activities are at an increased risk of data breaches. Such breaches can result in the exposure of sensitive environmental impact data and user information, eroding trust and confidence in these solutions.

Regulatory compliance and trust: To promote fintech adoption in GFN, companies must demonstrate a commitment to data privacy and security. Compliance with data protection regulations, similar to GDPR in Europe, is crucial. Transparent data handling practices and robust cybersecurity measures can enhance trust and encourage users to engage with green fintech solutions.

3.5.8 Competition from Big Tech

The entry of big tech companies into the fintech industry presents a challenge for GFN adoption through fintech solutions (Reimagining the future of Finance, 2023). While big tech's involvement can bring significant resources and innovation, it also raises concerns about market concentration and competition.

Monopolistic Environments: Big tech firms entering the fintech space may have the resources to drive down prices and potentially dominate the market. This concentration of power can limit opportunities for smaller fintech startups focused on green finance solutions, hindering overall innovation.

Impact on GFN Initiatives: The influence of big tech in fintech can affect the prioritization of GFN initiatives. In a highly competitive environment, there may be a shift away from sustainability-focused products and services if they are perceived as less profitable. This could slow down the integration of GFN into fintech offerings.

3.5.9 Interest Rate Volatility

Interest rate volatility can impact the funding and sustainability of fintech startups, including those operating in the GFN sector. Fintech companies often rely on external funding sources, and fluctuations in interest rates can affect their cost of capital and ability to innovate.

Access to Funding: Green fintech firms may face challenges in competing with traditional financial institutions that have access to cheaper funding sources. This can result in resource constraints and limit their ability to scale and develop sustainable finance solutions.

Innovation and GFN: Fintech startups play a crucial role in driving innovation in GFN. However, in an environment of interest rate volatility, securing funding for innovation becomes more challenging. This could potentially slow down the development and adoption of green fintech solutions.

3.5.10 Collaborative Solutions

Addressing these challenges requires collaboration among various stakeholders, including regulators, fintech firms, incumbents, and investors. Effective collaboration can lead to innovative solutions that promote GFN adoption through fintech.

Regulatory Cooperation: Regulators need to collaborate to create harmonized frameworks that facilitate GFN fintech adoption. Cross-border cooperation can ensure consistency in regulations and reduce compliance burdens on fintech firms.

Industry Partnerships: Fintech startups specializing in GFN can benefit from partnerships with traditional financial institutions. These partnerships can provide access to established customer bases and resources needed for scaling green fintech solutions.

Investor Engagement: Investors have a role in supporting green-fintech startups by providing the necessary capital and guidance. Investing in fintech firms with a clear focus on sustainability can drive innovation in green finance.

The challenges in fintech adoption for GFN are multifaceted, encompassing regulatory complexities, data privacy concerns, competition dynamics, and the impact of interest rate volatility. However, by recognizing these challenges and actively collaborating with stakeholders, the fintech industry can play a pivotal role in advancing GFN and contributing to sustainable development. Overcoming these challenges will require a concerted effort from regulators, fintech firms, incumbents, and investors to create a financial ecosystem that promotes both innovation and sustainability.

3.5.11 Conclusion

In conclusion, the intersection of fintech and GFN holds immense promise for addressing critical global challenges, including environmental sustainability and financial inclusion. Fintech's innovative capabilities offer opportunities to create a more sustainable financial ecosystem by promoting green investments, responsible consumption, and transparent reporting of environmental impacts. This fusion of fintech and GFN has the potential to revolutionize the way individuals and businesses interact with the financial sector while contributing to a more sustainable future.

However, this transformative potential is accompanied by several challenges that must be addressed to fully harness the benefits of fintech for GFN. Regulatory complexities, data privacy concerns, competition from big tech companies, and interest rate volatility pose significant obstacles to the adoption of green fintech solutions. These challenges require collaborative efforts from regulators, fintech firms, traditional financial institutions, and investors to create a conducive environment for innovation and sustainability.

3.5.12 Recommendations

1. Regulatory harmonization: regulators should collaborate across borders to develop harmonized frameworks that facilitate the integration of GFN into fintech solutions. Consistent regulations reduce compliance burdens on fintech firms and encourage cross-border green investments.
2. Industry partnerships: fintech startups specializing in GFN should actively seek partnerships with traditional financial institutions. These partnerships can provide access to established customer bases, financial resources, and expertise, enabling the scaling of green fintech solutions.
3. Investor engagement: investors play a crucial role in supporting green fintech startups by providing the necessary capital and guidance. They should consider investing in fintech firms with a clear sustainability focus, thereby driving innovation in GFN.
4. Mitigating big tech competition: regulators should monitor the entry of big tech companies into the fintech sector to ensure fair competition. Measures to prevent monopolistic practices can help maintain a level playing field for all fintech players, including those focusing on sustainability.
5. Addressing interest rate volatility: fintech startups, including those in GFN, should adopt risk management strategies to mitigate the impact of interest rate volatility. Diversifying funding sources and exploring innovative financial instruments can help ensure stability and support ongoing innovation.

6. Promoting GFN initiatives: fintech firms should continue to prioritize sustainability-focused products and services, even in competitive environments. Highlighting the long-term benefits of GFN can help maintain momentum and drive adoption.
7. Consumer education: fintech firms should invest in educating consumers about the environmental impact of their financial choices. Fintech apps can play a role in promoting eco-friendly purchases and responsible consumption patterns.

By addressing these challenges and implementing these recommendations, the fintech industry can fulfill its potential as a catalyst for GFN adoption. This collaboration-driven approach can contribute to a more sustainable and inclusive financial landscape, aligning with global efforts to address pressing environmental and social issues.

References

1. Calvin, K., Dasgupta, D., Krinner, G., Mukherji, A., Thorne, P.W., Trisos, C., Romero, J., Aldunce, P., Barrett, K., Blanco, G., Cheung, W.W.L., Connors, S., Denton, F., Diongue-Niang, A., Dodman, D., Garschagen, M., Geden, O., Hayward, B., Jones, C., Péan, C., IPCC, 2023: Climate Change 2023: Synthesis Report. *Contribution of Working Groups I, II and III to the Sixth Assessment Report of the Intergovernmental Panel on Climate Change*, First, Core Writing Team, H. Lee, J. Romero (Eds.), Intergovernmental Panel on Climate Change (IPCC), IPCC, Geneva, Switzerland, 2023, https://doi.org/10.59327/IPCC/AR6-9789291691647.
2. Chukwudi, U.M. and Ngepah, N., The drivers of environmental sustainability in BRICS economies: Do green finance and fintech matter? *World Dev. Sustain.*, 3, 1–16, 2023, https://doi.org/10.1016/j.wds.2023.100096.
3. Holden, E., Linnerud, K., Banister, D., Sustainable development: Our Common Future revisited. *Global Environ. Change*, 26, 130–139, 2014, https://doi.org/10.1016/j.gloenvcha.2014.04.006.
4. Awais, M., Afzal, A., Firdousi, S., Hasnaoui, A., Is fintech the new path to sustainable resource utilisation and economic development? *Resour. Policy*, 81, 103309, 2023, https://doi.org/10.1016/j.resourpol.2023.103309.
5. Mehta, K. and Sharma, R., *Sustainability, Green Management, and Performance of SMEs*, DeGruyter, USA, 2024.
6. G20-New-Delhi-Leaders-Declaration.pdf., https://www.mea.gov.in/Images/CPV/G20-New-Delhi-Leaders-Declaration.pdf.

7. Rao, A. and Kumar, S., Are environment-related technologies key to unlock the path towards sustainable development: An econometric analysis. *Geosci. Front.*, 15, 4, 101702, 2023, https://doi.org/10.1016/j.gsf.2023.101702.
8. Mehta, K., Sharma, R., Vyas, V., Efficiency and ranking of sustainability index of India using DEA-TOPSIS. *J. Indian Bus. Res.*, 11, 2, 179–199, 2019, https://doi.org/10.1108/JIBR-02-2018-0057.
9. Mehta, K. and Sharma, R., Unraveling quantum complexity: A fuzzy AHP approach to understanding software industry challenges, in: *Deep Learning Tools for Predicting Stock Market Movements*, pp. 39–60, 2024.
10. Vyas, V., Mehta, K., Sharma, R., Investigating socially responsible investing behaviour of Indian investors using structural equation modelling. *J. Sustain. Financ. Invest.*, 12, 1, 1–23, 2020.
11. Mehta, K., Sharma, R., Vyas, V., A quantile regression approach to study the impact of aluminium prices on manufacturing sector of India during COVID era. *Mater. Today Proc.*, 65, 7, 3506–3511, 2022.
12. Afzal, A., Firdousi, S.F., Waqar, A., Awais, M., The Influence of Internet Penetration on Poverty and Income Inequality. *SAGE Open*, 12, 3, 215824402211161, 2022, https://doi.org/10.1177/21582440221116104.
13. Abid, N., Ceci, F., Ikram, M., Green growth and sustainable development: Dynamic linkage between technological innovation, ISO 14001, and environmental challenges. *Environ. Sci. Pollut. Res.*, 29, 17, 25428–25447, 2022, https://doi.org/10.1007/s11356-021-17518-y.
14. Tao, R., Su, C.-W., Naqvi, B., Rizvi, S.K.A., Can Fintech development pave the way for a transition towards low-carbon economy: A global perspective. *Technol. Forecast. Soc. Change*, 174, 121278, 2022, https://doi.org/10.1016/j.techfore.2021.121278.
15. Sharma, R. and Mehta, K., Credit risk and bank specific factors: An empirical study using panel GMM. *Int. J. Econ. Bus. Res.*, 27, 2, 294–309, 2024.
16. Sharma, R., Mehta, K., Rana, R., Cryptocurrency adoption behaviour of millennial investors in India, in: *Perspectives on Blockchain Technology and Responsible Investing*, pp. 135–158, 2023.
17. Mehta, K., Sharma, R., Vyas, V., Kuckreja, J.S., Exit strategy decision by venture capital firms in India using fuzzy AHP. *J. Entrep. Emerg. Econ.*, 14, 4, 643–669, 2022.
18. Vyas, V., Mehta, K., Sharma, R., Are bitcoin prices isolated or co-integrated? *Int. J. Bus. Globalisation*, 35, 1–2, 5–19, 2023.
19. Sharma, R., Mehta, K., Chugh, A., Using Analytic Hierarchy Process to determine forex risk hedging strategies of SMEs. *AIP Conf. Proc.*, 2916, 1, 120008, 2023.
20. Nenavath, S. and Mishra, S., Impact of green finance and fintech on sustainable economic growth: Empirical evidence from India. *Heliyon*, 9, 5, e16301, 2023, https://doi.org/10.1016/j.heliyon.2023.e16301.

21. Arner, D.W., Barberis, J.N., Buckley, R.P., The Evolution of Fintech: A New Post-Crisis Paradigm? *SSRN Electron. J.*, 47, 4, 1271–1319, 2015, https://doi.org/10.2139/ssrn.2676553.
22. Sironi, P., *FinTech innovation: From robo-advisors to goal based investing and gamification*, Wiley, 2016.
23. https://www.bcg.com/publications/2023/future-of-fintech-and-banking#:~:text=3)%20Asia%2DPacific%2C%20historically,a%20projected%20CAGR%20of%2027%25.
24. Murinde, V., Rizopoulos, E., Zachariadis, M., The impact of the FinTech revolution on the future of banking: Opportunities and risks. *Int. Rev. Financ. Anal.*, 81, 102103, 2022, https://doi.org/10.1016/j.irfa.2022.102103.
25. Sharma, R. and Mehta, K., *Deep Learning Tools for Predicting Stock Market Movements*, pp. 1–460, Wiley-Scrivener Publishing, 2024.
26. https://www.google.com/search?q=%28Fintech+and+the+Future+of+Finance%2C+2023&sca_esv=61ba496ce5dbe72c&sxsrf=ADLYWIIcDj4ARSpsMW_gd77hwQmW_KlCrg%3A1733992388902&ei=xJ9aZ5jeNvyo2roPvaLO0AM&ved=0ahUKEwiY0IiD6aGKAxV8lFYBHT2REzoQ4dUDCBA&uact=5&oq=%28Fintech+and+the+Future+of+Finance%2C+2023&gs_lp=Egxnd3Mtd2l6LXNlcnAiKChGaW50ZWNoIGFuZCB0aGUgRnV0dXJlIG9mIEZpbmFuY2UsIDIwMjMyBRAhGJ8FMgUQIRifBTIFECEYnwUyBRAhGJ8FMgUQIRifBUjlBVAAWABwAHgAkAEAmAHpAaAB6QGqAQMyLTG4AQPIAQD4AQL4AQGYAgGgAvMBmAMAkgcDMi0xoAfvBQ&sclient=gws-wiz-serp.
27. https://assets.ey.com/content/dam/ey-sites/ey-com/en_gl/topics/banking-and-capital-markets/ey-global-fintech-adoption-index.pdf.
28. Mehta, K. and Sharma, R., Contrarian and momentum investment strategies: Evidence from Indian stock market. *Int. J. Appl. Bus. Econ. Res.*, 15, 2, 87–98, 2017.
29. https://assets.equifax.com/assets/india/face_26th_july_option_2_14-08-23.pdf.
30. https://www.wipro.com/content/dam/nexus/en/industries/securities-and-capital-markets/latest-thinking/future-of-robo-advisors-in-investment-and-wealth-management.pdf.
31. https://www2.deloitte.com/content/dam/Deloitte/global/Documents/Financial-Services/real-estate/gx-real-estate-predictions-2020.pdf.
32. https://www.mckinsey.com/~/media/mckinsey/industries/financial%20services/our%20insights/on%20the%20cusp%20of%20the%20next%20payments%20era%20future%20opportunities%20for%20banks/on-the-cusp-of-the-next-payments-era-future-opportunities-for-banks.pdf.
33. https://www.fintechcouncil.in/pdf/The%20Winds%20of%20Change-%20Edition%20II.pdf.

4

Decentralized Finance: Blockchain "Money Lego" System

Shivani Bajaj[1*], Anupam Sharma[2] and Ankit Saxena[3]

[1]*MM Institute of Management, Maharishi Markandeshwar (Deemed to be) University, Mullana, Ambala, India*
[2]*Chitkara Business School, Chitkara University, Punjab, India*
[3]*Institute of Business Management, GLA University, Mathura, Uttar Pradesh, India*

Abstract
As blockchain technology has grown, decentralized attempts have been made to give a lot of people access to banking, investment, and insurance services. But can decentralized finance (DeFi) replace the current financial system, or has it just given crypto-currency fans another "technology playground" to play in? The study looks at the main meanings of and then combines them to make a new term that is fuller. After that, the different stages of DeFi are shown, along with how popular each one is and what the pros and cons of each one are. The main idea of this chapter is that autonomous finance could provide financial services on a system that is strong, open, and easy to understand. It could also help a lot of people with simple money matters. But this cannot happen until the sector grows even more and knows how to handle new risks well.

***Keywords*:** Blockchain, crypto assets, smart contract, decentralized finance, Ethereum, liquidity mining

4.1 Introduction

4.1.1 Understanding Decentralized Finance

Decentralized finance, or DeFi, is a new way of thinking about money that has changed the way traditional money works by creating a decentralized

**Corresponding author*: bajaj.shivani53.sb@gmail.com

Renuka Sharma, Kiran Mehta, Vishal Vyas and Vinod Kumar Shukla (eds.) Decentralized Finance and Blockchain: A Game Changing Duo, (77–96) © 2025 Scrivener Publishing LLC

system that does not need approval to use. In its simplest form, decentralization in finance means getting rid of middlemen like banks, financial institutions, and officials so that people can directly manage their own money.

Blockchain technology is a key part of this decentralized environment because it lets smart contracts carry out conditions that have already been set without any help from a third party. This distributed ledger technology makes sure that financial transactions are clear, safe, and cannot be changed. This builds trust among players. Decentralized finance supports a truly open and inclusive financial ecosystem that anyone with an internet link can access by eliminating the need for centralized entities. People and money have changed along with new technology and ideas. It used to be that people just bartered, but now there is digital money.

A lot of new things have come about because of the internet, like smart gadgets, e-commerce, and telecommunications. But the internet has not changed the way money works. Credit cards, ATMs, online banking, peer-to-peer (P2P) loans, and PayPal (Nguyen, 2018) [1] are some of the most important changes. At the time, PayPal was just an application of the internet's brand-new technology. Blockchain makes the internet bigger, which adds many new assets and currencies to the current financial system (Alstyne, 2020) [2].

It is possible that the rise of blockchain and crypto currencies will help ease the stress that comes with a slump. Most economic downturns are caused by changes in aggregate demand. This means that the main cause is changes in the cost or availability of money (Bajaj S., 2023) [3]. The economy must be stable before monetary policy can be used. The amount of money in circulation can change when the economy does. This is possible if the government allows blockchain technologies to grow (Vyas, *et al.*, 2023) [4].

(Caton, 2019) [5] research shows that cryptocurrencies can be a great way to set rules that will help keep the economy stable in the long term. Based on this research, asset-backed cryptocurrencies might be a good way to get cheap cash during a disaster.

Artificial intelligence, blockchain, cloud, and data/distributed ledger technologies (DLT) are four new technologies that are at the heart of FinTech, RegTech, and DeFi. They can be summed up with the letters ABC. These technologies are completely changing the financial world by opening new ways to settle deals both within and between countries. Even though a lot of academic and professional study has been done on the subject, it is still not clear. We need to learn more about this subject to go beyond the basic ideas and improve the ways that blockchain is already being used.

Since the FinTech sector came into being a few years ago, the financial system has changed in big ways. Recently, new companies have been offering financial services and digital technologies together in a way that is better and more creative than any other answer we have seen so far. The financial environment is exposed to various types of risks (Sharma *et al.*, 2023; Mehta *et al.*, 2022) [6, 7]. The FinTech ecosystem is made up of a lot of different companies. Some offer new products and services, sometimes in ways that are not allowed by the rules, while others try to sell products that traditional banks give in new and different ways. Using distributed ledger technology and, more specifically, blockchain technology in this field can change the way the money, capital, and insurance markets work by cutting out middlemen. Researchers have examined cryptocurrency behavior as there is an increased interest of investors in this digital financial instrument (Vyas *et al.*, 2023; Sharma *et al.*, 2023) [4, 8]. Because of decentralization, new businesses models have come up that have not been tested yet but touch every part of the financial value chain. Because the network can safely and forever store records of past transactions, blockchains can easily be made better for a lot of different tasks and goals. This is why blockchain technology could be a "disruptive innovation" (Dell'Erba, 2019) [9]. If blockchain technology is used, it might "lead to a reduction of industry rents for the benefit of end investors and of the end users of finance (entrepreneurs and businesses), enhancing market welfare."

Blockchain technology can be used in all fields, especially in the service sector, according to the research team at Binance, one of the biggest trade platforms. This is because of the rise of crypto assets and the tokenization of real-world assets (Bullmann, 2019) [10] Anyone can join the public blockchain because it is open and used all over the world. Here, it is not the same as organized banking systems, which are closed. There is no one person or group in charge of decentralization, which means that information is spread out over many computer networks. This might create a system that is fair, clear, cannot be changed, and works well (Maker Team, 2020) [11]. Standardization is another great thing about public blockchains. Distributed ledger technology lets companies use their own business models in a way that does not cost a lot of money and works with other systems.

Programmability is linked to this because it lets things follow laws, rules, and other standards without being told to. Blockchain technology cuts transaction costs by getting rid of middlemen and making the system decentralized (Cong and Wang, 2022) [12]. You can find and pick a partner, sign a contract, and make a claim with less trouble. So, the two sides talk to each other directly and come up with new, creative ways to make deals.

Its goal is to combine platformization, open banking, and block chain technology to make a global, efficient, and decentralized market where anyone with an internet connection can pay for things and get more financial services like banking, investing, and insurance. The next question is whether all of this can be done with blockchain technology. Is it smart to make derivatives or run a decentralized trade site? Decentralized finance is working on these goals because it wants to be an alternative to the current system that uses cash. Is this really something that can be done, or is it just another "technology playground" for crypto asset fans? How will the block chain change the whole financial value chain? Or will it only be able to make one part of the chain or process better? This piece tries to answer this question, among other things.

4.2 Review of Literature and Methodology

4.2.1 Blockchain Technology

The blockchain is a shared, decentralized, and unchangeable database that keeps track of all currency exchanges. This blockchain keeps track of all activities and provides distributed trust around the world and across borders. Blockchain is a shared, spread database that keeps track of all the transactions that happen on the network and shares that information with other users (Schär, 2020) [13]. Blockchain wants to use cryptography instead of faith to replace it (de Vos, 2021) [14]. A lot of cryptocurrencies use this technology (Opare and Kim; 2020) [15]. Since it allows peer-to-peer transactions through distributed decentralized systems, it can get rid of the need for middlemen in financial transactions. In this way, blockchain can make business models that weren't possible before possible (Chen) [16].

Banks and other financial institutions are changing their old services to fit the needs of the block chain because it can be used (Alstyne) [2]. In the same way that the internet and social networks have changed the way people talk to each other, blockchain and distributed ledger technology are changing the way money is handled. This is a system that tells the network of networks how to send information. It is a system for blockchains that decides how to send value across the network. The first is the Internet of Things, and the second is the Internet of Things that are worth having.

The things that make blockchain unique have been put together into 4 main groups (Dos Santos *et al.*, 2022) [17]:

1. Persistence: Once data is written on the blockchain, it cannot be changed;
2. Consensus: All honest participants have the same set of information;
3. Liveliness: All participants can add new information; and
4. Openness: Any participant can add new information to the blockchain.

One big benefit of DeFi over centralized institutions is that all activities are open to everyone and are recorded on the blockchain that supports them. Some of the main ways it is used are (1) independence; (2) distributed ledger technology and blockchain; (3) smart contracts; (4) cutting out middlemen; and (5) open banking (Zetsche *et al.*, 2020) [18]. The World Economic Forum (2017) says that a distributed ledger is "a database that is shared and synchronized by everyone (Zetsche *et al.*, 2020) [18] that can have multiple (private or public) witnesses."

Below Table 4.1 summarizes the idea of DeFi from the extensive literature review.

The main method used to write this study was a descriptive and qualitative analysis, which was mixed with an analysis of indicators from public online databases. It is important that the language used in the analysis is easy to understand so that both professionals and non-professionals can learn more about this fairly new area of science. Since the subject is getting more famous in international literature, there are a lot of books and articles that meet the scientific standards. The internet is where most people in DeFi publish their work. Aside from papers with technical and fundamental analyses, which make up a big part of the online content in this area, both scientific and non-scientific content can be clearly split into two groups. Most of the sources are written materials that explain and analyze the initiatives. These include white papers, commonly asked questions, and answers to those questions. This is the starting place for critical analyses and summaries of them, as well as for studies that find out things about the DeFi ecosystem or its parts. There were a lot of sources written in English. This is because DeFi is built on technology layers and IT systems that are usually written in English. There is a range of scientific value in the sources, but the study only looked at the relevant papers that were both very scientific and written in more everyday language. This study uses scientific methods to try to explain what DeFi is.

Table 4.1 The following table shows these meanings in order of when they were first used.

Author	**Year**	**Definition**
Chen [16]	2018; 2020	It is different from both traditional finance and centralized banking because it could make finance and monetary policy more democratic by making it easier for more people to access them, getting rid of possible gatekeepers, and putting policy decisions in the hands of the system's actual users.
Sompolinsky [19]	2019; 2021	"DeFi services could open up completely new business models and completely change modern finance. They could lower transaction costs, make it easier for people to get financial services, and make it easier for entrepreneurs to invest."
(Zetsche *et al.*, 2020) [18]	2020	"Datasets don't have to be stored on just one server in one server center. Instead, they can be spread out across many server centers that users from all over the world can access through the internet, more or less at the same time."
(Cong) [12]	2022	Blockchain-based alternatives to standard financial services like banks, brokerages, and exchanges are offered by decentralized finance, or "DeFi."
P. Schueffel [20]	2021	"DeFi says that financial services shouldn't come from centralized middlemen but should be made by users for users." Putting software parts into an autonomous peer-to-peer system based on blockchain technology is how this is done.
Bullmann [10]	2019	Blockchain could play a part in the growth of decentralized finance in the future. Decentralized finance is a type of finance that does not use middlemen but instead uses smart contracts in decentralized settings.

4.3 Problem Statement, Study Questions, and the Structure of Analysis

The main goal of the study is to come up with a new, complete description of DeFi by looking into the idea and showing how the ecosystem is set up.

It looks at the most important definitions and tries to explain the idea with its own meaning by putting them all together. It is also worth asking what DeFi needs to grow to compete with the standard financial system and get more people to use it. To do this, the study looks at the different types of DeFi, how common they are, their benefits and possibilities, as well as the biggest risks that come with the system. Finally, the study results are shown, and conclusions are drawn from them.

4.4 DeFi in the Real World

Getting stocks could help you understand what DeFi means in the business world. In the past, buyers had to first make an account with a bank. Then they had to start the buy order through their bank. The bank would then tell a broker about the sale.

The seller then places the order with the stock exchange. This is the only time the client can buy shares from the market (B. Goff and M. Simpson, 2021) [21]. This is a very simple picture of how to buy stocks. The bank, the broker, and the market are the three people involved. On the other side, there were three middlemen: the bank, the broker, and yes, the exchange. Not only do so many middlemen raise prices for customers, but they might also get things wrong when buying and selling. The first thing a customer does with the DeFi method is log in to a "decentralized exchange" (DeX) on their computer or phone. In a DeFi market, a customer can make a purchase order for a "token" or digital object. This kind of token is like a claim to any kind of property (Schueffel, 2021) [20]. A smart contract will carry out a buy order as soon as the specifications of an asset match the order. The seller gives the token to the customer, who then puts it in their own collection. The token is never given to a third party, and the users' names are never shared or written down.

A digital token must be made to stand in for an object so that an autonomous system can handle it. This way of doing things, which is most like how banks make and give out money, is called "tokenization" or "dematerialization" (Schueffel, 2021) [20].

4.4.1 DeFi and its Main Benefits

As was said in the beginning, DeFi wants to build a new ecosystem based on global, decentralized financial services that everyone can easily reach and does not need a central government. Figure 4.1 shows the evidence of how transactions differ in traditional and decentralized financial systems. Traditional systems involve banks and intermediaries like Visa or PayPal, while decentralized systems allow direct peer-to-peer transfers using blockchain technology. Decentralized finance is a change from standard centralized financial systems to peer-to-peer financial solutions made possible by decentralized technologies mainly based on the Ethereum blockchain (Dos Santos, 2022) [17]. At the same time, DeFi systems have come out and work on other blockchains, like EOS, TRON, or Cosmos.

There is not a single agreed upon meaning of DeFi, but most literature and people in the market use the term to mean the same thing. It is kind of funny that "heads of DeFi companies seem unable to define the sector in a few sentences" (Binance, 2020) [22]. Decentralized finance "refers to a group of applications that are mainly based on blockchains and are becoming a choice to the traditional banking ecosystem" (Princeton, 2016) [23]. This means that DeFi apps do not use fiat currency for transactions, loans, or trading. Instead, they use stablecoins (like USDT, USDC, and Dai) and other crypto assets (like ETH, Wrapped Bitcoin, and 0x). Decentralized finance is an "ecosystem made up of financial applications that are being built on top of blockchain systems" (Binance Academy, 2020a) [24]. When it comes to rules, the Polish Financial Supervision Authority (UKNF) was

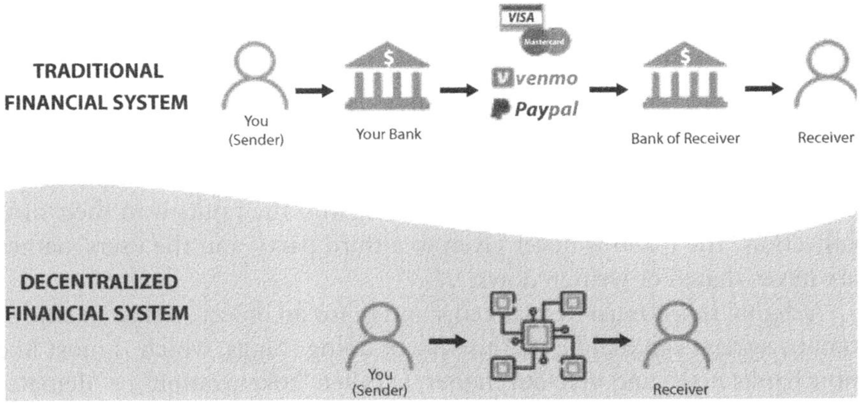

Figure 4.1 A comparison of the process of a transaction in traditional and decentralized finance. Source: Stably.

one of the first to describe DeFi as "an ecosystem of applications aimed at providing financial services on DLT.

In fact, the idea behind DeFi might also be summed up by the fact that the smart contract, which is computer code that runs itself, acts as a financial middleman. There is a similar description of DeFi: "an ecosystem made up of applications built on top of public distributed ledgers to make permission less financial services easier to use" [19, 25]. A similar language is used to describe DeFi: "open financial infrastructures built upon public smart contract platforms, such as the Ethereum blockchain" (Parlour, 2021) [26]. Banking services are not provided by a single organization (Zetzsche *et al.*, 2020) [18]. The authors say that at its heart are the markets, infrastructure, technology, methods, and applications that allow financial services to be provided in a decentralized way. The idea is looked at in terms of how well it works with other ideas: "DeFi is a financial ecosystem, where you can build tools, services, and smart contracts, and then connect them on a blockchain, like Lego" (Nartey, 2020) [27]. Putting together the different meanings given so far, DeFi can be thought of as the (eco)system that is public, permissionless, and DLT-based. The financial services that DeFi affects can be put into the following groups, which are also called DeFi functions in the literature (MakerDAO, 2024; Maker Blog, 2020) [11, 28]:

a) Servies like monetary banking (issuing stablecoins and running related payment systems)
b) Running decentralized trading platforms (such as DeX), which may include liquidity pooling services (like Uniswap, Curve Finance, Swerve, BurgerSwap, and PancakeSwap)
c) Offering peer-to-peer and liquidity pool lending and borrowing platforms (like Aave and Compound)
d) Offering higher-level, complex financial services such as derivatives trading, insurance protocols, asset management, and yield optimization platforms (e.g., Synthetix, Nexus Mutual, Yearn Finance).

The main goal of most DeFi projects is to do more than one thing or offer a "hybrid" service by mixing a few different features.

Blockchain technology and cryptocurrency are philosophically driven (Amler, 2021) [29]. Decentralized finance is "the movement that supports using decentralized networks and open-source software to make different kinds of financial products and services."

As was already said, the DeFi environment is different from the traditional financial system because it does not depend on centralized institutions and middlemen. Instead, it uses public protocols and decentralized apps. Transactions are carried out in a safe and predictable manner, and valid state changes are recorded on a public blockchain. So, this design can make a financial system that cannot be changed and works with a lot of other systems. It will be very open and give everyone the same rights to use it (Nartey, 2024) [27]. Also, this means that third parties like caretakers, central clearing houses, and others will be used less (Vyas, *et al.*, 2023) [30].

All the above meanings say that DeFi's goal is to offer financial services.

Let us look at the financial services that are available to get a better idea of the DeFi method.

4.4.2 Layers of DeFi: The Idea of Money Lego

A lot of people say that DeFi is like "money Lego." The idea behind it is that every protocol and app in a decentralized banking system can talk to each other and do work together. To get the best transaction results, you can mix and match different DeFi protocols and apps, just like you can mix and match Lego blocks (1, 2, 3). This not only gives users a great experience, but it also lets them make very difficult deals.

Check out the (Schar, 2020) [13] model to get a better idea of how DeFi works and how it changes money. It displays how every DeFi app and rule is made on top of the others, like a stack. The bottom layer, which is also known as the payment layer, is the block chain. It has rules for how the environment works. In fact, deals take place at this level. It is made up of crypto assets like ETH and Dai. This is the second layer, which is called the "asset" layer. On the third layer of the protocol, its main duties are laid out.

The next layer is the application layer, which is made up of user-friendly programs that connect the protocols and standards in the earlier levels. Smart contracts are linked together using a front-end interface that runs in a web browser. This makes the protocols simple to use and enjoyable for all users.

This layer is added on top of the application layer, making it more like an extra. When aggregators run platforms, they connect a lot of different systems and apps with users in mind. Most sites have tools that let users compare services and costs. This makes it easy to do things that would be hard to do otherwise. This is done by aggregators, which connect a lot of different protocols and important data from each site. People who use DeFi apps can make smart decisions and get the most out of them by running apps in this layer (Schar, 2020) [13].

Figure 4.2 shows the Schar model for Ethereum. More than one way makes it clear that the layers are stacked on top of each other. On the one

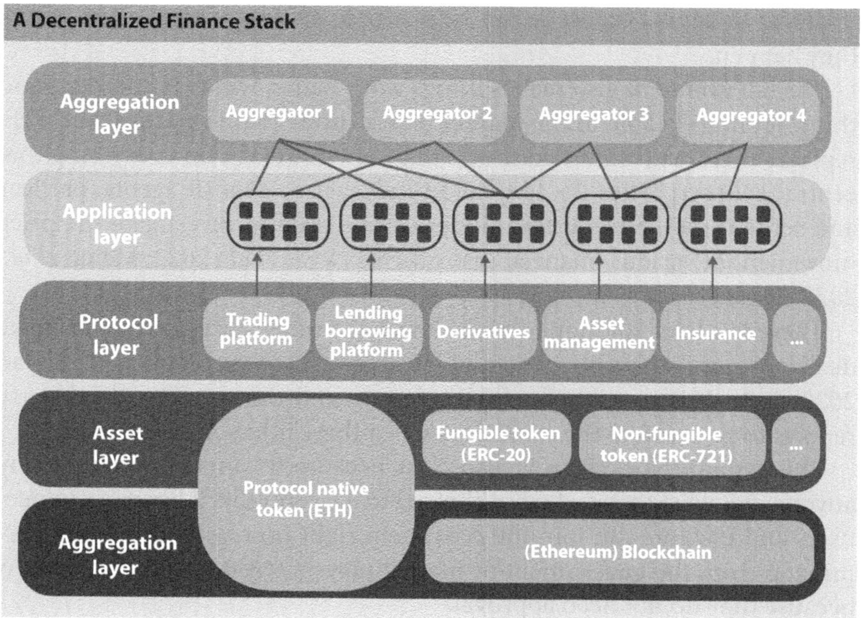

Figure 4.2 Decentralized finance stack. Source: Schar (2020).

hand, it is important to note that how each DeFi function is set up depends on how that layer interacts with and conducts business with the others. There are, however, some things that you should know about the underlying blockchain that determine how scalable, decentralized, or insecure a layer is (Hay, 2019; Amler *et al.*, 2021) [29].

As an example, in the DeFi ecosystem, users can borrow 100 USD worth of Dai stablecoin against their existing ETH. This allows them to do leveraged trading in another cryptocurrency asset, and they can then use a decentralized trading platform to trade their gains back to Dai and repay the loan.

4.4.3 Advantages and Opportunities of DeFi

There are quick, simple, and easy-to-use DeFi platforms that can be reached and used by anyone. Each platform can work with other platforms. Customers have a great time because of this. Users can decide which deals will be made and in what order. They can also choose how much the transaction fee will be. This is very helpful for deals that are hard to understand. It is also important to note the unprecedented level of openness: anyone can see and check all deals and smart contracts. This is different from most financial systems because it can help people avoid or lessen risks before they happen.

The environment also makes things work better, which is another good thing about it. People in the market trust central counterparties, but DeFi replaces them with smart contracts that can, in theory, do everything that central counterparties do, like hold funds, act as deposit agents, or clear and settle trades. Several techniques can be used to investigate the price movement of various financial instruments (Vyas *et al.*, 2023; Mehta *et al.*, 2022, Binance, 2024) [4, 7, 31]

These kinds of solutions should lower the other party's risk and make deals go more smoothly generally, no matter how you look at it (Schar, 2020) [13]. It is possible for legal pressure and the need for third-party reports to go down at the same time when there is less need for trust.

This type of blockchain is also clear because it cannot be changed by anyone, not even those who are allowed to. Decentralized finance protocol users and creators can join the ecosystem right now without getting permission from the government or market players (Goff, 2020) [21]. This is because they do not need approval.

Decentralized finance also lets users mix these strategies with others, such as liquidity mining, yield farming, and arbitrage, so it can be used for investment purposes, as well. Cryptocurrency users want to lock their funds. People who use secondary tokens may also get "cash flows" and see the value of their crypto assets go up if the platform's value goes up. Decentralized finance is not yet a good alternative to standard banking for people in developed economies. However, it is a great option for people in emerging economies like South America. Dai stablecoin, which is tied to the USD, has become a common way to save money in places where the economy is weak (Maker Blog, 2020) [11].

There are a lot of different types of transactions that can happen in both the standard financial system and DeFi. These transactions show that both are trying to help people with their money. People in the first area trust the "bank and its related actors," while people in the second area trust the block chain technology and protocols (Tayazime, 2023) [32]. The scene is different in each place, though. There are normal ways to handle money in the real world. Decentralized finance, on the other hand, is in charge of the block chains' value. The following are some parts of both standard banking and DeFi:

1. **Between authority and decentralization:** Traditional Financial System: The financial system is run and regulated by centralized officials, like

banks and governments. Decentralized Finance: DeFi uses block chain technology to do business, so there are no middlemen and deals can happen directly between users.

2. **Third parties:** Traditional Financial System: For deals and financial services, it relies on middlemen like banks, brokers, and clearing houses. Decentralized Finance: Does not use middlemen, so users can do business with each other directly through smart contracts on blockchain platforms.
3. **Access and Inclusion:** Traditional Financial System: Some people may not be able to get financial services because of where they live, how much money they make, or their credit background. Decentralized Finance: Anyone with an internet connection can use its banking services, which could lead to more people having access to money around the world.
4. **Censorship resistance:** Traditional Financial System: Authorities can freeze funds or limit access based on rules or court decisions. Decentralized Finance: Transactions cannot be censored because they are recorded on a blockchain, which means that anyone cannot quickly change them or stop them.
5. **Transparency:** Traditional Financial System: Some deals are not clear, and information is usually controlled by a few large institutions. Decentralized Finance: Blockchain transactions are clear and can be checked, which increases trust and lowers the risk of scams.
6. **Smart Contracts:** Traditional Financial System: Based on formal contracts and middlemen to make sure they are followed. Decentralized Finance: uses smart contracts, which are pieces of code that run themselves on the blockchain and automatically enforce the terms of contracts without the need for middlemen.
7. **Liquidity Pool:** Traditional Financial System: Most of the liquidity is held in a few central organizations. Decentralized Finance: uses decentralized liquidity pools so that users can give, borrow, and trade assets. This makes liquidity more spread out and flexible.
8. **Interest Rate:** Traditional Financial System: Banks and state banks decide how much interest it is to charge. Decentralized Finance: Interest rates in decentralized lending and borrowing systems are set by supply and demand.
9. **Accessibility around the world:** Traditional Financial System: Limited by countries and rules and regulations. Decentralized Finance: Available all over the world, pushing financial services that are not limited by location.

10. Safety and Risk: Traditional Financial System: The risks that come with having organized failure points like banks or clearing houses. Decentralized Finance: There are risks, like smart contracts being weak, but there are also perks, like blockchain technology's security.

It is important to remember that each method has its own pros and cons. Decentralized finance makes things easier to get to and lessens the need for middlemen, but it also brings new problems with security, rules, and how developed the technology is yet.

If the right changes are made to the system, DeFi could grow to be a very important part of blockchain. This could make it possible for billions of people around the world to get new, more complicated goods, and basic banking services at low costs. Also, the way banks work might change because of it (Amler *et al.*, 2020) [29]. The change in the way things work could make DeFi and centralized banking ecosystems want to work together. This might help make new business models that are safer and work better than the ones that are already in place (Maker Blog, 2020) [11]. In the last three months of 2020, it was already clear that they were going to work together. More big buyers are interested in crypto assets now than they were before (Zetzsche, 2020) [18]. Investors always look for various investment strategies to earn abnormal returns (Mehta and Sharma, 2017). More and more companies are either trying to get a license to offer financial services (Avgouleas, 2019) [33] or are about to release stablecoins after getting a banking license Avgouleas. Finally, it is important to remember that DeFi features have been made available to regular banks and institutional investors (Goff, 2021) [21]. It makes sense for the two places to work together and grow together, as shown by these points. In the long run, though, the rise of DeFi may also push other players to go digital and give better customer service.

4.4.4 Fundamental Risk Factors of DeFi

Here are some of the most important risks that come with DeFi:

1. Risks of smart contracts: There are bugs, security holes, and ways to take advantage of smart contracts. If someone takes advantage of a bug in the code, users could lose a lot of money.

   Example: In the 2016 DAO hack, a weakness in a smart contract was used to steal a lot of Ether.

2. Risks of Liquidity: Liquidity providers are very important to DeFi systems. When there are sudden changes in liquidity, like a lot of withdrawals, prices can slip, and the market can become less stable.
   Example: A sudden lack of liquidity can make it hard for users to make deals or get their money out of their accounts.
3. Risks for Oracle: Oracles give smart contracts information from outside sources. If oracles are hacked or changed, they can send wrong information into the system, which can stop smart contracts from being carried out.
   For example, if someone tampers with an oracle and gives out wrong price information for an asset, it could cause deals or liquidations on a DeFi platform to go wrong.
4. Uncertainty about regulations: DeFi works in a legal environment that is always changing. Regulatory actions or uncertainty can affect whether or not DeFi platforms are legal and how they work, which could lead to shutdowns or limits (Cong, L. W. and Wang, N., 2022) [12].
   For example, some DeFi services in some areas might have to shut down because of stricter rules or a quick change in the rules.
5. Short-Term Loss: In DeXs, liquidity providers may experience impermanent loss, which means that the value of their assets in the liquidity pool is not the same as the value of having those assets directly.
6. Risks of Collateralization: People who use assets as protection for loans run the risk of going bankrupt if the value of their collateral drops below a certain level. Market fluctuations can make this risk even greater.
7. Improvements to smart contracts: Adding new features to smart contracts can be hard and cause uncertainty. Users need to know how to update and what risks might be present during and after the upgrade.
8. Risks that are linked: Users can be exposed to systemic risks when different DeFi protocols and systems are linked to each other. If there is a bug or an attack in one protocol, it could affect other protocols.
   For example, if there is a flaw in a popular DeFi protocol, people may lose faith in the whole DeFi environment, which could affect many platforms.

9. Risks of User Error and Security: Phishing attacks, scams, or mistakes in how users handle secret keys could happen to them. When security is broken, money can be lost.
10. Problems with scalability: Some DeFi systems might have trouble with scalability, which could cause the blockchain network to get crowded, transaction fees to go up, and processing times to slow down.

    Example: When there is a lot of demand, like when the market is volatile, blockchain networks may get crowded, which can slow down deals and make them more expensive.
11. Coverage and availability of insurance: Some DeFi sites do offer insurance, but it may not be available to everyone or cover everything. Users should carefully look at their insurance choices and what they cannot do.
12. Risks of New Technologies: DeFi depends on new technologies a lot of the time. The fact that these technologies are still being tested means that there may be risks like unknown weaknesses and problems [25].

    For example, adding new consensus methods or cryptographic techniques to DeFi could have security effects that were not expected.

People who want to work or trade in the DeFi space should do their research, stay up to date on the risks, and only use money they can afford to lose. In addition, regulations and best practices in the DeFi space may continue to change, which makes it even more important to keep up with the latest news.

4.5 Results and Findings

The study's goal was to show that DeFi could be a new way to do things in the financial services field and could help make the area of those services truly open, clear, and strong. Anyone can see all the transactions, look at the data from those transactions, and learn from them for the future because the protocols can talk to each other. The study found that DeFi tells users everything they need to know about their transactions, and the users decide how much they want to handle it. As a whole, this is online, where people say they have a great time.

Making "trustless" versions of old banking systems is one way that DeFi has sparked a new wave of innovation. Also, by making new things possible that would not be possible without a public blockchain, such as liquidity pools and stablecoins. As the field grows, the risks we have already talked about might get smaller. Most of the time, this is because the area is still new. Better and more types of financial services are becoming available as more things come out. But people in the market should also be aware of the risks that have not been found yet. This is because new things are being made so quickly and are not being used much yet. Also, we should know that independence is not always what it seems to be. One way someone could get into the system is by having admin keys. They could then change a smart contract or start an emergency stop. You still have to believe in the system, and it was already said that each algorithm can have a different mix of centralized and decentralized parts.

The rise of DeFi could also be a wake-up call for organizations that are already in place. There is no "fire and water" between DeFi and the old way of doing business in our eyes. Decentralized financial solutions can be used in centralized FinTech frameworks. Some groups, like the Chicago DeFi Alliance, think that DeFi solutions can help the country get out of the economic downturn caused by the coronavirus. They also see the area in question as a possible path for future economic growth. Present players can make this more likely to happen if they are more open to the DeFi sector and willing to be more flexible in how they work together.

If technology keeps getting better, and especially if scale issues can be fixed, DeFi could grow to be one of the most important parts of blockchain. This might be a way for DeFi to reach even more people and make sure that everyone can use simple banking services. It could also change the way things are thought about in that area. People who work for centralized banks might also be pushed by this to come up with better and more efficient ways to run their businesses, or they might just look for ways to work with people in DeFi.

References

1. Nguyen, Q.K. and Dang, Q.V., Blockchain Technology for the Advancement of the Future, in: *2018 4th International Conference on Green Technology and Sustainable Development (GTSD)*, Nov. 2018, IEEE, Ho Chi Minh City, pp. 483–486, doi: 10.1109/GTSD.2018.8595577.
2. Alstyne, M.W.V., Parker, G.G., Choudary, S.P., Pipelines, Platforms, and the New Rules of Strategy. *Harv. Bus. Rev.*, 94, 4, 54–62, 2016.

3. Bajaj, S. and Saxena, A., An Empirical Investigation of Retail Investors' Sentiments: Role of Demographics. *Int. J. Prof. Bus. Rev.*, 8, 11, e03748–e03748, Nov. 2023.
4. Vyas, V., Mehta, K., Sharma, R., Are bitcoin prices isolated or co-integrated? *Int. J. Bus. Glob.*, 35, 1–2, 5–19, 2023.
5. Caton, J. L., Cryptoliquidity: the blockchain and monetary stability. *J. Entrep. Public Policy*, 9, 2, 227–252, 2020.
6. Mehta, K. and Sharma, R., Contrarian and momentum investment strategies: Evidence from indian stock market. *Int. J. Appl. Bus. Econ. Res.*, 15, 9, 107–118, 2017.
7. Mehta, K., Sharma, R., Vyas, V., A quantile regression approach to study the impact of aluminium prices on manufacturing sector of India during COVID era. *Mater. Today Proc.*, 65, 3506–3511, Jan. 2022, doi: 10.1016/j.matpr.2022.06.087.
8. Sharma, R., Mehta, K., Rana, R., Cryptocurrency adoption behaviour of millennial investors in India. in: *Perspectives on Blockchain Technology and Responsible Investing*, pp. 135–158, IGI Global, 2023.
9. Dell'Erba, M., Stablecoins in cryptoeconomics from initial coin offerings to central bank digital currencies. *NYUJ Legis. Pub. Pol'y.*, 22, 1, 2019.
10. Bullmann, D., Klemm, J., Pinna, A., In search for stability in crypto-assets: are stablecoins the solution? (No. 230). ECB Occasional Paper, 2019.
11. Maker Blog.pdf., MakerDAO's Gustav Arentoft: Decentralization Is Not a Binary Choice, Accessed: Dec. 04, 2024. [Online]. Available: https://cointelegraph.com/news/makerdaos-gustav-arentoft-decentralization-is-not-a-binary-choice.
12. Cong, L.W., Li, Y., Wang, N., Token-based platform finance. *J. Financ. Econ.*, 144, 3, 972–991, Jun. 2022, doi: 10.1016/j.jfineco.2021.10.002.
13. Nadler, M. and Schär, F., Decentralized finance, centralized ownership? An iterative mapping process to measure protocol token distribution, 2020, arXiv preprint arXiv:2012.09306.
14. de Vos, M.A., Decentralization and Disintermediation in Blockchain-based Marketplaces, Delft University of Technology, 2021, doi: 10.4233/UUID:A4F750B6-5AC5-4709-80C5-71EB71AC7B35.
15. Opare, E.A. and Kim, K., A Compendium of Practices for Central Bank Digital Currencies for Multinational Financial Infrastructures. *IEEE Access*, 8, 110810–110847, 2020, doi: 10.1109/ACCESS.2020.3001970.
16. Chen, Y. and Bellavitis, C., Blockchain disruption and decentralized finance: The rise of decentralized business models. *J. Bus. Ventur. Insights*, 13, e00151, 2020.
17. Dos Santos, S., Singh, J., Thulasiram, R.K., Kamali, S., Sirico, L., Loud, L., A New Era of Blockchain-Powered Decentralized Finance (DeFi) - A Review, in: *2022 IEEE 46th Annual Computers, Software, and Applications Conference (COMPSAC)*, Jun. 2022, pp. 1286–1292, doi: 10.1109/COMPSAC54236.2022.00203.

18. Zetzsche, D.A., Arner, D.W., Buckley, R.P., Decentralized Finance. *J. Financ. Regul.*, 6, 2, 172–203, Sep. 2020, doi: 10.1093/jfr/fjaa010.
19. Sompolinsky, Y. and Zohar, A., Bitcoin's Security Model Revisited, May 31, 2016, arXiv: arXiv:1605.09193. doi: 10.48550/arXiv.1605.09193.
20. Schueffel, P., DeFi: Decentralized Finance - An Introduction and Overview. *J. Innov. Manag.*, 9, 3, I–XI, Nov. 2021, doi: 10.24840/2183-0606_009.003_0001.
21. Goff, B. and Simpson, M. (Eds.), *Classicising Crisis: The Modern Age of Revolutions and the Greco-Roman Repertoire*, 1st ed., Routledge/Taylor & Francis Group, London; New York, NY, 2021, Series: Routledge monographs in classical studies: Routledge, 2020. doi: 10.4324/9781351115506.
22. Binance Academy 2020 Year in Review, Binance Academy, Accessed: Dec. 04, 2024. [Online]. Available: https://academy.binance.com/en/articles/binance-academy-2020-year-in-review.
23. *Bitcoin and cryptocurrency technologies: a comprehensive introduction*, Princeton University Press, Princeton (N.J.), 2016.
24. Binance Academy 2020 Year in Review, Binance Academy, Accessed: Dec. 04, 2024. [Online]. Available: https://academy.binance.com/en/articles/binance-academy-2020-year-in-review.
25. Blass, E.-O. and Kerschbaum, F., BOREALIS: Building Block for Sealed Bid Auctions on Blockchains, in: *Proceedings of the 15th ACM Asia Conference on Computer and Communications Security*, Oct. 2020, ACM, Taipei Taiwan, pp. 558–571, doi: 10.1145/3320269.3384752.
26. Lehar, A. and Parlour, C. A., Decentralized exchange: The uniswap automated market maker. *J. Finance Forthcoming*, 2021.
27. Nartey, J., Decentralized Finance (DeFi) and AI: Innovations at the Intersection of Blockchain and Artificial Intelligence, 2024. Available at SSRN 4781328, doi: 10.2139/ssrn.4781328.
28. MakerDAO's Gustav Arentoft: Decentralization Is Not a Binary Choice, Accessed: Dec. 04, 2024. [Online]. Available: https://cointelegraph.com/news/makerdaos-gustav-arentoft-decentralization-is-not-a-binary-choice.
29. Amler, H., Eckey, L., Faust, S., Kaiser, M., Sandner, P., Schlosser, B., DeFining DeFi: Challenges & Pathway, Jan. 14, 2021, arXiv: arXiv:2101.05589. doi: 10.48550/arXiv.2101.05589.
30. Vyas, V., Mehta, K., Sharma, R., Investigating socially responsible investing behaviour of Indian investors using structural equation modelling. *J. Sustain. Financ. Invest.*, 12, 1, 1–23, doi: 10.1080/20430795.2020.1790958.
31. Learn All About Blockchain & Cryptocurrency, Binance Academy, Accessed: Dec. 04, 2024. [Online]. Available: https://academy.binance.com/.
32. Tayazime, J. and Moutahaddib, A., DeFi, Blockchain and Cryptocurrencies: Proposing a Global Money Matrix for the Blockchain Era. *Eur. Sci. J. ESJ*, 19, 16, 160, Jun. 2023, doi: 10.19044/esj.2023.v19n16p160.
33. Avgouleas, E. and Kiayias, A., The promise of blockchain technology for global securities and derivatives markets: the new financial ecosystem and the 'holy grail'of systemic risk containment. *Eur. Bus. Organ. Law Rev.*, 20, 1, 81–110, 2019.

5

Blockchain and Cryptocurrency: Introduction to Decentralized Finance (DeFi)

Sonal Trivedi[1]*, Vinita Choudhary[2] and Neha Kamboj[3]

[1]School of Management & Commerce, Manav Rachna University, Faridabad, Haryana, India
[2]School of Leadership and Management, Manav Rachna International Institute of Research and Studies, Haryana, India
[3]IILM School of Management, IILM University Gurugram, Haryana, India

Abstract

Blockchain is considered to be the latest technology. Trust is a key factor in areas such as banking. Blockchain is a decentralized, encrypted security system that allows new digital platforms and services to be developed using this emerging technology. The cryptocurrency market has grown in popularity in recent years. With the availability of price data on cryptocurrency exchanges, it is possible to conduct statistical analysis to determine the features of the cryptocurrency market. Blockchain and cryptocurrency are foundational elements of decentralized finance (DeFi), playing essential roles in enabling the creation and functioning of various DeFi applications and services. This chapter aims to identify the characteristics of decentralized finance, blockchain, and cryptocurrency and how they are interrelated.

***Keywords*:** Cryptocurrency, blockchain, decentralization, decentralized finance, smart contract

**Corresponding author*: trivedi.sonal86@gmail.com

Renuka Sharma, Kiran Mehta, Vishal Vyas and Vinod Kumar Shukla (eds.) Decentralized Finance and Blockchain: A Game Changing Duo, (97–124) © 2025 Scrivener Publishing LLC

5.1 Introduction

This chapter aims to identify the characteristics of decentralized finance (DeFi), blockchain, and cryptocurrency and how they are interrelated. The first section presents the concept of DeFi, its key characteristics, and examples. The second section presents the concept of blockchain and its key characteristics. The third section presents the concept of cryptocurrency and its key characteristics. The fourth section presents the relationship between blockchain and cryptocurrency. The fifth section presents implications of DeFi. The sixth section presents current trends in DeFi. The seventh section presents future scope in DeFi followed by the conclusion.

The section below explains the concept of DeFi.

Decentralized finance is a term used to describe a movement within the crypto and blockchain space that seeks to create decentralized versions of traditional financial services [1]. These projects leverage blockchain technology to provide open, permissionless, and trustless alternatives to traditional financial intermediaries like banks, brokers, and other financial institutions [2]. From both the definitions, it can be drawn that usage of blockchain technology has transformed the traditional financial services into decentralized ones.

The section below presents the key characteristics of DeFi.

5.1.1 Key Characteristics of Decentralized Finance Include

1. Decentralization: DeFi platforms are made on networks of blockchain like Solana, Binance Ethereum, amd Smart Chain. These networks are decentralized, i.e. they do not depend on a solo central authority. As an alternative, transactions and operations are validated by a distributed network of nodes [3].
2. Open access: DeFi platforms are open to anyone with an internet connection and a compatible wallet. There are no restrictions or requirements to access DeFi services, making them inclusive and accessible to a global audience [4].
3. Interoperability: Many DeFi protocols and applications can interact with each other. This means users can move assets and data seamlessly between different platforms, creating a more interconnected and flexible financial ecosystem [5].
4. Smart contracts: A smart contract is a self-executing contract whose terms are directly written in the code. Decentralized

finance applications rely on smart contracts for automating processes, reduce the requirement for third-party mediators, and enable trustless interactions [6].

5. Liquidity provision: DeFi platforms often rely on liquidity provided by users. Users can lend, borrow, trade, and stake their assets, earning interest, rewards, or fees in return.
6. Decentralized exchanges (DEXs): They are platforms where investors can trade cryptocurrencies directly with each other without a centralized intermediary. The examples of popular DEXs are PancakeSwap, SushiSwap, and Uniswap [7].
7. Borrowing and lending: DeFi platforms permit people to provide their cryptocurrencies for earning yield or borrowing instruments using their property as collateral. MakerDAO, Compound, and Aave are examples of borrowing and lending platforms [8].
8. Monetization and contribution: Users can participate in monetization by providing liquidity to DeFi platforms and earning rewards such as additional tokens. Staking means holding and "predicting" tokens to support the network and operation and earn rewards [9].
9. Synthetic assets: Some DeFi platforms offer synthetic assets, which are tokenized representations of real-world assets like stocks, commodities, or even other cryptocurrencies. These tokens allow users to gain exposure to these assets without owning them directly.
10. Risk and challenges: while DeFi proposes stimulating openings, it is not without risks. Some of the challenges associated with DeFi are regulatory concerns, security breaches, smart contract vulnerabilities, and market volatility.

It is important to do meticulous research and apply caution when participating in DeFi activities, as the landscape can be complex and rapidly evolving. Always ensure that you are using reputable platforms and understand the risks involved before committing your assets.

5.1.2 Examples of Decentralized Finance

Decentralized finance is a rapidly growing cryptocurrency and blockchain sector. It aims to reinvent traditional financial services using decentralized technologies such as blockchain and smart contracts. Here are some examples of DeFi applications and platforms:

1. Decentralized Exchanges: DEXs permit people to trade cryptocurrencies openly among each other with no requirement of mediators. Examples include Uniswap, PancakeSwap, SushiSwap, and Curve [10].
2. Lending and lending platforms: These platforms permit investors to provide their crypto instruments and lend assets or earn interest against their holdings. Examples include Aave, Compound, MakerDAO, and Cream Finance [11].
3. Stablecoins: Stablecoins are cryptocurrencies designed to maintain a stable value, often tied to a traditional currency such as the US dollar. They are often used in DeFi for trading and as collateral. For example: DAI, USDC, and Tether.
4. Yield farming: Yield farming involves providing liquidity to various DeFi platforms and earning rewards in the form of additional tokens. Users can stake their assets in liquidity pools to earn returns. Platforms like Yearn Finance and Harvest Finance facilitate yield farming [12].
5. Synthetic assets: These platforms create tokens that represent the value of real-world assets like stocks, commodities, or even other cryptocurrencies. Examples include Synthetix and UMA.
6. Betting markets: Decentralized betting markets permit people to bet on the result of real actions like sporting events or elections. Auguro is an example of a decentralized prediction market platform.
7. Insurance protocols: DeFi insurance platforms provide protection against smart contract vulnerabilities and other risks in the DeFi ecosystem. Nexus Mutual is a notable example.
8. Decentralized Identity (DID): DID solutions offer users the capability of managing their personal information using blockchain technology. Sovrin and uPort are examples of DID platforms.
9. Decentralized asset management: These platforms provide automated portfolio management and investment strategies through smart contracts. Set Protocol and dHEDGE are examples.
10. Decentralized derivatives: Some platforms permit people to trade decentralized derivatives, including futures & options (F&O) on the blockchain.

11. Cross-chain platforms: These platforms enable interoperability between different blockchains, allowing assets to be transferred and used between different chains. Polkados and Cosmos are examples of such platforms.
12. Decentralized payment solutions: Projects like OMG Network (formerly OmiseGO) aim to provide scalable and affordable payment solutions on the blockchain.

These are just a few examples of the wide range of DeFi applications and platforms available. The DeFi space is constantly evolving, and new projects and innovations are constantly being developed. Blockchain technology is the core technology that enables the development of DeFi applications. The next section presents how these two concepts are interconnected.

5.2 Blockchain Technology

Blockchain is a decentralized and immutable digital ledger that records transactions securely and transparently [13]. It consists of a blockchain, each containing a set of transactions [14]. What makes blockchain unique is its decentralized nature and consensus mechanism that ensures that all participants in the network agree on the state of the ledger [15].

5.2.1 Key Features of Blockchain Technology

1. Decentralization: Blockchains are typically decentralized networks where multiple participants (nodes) work together for validating and recording transactions [16]. This removes the requirement for a central authority, building the system more challenging to censorship and individual failure [17].
2. Transparency: The transactions recorded on Blockchain are publicly recorded and evident to all participants in the network [18]. Such transparency increases trust and accountability.
3. Immutability: Once a transaction is recorded on the blockchain, it is very difficult to change or delete it. This immutability ensures the integrity of the event history [19].
4. Security: Blockchains use cryptographic techniques to protect transactions and data. Consensus mechanisms like Proof of Stake (PoS) or Proof of Work (PoW) ensure the correctness of transactions [20].

5.2.2 Decentralized Finance and Blockchain

Decentralized finance utilizes blockchain technology for creating an ecosystem of monetary applications and services that operate without conventional financial mediators. Here is how blockchain enables DeFi:

1. Smart contracts: DeFi applications are made by using smart contracts. They are coded on the blockchain, which is self-executing. These contracts mechanically perform predefined tasks when certain situations are met [21]. They permit the mechanization of monetary processes and eliminate the requirements for mediators.
2. Unauthorized access: An individual is required to have a well-suited wallet and internet connection to utilize DeFi platforms. Because the blockchain is decentralized, users can interact with DeFi applications without the permission of a central authority [22].
3. Trustless transactions: Blockchain's consensus mechanisms and cryptographic techniques allow users to engage in transactions without needing to trust a centralized entity. The blockchain's transparency and immutability ensure that transactions are secure and verifiable.
4. Interoperability: Many DeFi protocols and applications are built on the same blockchain or can communicate with each other across different blockchains. This interoperability allows for flawless movement of instruments and data between various DeFi services.
5. Custodial solutions: The independence of blockchain allows users to fully control their assets, reducing the risk that money remains with third parties.
6. Liquidity pools: In this, DeFi platforms often depend on liquidity provided by investors. Blockchain's tokenization capabilities allow users to invest their funds in liquidity pools, enabling trading, lending and borrowing [23].
7. Decentralization: DeFi platforms use the blockchain and decentralized features, ensuring that no single unit controls data or the network. Such decentralization promotes transparency, security, and trust in the ecosystem [24].
8. Immutability: Transactions and data stored on the blockchain are immutable, meaning they cannot be changed once

confirmed. This feature ensures the integrity of financial data and prevents fraud.
9. Transparency: Blockchain's public and transparent ledger permits participants to verify transactions and account balances, increasing trust and reducing the requirement for third-party verification [25].
10. Security: Blockchain's cryptographic techniques, consensus mechanisms, and decentralized structure contribute to the security of DeFi applications, making them resilient against attacks and breaches.

In summary, blockchain technology serves as the infrastructure that underpins the decentralized nature, security, and transparency of DeFi applications. It provides the foundation for creating a new paradigm of financial services that are open, inclusive, and accessible to a global audience.

Cryptocurrency and DeFi are closely intertwined concepts within the broader realm of blockchain technology. Let us explore how these two concepts relate to each other:

5.3 Cryptocurrency

Cryptocurrency refers to digital or virtual currencies that use encryption for secure transactions and control the creation of new units [26]. The most well-known cryptocurrency is Bitcoin, but there are thousands of other cryptocurrencies, often called altcoins, each with their own characteristics and uses [27]. The researchers have examined the cryptocurrency behavior as there is an increased interest of the investors in this digital financial instrument.

5.3.1 Key Features of Cryptocurrencies

1. Decentralization: Cryptocurrencies operate on decentralized networks, usually based on blockchain technology [28]. This means that no entity has currency control, and transactions are controlled by a network of decentralized nodes.
2. Digital ownership: Cryptocurrencies represent the ownership of digital assets stored in the blockchain. Ownership is controlled by cryptographic keys, giving users complete control over their money [29].

3. Global accessibility: Cryptocurrencies can and will be used by anyone with an internet connection. They enable cross-border transactions without intermediaries or currency conversion [30].
4. Anonymity and privacy: Although transactions are recorded on public ledgers, the identities are often pseudonyms. Some cryptocurrencies offer advanced privacy features that allow users and financial data [31].

5.3.2 Decentralized Finance and Cryptocurrency

Decentralized finance builds upon the principles of blockchain and cryptocurrency to create a new ecosystem of financial services that are open, permissionless, and trustless. Cryptocurrencies are integral to the DeFi space in several ways:

1. Native assets: Many DeFi protocols and applications are built on existing cryptocurrencies like Ethereum and Binance Coin. These native cryptocurrencies are used for various purposes within DeFi, such as providing liquidity, staking, and governance [32].
2. Liquidity pools: To smooth the progress of trading and lending activities, DeFi platforms rely on liquidity. Users contribute their cryptocurrencies for liquidity pools, to earn rewards or fees in exchange. These liquidity pools often involve pairing different cryptocurrencies to create trading pairs [33].
3. Collateral and borrowing: Cryptocurrencies are used as collateral to secure loans within DeFi platforms. Users can lock up their cryptocurrency holdings in smart contracts and borrow other assets against them, creating a decentralized lending and borrowing system.
4. Staking and yield farming: Investors can stake their cryptocurrencies in DeFi platforms for supporting network operations, participate in governance, and earn rewards. Yield farming involves providing liquidity to DeFi protocols and earning additional tokens as rewards.

5. Decentralized exchanges: DEXs are a crucial constituent of DeFi. These platforms enable users to trade cryptocurrencies directly with one another without relying on traditional centralized exchanges. Decentralized exchanges utilize smart contracts to facilitate peer-to-peer trading [34].
6. Cross-chain interoperability: Some DeFi projects are focused on enabling interoperability between different blockchains, allowing users to move their cryptocurrencies and assets seamlessly across various networks [35].
7. Tokenization of assets: Some DeFi projects tokenizing real-world assets, like commodities or real estate, using cryptocurrencies. This allows for fractional ownership and greater accessibility to traditionally illiquid assets.
8. Synthetic assets: Cryptocurrencies are used as collateral to mint synthetic assets, which are tokenized representations of real-world instruments, permiting users to gain exposure without owning the actual instrument.

In summary, cryptocurrency provides the underlying digital assets that power the various financial services and applications within the DeFi ecosystem. The combination of blockchain, cryptocurrencies, and smart contracts has paved the way for the creation of a more decentralized financial system, accessible and inclusive through DeFi.

5.4 Relationship Between Blockchain and Bryptocurrency

Based on the discussion above, here is a comparison table outlining the key differences between blockchain and cryptocurrency.

It can be concluded from Table 5.1 that while blockchain technology underlies many cryptocurrencies, not all cryptocurrencies use blockchain. For instance, some cryptocurrencies use directed acyclic graphs instead of traditional blockchain structures.

Table 5.1 A comparison between blockchain and cryptocurrency.

Aspect	**Blockchain**	**Cryptocurrency**
Definition	A decentralized, distributed digital ledger	A virtual or digital currency using cryptography
Purpose	Record and verify transactions across a network	Store of value or means of exchange
Technology	Distributed ledger technology	Encryption and consensus mechanisms
Components	Blocks, transactions, nodes, consensus mechanism	Coins/tokens, wallets, mining/proof of stake
Centralization	Decentralized and distributed	Decentralized, but can have centralized uses
Use Cases	Supply chain, finance, healthcare, voting, etc.	Payments, investment, smart contracts, etc.
Transparency	High transparency due to public ledger	Pseudonymous transactions
Security	High security due to cryptography and consensus	Security depends on the underlying blockchain technology
Energy Consumption	Varies by consensus mechanism (Proof of Work)	Varies by cryptocurrency (Proof of Stake, etc.)
Examples	Bitcoin, Ethereum, Hyperledger	Bitcoin, Ethereum, Ripple, Litecoin, etc.

5.5 Implications of Decentralized Finance

Decentralized finance has a major impact on various areas of the financial sector and beyond. Some of the key impacts are:

1. Financial inclusion: DeFi has the potential to fetch monetary services to underbanked and unbanked people around the globe. An internet connection allows individuals to participate in DeFi platforms and use financial services without relying on traditional banks.
2. The number of intermediaries is reduced: DeFi eliminates many intermediaries in financial transactions, which can reduce costs, increase efficiency, and minimize counterparty risk. Users can interact directly with smart contracts, reducing the requirement for traditional financial mediators like payment processors and banks.
3. Global accessibility: DeFi runs on blockchain networks, so it is reachable to anybody internet connectivity, despite their geographic location. This opens opportunities for cross-border transactions and financial communication without currency conversion or extensive regulatory processes.
4. Transparency and auditability: Transactions and operations on DeFi platforms are recorded on the blockchain, ensuring a high level of transparency and traceability. Such transparency can increase the trust of participants and enable better control of financial activities.
5. Programmable financial services: DeFi applications are built using smart contracts, which are self-executing contracts with predefined rules. It allows the automation of various financial processes such as borrowing, lending, trading and cultivation without intermediaries.
6. Market efficiency: DeFi platforms facilitate real-time trading and enable instant settlement of transactions, which increases market efficiency. In addition, liquid pools and automated market makers improve price discovery by reflecting supply and demand dynamics [36].
7. Control and ownership: DeFi permits users to control and own their assets. Users keep control of their private keys and can interact openly with DeFi protocols, reducing the risk of third parties owning assets [37].
8. Experimentation and innovation: The open-source nature of DeFi platforms encourages innovation, allowing developers to generate novel financial goods and services. This environment has led to the rapid emergence of various DeFi applications, each designed for different use cases.

9. Lower counterparty risk: DeFi protocols often require collateral to secure loans and transactions, reducing the risk of default. This collateral is held in smart contracts and is automatically liquidated if certain conditions are not met [38].
10. Challenges and risks: While DeFi offers many benefits, it also comes with challenges and risks such as smart contract vulnerabilities, regulatory uncertainty, and scalability issues. Users should be careful and do their due diligence before participating in DeFi activities [39].
11. Disruption of traditional financial institutions: DeFi can disrupt traditional financial institutions by providing alternative ways to access financial services, trade assets and manage investments. This disruption can change the financial landscape and force traditional players to adapt to the changing environment [40].
12. Regulatory considerations: As DeFi persists to grow, regulators are giving more consideration to its activities. The DeFi regulatory environment is still evolving, and the industry may face regulatory challenges and compliance requirements [41].

Overall, DeFi can transform traditional financial systems, increase financial inclusivity, and democratize finance. However, its rapid evolution also brings about various challenges and uncertainties that need to be carefully addressed as the space matures.

5.5.1 Relationship Between Decentralized Finance, Blockchain, and Cryptocurrency

The table below outlines the relationship between DeFi, blockchain, and cryptocurrency:

Table 5.2 A comparison between DeFi, blockchain, and cryptocurrency.

Aspect	Decentralized finance (DeFi)	Blockchain	Cryptocurrency
Definition	Decentralized financial systems built on blockchain	A decentralized, distributed digital ledger	A digital or virtual currency using cryptography

(Continued)

Table 5.2 A comparison between DeFi, blockchain, and cryptocurrency. (*Continued*)

Aspect	Decentralized finance (DeFi)	Blockchain	Cryptocurrency
Purpose	To reconstruct conventional financial services	Record and verify transactions across a network	Means of exchange or storage value
Technology	Built on blockchain technology	Distributed ledger technology	Encryption and consensus mechanisms
Components	Smart contracts, protocols, decentralized applications (dApps), tokens	Blocks, transactions, nodes, consensus mechanism	Coins/tokens, wallets, mining/ proof of stake
Centralization	Aimed at reducing reliance on central entities	Decentralized, but can have centralized uses	Decentralized, but can have centralized uses
Use Cases	Lending, borrowing, trading, yield farming, etc.	Supply chain, finance, healthcare, voting, etc.	Payments, investment, smart contracts, etc.
Transparency	High transparency due to public blockchain	High transparency due to public ledger	Pseudonymous transactions
Security	Relies on blockchain's security	High security due to cryptography and consensus	Security depends on the underlying blockchain technology
Energy Consumption	Varies based on underlying blockchain tech	Varies by consensus mechanism (Proof of Work)	Varies by cryptocurrency (Proof of Stake, etc.)
Examples	Compound, Uniswap, MakerDAO	Bitcoin, Ethereum, Hyperledger	Bitcoin, Ethereum, Ripple, Litecoin, etc.

It can be concluded from Table 5.2 that DeFi is a subset of applications and platforms built on top of blockchain technology, while cryptocurrencies are a form of digital assets that can be used in various ways, including within DeFi systems. Several techniques can be used to investigate the price movement of various financial instruments [42]. Blockchain technology provides the foundational infrastructure for both DeFi and cryptocurrencies.

Certainly, here is an overview of the development and evolution of blockchain, cryptocurrency, and DeFi:

5.5.2 Development of Blockchain, Cryptocurrency and Decentralized Finance

5.5.2.1 Blockchain

- Early concepts (before 2008): The idea of decentralized digital ledgers existed before the creation of Bitcoin. Notable concepts include Nick Szabo's Bit Gold and Wei Dai's B-money.
- Bitcoin and proof of concept (2008 to 2009): In 2008, a person or group using the pseudonym Satoshi Nakamoto published the Bitcoin White Paper, which introduced the concept of a peer-to-peer electronic cash system using blockchain technology. In 2009, Nakamoto mined the first Bitcoin block, known as the genesis block [43].
- Blockchain beyond Bitcoin (2010s): Developers began to explore blockchain applications beyond cryptocurrencies. Launched by Vitalik Buterin in 2015, Ethereum introduced smart contracts that allow developers for building decentralized applications (dApps) on its blockchain.
- Various use cases (2010s to present): Blockchain technology has found applications in various fields such as supply chain management, healthcare, finance, and voting systems. Private and permissioned blockchains have also emerged for commercial use.

5.5.2.2 Cryptocurrency

- Bitcoin's emergence (2009 to 2010): Bitcoin became the first functional cryptocurrency, gaining attention as a digital currency, which is decentralized. Bitcoin introduced the concept of using cryptographic techniques for secure transactions and consensus.

- Altcoins and diversification (2011 to 2013): Alternative cryptocurrencies (altcoins) like Litecoin (2011) and Namecoin (2011) were created, offering variations in mining algorithms and features. This marked the start of cryptocurrency diversification [44].
- Initial coin offerings (ICOs) and tokenization (2017 to 2018): ICOs gained popularity to fund new cryptocurrency projects. The ERC-20 standard of Ethereum allowed an easy formation of tokens, leading to a boom in token-based projects.
- Cryptocurrency as assets (2010s to present): Cryptocurrencies gained recognition as investable assets and a form of digital gold. Institutional interest, regulatory developments, and a wider acceptance contributed to mainstream adoption.

5.5.2.3 *Decentralized Finance*

- Early DeFi Concepts (2010s): The concept of creating decentralized financial applications using blockchain technology emerged. Some early projects attempted to build decentralized exchanges and lending platforms.
- Ethereum's role (2010s): Ethereum's smart contract capabilities enabled the creation of DeFi platforms. Compound (2018) introduced algorithmic lending, and Uniswap (2018) pioneered decentralized exchanges.
- Decentralized finance explosion (2020s): The DeFi sector saw explosive growth in 2020 and beyond, with projects offering yield farming, liquidity provision, decentralized stablecoins, derivatives, and more. Total value locked in DeFi protocols surged [45].
- Challenges and regulation (2020s to present): DeFi's rapid growth raised concerns about security, smart contract vulnerabilities, and regulatory challenges. Various DeFi platforms faced hacking incidents, emphasizing the need for robust security practices.

It is important to note that the development of these technologies is ongoing, and the landscape continues to evolve rapidly. Each area has its own challenges and opportunities, and their trajectories are intertwined as they shape the future of finance and technology.

5.5.2.4 *Process of Blockchain, Cryptocurrency and Decentralized Finance*

Decentralized finance, blockchain, and cryptocurrency processes are discussed as follows:

5.5.2.4.1 Blockchain Process

a. Event creation: Participants initiate events by creating digital records of their actions, such as sending cryptocurrency, executing a smart contract, or storing data [46].
b. Transaction confirmation: Transactions are sent to a network of nodes (computers) running blockchain software. Nodes verify the transaction and its validity, and check factors, such as digital signatures and available funds.
c. Formation of blocks: Valid events are grouped into a block. Each block carries a cryptographic reference to the preceding block, forming a blockchain (the term "blockchain").
d. Consensus mechanism: Nodes compete for solving a complex mathematical riddle (Proof of Work) or offer a contribution (Proof of Interest) to add the next block. This process ensures consent about the blockchain.
e. Adding a block: When a node successfully solves a puzzle or makes a required contribution, a new block is added to the blockchain. This process is also called mining.
f. Decentralization and security: The decentralized nature of blockchain and encryption technologies ensures data security, transparency, and immutability [47].

5.5.2.4.2 Cryptocurrency Process

a. Creation: Cryptocurrencies are created through processes such as mining (Proof of Work), where powerful computers solve complex mathematical puzzles to confirm and record transactions.
b. Distribution: New coins are rewarded to miners for their work. Alternatively, cryptocurrencies can be pre-mined or distributed through ICOs or token sales [48].

c. Wallets: Users need a digital wallet to store and manage their cryptocurrencies. To increase security, wallets can be software (online or offline) or hardware.
d. Transactions: Crypto transactions involve sending money from one wallet to another. Transactions are sent to the network and recorded on the blockchain.
e. Verification: Verification by miners or validators must be added to the blockchain for transactions to occur. The number of confirmations ensures the event and security [49].
f. Exchange: Cryptocurrencies can be exchanged in cryptocurrencies where users can buy, sell, or trade different currencies against each other or fiat currencies.

5.5.2.4.3 Decentralized Finance Process

a. Smart Contracts: DeFi applications are formed with smart contracts. They are self-executing contracts written in code. These agreements define the rules and processes for various economic activities [50].
b. Decentralization: DeFi platforms aim to reduce dependency on intermediaries by allowing participants to interact directly with smart contracts and protocols.
c. User Interaction: Users connect their crypto wallets to DeFi platforms, allowing them to interact with various financial services such as lending, borrowing, trading, and cropping.
d. Automated processes: Smart contracts automatically perform actions when predefined conditions are met. For example, a user can borrow their cryptocurrency to earn interest, which is automatically distributed by the smart contract.
e. Liquidity: DeFi platforms often use liquidity by allowing users to deposit their money for providing liquidity while trading. In exchange, they receive a fraction of transaction fees and commissions.
f. Risk management: Participants should be aware of the potential vulnerabilities of smart contracts and potential risks associated with DeFi platforms.

5.5.2.4.4 Adoption of Blockchain, Cryptocurrency, and Decentralized Finance

Adoption of blockchain, cryptocurrency and DeFi has grown significantly over the years. Here is an overview of their adoption trends:

1. Blockchain adoption: Business solutions: Various industries, including supply chain, logistics, healthcare and finance, have explored blockchain to improve transparency, traceability, and security. Companies such as IBM, Walmart, and Maersk have implemented blockchain-based solutions [51].
   - Government initiatives: Some governments have embraced blockchain for administrative efficiency, digital identity, and secure data management. Notable examples are the Estonian e-residence program and the Dubai blockchain strategy.
   - Consortia and partnerships: Consortia such as R3 Corda and Hyperledger have brought together companies, institutions, and developers to collaborate on blockchain projects and solutions.
   - Tokenization: In addition to cryptocurrencies, assets such as real estate, art, and goods are recognized, increasing fractional ownership and liquidity.
2. Adoption of cryptocurrencies: Payment options: Over the years, an increasing number of companies, online sellers and even brick-and-mortar stores have begun to accept cryptocurrencies as a means of payment. Companies like Tesla and Microsoft have accepted Bitcoin for some products and services [52].
   - Money transfers and cross-border payments: Cryptocurrencies are used to facilitate cross-border money transfers, providing a quicker and potentially cheaper substitute for traditional money transfers.
   - Financial inclusion: The potential of cryptocurrencies to fetch monetary services to underbanked and unbankedgroups, especially in areas with limited access to traditional banking infrastructure [53].
   - Investment and Trading: Cryptocurrencies have gained recognition as investable assets and are attracting private and institutional investors. Cryptocurrency exchanges and markets have proliferated to facilitate trading. Investors always look for various investment strategies to earn abnormal returns [54].

5.5.3 Implementation of Decentralized Finance

- Borrowing and lending: DeFi platforms such as Compound, Aave, and MakerDAO provide lending and lending services without intermediaries. Users can earn interest on their deposits or borrow against assets.
- Decentralized exchanges: Platforms like Uniswap, SushiSwap, and PancakeSwap allow users to trade cryptocurrencies directly from their wallets without a centralized exchange.
- Yield farming and liquidity mining: DeFi introduced the concept of yield farming where users provide liquidity to liquidity in exchange for payment. This has led to new opportunities to earn cryptocurrencies [55].
- Stable coins and payments: DeFi stable coins (e.g. USDC and DAI) enabled stable value transactions and acted as a bridge between traditional financial and blockchain ecosystems.
- Risks and challenges: While DeFi has gained traction, it also faced challenges such as the vulnerability of smart contracts, regulatory uncertainty, and the possibility of market manipulation.

Overall, adoption in all these sectors is driven by technological advances, use case innovation, investor interest, and the drive to create more efficient and inclusive financial systems. However, their adoption trajectory continues to be shaped by regulatory developments, safety concerns, and general understanding. The financial environment is exposed to various types of risks [56]. The following section presents current trends in DeFi.

5.6 Current Trends in Decentralized Finance

Here are some trends that were relevant in the DeFi space:

1. Liquidity aggregation and optimization: DeFi platforms were increasingly focusing on aggregating liquidity from various sources, including DEXs and automated market makers. This trend aimed at providing users with improved liquidity and more competitive pricing for their trades [57].
2. Layer 2 scaling solutions: To address the scalability challenges of blockchain networks, DeFi projects were exploring

and adopting layer 2 scaling solutions. These solutions aim to increase transaction throughput and reduce fees while maintaining the security of the underlying blockchain.

3. Cross-chain interoperability: With the proliferation of various blockchains, interoperability solutions were gaining traction. Projects were aiming to create bridges between different blockchains, enabling assets and data to move seamlessly between different networks [58].
4. Decentralized oracle networks: Reliable and secure external data is crucial for many DeFi applications. Decentralized oracle networks were being developed to provide accurate off-chain data to on-chain smart contracts, improving the reliability of DeFi protocols.
5. Stablecoin innovation: Stablecoins remained a fundamental component of DeFi ecosystems, and innovation was ongoing in this space. Algorithmic stablecoins, which aim to maintain their peg through algorithmic mechanisms, were gaining attention.
6. Regulatory scrutiny and compliance: As DeFi gained more mainstream attention, regulatory scrutiny was increasing. Projects and platforms were beginning to consider compliance measures and working with regulators to ensure a sustainable regulatory environment.
7. Institutional involvement: Traditional financial institutions and institutional investors were showing more interest in DeFi. This interest could potentially lead to increased adoption and integration of DeFi solutions within traditional financial markets.
8. Decentralized identity solutions: DID solutions aimed at giving users controlling power over their personal identity data. These solutions were being explored not only within the DeFi space but also in broader applications across industries.
9. Enhanced user experience: User experience and user interface improvements were becoming more important as DeFi projects sought to make their platforms more accessible to a wider audience. User-friendly interfaces and guides were being developed to simplify interactions with complex protocols [59].
10. Yield farming and staking innovations: Yield farming and staking continued to evolve with new strategies, protocols,

and incentive mechanisms. Projects were experimenting with different ways to attract liquidity providers and token holders.

11. Decentralized insurance solutions: The need for insurance coverage within the DeFi space was becoming apparent due to potential smart contract vulnerabilities and risks. Decentralized insurance platforms were being developed to offer coverage to users [60].
12. Non-fungible tokens (NFT) integration: While NFTs were initially associated with digital art and collectibles, they were finding applications in DeFi, as well. Non-fungible token-based collateral and unique financial products were being explored.

5.7 Future Scope in Decentralized Finance

The future scope in the field of DeFi is vast and holds potential for revolutionizing a diverse area of the financial sector and beyond. Here are some potential areas of growth and development in the DeFi space:

1. Mass adoption: DeFi has the potential to become more user-friendly, making it accessible to a wider audience. Improved user interfaces, reduced transaction fees, and seamless onboarding experiences could drive mass adoption of DeFi services [61].
2. Interoperability: Cross-chain interoperability solutions will likely become more sophisticated, enabling seamless value transfer and data sharing across different blockchain networks. This could lead to more efficient and interconnected DeFi ecosystems.
3. Regulatory maturation: Regulatory frameworks will likely evolve to address the unique challenges and opportunities it presents, as DeFi persists in gaining traction. Clarity in regulations could provide a more stable environment for innovation and growth [62].
4. Decentralized Identity (DID): DID solutions could expand beyond the realm of finance to revolutionize how individuals manage and control their online identification transversely assorted over online services and platforms.

5. Decentralized autonomous organizations (DAOs): DAOs could become more sophisticated and decentralized, allowing for decentralized decision-making and management of various projects and initiatives.
6. Decentralized governance: DeFi projects are increasingly adopting decentralized governance models where token holders participate in decision-making processes. This trend could lead to more community-driven development and decision-making.
7. Insurance and risk management: DeFi insurance platforms could mature and presents more comprehensive coverage not in favor of smart contract susceptibilities, hacks, and market risks. These platforms could turn into an essential element of the DeFi ecosystem.
8. Stablecoin innovation: Stablecoins could continue to evolve with more advanced algorithmic mechanisms, reducing their reliance on centralized assets while maintaining stability [63].
9. Decentralized derivatives: The market for decentralized derivatives, including options and futures, could grow as users seek more accessible and transparent ways to hedge and speculate on price movements.
10. Environmental sustainability: DeFi protocols could explore more environmentally friendly consensus mechanisms to address concerns about energy consumption, aligning with broader sustainability goals.
11. Privacy solutions: Improved privacy solutions could emerge, allowing users to transact and interact with DeFi platforms without compromising their personal data.
12. Integration with traditional finance: Collaboration between traditional financial institutions and DeFi platforms could increase, leading to hybrid solutions that leverage the strengths of both ecosystems.
13. Tokenization of real-world financial instruments: DeFi could facilitate the tokenization of real-world instruments such as real estate, commodities, and intellectual property, making these assets more accessible and tradable.
14. Education and awareness: As DeFi becomes more complex, educational resources and initiatives could increase to empower users with the comprehension and proficiency required to safely and effectively find the way.

15. Yield farming innovation: Yield farming strategies and platforms could continue to evolve, providing users with new ways to earn rewards and incentives for providing liquidity.
16. Decentralized credit and lending: DeFi lending platforms could expand to offer more sophisticated credit solutions, potentially bridging the gap between DeFi and traditional lending markets.

It is significant to note that the DeFi landscape is constantly budding, and the future scope will be influenced by technological advancements, regulatory developments, market trends, and user demands. As with any rapidly developing field, there will be hurdles and uncertainties in the future, but the latent for positive disruption and innovation in the financial industry is substantial.

5.8 Conclusion

In conclusion, the research study provides a comprehensive analysis of the relationship between blockchain, cryptocurrency, and DeFi. The comparison tables clearly outline the distinctions between blockchain and cryptocurrency, emphasizing that while blockchain serves as the foundational technology for many cryptocurrencies, not all cryptocurrencies rely on traditional blockchain structures. The implications of DeFi are explored in-depth, revealing its transformative potential across various facets of the financial industry. Decentralized finance's advantages, such as financial inclusion, reduced intermediaries, global accessibility, transparency, programmable financial services, market efficiency, ownership control, innovation, and reduced counterparty risk, are meticulously discussed. However, the study also highlights the challenges and risks associated with DeFi, including smart contract vulnerabilities, regulatory uncertainties, and scalability issues.

Furthermore, the research traces the development of blockchain, cryptocurrency, and DeFi over time, from their early conceptualization to their current state, noting significant milestones and trends. The processes of blockchain, cryptocurrency, and DeFi are elucidated, providing a clear understanding of how each component functions within its respective ecosystem. The adoption trends underscore the growing acceptance and integration of these technologies across various sectors, with a particular emphasis on the increasing interest from traditional financial institutions in DeFi.

The study also provides insights on current trends in DeFi sheds light on the dynamic nature of the ecosystem, highlighting key areas such as liquidity aggregation, layer 2 scaling solutions, cross-chain interoperability, decentralized oracle networks, stablecoin innovation, regulatory scrutiny, institutional involvement, decentralized identity solutions, enhanced user experience, yield farming and staking innovations, decentralized insurance solutions, and NFT integration. These trends reflect the ongoing evolution and maturation of the DeFi space.

Finally, the research outlines the future scope of DeFi, pointing towards potential areas of growth and development. Key areas of focus include mass adoption, interoperability, regulatory maturation, decentralized identity, DAOs, decentralized governance, risk management and insurance, stablecoin innovation, decentralized derivatives, environmental sustainability, privacy solutions, integration with traditional finance, tokenization of real-world assets, education and awareness, and continued innovation in yield farming. The study acknowledges the ever-changing landscape of DeFi and the need for addressing challenges while harnessing the substantial potential for positive disruption and innovation in the financial industry.

References

1. Chen, Y. and Bellavitis, C., Blockchain disruption and decentralized finance: The rise of decentralized business models. *J. Bus. Ventur. Insights*, 13, e00151, 2020.
2. Ozili, P.K., Decentralized finance research and developments around the world. *J. Banking Financ. Technol.*, 6, 2, 117–133, 2022.
3. Ozcan, R., Decentralized finance, in: *Financial Ecosystem and Strategy in the Digital Era: Global Approaches and New Opportunities*, pp. 57–75, Springer International Publishing, Cham, 2021.
4. Bartoletti, M., Chiang, J.H.Y., Lafuente, A.L., Towards a theory of decentralized finance, in: *Financial Cryptography and Data Security. FC 2021 International Workshops: CoDecFin, DeFi, VOTING, and WTSC, Virtual Event*, March 5, 2021, Revised Selected Papers 25, pp. 227–232, Springer Berlin Heidelberg, 2021.
5. Bartoletti, M., Chiang, J., Junttila, T., LluchLafuente, A., Mirelli, M., Vandin, A., Formal analysis of lending pools in decentralized finance, in: *International Symposium on Leveraging Applications of Formal Methods*, 2022, October, Springer Nature Switzerland, Cham, pp. 335–355.
6. Anoop, V.S. and Goldston, J., Decentralized finance to hybrid finance through blockchain: a case-study of acala and current. *J. Banking Financ. Technol.*, 6, 1, 109–115, 2022.

7. Grassi, L., Lanfranchi, D., Faes, A., Renga, F.M., Do we still need financial intermediation? The case of decentralized finance–DeFi. *Qual. Res. Account. Manage.*, 19, 3, 323–347, 2022.
8. Pineiro-Chousa, J., Cabarcos, A.L., Gonzalez, I., DeFi and start-ups: revolution in finance, in: *Financing Startups: Understanding Strategic Risks, Funding Sources, and the Impact of Emerging Technologies*, pp. 163–184, Springer International Publishing, Cham, 2022.
9. Pineiro-Chousa, J., Sevic, A., Gonzalez-Lopez, I., Impact of social metrics in decentralized finance. *J. Bus. Res.*, 158, 113673, 2023.
10. Amler, H., Eckey, L., Faust, S., Kaiser, M., Sandner, P., Schlosser, B., Definingdefi: Challenges & pathway, in: *2021 3rd Conference on Blockchain Research & Applications for Innovative Networks and Services (BRAINS)*, 2021, September, IEEE, pp. 181–184.
11. Wronka, C., Financial crime in the decentralized finance ecosystem: new challenges for compliance. *J. Financ. Crime*, 30, 1, 97–113, 2023.
12. Popescu, A.D., Decentralized finance (defi)–the lego of finance. *Soc. Sci. Educ. Res. Rev.*, 7, 1, 321–349, 2020.
13. Popescu, A.D., Understanding FinTech and Decentralized Finance (DeFi) for Financial Inclusion, in: *FinTech Development for Financial Inclusiveness*, pp. 1–13, IGI Global, USA, 2022.
14. Bonnet, S. and Teuteberg, F., Impact of blockchain and distributed ledger technology for the management of the intellectual property life cycle: A multiple case study analysis. *Comput. Ind., 144*, 103789, 2023.
15. Breidbach, C.F. and Tana, S., Betting on Bitcoin: How social collectives shape cryptocurrency markets. *J. Bus. Res., 122*, 311–320, 2021.
16. Dinh, T.T.A., Liu, R., Zhang, M., Chen, G., Ooi, B.C., Wang, J., Untangling blockchain: A data processing view of blockchain systems. *IEEE Trans. Knowl. Data Eng., 30*, 7, 1366–1385, 2018.
17. Dos Santos, S., Singh, J., Thulasiram, R.K., Kamali, S., Sirico, L., Loud, L., A new era of blockchain-powered decentralized finance (DeFi)-a review, in: *2022 IEEE 46th Annual Computers, Software, and Applications Conference (COMPSAC)*, 2022, June, IEEE, pp. 1286–1292.
18. Malherbe, L., Montalban, M., Bédu, N., Granier, C., Cryptocurrencies and blockchain: Opportunities and limits of a new monetary regime. *Int. J. Political Econ., 48*, 2, 127–152, 2019.
19. Mehta, K. and Sharma, R., Contrarian and momentum investment strategies: Evidence from Indian stock market. *Int. J. Appl. Bus. Econ. Res.*, 15, 2, 87–98, 2017.
20. Aoun, A., Ilinca, A., Ghandour, M., Ibrahim, H., A review of Industry 4.0 characteristics and challenges, with potential improvements using blockchain technology. *Comput. Ind. Eng., 162*, 107746, 2021.
21. Aste, T., Tasca, P., Di Matteo, T., Blockchain technologies: The foreseeable impact on society and industry. *Computer, 50*, 9, 18–28, 2017.

22. Rawat, B., Chaudhary, V., Doku, R., Blockchain technology: Emerging applications and use cases for secure and trustworthy smart systems. *J. Cybersecur. Privacy*, *1*, 1, 4–18, 2020.
23. Mehta, K., Sharma, R., Vyas, V., A quantile regression approach to study the impact of aluminium prices on manufacturing sector of India during COVID era. *Mater. Today Proc.*, 65, 7, 3506–3511, 2022.
24. Baum, C., Hsin-yu Chiang, J., David, B., Frederiksen, T.K., Gentile, L., Sok: Mitigation of front-running in decentralized finance, in: *International Conference on Financial Cryptography and Data Security*, 2022, May, Springer International Publishing, Cham, pp. 250–271.
25. Bhowmik, D., Crypto-Currency: Trends and Determinants. *Saudi J. Econ. Fin.*, 6, 2, 37–50, 2022.
26. Makridis, C.A., Fröwis, M., Sridhar, K., Böhme, R., The rise of decentralized cryptocurrency exchanges: Evaluating the role of airdrops and governance tokens. *J. Corp. Finance*, 79, 102358, 2023.
27. Mehta, K. and Sharma, R., Unraveling quantum complexity: A fuzzy AHP approach to understanding software industry challenges, in: *Deep Learning Tools for Predicting Stock Market Movements*, pp. 39–60, 2024.
28. Casino, F., Dasaklis, T.K., Patsakis, C., A systematic literature review of blockchain-based applications: Current status, classification and open issues. *Telemat. Inform.*, *36*, 55–81, 2019.
29. Choudhary, V., Kamboj, N., Trivedi, S., Scoping Review of Literature on the Application of Blockchain in Finance, in: *Perspectives on Blockchain Technology and Responsible Investing*, pp. 1–28, 2023.
30. Saengchote, K., Decentralized lending and its users: Insights from Compound. *J. Int. Financ. Mark. Inst. Money*, 101807, 2023.
31. Scharfman, J. and Scharfman, J., Decentralized finance (DeFi) compliance and operations, in: *Cryptocurrency Compliance and Operations: Digital Assets, Blockchain and DeFi*, pp. 171–186, 2022.
32. Clohessy, T., Acton, T., Rogers, N., Blockchain adoption: Technological, organisational and environmental considerations, in: *Business Transformation through Blockchain*, vol. 1, pp. 47–76, 2019.
33. Dupuis, D. and Gleason, K., Money laundering with cryptocurrency: open doors and the regulatory dialectic. *J. Financ. Crime*, *28*, 1, 60–74, 2020.
34. Sharma, R. and Mehta, K., Credit risk and bank specific factors: An empirical study using panel GMM. *Int. J. Econ. Bus. Res.*, 27, 2, 294–309, 2024.
35. Sharma, R. and Mehta, K., *Deep Learning Tools for Predicting Stock Market Movements*, John Wiley & Sons, 2024.
36. Fan, S., Min, T., Wu, X., Wei, C., Towards understanding governance tokens in liquidity mining: a case study of decentralized exchanges. *World Wide Web*, 26, 3, 1181–1200, 2023.
37. Ghosh, A., Gupta, S., Dua, A., Kumar, N., Security of Cryptocurrencies in blockchain technology: State-of-art, challenges and future prospects. *J. Network Comput. Appl.*, *163*, 102635, 2020.

38. Gudgeon, L., Perez, D., Harz, D., Livshits, B., Gervais, A., The decentralized financial crisis, in: *2020 crypto valley conference on blockchain technology (CVCBT)*, 2020, June, IEEE, pp. 1–15.
39. Harwick, C. and Caton, J., What's holding back blockchain finance? On the possibility of decentralized autonomous finance. *Q. Rev. Econ. Finance*, 84, 420–429, 2022.
40. Johnson, K.N., Decentralized finance: Regulating cryptocurrency exchanges. *Wm. Mary L. Rev.*, 62, 1911, 2020.
41. Kamath, R.R. and Habeeb, M., Cryptocurrency and the Indian Monetary System, in: *Advanced Machine Learning Algorithms for Complex Financial Applications*, pp. 31–42, IGI Global, USA, 2023.
42. Vyas, V., Mehta, K., Sharma, R., Are bitcoin prices isolated or co-integrated? *Int. J. Bus. Globalisation*, 35, 1–2, 2023.
43. Trivedi, S. and Malik, R., Blockchain Technology as an Emerging Technology in the Insurance Market, in: *Big Data: A Game Changer for Insurance Industry*, pp. 81–100, Emerald Publishing Limited, UK, 2022.
44. Zheng, P., Su, B., Jiang, Z., Yang, C., Chen, J., Wu, J., Exploring Heterogeneous Decentralized Markets in DeFi and NFT on EthereumBlockchain, in: *2023 IEEE 10th International Conference on Cyber Security and Cloud Computing (CSCloud)/2023 IEEE 9th International Conference on Edge Computing and Scalable Cloud (EdgeCom)*, 2023, July, IEEE, pp. 259–267.
45. Klarin, A., The decade-long cryptocurrencies and the blockchain roller-coaster: Mapping the intellectual structure and charting future directions. *Res. Int. Bus. Finance, 51*, 101067, 2020.
46. Mehta, K., Sharma, R., Vyas, V., Kuckreja, J.S., Exit strategy decision by venture capital firms in India using fuzzy AHP. *J. Entrep. Emerg. Econ.*, 14, 4, 643–669, 2022.
47. Patel, R., Migliavacca, M., Oriani, M.E., Blockchain in banking and finance: A bibliometric review. *Res. Int. Bus. Finance*, 62, 101718, 2022.
48. Shakya, V., Kumar, P.P., Tewari, L., Blockchain-based cryptocurrency scope in India, in: *2021 5th International Conference on Intelligent Computing and Control Systems (ICICCS)*, 2021, May, IEEE, pp. 361–368.
49. Trivedi, S., Blockchain Framework for Insurance industry. *Int. J. Innov. Technol. Manage.*, 2350034, 2023.
50. Trivedi, S., Mehta, K., Sharma, R., Systematic literature review on application of blockchain technology in E-finance and financial services. *J. Technol. Manage. Innov.*, 16, 3, 89–102, 2021.
51. Shanaev, S., Sharma, S., Ghimire, B., Shuraeva, A., Taming the blockchain beast? Regulatory implications for the cryptocurrency Market. *Res. Int. Bus. Financ., 51*, 101080, 2020.
52. Sharma, R., Mehta, K., Chugh, A., Using Analytic Hierarchy Process to determine forex risk hedging strategies of SMEs. *AIP Conf. Proc.*, 2916, 1, 120008, 2023.

53. Sharma, R., Mehta, K., Rana, R., Cryptocurrency adoption behaviour of millennial investors in India, in: *Perspectives on Blockchain Technology and Responsible Investing*, pp. 135–158, IGI Global, USA, 2023.
54. Trivedi, S., Cryptocurrency as an Emerging and Modern Investment Avenue in India, in: *Handbook of Research on Stock Market Investment Practices and Portfolio Management*, pp. 329–347, IGI Global, USA, 2022.
55. Sriman, B. and Kumar, S.G., Decentralized finance (defi): the future of finance and defi application for Ethereumblockchain based finance market, in: *2022 International Conference on Advances in Computing, Communication and Applied Informatics (ACCAI)*, 2022, January, IEEE, pp. 1–9.
56. Trivedi, S. and Malik, R., Role of Cryptocurrency in Digital Marketing, in: *Blockchain Technology and Applications for Digital Marketing*, pp. 175–185, IGI Global, USA, 2021.
57. Umar, Z., Polat, O., Choi, S.Y., Teplova, T., Dynamic connectedness between non-fungible tokens, decentralized finance, and conventional financial assets in a time-frequency framework. *Pac.-Basin Finance J.*, 76, 101876, 2022.
58. Vyas, V., Mehta, K., Sharma, R., Investigating socially responsible investing behaviour of Indian investors using structural equation modelling. *J. Sustain. Financ. Invest.*, 12, 1, 1–23, 2020.
59. Wątorek, M., Drożdż, S., Kwapień, J., Minati, L., Oświęcimka, P., Stanuszek, M., Multiscale characteristics of the emerging global cryptocurrency market. *Phys. Rep.*, 901, 1–82, 2021.
60. Wieandt, A. and Heppding, L., Centralized and decentralized finance: Coexistence or convergence?, in: *The Fintech Disruption: How Financial Innovation Is Transforming the Banking Industry*, pp. 11–51, Springer International Publishing, Cham, 2023.
61. Zetzsche, D.A., Arner, D.W., Buckley, R.P., Decentralized finance (defi). *J. Financ. Regul.*, 6, 172–203, 2020.
62. Zhang, Y., Chan, S., Chu, J., Shih, S.H., The adaptive market hypothesis of Decentralized finance (DeFi). *Appl. Econ.*, 55, 42, 4975–4989, 2023.
63. Zutshi, A., Grilo, A., Nodehi, T., The value proposition of blockchain technologies and its impact on Digital Platforms. *Comput. Ind. Eng.*, 155, 107187, 2021.

6

Unraveling the Impact of Cryptocurrencies on the Indian Economy: A PESTLE Approach

Jyoti Verma[1]*, Gagandeep[1] and Anjali Sharma[2]

[1]Chitkara Business School, Chitkara University, Punjab, India
[2]Mittal School of Business, Lovely Professional University, Phagwara, Punjab, India

Abstract
Cryptocurrencies, such as Bitcoin, emerged as a decentralized digital form of currency that operates on blockchain technology. In recent years, cryptocurrency has drawn a lot of interest as a digital form of money that uses cryptographic methods to safeguard financial transactions. The rapid growth and increasing popularity of cryptocurrencies worldwide underscore the need to understand their implications for the Indian economy. This chapter aims to unravel the impact of cryptocurrencies on the Indian economy using a Political, Economic, Social, Technological, Legal, and Environmental (PESTLE) approach. A comprehensive analysis of the various PESTLE factors has been done to assess how cryptocurrencies influence different aspects of the Indian economy. By conducting a comprehensive PESTLE analysis, this chapter provides a holistic understanding of the impact of cryptocurrencies on the Indian economy, enabling policymakers, researchers, and stakeholders to make informed decisions and develop appropriate strategies to navigate this evolving landscape.

***Keywords*:** Cryptocurrencies, economic factors, environmental factors, political factors, sociocultural factors, technological factors

**Corresponding author*: jyoti.verma@chitkara.edu.in

Renuka Sharma, Kiran Mehta, Vishal Vyas and Vinod Kumar Shukla (eds.) Decentralized Finance and Blockchain: A Game Changing Duo, (125–142) © 2025 Scrivener Publishing LLC

6.1 Introduction

Using blockchain technology, cryptocurrencies like Bitcoin have arisen as a decentralized digital form of money. Satoshi Nakamoto, who also described the blockchain technology that underpins it, introduced the first cryptocurrency [1], Bitcoin, in this important white paper. It explains how a decentralized electronic currency system is made possible by the usage of blockchain [2]. Cryptographic methods are used by cryptocurrencies to safeguard transactions and uphold transparency without the need for intermediaries like banks. Blockchain, the underlying technology, permits a distributed, unchangeable ledger that keeps track of all transactions. One important topic of continuing discussion and debate is the effect of cryptocurrencies on the Indian economy. Even if cryptocurrencies are becoming more popular in India, they have not had much of an influence on the overall economy.

However, there are a few possible ways that cryptocurrencies may have impacted the Indian economy:

- **Investments and speculation** – Investors and merchants in India have shown a lot of interest in cryptocurrencies. Some individuals and businesses have made large investments in cryptocurrencies in hopes of profiting from the increase in prices [3, 4]. Although the entire scale is still rather small in comparison to traditional investment assets, the increasing investment activity may have effects on capital flows and investor behavior.
- **Fintech innovation** – Blockchain technology, which underpins cryptocurrencies, has sparked innovation in the financial technology (Fintech) industry [5, 6]. Startups in India are investigating blockchain-based solutions for a range of uses, including identity verification, cross-border payments, and supply chain management. The Indian financial system might become more effective and transparent because of these developments.
- **Financial inclusion** – Cryptocurrencies have the potential to improve financial inclusion by providing underbanked or unbanked people with access to financial services. Individuals can engage in the global digital economy using cryptocurrencies without using conventional banking infrastructure [3]. This may be especially important in a nation

like India where a sizable segment of the populace continues to live in poverty.
- **Regulatory challenges** – Governments all over the globe, including India, are facing regulatory difficulties because of the advent of cryptocurrencies. The Indian government and regulatory authorities have been cautious about cryptocurrencies due to concerns related to money laundering, tax evasion, and investor protection [4]. Regulatory uncertainties and restrictions on cryptocurrencies may impact the growth and adoption of cryptocurrencies in India.
- **International trade and remittances** – In contrast to conventional remittance routes, cryptocurrencies may provide a more cost-effective and swifter option for international transactions and remittances. India, which receives many remittances, might gain from the use of cryptocurrencies to speed up cross-border transactions.

6.2 Evolution of Cryptocurrency

The development of cryptocurrencies is a story of transformation that has altered preconceived ideas about money, finance, and commerce. Everything started when Satoshi Nakamoto [1], an unidentified person, introduced Bitcoin in 2009. Since then, the world of cryptocurrencies has expanded quickly, as seen by the birth of a large number of altcoins, the advancement of blockchain technology, and the increasing awareness of the potential effects on a range of sectors.

The financial environment is exposed to various types of risks [7–9]. Cryptocurrency development has not been without difficulties. The sector is nevertheless affected by price volatility, security concerns, and regulatory difficulties. However, as the industry matured, there have been more attempts to overcome these issues. While advances in blockchain technology promise to improve security and scalability, stablecoins, which are backed by regular fiat currencies, are designed to reduce volatility. The cryptocurrency scene is expected to continue developing in the future. Governments looking into the idea of issuing their digital currency are starting to take interest in central bank digital currencies, or CBDCs. Furthermore, continuous research and development endeavors to tackle challenges related to scalability, improve privacy features, and expand the integration of blockchain technology across diverse industries such as voting systems, healthcare, and supply chain management.

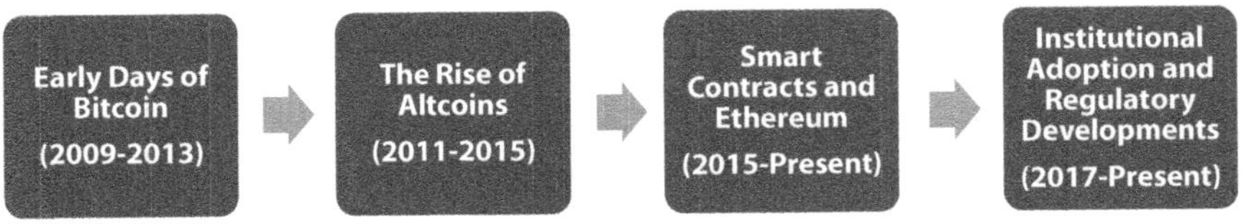

Figure 6.1 The evolution of cryptocurrency. Source: Author's compilations.

From Bitcoin's inception to the present, the history of cryptocurrencies reveals a dynamic and revolutionary path. The notion of cryptocurrencies has evolved from a specialized idea to a widely acknowledged asset class, highlighting its adaptability and capacity to transform conventional financial institutions. Future advancements in technology, institutional acceptance, and legal frameworks point to a potential role for cryptocurrencies in the global economy, both challenging and enhancing established financial institutions. To fully realize the promise of decentralized digital currencies, it is still imperative to keep an eye on obstacles, take appropriate action, and encourage creativity as we proceed. Figure 6.1 represents the evolution of cryptocurrency.

Let us discuss the evolution of cryptocurrency in brief:

6.2.1 Early Days of Bitcoin (2009–2013)

The emergence of decentralized digital currencies was signalled by the creation of Bitcoin. When it first started off, the main function of Bitcoin was as a peer-to-peer electronic cash system that let users deal without the involvement of intermediaries like banks. Blockchain, the underlying technology that ensures decentralization, security, and transparency, became the mainstay of Bitcoin's success [10–12]. 'Bitcoin: A Peer-to-Peer Electronic Cash System,' a white paper written by Satoshi Nakamoto, served as the inspiration for the concept and concepts of cryptocurrencies [1]. A community of enthusiasts, developers, and early users were drawn to Bitcoin because of its decentralized character, which they believed had the potential to upend established financial institutions. Because Bitcoin is anonymous, at this time it was frequently linked to the dark web and illegal activity. However, as a decentralized digital money, its acceptance increased over time, opening the door for the emergence of competing cryptocurrencies.

6.2.2 The Rise of Altcoins (2011–2015)

The emergence of alternative cryptocurrencies, or altcoins, was spurred by the popularity of Bitcoin [13]. These digital assets aim to offer novel functionality or remedy alleged design flaws in Bitcoin. One of the first cryptocurrencies, Litecoin, was developed by Charlie Lee in 2011 and included a new hashing algorithm and a quicker block generation time. In the years that followed, other altcoins with distinct value propositions came into being. Namecoin was focused on decentralized domain registration, whereas Ripple was more concerned with making cross-border transactions quick and affordable. The variety of cryptocurrencies allowed for more options than only peer-to-peer trades, which encouraged exploration and creativity in the field of cryptocurrencies.

6.2.3 Smart Contracts and Ethereum (2015–Present)

The launch of Ethereum in 2015 was a pivotal point in the development of cryptocurrencies. The notion of smart contracts—self-executing contracts with terms explicitly encoded into code—was first proposed by Vitalik Buterin's Ethereum. With the help of this breakthrough, developers were able to create decentralized apps (DApps) on the Ethereum blockchain, expanding the potential uses of blockchain technology beyond straightforward financial transactions [14, 15]. It turned out that smart contracts were revolutionary, paving the way for the creation of non-fungible tokens, decentralized finance apps, and other blockchain-based solutions. Because of Ethereum's success, the cryptocurrency industry has matured overall as a thriving ecosystem of initiatives and decentralized autonomous organizations has grown.

6.2.4 Institutional Adoption and Regulatory Developments (2017–Present)

From 2017 onward, institutional investors began paying more attention, indicating a move from a specialized interest to a more widely acknowledged one. Institutional investors now have ways to get exposure to cryptocurrencies while still meeting regulatory requirements thanks to the introduction of Bitcoin futures on well-known platforms like the Chicago Mercantile Exchange. Governments and regulatory agencies started debating the necessity of creating frameworks for emerging cryptocurrency business at the same time [16–18]. While some nations welcomed cryptocurrencies and created clear regulations, others viewed the industry warily, raising worries about possible dangers including money laundering and manipulation of the markets.

6.3 Blockchain Technology and its Role in Cryptocurrencies

Blockchain technology acts as a foundational infrastructure for the functioning of cryptocurrencies. Here is an overview of blockchain's role in cryptocurrencies:

- **Security and immutability** – Cryptocurrencies use blockchain's cryptographic algorithms to safeguard transaction data, ensuring security and immutability. A chain of blocks is created by a series of transactions that are cryptographically connected. A transaction becomes difficult to change or tamper with once it is included in a block and uploaded to the blockchain. Because of its immutability, these transactions are more secure and reliable.
- **Decentralized ledger** –The decentralized, open, and immutable blockchain is the primary recorder of all transactions that take place inside a cryptocurrency network [4, 19, 20]. It does away with the requirement for a central authority, like a bank, to verify and keep track of transactional data. Instead, network users called nodes collaboratively maintain the blockchain.
- **Transparency** – Blockchain promotes transparency by making transaction histories available to the public. On the blockchain, all transaction records are publicly accessible, promoting transparency and ensuring accountability [3, 4, 21]. Participants may independently verify transactions and keep an eye on the network's integrity thanks to this feature, which increases participant confidence.
- **Transaction validation** – To validate transactions and guarantee their integrity, blockchain uses consensus techniques like Proof of Work (PoW) or Proof of Stake (PoS). These controls stop users from trying to spend the same Bitcoin unit more than once, a practice known as double-spending.

To confirm transactions and add them to the blockchain, validators on the network compete to solve challenging mathematical problems or stake their Bitcoin holdings.

- **Tokenization and asset management** – On the blockchain, real-world assets may be tokenized and represented as digital tokens. As a result, it is simpler to efficiently transfer and manage assets utilizing cryptocurrencies, such as stocks or real estate. Tokenization improves liquidity, eliminates intermediaries, and opens new possibilities for international asset accessibility and fractional ownership.
- **Smart contracts** – Blockchain technology enables smart contracts, self-executing agreements with predetermined terms and circumstances. Smart contracts automatically carry out transactions and uphold contractual commitments whenever the preset conditions are met. They make it possible for the complex financial systems and DApps of the Bitcoin ecosystem to operate [22].

6.4 Economic Implications of Cryptocurrency

Figure 6.2 shows the evidence of Global Crypto Industry. By 2026, the worldwide cryptocurrency industry is expected to surpass $1.8 billion and reach $2.3 billion. Globally, 3.9% of individuals have cryptocurrency, with Bitcoin being the fifth-largest cryptocurrency by market capitalization.

Some researchers focused on how blockchain technology can disrupt conventional intermediaries and lead to the development of alternative

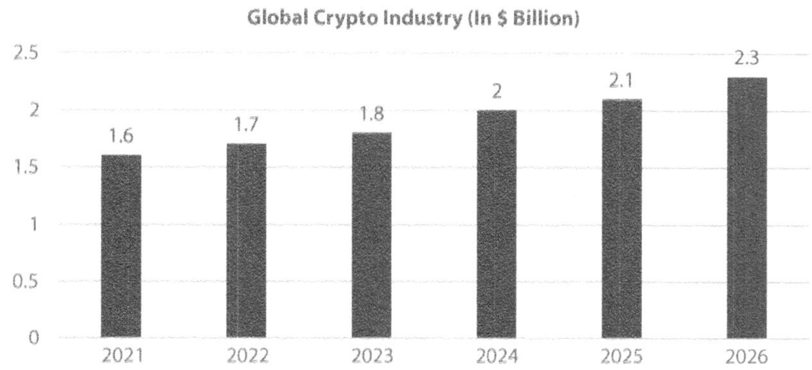

Figure 6.2 The global crypto industry [58].

economic models [23]. The study examines blockchain's potential uses across a range of sectors. It also addresses how it affects transaction costs, trust, and innovation, whereas some investigated Bitcoin's economics and determined if it qualifies as a true form of money [24]. The research investigates the features of Bitcoin, its potential influence on conventional monetary systems, and the economic effects of its adoption. The existence of price manipulation in the Bitcoin ecosystem [25]. It investigates the effects of shady trading practices and the financial ramifications of such manipulation on the efficiency and stability of Bitcoin marketplaces. Some researchers [19, 26] examined the economics of digital currencies, including cryptocurrencies issued by the Bank of England. They addressed the consequences for monetary policy and financial stability, as well as any potential advantages, dangers, and difficulties connected with the widespread use of digital currencies [27, 59].

6.5 PESTLE Analysis

The PESTLE analysis is a framework used to assess the macro-environmental factors that can affect an industry or a country's economy. It aims to answer to the following queries:

- What effects will regulation have on the cryptocurrency?
- How does it affect the economy?
- What are the sociocultural factors related to cryptocurrency?
- What are the technical issues related to cryptocurrencies?
- What are the legal issues related to cryptocurrencies?
- How does it affect the environment?

Let us analyze the impact of cryptocurrencies on the Indian economy using the PESTLE model:

6.5.1 Political Factors

Being a new product on the market, cryptocurrencies face several obstacles, particularly restrictions from the government. Government support or opposition will have a significant impact on how the cryptocurrency business is regulated and how the public sector uses blockchain technology in the future [19, 27]. Cryptocurrencies may have positive and negative repercussions from regulation, depending on the nature of the regulations and how they are implemented. Market stability, investor confidence, and legitimacy are all improved by effective regulation. Fraud is reduced, consumer rights are upheld, and innovation is encouraged within limits. However, many regulations may cost firms cash for compliance fees and inhibit innovation. It is essential to strike a balance between regulatory control and technical development if one can understand the value of cryptocurrencies while minimizing hazards. Regulations might help or hinder the growth and mass acceptance of cryptocurrencies since the government could support or oppose their entry into the market. The Indian government has voiced worries about the hazards connected to cryptocurrencies, such as tax fraud and money laundering [28, 29]. Some authors emphasized the importance of political choices and stressed how regulatory clarity or ambiguity may have a significant impact on the uptake of cryptocurrencies [30], and some have examined the differences in regulatory strategies between nations, examining the effects of regulatory pronouncements on cryptocurrency markets and identifying significant market responses [31]. To make matters more complicated, governments also play a part in the issuance of CBDCs. In their discussion of the effects of CBDCs on the cryptocurrency ecosystem, authors draw attention to the possible interactions between decentralized cryptocurrencies and state-backed digital currencies [32].

6.5.2 Economic Factors

Cryptocurrencies have affected established financial institutions and currencies by adding a new dimension to economic issues. The economic feasibility of cryptocurrencies has been examined [33], and it considers Bitcoin's potential as a haven asset in times of economic turmoil. Monetary policy, inflation rates, and economic stability all impact how appealing cryptocurrencies are as an alternative investment. An emerging trend in the economy is the growth of token economies and initial coin offerings (ICOs). In the analysis of the financial effects of tokenization, the author highlights the possibility that blockchain-based tokens will lead to the emergence of decentralized economies [34].

Regulation of cryptocurrencies has a big impact on economies. Economic growth is fueled by investments attracted by transparent legislation. Investors always look for various investment strategies to earn abnormal returns [35]. Institutional participation is increased by legitimacy, which increases market stability. Overregulation, however, may restrict economic potential by stifling innovation and discouraging enterprises.

It is critical to strike a balance between regulating and promoting a vibrant crypto ecosystem to maximize advantages while minimizing negative consequences on economic growth.

Banks are crucial financial institutions in modern economies. The global financial crisis increased people's mistrust of financial markets and those in control of them. The Great Recession unleashed those who should have been held accountable: the bankers, the intermediaries, and the third parties who simply served to squeeze profits out of transactions. Several techniques can be used to investigate the price movement of various financial instruments [8, 36, 37]. The most important element of the financial industry and the reason banks exist is trust. Cryptocurrencies are able to introduce a reliable mechanism into the system since no single entity is in charge of directing and controlling it. The unbanked population in India may access financial services and participate in the digital economy with the help of cryptocurrencies. Because of their extreme volatility, cryptocurrencies might encourage speculative trading [38]. The researchers have examined the cryptocurrency behavior as there is an increased interest of the investors in this digital financial instrument [7, 39, 60]. Investors may face risks as a result, and the stability of the Indian financial system as a whole may be affected. On the other hand, distributed ledger technology provides a lot of efficiency and cost-cutting possibilities for the banking industry [40].

6.5.3 Sociocultural Factors

Cryptocurrencies are intertwined with sociocultural influences. Authors, who also consider how they could promote financial inclusion [32], examine the social impact of cryptocurrencies. Usability and accessibility are highlighted as critical social considerations, particularly for the unbanked population. Furthermore, the popularity and adoption of cryptocurrencies are influenced by public opinion and perception. Studies on sentiment analysis on Twitter data have been conducted [41], and the results show how social media sentiments and changes in the Bitcoin market interact. Adoption rates are influenced by public perception and acceptability. Cultural norms affect how people feel about digital assets. Socioeconomic differences have an impact on comprehension and accessibility. Education and digital literacy are important to close disparities. The decentralized nature of cryptocurrencies disrupts established financial assumptions and generates discussion. These elements influence how cryptocurrencies are integrated into society norms, financial institutions, and day-to-day living as social attitudes change. India still has a low acceptance rate for cryptocurrencies when compared to other nations. The acceptability and adoption of cryptocurrencies among the Indian populace may be influenced by cultural variables including confidence in and experience with established banking systems. However, India's digital divide and the lack of internet connection in rural regions might prevent broad acceptance and usage of cryptocurrencies.

6.5.4 Technological Factors

Cryptocurrencies are prone to technological problems. Scalability concerns arise due to network congestion and transactional speed. User funds are at risk from security flaws like hackers and breaches. Funds are lost because of private key management complexities. Barriers to interoperability prevent seamless communication between various blockchains. Forks and upgrades may cause community fragmentation. The long-term health and efficiency of cryptocurrency systems depend on creative responses to these technological problems in fields like consensus algorithms, security protocols, and sustainable energy sources.

Blockchain technology, on which cryptocurrencies are based, has the potential to completely transform several industries in India, including banking, supply chain management, and governance [42]. An electronic document saves information and then disseminates it through a computer network. This data is authenticated and encrypted. Once a transaction has been uploaded to the blockchain system, it cannot be altered or deleted. A multitude of industries, including banking, e-commerce, healthcare, logistics, and real estate, stand to benefit from blockchain technology's ability to reduce corruption. The security and openness of data stored in a blockchain enable people to interact with one another in an efficient and never-before-seen way while also building trust [43–46]. A flourishing cryptocurrency ecosystem depends on the creation of infrastructure, such as safe exchanges and wallets, as well as the accessibility of technical knowledge.

6.5.5 Legal Factors

Cryptocurrencies are surrounded by legal difficulties. Uncertainty in categories (commodity, security, currency) is caused by regulatory ambiguity. Decentralized systems have difficulties with respect to Know Your Customer (KYC) and anti-money laundering (AML) compliance. Consumer protection gaps increase the likelihood of fraud. Different legal systems apply to international commerce [47, 48]. Tax laws governing digital assets are changing. Concerns about investor rights are raised by ICOs. Legally speaking, smart contract enforceability is murky. For the cryptocurrency ecosystem to flourish sustainably within the confines of current legal frameworks, it is essential to strike a balance between encouraging innovation and guaranteeing legal compliance. Cryptocurrencies are much like other kinds of money in that they may be used for bad things. A secure and completely anonymous system of Bitcoin trading would considerably hinder government agencies' efforts to find criminals. Bitcoin may be used to launder money and to finance unlawful activities. To reduce the dangers related to cryptocurrencies, the government may impose stronger KYC and AML legislation [49–51]. A thorough historical review of regulatory trends has been conducted, highlighting the necessity of a well-rounded strategy that takes consumer protection and money laundering issues into account [52].

Authors examined the legal difficulties in implementing rules in a decentralized economy [32]. Research has also been done on the effects of legal pronouncements on cryptocurrency markets, showing how court rulings may have a big impact on market dynamics [31].

6.5.6 Environmental Factors

The environmental effects of cryptocurrencies are caused by their energy-intensive mining procedures. The PoW consensus processes need a lot of power, which raises greenhouse gas emissions. Mining activities frequently cluster in areas with inexpensive energy, placing pressure on regional resources. Mining for cryptocurrencies uses a lot of energy. The acceptance and regulation of cryptocurrencies may be influenced by India's energy infrastructure and environmental sustainability objectives. These currencies are produced through an energy-intensive 'mining' process that employs powerful computers to solve a challenging mathematical equation, guaranteeing an anonymous miner adheres to the protocol chosen by the network to build the blockchain record of transactions. Then, as payment for successfully solving the equation, miners receive these coins [53–55]. The significant energy footprint exacerbates environmental problems worldwide and casts doubt on sustainability [56]. These consequences might be reduced by switching to more energy-efficient consensus processes like PoS and investigating renewable energy sources, fostering a greener and more environmentally conscious Bitcoin economy. The study conducted by [57, 61] examines the carbon footprint associated with Bitcoin mining, providing insight into the environmental effects of proof-of-work consensus algorithms. The comprehension of the environmental effects of various technology decisions made in the Bitcoin area is aided by these publications.

6.6 Conclusion

In conclusion, the dynamic interaction of variables is highlighted by the assessment of the link between cryptocurrencies and the Indian economy using the PESTLE framework. Regarding political considerations, the study looks at how the government stands about cryptocurrencies and possible legislation that may be put in place to track and manage their use. To comprehend how cryptocurrencies will affect financial inclusion, investment opportunities, and the general stability of the Indian financial system, economic issues are examined. To ascertain the acceptance and adoption of cryptocurrencies among the Indian people, sociocultural aspects are examined while taking into account cultural attitudes and preferences. The chapter also examines technological issues, concentrating on how blockchain technology, which forms the basis of cryptocurrencies, might transform India's banking, supply chain, and governance industries. Legal considerations are evaluated in order to examine potential taxation laws, AML rules, and KYC regulations that may be applied to Bitcoin transactions. Additionally, environmental issues are taken into account to assess how the energy requirements of cryptocurrency mining correspond with India's sustainability objectives. This chapter does a thorough PESTLE analysis to give policymakers, researchers, and stakeholders a holistic knowledge of the influence of cryptocurrencies on the Indian economy. With this insight, they can design effective strategies to manage this changing environment.

References

1. Nakamoto, S., Bitcoin: A peer-to-peer electronic cash system, in: *Decentralized business review*, 2008.
2. Swan, M., *Blockchain: Blueprint for a new economy*, O'Reilly Media, Inc, California, USA, 2015.
3. Xi, D., O'Brien, T.I., Irannezhad, E., Investigating the investment behaviors in cryptocurrency. *J. Altern. Invest.*, 23, 2, 141–160, 2020.
4. Chuen, D.L.K., Guo, L., Wang, Y., Cryptocurrency: A new investment opportunity? *J. Altern. Invest.*, 20, 3, 16–40, 2017.

5. Verma, J., Sharma, J., Gupta, M., Digital Currency and Blockchain Technology in the Financial World, in: *Perspectives on Blockchain Technology and Responsible Investing*, pp. 216–225, IGI Global, Hershey, Pennsylvania, 2023.
6. Varma, P., Nijjer, S., Sood, K., Grima, S., Rupeika-Apoga, R., Thematic Analysis of Financial Technology (Fintech) Influence on the Banking Industry. *Risks*, 10, 10, 186, 2022.
7. Sharma, R., Mehta, K., Chugh, A., Using Analytic Hierarchy Process to determine forex risk hedging strategies of SMEs. *AIP Conf. Proc.*, 2916, 1, 120008, 2023.
8. Sharma, R. and Mehta, K., *Deep Learning Tools for Predicting Stock Market Movements*, John Wiley & Sons, New Jersey, USA, 2024.
9. Mehta, K., Sharma, R., Vyas, V., Kuckreja, J.S., Exit strategy decision by venture capital firms in India using fuzzy AHP. *J. Entrep. Emerg. Econ.*, 14, 4, 643–669, 2022.
10. ElBahrawy, A., Alessandretti, L., Kandler, A., Pastor-Satorras, R., Baronchelli, A., Evolutionary dynamics of the cryptocurrency market. *R. Soc. Open Sci.*, 4, 11, 170623, 2017.
11. Mishra, D., Patro, G.J., Acharjya, S., The Evolution and Growth of Cryptocurrency. *Globsyn Manage. J.*, 15, 1/2, 241–253, 2021.
12. Syed, A.M., Moge, J.A., Siddiqui, M.S., Cryptocurrency: Next Level in the Evolution of Money. *Asia. J. Res. Bus. Econ. Manag.*, 6, 11, 53–63, 2016.
13. Rose, C., The evolution of digital currencies: Bitcoin, a cryptocurrency causing a monetary revolution. *Int. Bus. Econ. Res. J. (IBER)*, 14, 4, 617–622, 2015.
14. Angotti, A., Klauder, A., Bjelland, K., A new regulatory evolution: Cryptocurrency and the securities industry at the crossroads. *J. Financ. Compliance*, 2, 4, 318–329, 2019.
15. Liu, J. and Serletis, A., Volatility in the cryptocurrency market. *Open Econ. Rev.*, 30, 779–811, 2019.
16. Shilov, K.D. and Zubarev, A.V., Evolution of Bitcoin as a financial asset. *Finance: Theory Pract.*, 25, 5, 150–171, 2021.
17. Hossain, M.S., What do we know about cryptocurrency? Past, present, future. *China Finance Rev. Int.*, 11, 4, 552–572, 2021.
18. Sharma, S. and Sood, R., Evolution of Cryptocurrency: Analysing the Utility, Legality, and Regulatory Framework in India, in: *Handbook of Research on Cyber Law, Data Protection, and Privacy*, pp. 137–160, IGI Global, Hershey, Pennsylvania, 2022.
19. Verma, J., Factors' influencing driving demand of cryptocurrency and its impact on behavioral intention: An Indian perspective. *Rev. Financ. Bank.*, 14, 1, 35–43, 2022.
20. Mikhaylov, A., Cryptocurrency market analysis from the open innovation perspective. *J. Open Innov.: Technol. Mark. Complex.*, 6, 4, 197, 2020.
21. Anson, M., Initial exchange offerings: The next evolution in cryptocurrencies. *J. Altern. Invest.*, 23, 4, 110–121, 2021.

22. Papadimitriou, T., Gogas, P., Gkatzoglou, F., The evolution of the cryptocurrencies market: A complex networks approach. *J. Comput. Appl. Math.*, 376, 112831, 2020.
23. Catalini, C., de Gortari, A., Shah, N., Some simple economics of stablecoins. *Annu. Rev. Financ. Econ.*, 14, 117–135, 2022.
24. Yermack, D., Is Bitcoin a real currency? An economic appraisal, in: *Handbook of digital currency*, pp. 31–43, Academic Press, California, USA, 2015.
25. Gandal, N., Hamrick, J.T., Moore, T., Oberman, T., Price manipulation in the Bitcoin ecosystem. *J. Monet. Econ.*, 95, 86–96, 2018.
26. Ali, R., Barrdear, J., Clews, R., Southgate, J., The economics of digital currencies. *Bank of England Quarterly Bulletin, Q3*, 2014.
27. Trivedi, S. and Malik, R., Role of Cryptocurrency in Digital Marketing, in: *Blockchain Technology and Applications for Digital Marketing*, pp. 175–185, IGI Global, Hershey, Pennsylvania, 2021.
28. Colon, F., Kim, C., Kim, H., Kim, W., The effect of political and economic uncertainty on the cryptocurrency market. *Finance Res. Lett.*, 39, 101621, 2021.
29. Zhao, H. and Zhang, L., Financial literacy or investment experience: which is more influential in cryptocurrency investment? *Int. J. Bank Mark.*, 39, 7, 1208–1226, 2021.
30. Nabilou, H., How to regulate bitcoin? Decentralized regulation for a decentralized cryptocurrency. *Int. J. Law Inf. Technol.*, 27, 3, 266–291, 2019.
31. Foley, S., Karlsen, J.R., Putniņš, T.J., Sex, drugs, and bitcoin: How much illegal activity is financed through cryptocurrencies? *Rev. Financ. Stud.*, 32, 5, 1798–1853, 2019.
32. Narayanan, A., Bonneau, J., Felten, E., Miller, A., Goldfeder, S., *Bitcoin and cryptocurrency technologies. A comprehensive*, Princeton University Press, Princeton, NJ, 2021.
33. Corbet, S., Lucey, B., Urquhart, A., Yarovaya, L., Cryptocurrencies as a financial asset: A systematic analysis. *Int. Rev. Financ. Anal.*, 62, 182–199, 2019.
34. Mougayar, W., *The business blockchain: promise, practice, and application of the next Internet technology*, John Wiley & Sons, Hoboken, New Jersey, 2016.
35. Mehta, K. and Sharma, R., Contrarian and momentum investment strategies: Evidence from Indian stock market. *Int. J. Appl. Bus. Econ. Res.*, 15, 2, 87–98, 2017.
36. Vyas, V., Mehta, K., Sharma, R., Investigating socially responsible investing behaviour of Indian investors using structural equation modelling. *J. Sustain. Finance Invest.*, 12, 1, 1–23, 2020.
37. Mehta, K., Sharma, R., Vyas, V., A quantile regression approach to study the impact of aluminium prices on manufacturing sector of India during COVID era. *Mater. Today: Proc.*, 65, 7, 3506–3511, 2022.
38. Yue, Y., Li, X., Zhang, D., Wang, S., How cryptocurrency affects economy? A network analysis using bibliometric methods. *Int. Rev. Financ. Anal.*, 77, 101869, 2021.

39. Vyas, V., Mehta, K., Sharma, R., Are bitcoin prices isolated or co-integrated? *Int. J. Bus. Glob.*, 35, 1–2, 2023.
40. Haq, I.U., Maneengam, A., Chupradit, S., Suksatan, W., Huo, C., Economic policy uncertainty and cryptocurrency market as a risk management avenue: A systematic review. *Risks*, 9, 9, 163, 2021.
41. Garcia, D. and Schweitzer, F., Social signals and algorithmic trading of Bitcoin. *R. Soc. Open Sci.*, 2, 9, 150288, 2015.
42. Verma, J., Sharma, J., Sharma, A., Kaur, J., Does Metaverse a Technological Revolution in Artificial Intelligence? A Bibliometric Analysis, in: *2022 Seventh International Conference on Parallel, Distributed and Grid Computing (PDGC)*, IEEE, pp. 425–428, 2022.
43. Mazure, G. and Kalnina, A., Analysis of Potential Application of Blockchain Technology in Renewable Energy Sector. *International Multidisciplinary Scientific GeoConference: SGEM*, vol. 22, 5.1, pp. 523–532, 2022.
44. Junlakarn, S., Kokchang, P., Audomvongseree, K., Drivers and challenges of peer-to-peer energy trading development in Thailand. *Energies*, 15, 3, 1229, 2022.
45. Bonnet, S. and Teuteberg, F., Impact of blockchain and distributed ledger technology for the management, protection, enforcement and monetization of intellectual property: a systematic literature review. *Inf. Syst. e-Bus. Manag.*, 21, 2, 229–275, 2023.
46. Canh, N.P., Binh, N.Q., Thanh, S.D., Cryptocurrencies and investment diversification: empirical evidence from seven largest cryptocurrencies. *Theor. Econ. Lett.*, 9, 03, 431, 2019.
47. Martínez-López, F.J., Li, Y., Young, S.M., Business Model Design for Social Media Companies, in: *Social Media Monetization: Platforms, Strategic Models and Critical Success Factors*, pp. 151–167, Springer International Publishing, Cham, 2022.
48. Noda, A., On the evolution of cryptocurrency market efficiency. *Appl. Econ. Lett.*, 28, 6, 433–439, 2021.
49. Eierle, B., Hartlieb, S., Hay, D.C., Niemi, L., Ojala, H., External factors and the pricing of audit services: A systematic review of the archival literature using a PESTLE analysis. *Auditing: J. Pract. Theory*, 41, 3, 95–119, 2022.
50. Oğhan, V., Environmental policies for green cryptocurrency mining, in: *Handbook of research on challenges in public economics in the era of globalization*, pp. 217–227, IGI Global, Hershey, Pennsylvania, 2022.
51. Aziz, A.T.I.F., Cryptocurrency: Evolution & legal dimension. *Int. J. Bus. Econ. Law*, 18, 4, 31–33, 2019.
52. Zohar, A., Bitcoin: under the hood. *Commun. ACM*, 58, 9, 104–113, 2015.
53. Gursoy, S., Akkus, H.T., Dogan, M., The causal relationship between bitcoin energy consumption and cryptocurrency uncertainty. *J. Bus. Econ. Finance*, 11, 1, 58–67, 2022.
54. Boukis, A., Exploring the sources of consumer-based brand equity in the cryptocurrency market. *Rev. Mark. Sci.*, 20, 1, 233–255, 2022.

55. Yan, L., Mirza, N., Umar, M., The cryptocurrency uncertainties and investment transitions: Evidence from high and low carbon energy funds in China. *Technol. Forecast. Soc. Change*, 175, 121326, 2022.
56. Marzo, G.D., Pandolfelli, F., Servedio, V.D., Modeling innovation in the cryptocurrency ecosystem. *Sci. Rep.*, 12, 1, 12942, 2022.
57. Krause, M.J. and Tolaymat, T., Quantification of energy and carbon costs for mining cryptocurrencies. *Nat. Sustain.*, 1, 11, 711–718, 2018.
58. Global Crypto Industry- NASSCOM retrieved from https://www.moneycontrol.com/news/business/companies/in-charts-growth-of-the-crypto-tech-market-in-india-7513551.html
59. Trivedi, S. and Malik, R., Blockchain Technology as an Emerging Technology in the Insurance Market, in: *Big Data: A Game Changer for Insurance Industry*, pp. 81–100, Emerald Publishing Limited, Bingley, UK, 2022.
60. Mehta, K. and Sharma, R., Unraveling quantum complexity: A fuzzy AHP approach to understanding software industry challenges, in: *Deep Learning Tools for Predicting Stock Market Movements*, pp. 39–60, 2024.
61. Sharma, R., Mehta, K., Rana, R., Cryptocurrency adoption behaviour of millennial investors in India, in: *Perspectives on Blockchain Technology and Responsible Investing*, pp. 135–158, 2023.

7

The Role of Blockchain in Disrupting Traditional Banking with Decentralized Finance

Tarun Kumar Vashishth[1]*, Vikas Sharma[1], Kewal Krishan Sharma[1], Bhupendra Kumar[1], Sachin Chaudhary[1] and Vineet Kaushik[2]

[1]School of Computer Science and Applications, IIMT University, Meerut, U.P., India
[2]School of Commerce and Management, IIMT University, Meerut, U.P., India

Abstract
Blockchain appeared as a transformative power in the financial sector, enabling the development of decentralized finance (DeFi) applications that challenge the traditional banking system. This paper explores the role of blockchain in disrupting traditional banking through the lens of DeFi. It examines the key features of blockchain technology that empower DeFi platforms, such as transparency, immutability, and decentralized governance. Additionally, it highlights potential benefits and challenges associated with the adoption of decentralized financial solutions in the banking industry. The study concludes by discussing implications of blockchain-driven DeFi for traditional banking institutions and offering insights into the future of this game-changing duo.

***Keywords*:** Blockchain, decentralized finance, traditional banking, disruption, transparency, immutability, decentralized governance

Abbreviations

DeFi	Decentralized Finance
AML	Anti-money laundering
KYC	Know Your Customer
DEXs	Decentralized exchanges

**Corresponding author*: tarunvashishth@gmail.com

Renuka Sharma, Kiran Mehta, Vishal Vyas and Vinod Kumar Shukla (eds.) Decentralized Finance and Blockchain: A Game Changing Duo, (143–174)

CBDCs Central Bank Digital Currencies
DAOs Decentralized Autonomous Organizations
DApps Decentralized Applications

7.1 Introduction

The traditional banking industry has long been characterized by centralized intermediaries, lengthy transaction processes, and limited access. However, with the advent of blockchain skills, a paradigm shift is underway. Decentralized finance (DeFi) applications built on blockchain networks offer a new approach to financial services, challenging the status quo of traditional banking [21]. This chapter delves into the role of blockchain in disrupting traditional banking through the lens of DeFi.

7.1.1 Significance and Background of Blockchain Technology

Blockchain has arisen as a transforming power to revolutionize various industries, including finance and banking. Understanding the background and significance of blockchain is critical in comprehending its disruptive potential in traditional banking and the rise of DeFi [7].

Background of blockchain technology: Blockchain technology originated with the arrival of Bitcoin, an initial non-centralized digital currency [31] presented by an anonymous person or group of persons adopting the pseudonym Satoshi Nakamoto in 2008. Its underlying technology, Bitcoin, known as blockchain, gained attention for its ability to provide a safe, see-through way to record and authenticate transactions without the necessity for intermediaries. Researchers have examined the cryptocurrency behavior as there is an increased interest from investors in this digital financial instrument [26, 27, 34].

Definition and functionality of blockchain: Blockchain is a defined as a distributed and non-centralized digital ledger that keeps records of transactions across multiple computers or nodes. It works with consensus machinery, where participants over the network collectively validate and agree on the state of the ledger [2]. The financial environment is exposed to various types of risks [16, 24–27]. Every transaction is securely recorded in a distributed block, and these blocks are connected in a chronological and immutable block of chain.

Key characteristics of blockchain:

- Decentralization: Blockchain eliminates the requirement for a dominant/intermediary authority, enabling peer-to-peer transactions and consensus-based decision-making.
- Transparency and immutability: Transactions stored over blockchain are transparent and accessible to participants. Once recorded, data over the blockchain cannot be altered or tampered with, improving the integrity and trustworthiness of the system.
- Security: Blockchain utilizes cryptology techniques to ensure the safety and authenticity of transactions. The distributed nature of a digital ledger makes it resistant to hacking and fraudulent activities.
- Cost and efficacy reduction: Blockchain eradicates prerequisites for intermediaries in transactions, reducing costs and streamlining processes. Smart contracts (s-contract), programmable self-executing contracts on blockchain, automate various functions and further enhance efficiency [2].

Significance of blockchain for financial and banking:
The significance of blockchain in finance is transformative, revolutionizing traditional processes and fostering a new era of security, efficiency, and transparency. At its core, blockchain, a non-centralized and distributed ledger technology [5], eradicates the need for intermediaries in financial transactions. This does not only reduce transaction costs, but it also expedites the settlement process, enabling near-instantaneous, cross-border transfers. The immutable and transparent nature of blockchain ensures a tamper-proof record of transactions, minimizing the risk of fraud and enhancing the overall security of financial data. Smart contracts, self-executing agreements written into code on the blockchain, automate and enforce contractual obligations, eradicating the need for manual intervention and reducing the potential in creating errors. This not only streamlines processes but also enhances the overall efficiency of financial operations. Furthermore, blockchain technology enables an enhanced financial inclusion by providing secure and accessible financial services to unbanked and underbanked populations [3, 14].

Decentralization and cryptographic security ensure that people have great control over monetary assets and identities. Moreover, blockchain's traceability facilitates efficient auditing and compliance, reducing attacks of monetary crimes and ensuring adherence to regulatory standards [6].

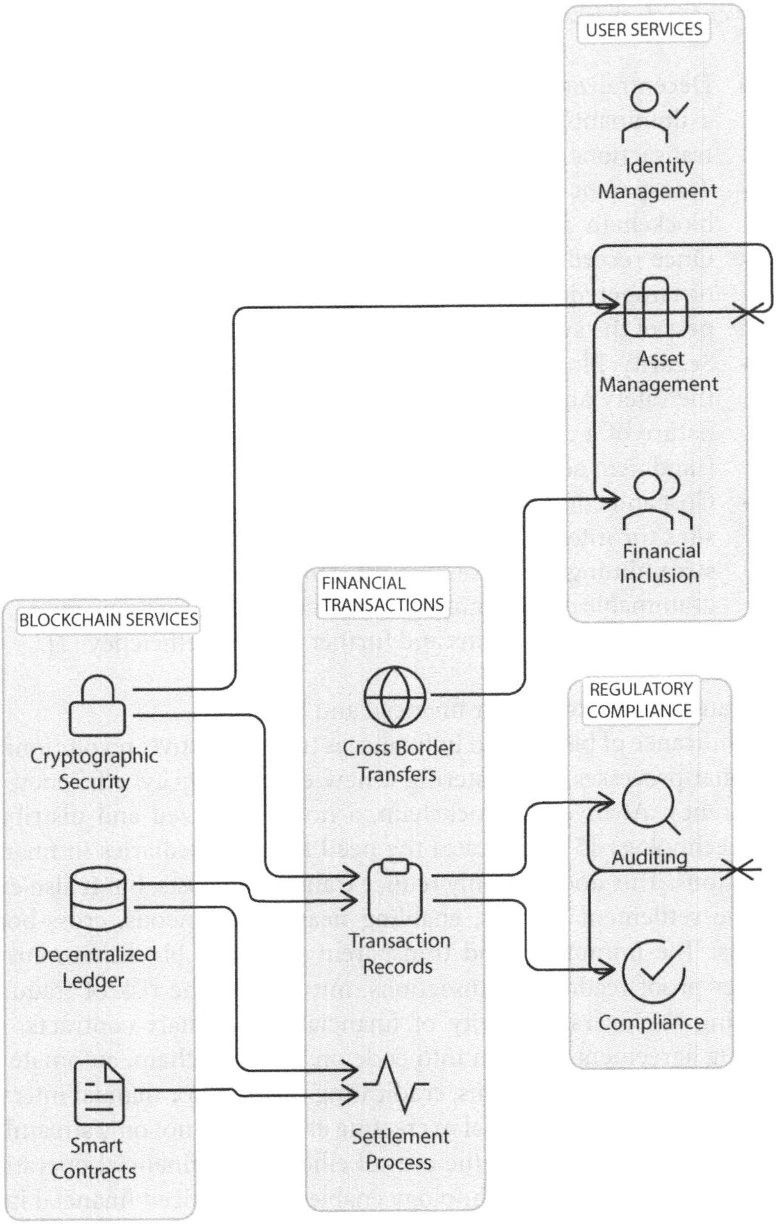

Figure 7.1 Blockchain in finance and banking.

The implementation of blockchain in finance and banking is not only a technical upgrade but a paradigm move toward a more inclusive, secure, and efficient financial ecosystem. As financial institutions increasingly recognize the value of blockchain, this technology stands poised to redefine the very foundations of the financial industry, promoting trust, reducing friction, and revealing a new potential for innovation [18]. Figure 7.1 depicts the blockchain technology revolutionizes finance and banking by enhancing transparency, reducing transaction costs, and ensuring secure, tamper-proof records.

7.1.2 Overview of Traditional Banking and its Limitations

Traditional banking, characterized by brick-and-mortar branches, face-to-face interactions, and paper-based transactions, has long been the bedrock of financial services. While providing a sense of familiarity and physical presence, traditional banking models come with inherent limitations. One of the primary drawbacks is geographical constraints, as customers are tethered to physical branches, leading to inconvenience, especially in remote areas. The operational hours of traditional banks also pose challenges, restricting access for those with time constraints or unconventional working hours. Moreover, the paperwork-intensive processes contribute to delays and inefficiencies, hampering the speed of transactions. Traditional banks often struggle with legacy systems, making it challenging to adapt swiftly to evolving customer expectations and technological advancements. Additionally, the rigid and bureaucratic nature of traditional banking can result in a lack of innovation, hindering the development of customer-centric solutions. Security concerns in traditional banking, predominantly reliant on physical documents and signatures, also persist, with the potential for fraud and unauthorized access. The emergence of digital transformation and fintech disruptors has underscored these limitations, emphasizing the need for the banking sector to embrace technological advancements and shift towards more agile, customer-centric, and secure alternatives. As technology continues to reshape the financial landscape, traditional banks must navigate these challenges to remain relevant and competitive in a rapidly evolving industry [10].

7.1.3 Introduction to Decentralized Finance and its Potential Benefits

Decentralized finance is a rapidly growing ecosystem of fiscal uses and services built over blockchain, specifically utilizing s-contracts. Unlike traditional banking systems, DeFi aims to give less open permission and DeFi services accessible to anyone with an internet connection. Here is an introduction to DeFi and its potential benefits:

Open and permissionless access: DeFi protocols are accessible to anyone, regardless of their geographic location, socioeconomic status, or identification. The only requirements are an internet connection and a compatible wallet to interact with DeFi applications. This inclusivity allows individuals, who are unbanked or underbanked, to take part in financial activities and access various services, like lending, borrowing, and investing [1].

Trustless transactions: DeFi applications utilize s-contracts, which are auto executing agreements that automatically execute predefined actions when specific conditions are met. These s-contracts are stored on the blockchain, ensuring transparency and eliminating the need to rely on a single authority. By removing the requirement of trust in its central authority, DeFi enables any to transaction directly, enhancing security and reducing counterparty risks.

Financial empowerment: DeFi provides individuals with greater control over their financial activities. Users can manage their assets, invest in various financial instruments, and earn interest without relying on traditional financial institutions. Through DeFi, individuals can become their bank, managing their funds and making financial decisions according to their preferences [4].

Enhanced liquidity and efficiency: DeFi requests are built on blockchain on digital networks that allow seamless and instant transactions. Moreover, DeFi protocols enable the interoperability of different platforms, aggregating liquidity from various sources. This results in increased liquidity and efficiency in trading and lending, as users can access a larger pool of funds for their financial activities.

Programmability and innovation: DeFi leverages the programmability of smart contracts to create innovative financial products and services. Developers can build new protocols, decentralized exchanges, lending platforms, prediction markets, and more. This flexibility allows for the creation of customizable and automated financial solutions, which were previously impossible within the traditional banking system [28].

Cost reduction: Decentralized finance aims to reduce costs associated with traditional financial services. By removing in-between and automating processes via s-contracts, DeFi applications can provide financial services at lower fees compared to traditional banks. This cost reduction benefits both users and businesses, making financial services more accessible and affordable.

Transparency and auditability: Decentralized finance works on public blockchains, allowing transparent and auditable transactions. In every transaction, activities are marked on the blockchain, providing a permanent

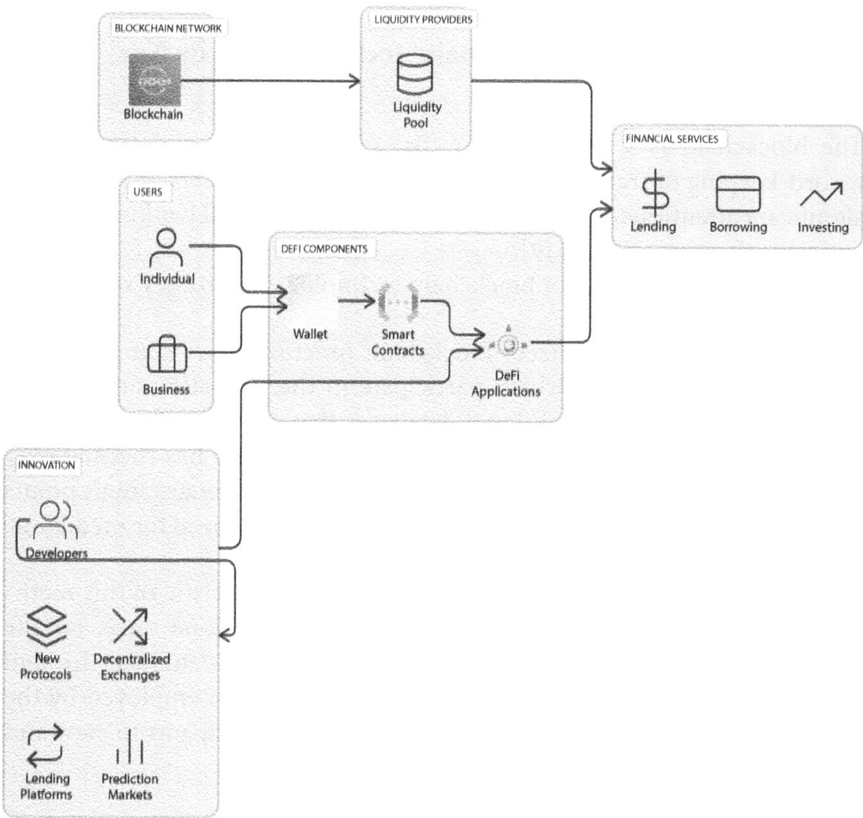

Figure 7.2 Decentralized finance (DeFi).

and immutable record. It reduces the risk of fraud and enhances accountability, as handlers can verify and audit transactions independently.

Decentralized finance introduces a new paradigm in finance by leveraging blockchain expertise and s-contracts to provide open, permissionless services. It offers benefits such as open access, trustless transactions, financial empowerment, liquidity, programmability, cost reduction, and transparency. As DeFi continues to evolve, it has the power to disrupt traditional banking systems by contributing innovative, inclusive, and efficient financial solutions to individuals and businesses globally [11]. Figure 7.2 depicts Decentralized Finance (DeFi) eliminates intermediaries by utilizing blockchain-based smart contracts, enabling peer-to-peer financial transactions and services.

7.2 Blockchain Technology in Banking

7.2.1 Explanation of Blockchain Technique and its Key Features

The blockchain is a digital ledger that gives a secure and transparent record-keeping of transactions through multiple computers. It has gained significant attention for its potential to disrupt traditional banking systems and pave the way for DeFi [9].

Here is an explanation of blockchain technology and its key structures:

Distributed and decentralized: Blockchain functions over computer networks, known as nodes, which participate in the validation and storage of transactions. Unlike traditional databases that are centrally controlled, blockchain is decentralized, meaning that no one entity has rheostat over the network. Non-centralization improves security, eliminates single points of failure, and allows peer-to-peer interactions with no need for mediators.

Immutable and transparent: The fundamental characteristic of this methodology is its immutability and if a transaction is done once, on the blockchain, it becomes impossible to tamper with. It is attained through crypto-graphic techniques and a consensus mechanism employed by the network. The transparency of blockchain enables participants to view and verify transactions, ensuring trust and accountability.

Consensus mechanisms: Blockchain networks rely on agreement mechanisms to achieve a consensus among network participants about the state of the ledger. Different consensus algorithms, such as Proof of Work or Proof of Stake, are used to validate transactions and add new blocks to the chain. These mechanisms ensure that all nodes in the network agree on the validity of the transactions, maintaining the integrity of the blockchain.

Security and cryptography: Blockchain employs cryptographic algorithms to secure transactions and data stored on the network. Transactions are cryptically signatured, ensuring that they are authentic and tamperproof. Decentralized nature of blockchain, coupled with cryptographic techniques, makes it highly secure against hacking and fraudulent activities.

Smart contracts: These are self-executing contracts that are coded on the blockchain. It automatically runs in a pre-defined manner when specific situations happen. They enable the automation of business processes, removing the need for intermediaries and facilitating trustless transactions [17]. They can be used to create decentralized applications (DApps) and complex financial instruments in the DeFi space.

Privacy and identity protection: The blockchain provides varying levels of privacy depending on the specific blockchain architecture. While some public blockchains provide fakes, others, such as private or permissioned blockchains, offer enhanced privacy and access controls. Blockchain also has the potential to address identity organization challenges by providing secure and verifiable digital identities, empowering anyone to have control over personal data [18].

Interoperability and scalability: Blockchain networks can be designed to be interoperable, enabling seamless communication and transactions between different blockchain platforms. It allows for the integration of various DeFi applications and the aggregation of liquidity. Scalability, the ability to handle a huge transaction, is a significant challenge for blockchain technology.

Blockchain technology offers a distributed and decentralized approach to record-keeping and transaction verification. Its key features include decentralization, immutability, transparency, consensus mechanisms, privacy, and scalability. These features form the foundation for disruptive innovations in traditional banking through the emergence of DeFi and the potential to redefine financial systems worldwide [20].

7.2.2 Application of Blockchain in Traditional Banking Processes

Blockchain has power to transform traditional banking processes, introducing efficiency, transparency, and cost savings. Here are some key areas where blockchain can be applied in traditional banking:

Payments and remittances: Blockchain can streamline and enhance payment and remittance processes, both domestically and internationally. By leveraging blockchain's distributed ledger, connections can be settled directly among parties without the need for intermediaries, dropping costs and transaction times. Blockchain-based payment solutions can enable faster cross-border transfers, real-time settlement, and an improved traceability of transactions, ensuring greater transparency and security.

Clearing and settlement: The traditional clearing and settlement processes in banking often involve multiple intermediaries, manual reconciliation, and lengthy settlement periods. Blockchain can provide a decentralized and transparent platform for the automation of clearing and settlement, eliminating the need for intermediaries and reducing the time and costs associated with the process. The s-contracts on blockchain can enable automated and secure settlements, ensuring timely and accurate transactions.

Trade finance and supply chain: It can significantly improve the efficiency and transparency of trade finance processes, including the letter of credit, bill of lading, and documentation management. By utilizing blockchain, trade finance transactions can be recorded, verified, and shared among relevant parties in a secure and immutable manner. It enhances trust, reduces fraud, and streamlines the overall trade finance ecosystem, benefiting both banks and businesses involved in international trade [29].

Anti-money laundering (AML) and Know Your Customer (KYC): Blockchain-grounded solutions can simplify and augment the AML and KYC processes, which are critical in mitigating risks and complying with regulatory requirements [22]. Blockchain allows for the secure storage and sharing of customer identity information, eliminating the need for repetitive customer verification across multiple institutions. This can lead to improved customer experience, reduced costs, and enhanced data privacy and security.

Syndicated loans and debt issuance: Blockchain has the capacity to streamline the process of syndicated loans and debt issuance, making it efficient

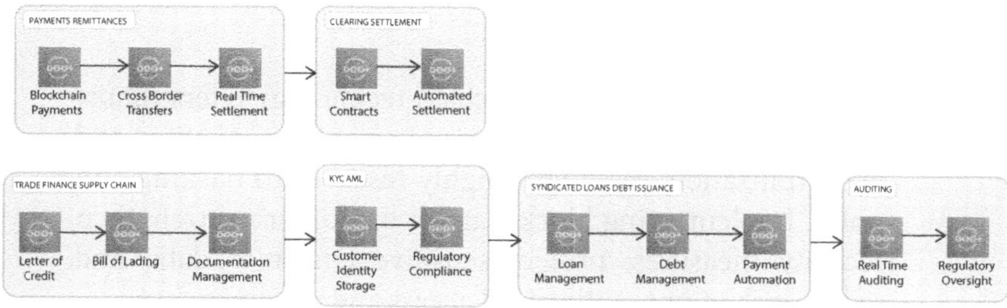

Figure 7.3 Applications of blockchain in a traditional banking system.

and cost-effective. By digitizing the issuance, management, and settlement of loans and debts on the blockchain, multiple parties involved in the process can access a single source of truth, reducing paperwork, improving transparency, and automating interest and principal payments. This can enhance the speed, accuracy, and liquidity of loan and debt markets.

Auditing and regulatory compliance: Immutability in the transparent landscape of blockchain makes it well-suited for auditing and regulatory compliance purposes. Banks can utilize the blockchain to securely record and store financial transactions, enabling auditors and regulators to access real-time and tamperproof information. This improves the efficiency of audits and enhances regulatory oversight. Figure 7.3 illustrates the blockchain technology finds multiple applications within traditional banking systems, including secure transactions, fraud prevention, identity verification, and efficient cross-border payments.

Blockchain can revolutionize traditional banking processes by introducing transparency, efficiency, and cost savings. Its applications in payments, remittances, clearing and settlement, trade finance, KYC/AML, syndicated loans, debt issuance, auditing, and regulatory compliance offer significant potential to disrupt and improve traditional banking practices, leading to a more efficient and inclusive financial ecosystem.

7.2.3 Benefits and Issues to Use Blockchain in Traditional Banking

Blockchain holds immense potential to transform traditional banking systems, introducing numerous benefits [8]. However, its implementation in the banking sector also comes with certain challenges. Here are the key pros and cons of implementing blockchain in traditional banking:

Benefits:

- Security enhancement: Blockchain technology offers robust security features, including cryptographic encryption and decentralization, making it highly resistant to hacking and fraud. Implementing blockchain in banking can strengthen security measures, protect sensitive customer data, and reduce risk of non-authorized access and data breaches.
- Improved efficiency and cost savings: Blockchain streamlines and automates various banking processes, eliminating the need for manual reconciliation. This reduces operational costs, minimizes errors, and accelerates transaction settlement. By leveraging blockchain, traditional banks can achieve greater efficiency, lower costs, and faster processing times.
- Increased transparency and trust: The nature of blockchain enables all participants to have real-time visibility into transactions and a shared view of the ledger. This transparency enhances trust between parties, reduces disputes, and provides a tamper-proof audit trail. Customers can have greater confidence in the integrity of the banking system, leading to improved faith and customer satisfaction.
- Financial inclusion: Blockchain technology has the strength to extend services to underserved populations. By allowing access to decentralized financial services through blockchain-based applications, traditional banks can reach individuals who have less access to banking services, thereby promoting financial inclusion [29].
- Innovation and new revenue streams: Implementing blockchain allows traditional banks to explore and develop innovative financial services. The s-contracts and non-centralized applications built on blockchain enable the creation of new revenue streams, such as tokenized assets, decentralized lending, and digital identity solutions. It opens opportunities for banks to step into the growing DeFi market [12].

Challenges:

- Regulatory and compliance frameworks: Blockchain implementation in traditional banking requires navigating complex regulatory and compliance frameworks. As technology is still evolving, regulatory guidelines for blockchain-based financial services are not fully established. Banks must work closely with regulators to ensure compliance with existing regulations and address concerns regarding privacy, identity verification, AML, and customer protection.

- Scalability and performance: Blockchain faces encounters related to scalability and performance, mainly in handling a large number of transactions concurrently. Traditional banking systems are required to process high volumes of transactions efficiently, and blockchain networks must demonstrate scalability to handle such demands without compromising speed, security, or cost-effectiveness.
- Integration with legacy systems: Many traditional banks operate on legacy systems not designed to integrate with blockchain technology seamlessly. Implementing blockchain may require significant modifications or replacements of existing systems, posing technical challenges and requiring substantial investment. Ensuring interoperability between blockchain and heritage systems is crucial for a smooth transition.
- Governance and standardization: Blockchain governance models and standards are still evolving. Traditional banks must establish robust governance frameworks for blockchain implementation, addressing issues such as consensus mechanisms, network upgrades, and decision-making processes. Standardization efforts are to ensure compatibility and interoperability between unlike blockchain networks and applications.
- Adoption and user education: Successful implementation of blockchain in traditional banking needs user adoption and education. Banks need to invest in customer education programs to familiarize users with blockchain technology and its benefits. The resistance to change and the need to shift customer behavior from traditional banking to blockchain-based systems can present significant challenges.

In summary, implementing blockchain in traditional banking offers several benefits, including enhanced security, improved efficiency, increased transparency, financial inclusion, and innovation. However, challenges related to regulations, scalability, legacy system integration, governance, and user adoption must be overcome for successful implementation. By handling these challenges, traditional banks may harness the disruptive potential of blockchain and leverage it to provide more secure, efficient, and customer-centric financial services.

7.3 Decentralized Finance

7.3.1 Definition and Principles of DeFi

Decentralized finance refers to an ecosystem of monetary applications and services built over blockchain technology, specifically leveraging the principles of decentralization, transparency, and open access. It aims to create a financial system that operates without intermediaries, providing individuals with more control over their financial activities and promoting inclusiveness. Here are the key definitions and principles that underpin DeFi:

Definition of DeFi: DeFi can be defined as a set of financial applications and protocols that operate on decentralized networks, primarily utilizing this technology. These applications aim to offer open and permissionless access to several financial services, including lending, borrowing, trading, investing, and asset management. Decentralized finance leverages s-contracts to automate and enforce execution of financial agreements, removing the requirement for intermediaries.

Principles of DeFi:

Decentralization: DeFi is built on decentralized networks, typically public blockchains, where control is dispersed among several participants or nodes. It eradicates the need for centralized authorities, such as banks or financial institutions, allowing for peer-to-peer interactions and decision-making through consensus mechanisms.

Open access: DeFi emphasizes inclusivity, allowing all with an internet to access and utilize services. It removes barriers to entry, enabling individuals from underserved regions or with limited financial resources to participate in the ecosystem. Decentralized finance applications are typically open-source, enabling community-driven development and innovation.

Transparency: DeFi promotes transparency by recording financial transactions and data on public blockchains, visible to all participants. This enables users to verify and audit transactions, ensuring trust and accountability.

Additionally, the transparency of DeFi protocols allows real-time monitoring and reduces the potential for fraud or manipulation.

Interoperability: DeFi protocols strive for interoperability, allowing different uses and platforms to seamlessly communicate and interact. This interoperability enables users to access a wide range of services and facilitates the movement of assets across different protocols and networks, creating a more integrated and interconnected ecosystem.

Programmability: DeFi leverages the programmability of s-contracts, enabling the automation of financial agreements and the creation of complex instruments. Smart contracts execute predefined actions based on predetermined conditions, providing efficiency, accuracy, and reliability in executing financial transactions without the need for intermediaries.

Security: DeFi prioritizes security by leveraging cryptographic techniques, consensus mechanisms, and decentralized networks. The use of public-private key encryption ensures the secure storage and transfer of assets. Decentralization and consensus mechanisms make the system more resilient to attacks, reducing risk of unauthorized access, fraud, and manipulation.

Decentralized finance denotes a paradigm shift in financial industry, leveraging blockchain and principles such as decentralization, open access, transparency, interoperability, programmability, and security. By embracing these principles, DeFi aims to disrupt traditional banking systems, empower individuals with additional control over their finances, and foster an inclusive and transparent financial ecosystem [8].

7.3.2 Overview of DeFi Ecosystem and its Components

Decentralized finance has come up as a rapidly growing ecosystem that leverages blockchain technology to create open, permissionless, and decentralized financial services [19]. Within the DeFi ecosystem, various components work together to enable innovative and disruptive financial solutions. Here is an overview of key components in the DeFi ecosystem:

Smart contracts: Self-executing contracts are encoded on the blockchain. They automatically execute predefined actions when specific conditions are met. Smart contracts serve as the building blocks for many DeFi applications, enabling automation, trustless transactions, and the elimination of intermediaries. They facilitate the creation of DApps that can provide financial services without relying on traditional intermediaries.

Decentralized exchanges (DEXs): DEXs allow users to trade digital assets directly with one another without the need for controlling authorities. Decentralized exchanges operate on blockchain networks and utilize s-contracts to execute and settle trades. They provide a more secure, transparent, and censorship-resistant alternative to centralized exchanges, enabling users to maintain control of their funds and trade without relying on a centralized order book.

Lending-borrowing platforms: Such platforms enable users to lend digital assets and earn interest or borrow assets by leveraging their existing holdings as collateral. Such platforms utilize s-contracts to automate loan issuance, interest calculation, and collateral management. By eliminating the need for traditional intermediaries, DeFi lending platforms offer increased accessibility, lower barriers to entry, and competitive interest rates compared to traditional lending services [32].

Stablecoins: They are cryptocurrencies intended to preserve a stable value by pegging them to a reserve asset or algo-managing their supply. Stablecoins play a vital role in the DeFi ecosystem by providing price stability and a familiar unit of accounts for financial transactions. They enable users to hedge against volatile cryptocurrencies and facilitate seamless transactions within DeFi applications, such as lending, trading, and payments.

Decentralized asset management: DeFi also encompasses decentralized asset management platforms that enable users to invest, diversify, and manage its digital assets through automated or user-driven strategies. These platforms utilize s-contracts to create decentralized investment funds, index funds, and yield farming strategies. They offer users greater control, transparency, and potential for higher returns compared to traditional asset management services.

Oracle networks: Oracle networks play a role in the DeFi ecosystem by providing external data to s-contracts. They work as bridges between blockchain and the real world, delivering real-time price feeds, market data, and other off-chain information required for smart contracts to execute and make informed decisions. It ensures the accuracy and reliability of data used within DeFi applications, giving them to interact with external systems and real-world events.

Governance and decentralized autonomous organizations (DAOs): Governance mechanisms and DAOs are components that allow participants in the DeFi ecosystem to collectively make decisions and shape the development of protocols. Through voting and governance tokens, users can participate in decision processes such as protocol upgrades, fee distribution, and parameter adjustments. Decentralized autonomous organizations aim to foster community governance and create more decentralized and inclusive financial systems.

Table 7.1 Comparison of DeFi with traditional financial systems.

Key aspect	DeFi	Traditional financial systems
Centralization	Decentralized, no central authority governs the system.	Centralized, controlled by banks and financial institutions.
Access & inclusion	Open and access to all with an internet. No need for a bank account.	Restricted access, requiring a bank account and compliance with regulatory requirements.
Intermediaries	Minimized or eliminated, peer-to-peer transactions.	Reliant on intermediaries like banks, clearing houses, and payments.
Transparency	Transparent, transactions recorded on a public block-chain.	Limited transparent, with access to detailed transaction information often restricted.
Censorship resistance	Censorship-resistant, transactions are not subject to approval by any central authority.	Subject to censorship and approval processes, especially in politically sensitive regions.
Smart contracts	Utilizes smart contracts to automate and enforce agreements.	Limited use of smart contracts, with most agreements requiring manual processing.

(Continued)

Table 7.1 Comparison of DeFi with traditional financial systems. (*Continued*)

Key aspect	DeFi	Traditional financial systems
Global accessibility	Globally accessible, available to anyone with an internet connection.	Global, but access may be restricted based on regulatory compliance and geographical location.
Speed of transactions	Generally faster due to automation and fewer intermediaries.	Can be slower, especially for cross-border transactions, due to multiple intermediaries and regulatory compliance checks.
Costs	Generally lower costs as it eliminates intermediary fees.	May have higher transaction costs due to the involvement of intermediaries.
Innovation	Rapid innovation, with the ability to experiment and deploy new financial products and services.	Innovation may be slower due to regulatory constraints and established systems.
Security	Relies on blockchain security, cryptography, and decentralized consensus.	Security relies on traditional cybersecurity measures and centralized controls.
Risk	A new and evolving space, may be subject to smart contract vulnerabilities.	Established, but still subject to risks such as economic downturns and systemic failures.

The DeFi ecosystem comprises various components, including s-contracts, DEXs, lending platforms, stablecoins, decentralized asset management, oracle networks, and governance mechanisms. These components work together to enable open, transparent, and decentralized financial services, empowering individuals with greater control over their financial activities and disrupting traditional banking systems [9].

7.3.3 Comparison of DeFi with Traditional Financial Systems

Decentralized finance presents a distinct alternative to traditional financial systems, offering unique characteristics and advantages. Table 7.1 highlights the DeFi differs significantly from traditional financial systems in terms of accessibility, transparency, control, and operational efficiency. Here is a comparison between DeFi and traditional financial systems in several key aspects:

7.3.4 Advantages and Potential Risks of DeFi Applications

Decentralized finance applications have gained traction for their potential to revolutionize the financial industry. While they offer numerous

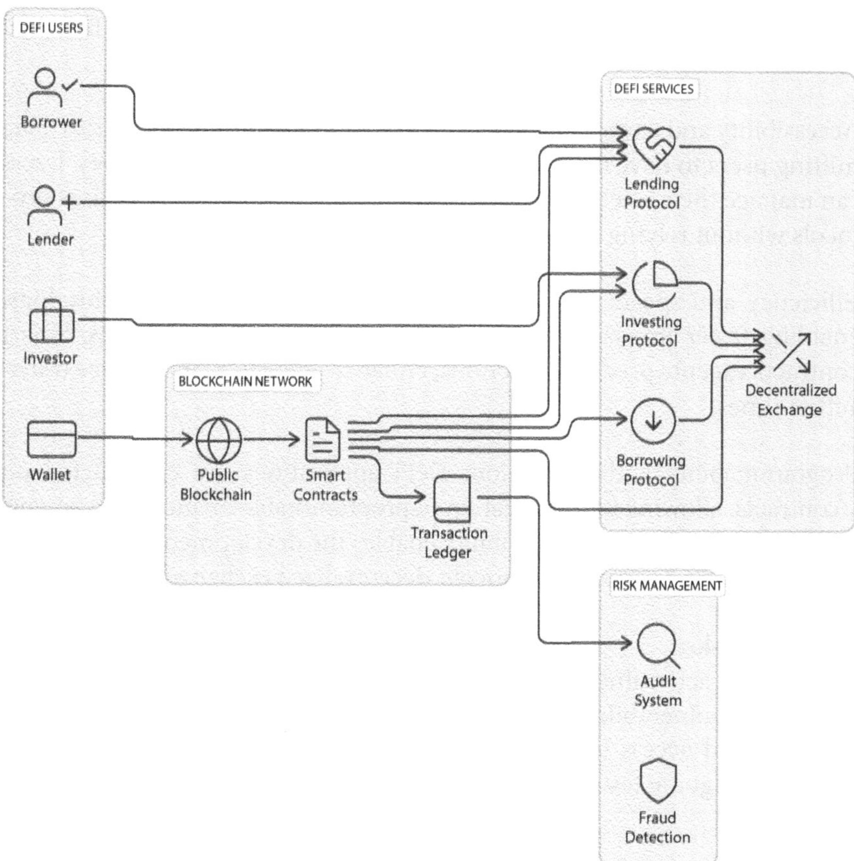

Figure 7.4 Decentralized finance applications architecture.

advantages, it is significant to consider the potential risks associated with applications [19]. Here are the key advantages and potential risks of DeFi applications:

Advantages:
Financial Inclusion: DeFi applications aim to provide financial services to anyone with an internet, promoting the inclusion of finance. Individuals who have deficient access to old banking systems can participate in DeFi, accessing services like lending/borrowing.

Transparency: DeFi applications operate on public blockchains, making transaction data accessible to all participants. Transparency improves trust, as users can independently verify and audit transactions. It also decreases the potential for fraud. Figure 7.4 illustrates, the architecture of decentralized finance applications consists of layered protocols, smart contracts, and blockchain infrastructure enabling trustless and automated financial services.

Accessibility and control: DeFi eliminates the need for intermediaries, permitting users to have direct control of funds and financial activities. Users can manage their assets, make transactions, and participate in various protocols without relying on third-party entities.

Efficiency and speed: DeFi applications leverage blockchain technology, enabling faster transaction settlements and automated processes. Smart contracts execute predefined actions, enhance efficiency, and reduce transaction times.

Programmability and innovation: DeFi applications are constructed on s-contracts, allowing for the creation of programmable financial agreements and protocols. This programmability enables the development of innovative financial products, lending protocols, decentralized exchanges, and more.

Potential risks:
Smart contract vulnerabilities: S-contracts are not immune to error. Exploiting vulnerabilities in s-contracts can lead to financial losses or unauthorized access to funds. Thorough code audits, security top practices, and ongoing testing are necessary to mitigate these risks.

Market volatility and asset risks: DeFi applications often involve the use of cryptocurrencies and digital assets, which are subject to high volatility. Several techniques can be used to investigate the price movement of various financial instruments [14–16, 33]. Users should be aware of the risks associated with price fluctuations, market manipulation, and potential asset value depreciation.

Regulatory and compliance risks: DeFi operates in a speedily evolving regulatory landscape. Uncertainty regarding regulatory frameworks can introduce compliance risks for both users and developers. Compliance with AML and KYC regulations leftovers a challenge for DeFi users.

Centralization of power: While DeFi aims to eliminate intermediaries, certain DeFi protocols and platforms may become centralized over time. The concentration of governance power or control in the hands of a few participants can undermine the decentralized nature of DeFi.

User error and security risks: Such applications want users to achieve their private keys and s-contracts. User errors, such as incorrect addresses or missteps in transaction execution, can lead to irreversible losses. Users must prioritize security practices, such as secure key management and verifying contract details.

Scalability and network congestion: As DeFi gains popularity, scalability becomes a challenge. Network congestion and high gas fees can impact the usability and affordability of DeFi applications. Scaling solutions and optimizations are necessary to improve the overall user experience.

Decentralized finance applications offer advantages such as financial inclusion, transparency, accessibility, efficiency, and innovation. However, potential risks exist, including smart contract vulnerabilities, market volatility, regulatory uncertainty, centralization risks, user errors, and scalability challenges. Users and developers must be mindful of risks and implement security measures and due diligence to mitigate them effectively.

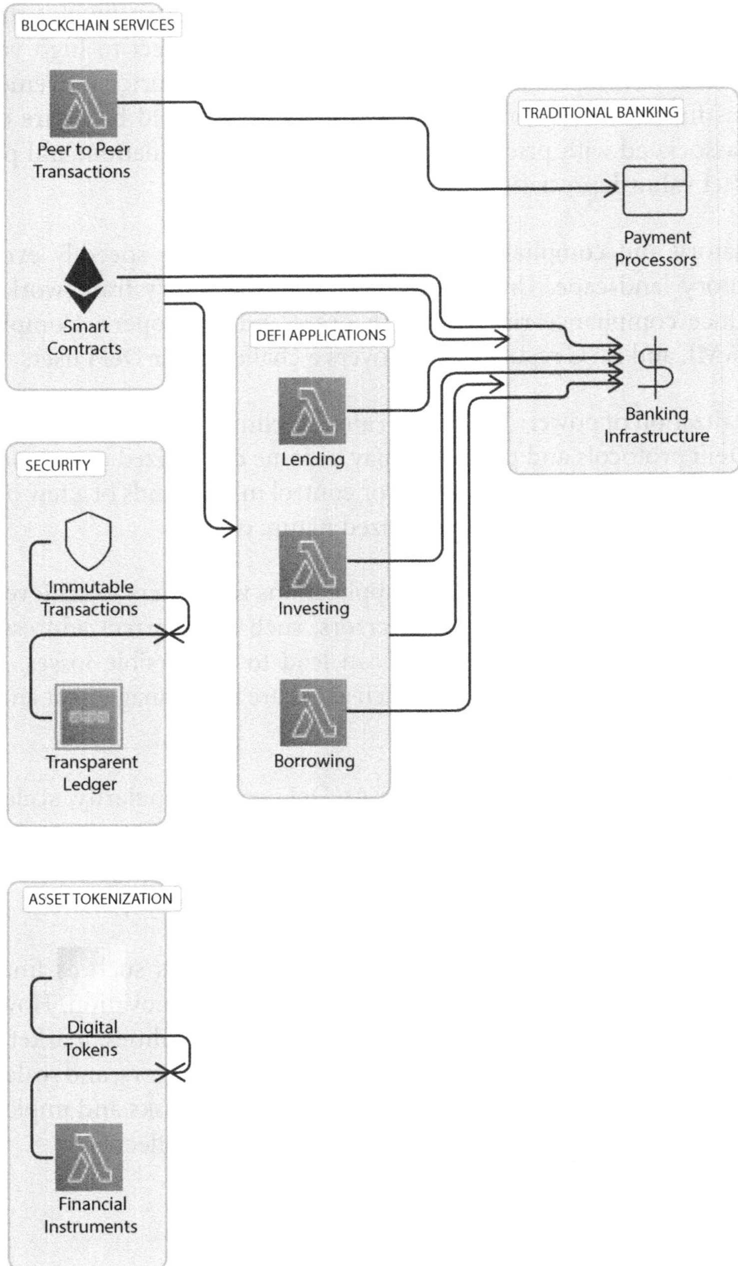

Figure 7.5 The disruptive potential of blockchain and DeFi in traditional banking.

7.4 Disruptive Potential of Blockchain and DeFi in Traditional Banking

7.4.1 Disintermediation: Removing Intermediaries and Reducing Costs in Financial Transactions

Blockchain and DeFi have the potential to disrupt traditional banking by eradicating the necessity for intermediaries. Through decentralized networks and smart contracts, blockchain enables direct peer-to-peer transactions, reducing the reliance on banks and payment processors. This disintermediation can proceed to lower transaction costs, fasten settlements, and increase efficiency in financial transactions.

7.4.2 Financial Inclusion: Outspreading Access to Financial Facilities to Unbanked and Underbanked Populations

Old banking systems often exclude segments of the population that lack access to banking services. Blockchain and DeFi can bridge this gap by providing inclusive financial services to unbanked and underbanked populations. With an internet connection, individuals can access similar services in a traditional banking infrastructure. Its expanded access to financial services promotes financial inclusion and economic empowerment. Figure 7.5 depicts the blockchain and DeFi possess significant disruptive potential in traditional banking by decentralizing control, enhancing transparency, and enabling faster, low-cost financial services.

7.4.3 Transparency and Security: Enhancing Trust and Reducing Fraud through Blockchain's Immutability and Lucidity

Blockchain's decentralized and transparent nature introduces greater trust and security into financial transactions. Transactions recorded on blockchain are immutable, dipping the risk of fraud. This transparency allows participants to independently verify and audit transactions, fostering trust and accountability. By leveraging blockchain technology, traditional banking processes can become more transparent, secure, and resistant to fraudulent activities.

7.4.4 Liquidity and Market Efficiency: Enabling New Forms of Asset Tokenization and Improving Market Liquidity

Blockchain and DeFi enable the tokenization of assets, converting physical or illiquid assets into digital tokens. Investors always look for various investment strategies to earn abnormal returns [13]. This tokenization allows for the creation of new fiscal instruments with investment opportunities. It also improves market liquidity by facilitating the seamless trading of digital assets. Investors can access a wider range of assets and benefit from increased market efficiency, as blockchain enables fractional ownership, reduces barriers to entry, and enables faster settlement times.

The capacity of blockchain and DeFi to disintermediate financial transactions, expand financial services to disadvantaged people, increase security and transparency, and boost liquidity and market efficiency presents blockchain and DeFi with significant disruptive potential for traditional banking. Embracing blockchain technology and the principles of DeFi can lead to a more inclusive, efficient, and secure financial ecosystem, transforming traditional banking systems in profound ways.

7.5 Challenges and Risks in Implementing Blockchain and DeFi in Banking

7.5.1 Regulatory and Compliance Disputes: Addressing Legal and Regulatory Frameworks for DeFi Applications

Implementing blockchain and DeFi in traditional banking systems poses regulatory challenges due to the evolving nature of these technologies. Decentralized finance applications may need to navigate complex and varying regulatory frameworks, including obedience to AML and KYC clear guidelines that ensure compliance while fostering innovation [35].

7.5.2 Security Concerns: Mitigating Risks Associated with S-Contract Weaknesses and Hacking Occurrences

Smart contracts, the foundation for DeFi applications, can contain coding vulnerabilities that hackers may exploit. Security risks include potential financial losses or unauthorized access to funds. Thorough code audits, robust security protocols, and ongoing testing are crucial to identify and mitigate smart contract vulnerabilities. Additionally, implementing secure key management practices/educating users for security good practices are indispensable to safeguarding assets and mitigating risks.

7.5.3 Scalability and Interoperability: Overcoming Limitations in Blockchain Scalability and Ensuring Interoperability Between Different DeFi Platforms

Scalability is a significant challenge for blockchain and DeFi applications. As user adoption increases, network congestion and high transaction fees may hinder the scalability and usability of DeFi platforms. Scaling solutions, like layer-2 protocols or sharding, are being developed to address these challenges. Furthermore, ensuring interoperability between different networks and DeFi platforms is crucial for creating a cohesive ecosystem that allows the seamless transfer of assets and information.

7.5.4 Governance and Risk Management: Establishing Robust Governance Mechanisms and Risk Management Frameworks for DeFi Protocols

Decentralized finance protocols often operate in a decentralized manner, making governance and risk management complex. Decisions related to protocol upgrades, fee distributions, and risk mitigation strategies need to be addressed in a decentralized and transparent manner. Developing effective governance models, consensus mechanisms, and management of risk frameworks are necessary to ensure the stability, security, and long-term sustainability of DeFi protocols.

7.5.5 User Education and Adoption: Overcoming Barriers to User Understanding and Adoption of Blockchain and DeFi Applications

Blockchain and DeFi concepts may be unfamiliar to many users, posing challenges in user education and adoption. The lack of understanding, improper use of wallets, and mistakes in transaction execution can lead to irreversible losses. Promoting user education, creating user-friendly interfaces, and simplifying onboarding processes are crucial to enhance user adoption and ensure that users can confidently navigate the DeFi ecosystem.

In summary, implementing blockchain and DeFi in traditional banking systems faces challenges related to regulatory compliance, security vulnerabilities, scalability, interoperability, governance, and user adoption. Addressing these challenges requires collaboration between industry participants, regulators, and policymakers, as well as continuous innovation, security measures, and user education. Overcoming these hurdles can unlock the transformative potential of blockchain and DeFi, enabling a secure, efficient, and financial ecosystem.

7.6 Future Perspectives and Recommendations

The future perspectives of blockchain and DeFi present an exciting landscape of continuous innovation, transformative shifts, and the potential for redefining the global financial system. As we look forward, several key trends are likely to shape the trajectory of these technologies. Firstly, the integration of blockchain and DeFi into mainstream financial institutions is anticipated to gather momentum. Traditional banks may leverage blockchain for enhanced security, transparency, and efficiency, adopting DeFi principles to streamline processes like lending, borrowing, and trading. Additionally, the development of scalable and interoperable blockchain solutions is crucial for addressing current limitations such as network congestion and high transaction costs. The maturation of regulatory frameworks is another pivotal aspect that will influence the future of blockchain and DeFi. Clear and globally harmonized regulations will provide a conducive environment for innovation while ensuring consumer protection and financial stability [23].

Moreover, the evolution of decentralized identity solutions on the blockchain is poised to revolutionize the way personal data is managed. Decentralized identity, allowing individuals to control and share their information securely, aligns with principles of privacy and consent, addressing concerns related to data breaches and identity theft. The emergence of DAOs as a governance model is a trend to watch. The DAOs, enabled by blockchain, facilitate decentralized decision-making and operations, challenging traditional hierarchical structures.

In terms of recommendations, fostering collaboration between the blockchain and traditional finance sectors is crucial. Open dialogue, partnerships, and knowledge exchange will accelerate the integration of these technologies into mainstream financial services. Additionally, proactive engagement with regulators to establish clear and adaptive frameworks is essential for building a robust foundation for the future of blockchain and

DeFi. Educating all stakeholders about benefits, risks, and best practices in this evolving landscape is paramount to ensuring responsible adoption. The industry should give priority to the development of friendly interfaces and comprehensive security measures to improve overall user experience and address concerns surrounding potential vulnerabilities [30].

In conclusion, the future perspectives of blockchain and DeFi hold immense promise for reshaping financial systems globally. Strategic collaborations, regulatory clarity, technological advancements, and a commitment to user education are imperative to realizing the full potential of these transformative technologies in creating a more inclusive, efficient, and secure financial ecosystem. The landscape continues to come. Adaptability and foresight will be key drivers of success in navigating the dynamic future for blockchain and DeFi.

7.7 Conclusion

Blockchain technology with DeFi is transforming the financial sector, challenging the traditional banking system. The features of blockchain, including transparency, immutability, and decentralized governance, provide the foundation for DeFi platforms to operate efficiently and securely. Decentralized finance offers numerous benefits, including financial inclusion, faster transactions, and worldwide accessibility. Challenges such as security vulnerabilities, scalability issues, and regulatory considerations must be tackled. Traditional banking institutions need to embrace blockchain technology and explore partnerships and collaborations to leverage the potential of DeFi. The journey towards a decentralized future in finance is underway, and understanding the role of blockchain is essential for navigating this evolving landscape.

7.7.1 Recap of Key Findings and Insights

Throughout this exploration of blockchain and DeFi in traditional banking, several key findings and insights have emerged. We have examined the advantages and challenges of implementing blockchain and DeFi, the disruptive potential they hold, and the future perspectives for their adoption. The following recap highlights the key takeaways:

Advantages of blockchain and DeFi: Blockchain and DeFi offer benefits such as disintermediation, financial inclusion, transparency, security, and improved liquidity and market efficiency.

Challenges and risks: Implementing blockchain and DeFi in traditional banking involves challenges related to regulatory compliance, security vulnerabilities, scalability, interoperability, governance, and user adoption. These challenges require collaboration, innovation, security measures, and user education for effective mitigation.

Disruptive potential: Blockchain and DeFi have the potential to disrupt traditional banking by removing intermediaries, extending financial services to the unbanked, enhancing transparency and security, and enabling new forms of asset tokenization and market liquidity.

7.7.2 Summary of the Disruptive Potential of Blockchain and DeFi in Traditional Banking

The disruptive potential of blockchain and DeFi in traditional banking falls in its ability to challenge and change over the established fiscal paradigm. Blockchain, as the underlying technology of cryptocurrencies, introduces decentralization and security features that question the necessity of intermediaries in financial transactions. Decentralized finance builds upon blockchain, reimagining financial services in a trustless, automated, and permissionless environment. This disruption is multifaceted.

Firstly, financial inclusion is expanded as DeFi permits everyone with an internet to get connected money related services, overcoming barriers present in traditional banking. The democratization of finance is particularly impactful for the unbanked and underbanked populations.

Secondly, automation and s-contracts within DeFi bring efficiency and speed to financial processes, reducing requirements for intermediaries and minimizing the jeopardy of human-produced mistakes. The programmability of smart contracts enables self-executing agreements, challenging traditional banking reliance on manual processes.

Decentralized lending and borrowing platforms in DeFi provide an alternative to traditional banking loans, fostering a peer-to-peer model that operates in the absence of central checkpoints. Additionally, DEXs offer alternatives for asset trading outside of traditional stock markets.

While the disruptive potential is evident, challenges like regulatory uncertainties and security concerns persist. However, the ongoing integration of blockchain and DeFi into mainstream financial institutions, the development of scalable solutions, and the maturation of regulatory frameworks are likely future trends. Furthermore, the evolution of decentralized identity solutions and the upcoming DAOs present new avenues for transformation.

Recommendations for the future include fostering the collaboration between blockchain and traditional finance, engaging with regulators to establish clear frameworks, and prioritizing user education and security measures. The future of blockchain and DeFi promises to reshape the global financial system, emphasizing inclusivity, efficiency, and security. The successful navigation of this evolving landscape requires adaptability, foresight, and a commitment to responsible adoption.

7.7.3 Final Remarks for the Future of Banking with Non-Centralized Finance

The future for banking with non-centralized finance holds immense potential for innovation, efficiency, and inclusion. As blockchain and DeFi continue to mature, the following considerations become crucial:

Collaboration and regulation: Collaboration among the industry, regulators, and policymakers is essential to establish clear regulatory frameworks that foster innovation while ensuring consumer protection.

Technical advancements: Continued technical advancements addressing scalability, interoperability, privacy, and security may contribute to a broader acceptance of blockchain and DeFi in banking.

User skill enhancement and experience: Prioritizing user education, creating user-friendly interfaces, and simplifying onboarding processes are vital for widespread adoption and optimal user experiences.

Ongoing evaluation and adaptation: The landscape of blockchain and DeFi is continuously evolving. Banks must regularly evaluate and adapt their strategies to leverage emerging technologies and seize new opportunities.

In conclusion, the disruptive potential of blockchain and DeFi in traditional banking is poised to revolutionize the industry. By embracing the advantages, addressing the challenges, and adapting to the changing landscape, banks can use their transformative power for blockchain and DeFi to generate more efficient, inclusive, and customer-centric financial systems.

References

1. Abdulhakeem, S.A. and Hu, Q., Powered by Blockchain Technology, DeFi (Decentralized Finance) Strives to Increase Financial Inclusion of the Unbanked by Reshaping the World Financial System. *Mod. Econ.*, 12, 01, 1–16, 2021, doi: 10.4236/me.2021.121001.
2. Ahluwalia, S., Mahto, R.V., Guerrero, M., Blockchain technology and startup financing: A transaction cost economics perspective. *Technol. Forecast. Soc. Change*, 151, 119854, Feb. 2020, doi: 10.1016/j.techfore.2019.119854.
3. Ali, S. and Rangone, A., The Role of Decentralized Finance in Emerging Financial Services. *Economia Aziend. Online*, 14, 4, 863–885, 2023, doi: DOI: http://dx.doi.org/10.13132/2038-5498/14.4.863-885.
4. Anoop, V.S. and Goldston, J., Decentralized finance to hybrid finance through blockchain: a case-study of acala and current. *J. Banking Financ. Technol.*, 6, 1, 109–115, Apr. 2022, doi: 10.1007/s42786-022-00041-0.
5. B.R. and Aithal, P.S., RBI Distributed Ledger Technology and Blockchain-A Future of Decentralized India. *Int. J. Manag. Technol. Soc. Sci.*, 5, 1, 227–237, May 2020, doi: 10.47992/ijmts.2581.6012.0091.
6. Cai, C.W., Disruption of financial intermediation by FinTech: a review on crowdfunding and blockchain. *Account. Financ.*, 58, 4, 965–992, Sep. 2018, doi: 10.1111/acfi.12405.
7. Chen, Y. and Bellavitis, C., Blockchain disruption and decentralized finance: The rise of decentralized business models. *J. Bus. Ventur. Insights*, 13, e00151, Jun. 2020, doi: 10.1016/j.jbvi.2019.e00151.
8. De Meijer, C.R.W., DeFi and banks: Is this the end of traditional banking? *J. Sec. Oper. Custody*, 14, 3, 231, Aug. 2022, doi: 10.69554/hqix9853.
9. Friesendorf, C. and Blütener, A., Decentralized Finance: How dApps Disrupt Banking, in: *Decentralized Finance (DeFi)*, pp. 1–9, 2023.
10. Guo, Y. and Liang, C., Blockchain application and outlook in the banking industry. *Financ. Innov.*, 2, 1, 24, Dec. 2016, doi: 10.1186/s40854-016-0034-9.
11. Kumar, B., Sharma, V., Vashishth, T.K., Panwar, R., Sharma, K.K., Chaudhary, S., Exploring the Transformative Power of Internet of Things (IoT) Technologies in the Age of Industry 4.0, in: *Advanced IoT Technologies and Applications in the Industry 4.0 Digital Economy*, pp. 42–59, Jan. 2024.
12. Marecki, K. and Wójcik-Czerniawska, A., Defi (decentralized finance) will lead to a revolution in the world of financial services. *Econ. Bus. J.*, 15, 1, 284–290, 2021.
13. Mehta, K. and Sharma, R., Contrarian and momentum investment strategies: Evidence from Indian stock market. *Int. J. Appl. Bus. Econ. Res.*, 15, 2, 87–98, 2017.
14. Mehta, K. and Sharma, R., Unraveling Quantum Complexity, in: *Deep Learning Tools for Predicting Stock Market Movements*, pp. 39–60, Apr. 2024.
15. Mehta, K., Sharma, R., Vyas, V., A quantile regression approach to study the impact of aluminium prices on manufacturing sector of India during

COVID era. *Mater. Today: Proc.*, 65, 3506–3511, 2022, doi: 10.1016/j.matpr.2022.06.087.
16. Mehta, K., Sharma, R., Vyas, V., Kuckreja, J.S., Exit strategy decision by venture capital firms in India using fuzzy AHP. *J. Entrep. Emerg. Econ.*, 14, 4, 643–669, Jul. 2021, doi: 10.1108/jeee-05-2020-0146.
17. Nowiński, W. and Kozma, M., How Can Blockchain Technology Disrupt the Existing Business Models? *Entrep. Bus. Econ. Rev.*, 5, 3, 173–188, 2017, doi: 10.15678/eber.2017.050309.
18. Ozcan, R., Decentralized Finance, in: *Financial Ecosystem and Strategy in the Digital Era*, pp. 57–75, 2021.
19. Pakenaite, S. and Taujanskaite, K., Investigation of the Blockchain's Influence on Traditional Banking: Challenges and Opportunities. *Eur. Sci. J. ESJ*, 15, 10, 1, Apr. 2019, doi: 10.19044/esj.2019.v15n10p1.
20. Patel, R., Migliavacca, M., Oriani, M.E., Blockchain in banking and finance: A bibliometric review. *Res. Int. Bus. Finance*, 62, 101718, Dec. 2022, doi: 10.1016/j.ribaf.2022.101718.
21. Popescu, A.D., Transitions and concepts within decentralized finance (Defi) Space. *Research Terminals in the social sciences*, 2020.
22. Ross, E.S., Nobody puts blockchain in a corner: The disruptive role of blockchain technology in the financial services industry and current regulatory issues. *Catholic Univ. J. Law Technol.*, 25, 2, 7, 2017, https://scholarship.law.edu/jlt/vol25/iss2/7.
23. Schueffel, P., DeFi: Decentralized Finance - An Introduction and Overview. *J. Innov. Manage.*, 9, 3, I–XI, Nov. 2021, doi: 10.24840/2183-0606_009.003_0001.
24. Sharma, R. and Mehta, K., Credit risk and bank specific factors: an empirical study using panel GMM. *Int. J. Econ. Bus. Res.*, 27, 2, 294–309, 2024, doi: 10.1504/ijebr.2024.136496.
25. Sharma, R. and Mehta, K. (Eds.), *Deep Learning Tools for Predicting Stock Market Movements*, Wiley, Apr. 2024.

26. Sharma, R., Mehta, K., Chugh, A., Using analytic hierarchy process to determine forex risk hedging strategies of SMEs, in: *Applied Data Science and Smart Systems*, vol. 2916, p. 120008, 2023.
27. Sharma, R., Mehta, K., Rana, R., Cryptocurrency Adoption Behaviour of Millennial Investors in India, in: *Perspectives on Blockchain Technology and Responsible Investing*, pp. 135–158, Jun. 2023.
28. Tumasjan, A., The Promise and Prospects of Blockchain-Based Decentralized Business Models, in: *Knowledge and Digital Technology*, pp. 203–224, 2024.
29. Vashishth, T.K. and Chaudhary, S., Privacy and Confidentiality in Permissioned Blockchain Networks: Evaluating Security Models. *Future Trends in Business: Knowledge, Skills, Sustainability, Innovation and Technology*, 2023.
30. Vashishth, T.K., Kumar, B., Alam, M.S., Sharma, V., Chaudhary, S., The Impact of Artificial Intelligence on the Future of Computing: A Comparative Study, in: *Applications of Block Chain technology and Artificial Intelligence*, pp. 1–17, 2024.
31. Vashishth, T.K., Sharma, V., Kumar, B., Chaudhary, S., Panwar, R., Sharma, K.K., Guarding Finances: The Role of Image Processing in Unmasking Counterfeit Currency. *2024 2nd International Conference on Advancement in Computation Computer Technologies (InCACCT)*, May 2024, pp. 668–671, doi: 10.1109/incacct61598.2024.10551141.
32. Kumar Vashishth, T., Sharma, V., Kumar, B., Krishan Sharma, K., Cloud-Based Data Management for Behavior Analytics in Business and Finance Sectors, in: *Data-Driven Modelling and Predictive Analytics in Business and Finance*, pp. 133–155, May 2024.
33. Vyas, V., Mehta, K., Sharma, R., Investigating socially responsible investing behaviour of Indian investors using structural equation modelling. *J. Sustain. Finance Invest.*, 12, 2, 570–592, Jul. 2020, doi: 10.1080/20430795.2020.1790958.
34. Sharma, R., Vyas, V., Mehta, K., Are bitcoin prices isolated or co-integrated. *Int. J. Bus. Globalisation*, 35, 1/2, 5–19, 2023, doi: 10.1504/ijbg.2023.10059854.
35. Zetzsche, D.A., Arner, D.W., Buckley, R.P., Decentralized Finance. *J. Financ. Regul.*, 6, 2, 172–203, Sep. 2020, doi: 10.1093/jfr/fjaa010.

8

Kinship of Decentralized Finance (DeFi) and Blockchain: Empowering Safe-Haven Assets

Chitra Devi Nagarajan* **and Jenifer Rajkumar**

VIT Business School, Vellore Institute of Technology, Chennai, India

Abstract
Integrating blockchain technology with decentralized finance (DeFi) [1] has ignited a remarkable and profound revolution in the global financial landscape. This paper embarks on a journey into the intricate and interconnected relationship between DeFi and blockchain, focusing toward the captivating concept of DeFi safe-haven assets that flourish within the vast and intricate financial ecosystem. Within this scholarly study, a comprehensive and in-depth analysis is conducted on the diverse and multifaceted categories of DeFi assets, which have been meticulously identified as coveted safe havens. Furthermore, this research endeavor conscientiously evaluates and scrutinizes obstacles that investors inevitably encounter when engaging in the alluring realm of investing in DeFi assets and unraveling the boundless potential of blockchain solutions.

***Keywords*:** Decentralized finance, blockchain technology solutions, safe-haven assets

8.1 Introduction

Safe-haven assets are recognized for their ability to appreciate during economic upheavals. Established assets like gold (Baur and Lucey, 2010; Baur and McDermott, 2010) [2, 3], Bitcoin (Bouri *et al.*, 2017 [8]; Urquhart and Zhang, 2019 [54]), and foreign exchange currencies (referred to as Forex) (Grisse and Nitschka, 2015) [23] have gained prominence as secure

**Corresponding author*: chitradevi.n@vit.ac.in

Renuka Sharma, Kiran Mehta, Vishal Vyas and Vinod Kumar Shukla (eds.) Decentralized Finance and Blockchain: A Game Changing Duo, (175–192)

investment options due to their propensity to retain or increase in value during periods of financial instability. A crucial criterion for identifying safe-haven assets is their ability to exhibit either no correlation or negative correlation with other assets or portfolios amid economic turmoil (Baur and Lucey, 2010 [2]; Bouri *et al.*, 2020 [9]). Recently, decentralized finance (DeFi) [1] fundamentally transformed the process of financial intermediation, allowing it to function in innovative decentralized manners that prevent any individual entity from possessing excessive power or monopolizing the system (Grassi *et al.*, 2021) [22]. During periods of economic turmoil, especially the COVID-19 pandemic, DeFi investment has gained significance in emphasizing safe-haven characteristics (Piñeiro–Chousa *et al.*, 2023 [39]). It has been tested and proven that DeFi assets are safe-haven assets within strategic commodity markets such as crude oil and gold (Cevik *et al.*, 2022 [12]). During the crisis periods, DeFi has emerged, showcasing its resilience and potential to provide stability and security in uncertain financial landscapes.

A concise term denoting the concept of decentralized finance, DeFi exemplifies a rapidly growing digital ecosystem in which individuals are empowered to engage in transactions and exchange financial assets without relying on traditional financial institutions such as banks, brokerages, or exchanges. The progression of digital enterprises highlights the emergence of DeFi-based technologies, including GameFi, SciFi, and SocialFi, as foundational components for future economic activities, in conjunction with the expansion of employment opportunities and businesses based on the Metaverse (Far *et al.*, 2023 [19]). Decentralized financial markets exert influence on asset valuation, intersecting with the principles of behavioral finance (BeFi), and prompting a more profound investigation into how DeFi protocols can be harnessed for innovation and the development of novel financial products (Bennett *et al.*, 2023 [5]; Shah *et al.*, 2023 [45]). The extraordinary expansion of DeFi is credited to a vast array of fiscal offerings that encompass the domains of loans, debt acquisition, instantaneous transactions, cyber pockets, and financial instruments between individuals, all while harnessing the power of blockchain technology, without any reliance on a central governing body (Gubareva, 2021 [24]; Schär, 2021 [44]; Yousaf and Yarovaya, 2022 [60]).

The financial environment is exposed to various types of risks (Sharma and Mehta, 2024 [47], 2024 [46]; Sharma *et al.*, 2023 [49]; Mehta *et al.*, 2022 [34]). During economic crises and the COVID-19 pandemic, when investors sought alternative assets to diversify their portfolios beyond Bitcoin, oil, gold, and stocks, DeFi assets emerged as a secure sanctuary for their investments (Chopra *et al.*, 2024 [15]). Decentralized finance serves as a sanctuary, akin to the precious metal of gold, as its influence on DeFi is undeniable, while the Volatility Index (VIX) holds an opposing effect on DeFi. Decentralized finance assumes the role of a secure refuge and a safeguard against the unpredictable nature of the stock market (Piñeiro-Chousa *et al.*, 2021 [37]). The realm of DeFi and cryptocurrency asset markets manifests robust spillovers both within and between markets, whereas the stock market and the safe-haven markets exhibit feeble interconnectedness. Therefore, DeFi becomes a safe haven and a hedge against stock market volatility. Researchers have examined cryptocurrency behavior as there is an increased interest from the investors in this digital financial instrument (Vyas *et al.*, 2023 [56]; Sharma *et al.*, 2023 [48]); Piñeiro-Chousa *et al.*, 2021 [37]). Decentralized finance is built upon cryptography, blockchain technology, and smart contracts. However, DeFi applications run on smart contracts that allow sophisticated functionality to a blockchain beyond simple transactions. For example, the application has created a way for two anonymous parties mutually involved in the loan process to proceed without the intermediation of banks (Catchlove, 2017 [11]; Chen and Bellavitis, 2019 [13]; Schär, 2021 [44]; Wang *et al.*, 2021 [57]). However, DeFi has introduced risks due to the occurrence of cyber-attacks on the DeFi-specific service known as flash loans (Gudgeon *et al.*, 2020 [25]; Qin *et al.*, 2021 [41]). Decentralized finance platforms are susceptible to hacking and vulnerabilities in smart contracts (Qin *et al.*, 2021 [41]). Similarly, the stablecoins are pegged to cryptocurrency, and flat money is backed by the US dollar. The most popular stablecoin is DAI, which is equal to the US dollar. It uses a stabilization mechanism against volatility. When collateral cryptocurrency devaluates about the US dollar, the borrower must increase the amount of collateral to keep the ratio above the liquidation, and it attracts a penalty fee (Qin *et al.*, 2021 [41]). Additionally, the scalability and security issues faced by DeFi assets, which were initially perceived as safe-haven assets, hinder the maintenance of decentralization (Li *et al.*, 2022 [28]). Hence, the incorporation of a privacy-preserving system for smart contracts becomes an imperative requirement in the realm of DeFi, utilizing the blockchain model of cryptography (Androulaki *et al.*, 2013) [64]. Furthermore, transparency plays a pivotal role in ensuring trust among users in DeFi. The transparent and auditable nature of blockchain technology allows for the recording of all transactions and activities on public ledgers within DeFi platforms. This enables users to verify real-time transactions, thus enhancing transparency and accountability within the ecosystem. The networking environment of DeFi built on blockchain technology offers financial services and products that are transparent, reliable, and decentralized (Benedetti and Labbé, 2022 [4]). This research aims to assess DeFi as a safe-haven assets and its potential obstacles and identify strategies for overcoming them through the strategic implementation of blockchain technology.

8.2 DeFi as Safe-Haven Assets

8.2.1 DeFi Crypto Tokens

Decentralized finance tokens, more commonly known as DeFi tokens, are decentralized applications that run on blockchains with smart contracts. They aim to transform banks, exchanges, and other traditional financial systems using cryptocurrencies, reducing or eliminating the need for third parties (Gogol *et al.*, 2024 [20]). Decentralized finance crypto tokens are a new form of financial instruments that utilize blockchain technology and smart contracts. They aim to create a decentralized financial system by extending the concept of digital currencies. Decentralized finance tokens, such as those used in borrowing, lending, and providing liquidity, have monetary value and can be traded on specialized decentralized exchanges (DEXs). The efficiency of the DeFi market varies over time, with short periods of inefficiency and predictability in token prices each year (Zhang *et al.*, 2023 [63]). The returns of DeFi tokens are influenced by factors such as investor attention, exposure to the cryptocurrency market, and network effects (Şoiman *et al.*, 2022 [51]). Additionally, DeFi tokens are distinct from nonfungible tokens and show limited correlation with major cryptocurrencies like Bitcoin and Ethereum, making them potentially attractive for portfolio diversification. As of January 2022, the total value of tokens deposited on DeFi-focused blockchains has risen by approximately 40% since November, reaching about $60 billion. This surge represents and attracts significant interest and investment as it offers various financial services and products without traditional intermediaries. These tokens are typically built on blockchain networks such as Ethereum and are used to facilitate various financial activities within the DeFi ecosystem. Decentralized financial assets exhibit a strong correlation with currency markets (Yousaf and Yarovaya, 2022 [60]). Conversely, it is not correlated with conventional cryptocurrencies (Corbet *et al.*, 2023 [16]). This unique characteristic of DeFi assets presents a promising opportunity for digital investors.

8.2.2 Stablecoins

Decentralized finance stablecoins are digital assets that are designed to mitigate the risks associated with price fluctuations in cross-chain transactions. These stablecoins are pegged to nonvolatile assets, such as the US dollar, and aim to facilitate cross-chain commerce without the need for trusted intermediaries or complex protocols (Daniel, *et al.*, 2023 [17]). Their purpose is crucial in reducing trading expenses, and they operate solely on the blockchain, ensuring transparency and efficiency in transactions. The stability of stablecoins is closely linked to the growth of cryptocurrencies (Lyons and Viswanath–Natraj, 2020 [30]).

These coins are exchanged for a predetermined value against assets held by the issuer, often maintaining a 1:1 ratio with secure assets (Gorton and Zhang, 2023 [21]). The two major stablecoins, Tether (USDT) and USD Coin (USDC), are backed by assets in this manner. Tether, an early participant in the stablecoin market, currently holds a market capitalization of $62 billion as of July 2021, with USD Coin following closely behind at a market capitalization of $26.8 billion. These stablecoins are essential components of the DeFi ecosystem, facilitating seamless transactions and providing stability amid the volatile cryptocurrency landscape. Decentralized finance stablecoins serve as safe-haven assets within the cryptocurrency realm due to their stability and pegging to low-volatility assets like the US dollar. Unlike volatile cryptocurrencies, stablecoins offer investors and users a reliable store of value during market turbulence.

8.2.3 Synthetic Assets

Decentralized finance synthetic assets represent digital assets that derive their value from underlying assets or indexes without direct ownership of the underlying assets. These assets are created through smart contracts and protocols on DeFi platforms, enabling users to gain exposure to a wide range of assets, including traditional stocks, commodities, and currencies, within the blockchain ecosystem. By leveraging synthetic assets, users can access markets that may be otherwise inaccessible due to regulatory constraints or geographical limitations. Furthermore, synthetic assets enable investors to hedge against risks, diversify their portfolios, and participate in decentralized financial activities such as trading, lending, and derivatives markets. However, the use of synthetic assets also comes with risks, including smart contract vulnerabilities and potential manipulation. As DeFi continues to evolve, synthetic assets play a significant role in expanding the accessibility and versatility of DeFi, offering users innovative ways to engage with global financial markets.

Synthetic assets within the realm of DeFi obtain their value from the assets that underlie them or from derivatives that are directly associated with said assets. These assets come into existence through the utilization of intelligent contracts and protocols on platforms dedicated to DeFi, thereby providing investors with the opportunity to engage with stocks, commodities, and currencies within the blockchain ecosystem. They signify a notable progression in the realm of conventional derivative products, as they establish cryptocurrency-based counterparts that steadfastly monitor the oscillations of the original asset within the blockchain. Investing in synthetic asset derivatives allows for the formation of hybrid portfolios that function as a hedge against the volatility of cryptocurrencies by incorporating TradeFi options. Synthetic assets possess numerous advantages, such as being traded in secure, unchangeable, and decentralized environments on the blockchain. In contrast, conventional derivatives typically occur through regulated stock exchanges. This distinction highlights the innovative nature of synthetic assets within DeFi, offering investors alternative avenues to effectively manage risk and diversify their portfolios in the rapidly evolving digital asset landscape.

While synthetic assets offer certain advantages, such as accessibility and programmability within DeFi platforms, they also come with risks. These risks include smart contract vulnerabilities, liquidity issues, and the potential for tracking errors between the synthetic asset and its underlying reference. Investors should be cautious when considering synthetic assets as safe-haven assets and carefully assess their risk tolerance, investment goals, and the specific characteristics of the synthetic assets.

8.2.4 Wrapped Assets

The concept of DeFi-wrapped assets has gained attention because it allows integrating traditional financial assets into the DeFi space, expanding the range of financial services and opportunities. The original asset is 'wrapped' into a digital vault, and a newly minted token is created to transact on other platforms. Wrapped tokens allow non-native assets to be used on any blockchain, build bridges between networks and implement interoperability in the cryptocurrency space. They can represent anything from arts and collectibles, commodities, crypto assets, equity, and stocks to fiat currencies and real estate. Since wrapped tokens are pegged to another asset, they necessarily need to be regarded and managed by a custodian entity that will wrap and unwrap the asset. The DeFi-wrapped assets, also known as wrapped tokens, are digital representations of assets from other blockchains, which have been tokenized and made compatible with DeFi platforms, typically on the Ethereum blockchain. Examples of wrapped assets include Wrapped Bitcoin, Wrapped Ethereum, and Wrapped Litecoin. These tokens enable users to bring liquidity and utility from other blockchain networks into the Ethereum DeFi ecosystem.

Furthermore, (Yousaf *et al.*, 2022) [61] assert that DeFi assets are completely disassociated from traditional asset classes. This divergence from conventional assets becomes even more evident when considering the potential of DeFi assets to serve as safe-haven assets against stock market volatility (Piñeiro–Chousa *et al.*, 2022 [38] (Bouri *et al.*, 2019) [7]). Decentralized financial assets can be utilized as a reliable refuge for investors seeking shelter from the unpredictable fluctuations in the stock market. Additionally, DeFi assets can also serve as safe-haven assets in the crude oil and gold markets (Cevik *et al.*, 2022 [12]). These findings further support the notion that DeFi assets possess the potential to provide stability and security in various investment scenarios. However, DeFi investors are facing many challenges in considering DeFi assets as safe-haven assets.

8.3 Challenges of DeFi as Safe-Haven Assets and Blockchain Solutions

8.3.1 Transparency

The primary challenge that currently confronts DeFi platforms is rooted in the reality that decentralized applications are not bound by any obligation to fulfill customer requirements. One such requirement, for instance, is the imperative for these platforms to adhere to the meticulous Know Your Customer (KYC) processes, which are specifically designed to ensure the verification and authentication of customer information. Consequently, it becomes necessary for all parties involved in transactions on these platforms to diligently submit their identification documentation before engaging in investment activities or initiating the process of opening new accounts. In addition to this, it is also incumbent upon users to retain a certain amount of their crypto assets in a private wallet, as this is a prerequisite for interacting with decentralized applications. This requirement effectively facilitates anonymous transactions within the DeFi platform, thereby potentially enabling the occurrence of illicit activities. Furthermore, it is important to note that transparency issues further exacerbate the concerns of consumers. The overall safety and security of the protocol employed by such platforms are intrinsically tied to the reliability of the underlying smart contracts that govern their operations. It is crucial to acknowledge the fact that these smart contracts serve as the foundation upon which the entire system is built. Therefore, any flaws or vulnerabilities in these contracts would directly compromise the safety and security of the DeFi platform, thereby heightening consumer apprehensions (Borisov, 2022 [6]).

Blockchain is decentralized, which means any network member can verify data recorded into the blockchain. Another important thing relates to transparency, as it has a counterpart in possible privacy problems. If everything is recorded on public ledgers, there is anonymity but not necessarily privacy. All of this bears on the future of any project based on cryptocurrencies as it is always under the threat of government regulations, for example, by banning or constraining their use, similar to what happened to Initial Coin Offerings (ICOs) (Piñeiro-Chousa *et al.*, 2022) [38]. This can increase the confidence and satisfaction of the safe-haven asset users who want to access or monitor their assets or services on the blockchain. Decentralized insurance acts as a safety net for the DeFi ecosystem. From wallet insurance to smart contract insurance, the comfort of knowing that your assets are protected in the case of a bug or a hack creates peace of mind for crypto investors (Popescu, 2020 [40]).

8.3.2 Fraud

Decentralized finance-related crimes can generally be categorized into two types: external agent hacks of DeFi protocols and insider rug pulls. In 2021, the majority of DeFi network attacks were carried out by external agents. These attacks resulted in a staggering $361 million in DeFi-related losses, accounting for 76% of all such crimes that occurred during that time (Wronka, 2023 [59]). The remaining 24% of the crimes were attributed to insider activities, which led to losses amounting to over $113 million on an annual basis. It is important to note that the nature of blockchain transactions is irreversible, meaning that fraudulent or fake transactions cannot be undone. This highlights the significant reliance that DeFi platforms place on the integrity of underlying blockchain protocols and smart contracts. Any programming flaws in these protocols and contracts can potentially result in hacks and substantial losses for the users (Wronka, 2023 [59]). Moreover, the presence of Bitcoin-controlled addresses associated with darknet markets, ransomware, hackers, and fraudsters further contributes to the security concerns surrounding DeFi platforms.

In the context of blockchain technology, security refers to the measures taken to safeguard the system from malicious attacks or technical failures that could compromise its integrity or availability. This encompasses the security of underlying codes, cryptographic algorithms, and consensus mechanisms. It is crucial to address security as a major concern and challenge in blockchain technology, as it involves complex trade-offs between decentralization, performance, and usability. Failure to adequately address security concerns can potentially expose safe-haven assets or services on the blockchain to various threats, such as hacking, bugs, or human errors (Li *et al.*, 2021 [27]). Therefore, DeFi platforms must prioritize the implementation of robust security measures to ensure the protection of user assets and the overall integrity of the system with the help of blockchain technology.

8.3.3 Volatility

Price volatility in many DeFi systems highlights the crucial significance of oracles, which play a pivotal role in introducing accurate and reliable data from external sources into smart contracts. These oracles serve as the guardians of precision, ensuring that the information integrated into DeFi platforms is trustworthy and dependable, thereby safeguarding the integrity of the entire system (Liu *et al.*, 2020 [29]). Several techniques can be used to investigate the price movement of various financial instruments (Mehta and Sharma, 2024 [33]; Vyas *et al.*, 2020 [55]; Mehta *et al.*, 2022 [35]). In light of the current emphasis on implied volatility, it becomes crucial to delve deeper into the intricate relationship between traditional stock volatility and the volatility inherent in the realm of DeFi (Piñeiro-Chousa, 2022 [38]). Stablecoins, a category of digital assets meticulously crafted to maintain a stable value pegged to traditional fiat currencies, serve as invaluable safe havens within the volatile realm of the cryptocurrency market. They offer a sanctuary from the erratic fluctuations witnessed in numerous cryptocurrencies, providing investors with a sense of security and stability that is often elusive in the fast-paced world of digital assets. As the absence of central bank digital currencies becomes increasingly apparent, the demand for stablecoins, particularly those intricately woven into the fabric of DeFi applications through the utilization of smart contracts, has skyrocketed.

These private stablecoins native to cryptocurrency protocols have emerged as a beacon of reliability, assuring users that their value remains unaffected by the turbulent tides of the crypto market (Makarov and Schoar, 2022 [31]). It is worth noting that the presence of high leverage in the crypto market exacerbates the already rampant volatility, leading to cascading waves. Investors always look for various investment strategies to earn abnormal returns (Mehta and Sharma, 2017 [32]). Nevertheless, it is important to acknowledge that some stablecoins deviate from this convention and are instead linked to alternative cryptocurrencies or even tangible commodities like silver or gold. It is within this backdrop that stablecoins can be classified into three primary types, each distinguished by their unique characteristics and underlying mechanisms. The first category encompasses centralized or fiat-backed stablecoins, which are issued and controlled by private entities. Ideally, these stablecoins are backed on a one-to-one ratio, meaning that for every stablecoin in circulation, an equivalent amount of fiat currency is held in reserve within a secure bank account.

Volatility in the the DeFi realm is effectively controlled and regulated through the ingenious utilization of blockchain technology. This is achieved using liquidity pools, automated market makers (AMMs), stablecoins, smart contract governance, hedging instruments, volatility indexes, and oracles. These sophisticated mechanisms collectively contribute to the stabilization of asset values, the seamless facilitation of trading activities, and the overall enablement of risk management within the decentralized financial ecosystems. It is truly awe-inspiring to witness how self-executing smart contracts and decentralized governance empower participants to actively exert their influence over the protocols, thereby allowing them to dynamically adapt to the ever-fluctuating market conditions. By harnessing the immense power of blockchain's inherent transparency and decentralized nature, DeFi platforms aspire to successfully mitigate the inherent volatility risks that underlie this domain, while simultaneously empowering users with an unprecedented level of control over their financial undertakings. However, it is crucial to acknowledge the perpetual evolution and the inherent risks that inherently exist within the DeFi landscape, as this acknowledgement serves as a testament to the continuously evolving nature of this nascent ecosystem.

8.3.4 Liquidity

Liquidity providers are people who supply funds to DeFi protocols that facilitate the exchange of assets, such as DEXs or lending platforms. They may seek a safe haven in DeFi because they can earn fees, support the network, or access new markets. The dynamics of transaction fees in Bitcoin and their implications from mining and markets are in DEXs (Easley *et al.*, 2019 [18]). Liquidity providers or users may also seek safe-haven assets that can help them enhance their liquidity, avoid slippage, or mitigate impermanent loss, such as Uniswap, Balancer, or Aave. Any decentralized finance project has liquidity mining at its core. This is because liquidity pools are crucial parts of the DeFi ecosystem. Liquidity pools are locked in a smart contract and used to facilitate trades between assets. Instead of traditional buyer and seller markets, many DeFi platforms use AMMs, which use liquidity pools to allow digital assets to be exchanged.

Blockchain technology addresses the issue of liquidity risk in DeFi assets by utilizing liquidity pools, AMMs such as Uniswap, stablecoins, opportunities for arbitrage, and decentralized governance. These innovative mechanisms ensure a consistent provision of liquidity and maintain price stability, effectively minimizing the possibility of sudden liquidity shortages. By enabling transparent and instantaneous transactions, blockchain facilitates the efficient determination of prices and encourages arbitrage, which in turn helps maintain a balanced liquidity distribution across DEXs. The implementation of decentralized governance empowers the community to enact measures that promote liquidity enhancement and risk mitigation, ultimately fostering a DeFi ecosystem that is more robust and stable. Nevertheless, it is important to acknowledge that liquidity risk remains a concern, particularly during periods of heightened market volatility or in less liquid markets within the DeFi space.

8.3.5 Accountability

Decentralized finance also raises accountability and enforcement issues around issues of both public and private ordering (Zetzsche *et al.*, 2020 [62]). A challenge for any blockchain project in this layer is the choice of jurisdiction or accountability over multiple jurisdictions (West, 2018 [58]) in combination with the product or service offered. The challenge is predominately that, in this early stage of the technology, laws and regulations toward products and services like ICOs can alter much in time (Salmon, 2018 [43]) and even in hindsight be enforced.

Blockchain technology nurtures responsibility in DeFi transactions by guaranteeing openness, unchangeability, and cryptographical validation. *Via* blockchain's lucid register, participants can monitor transactions in real-time, while the unalterable essence of blockchain ensures that documents remain untamable and provable. Cryptographic autographs and intelligent agreements further heighten responsibility by certifying transaction genuineness and automating rule enforcement without the requirement of intermediaries. These attributes empower users to place trust in the integrity of DeFi ecosystems, cultivating a more lucid and answerable financial milieu.

8.3.6 Regulations

As long as DeFi is subjected to new regulations (virtually daily), such as permitting banks to be cryptocurrency custodians, the market outlook for these institutions is murky (Borisov, 2022 [6]). Due to the global nature of crypto-asset transactions and, in particular, DeFi transactions, there is a strong need for a robust global regulatory framework for the prevention of financial crime such as money laundering and terrorism financing, international financial instability, and risks to investors globally (Salami, 2021 [42]). Decentralized finance requires careful regulatory attention. In situations where DeFi produces new forms of technological reliance, regulation must focus on the reconcentrated portion of the value chain to ensure effective oversight and risk control: in this framework, regulation is necessary to support decentralization (Salami, 2021), in the same way that regulation is at the core of securities markets and other financial services (Zetzsche *et al.*, 2020 [62]). Thereby potentially decentralizing both finance and its regulation in the ultimate expression of RegTech; not only 'embedded supervision' but in fact 'embedded regulation (Zetzsche *et al.*, 2020 [62]).

Blockchain technology mitigates regulatory risks by providing transparency, traceability, and automated mechanisms for compliance. Through its transparent ledger, regulators can gain real-time insights into transactions, thereby enabling effective oversight and monitoring of compliance. The unchangeable nature of blockchain ensures records are impervious to tampering, thus facilitating audits and investigations while simultaneously reducing the risk of fraud. Smart contracts that are embedded with regulatory requirements automate compliance, thus minimizing the potential for noncompliance and breaches of regulatory standards. Privacy features that have been enhanced safeguard sensitive information, and interoperability standards streamline transactions that occur across national borders, thereby fostering collaboration in the realm of regulation. By employing regulatory sandboxes and collaboration, regulators can explore the potential of blockchain technology within controlled environments, thus encouraging innovation while simultaneously maintaining regulatory oversight.

8.3.7 Trust

The DeFi ecosystem, which is rapidly expanding, operates on a unique model in which financial obligations are established within "smart contracts." These are computer codes stored on the blockchain. These contracts are enforced by a decentralized network of computers. An important aspect of this model is that participants no longer need to rely on trust among individuals, and individual identities become inconsequential. Instead, participants place their trust in computer codes and the decentralized network of the blockchain to ensure that the code's enforcement is upheld. This paradigm shift has significant implications as it enables financing and trade in situations where traditional methods were previously impractical. Advocates of DeFi often refer to this as "code is law," but is this principle applicable in practical scenarios? Can a financial system operate without the need for trust among individuals? Immunity is a crucial advantage of blockchain. It guarantees that data recorded on the blockchain cannot be altered. It serves as a secure mechanism for sharing information among parties that do not trust each other (Castonguay and Stein Smith, 2020 [10]). As a result, blockchain prevents any tampering with data within the network, thereby enhancing the credibility and reliability of the safe-haven assets or services stored on the blockchain (Sherimon *et al.*, 2022) [50]).

8.3.8 Inflexibility

The main impediment faced by emerging technologies such as blockchain is the scarcity of funds and the inflexibility in regulatory frameworks (Toufaily *et al.*, 2021 [53]). Although the immutability of public ledgers and smart contracts improves transparency and trust, it can also result in rigidity and inflexibility (Murray *et al.* 2021 [36]). Financial services that are decentralized and rely on blockchain technology frequently encounter inherent inflexibility, which obstructs the advancement of their products and their ability to adapt to evolving market dynamics (Tian *et al.*, 2010 [52]). This inflexibility poses challenges for experimentation and innovation in DeFi, as modifications to smart contracts and platforms necessitate broad consensus among stakeholders (Chen and Bellavitis, 2020 [14]). The governance structure of Ethereum and the concept of "governance through technical code" contribute to this inflexibility, potentially jeopardizing the security of the system (Lehdonvirta and Ali, 2016 [26]).

8.4 Conclusion

The fusion of DeFi and blockchain technology with safe-haven assets signifies an enthralling chapter in the continuous progression of finance. At its essence, this convergence denotes a transformative shift in how individuals and institutions perceive and engage with safe-haven assets. The emergence of blockchain has fortified the security and dependability of these assets, while DeFi has redefined their accessibility and usefulness. However, embarking on this extraordinary odyssey is not devoid of its perils. The intricate essence of DeFi protocols, intricately woven with the tapestry of smart contracts, lays bare the participants to potential vulnerabilities and financial losses. The ever-evolving realm of regulations raises profound inquiries regarding the enduring sustainability and authenticity of blockchain-infused DeFi assets. The inherent unpredictability that permeates the cryptocurrency realm remains an unwavering challenge for both astute investors and visionary asset issuers. Challenges in the realm of cryptocurrency present formidable obstacles, encompassing issues such as deceitful practices, wild fluctuations, usability concerns, uncertain regulatory frameworks, anxieties surrounding privacy, the establishment of trust in a decentralized manner, the inflexibility of existing systems, the absence of accountability, and the void in the digital domain (Chen and Bellavitis, 2020 [14]; Qin *et al.*, 2021 [41]).

Hence, it becomes imperative to directly confront and tackle these impediments head-on when embarking on any novel crypto venture, to establish a robust ecosystem capable of navigating the ever-evolving crypto landscape. The primary hurdles that emerge are the inflexibility of funding and regulations towards emerging technologies (Toufaily *et al.*, 2021 [53]). While the immutability of public ledgers and smart contracts bolsters transparency and trust, it also introduces rigidity (Murray *et al.*, 2019). Decentralized financial services, built on blockchain technology, often grapple with this inherent inflexibility, leading to challenges in product upgrades and adaptability (Tian *et al.*, 2010 [52]). Despite the potential for upgrades through distributed consensus, attaining broad stakeholder agreement for significant changes remains an arduous task (Chen and Bellavitis, 2020 [14]). The Ethereum governance structure's inflexibility and the "ruling *via* technical code" principle strain the system, potentially jeopardizing infrastructure security (Lehdonvirta and Ali, 2016 [26]).

As we draw this investigation to a close, one aspect emerges with great clarity: the undeniable potential for transformation offered by blockchain-linked, safe-haven assets. These assets provide a mechanism for the preservation of wealth, the diversification of portfolios, and the exploration of novel and stimulating avenues within financial markets. This symbiosis of technology and fiscal prudence is anticipated to remain a central focus of research, innovation, and industry advancement for the foreseeable future. In this ever-evolving panorama, various stakeholders – ranging from investors and developers to regulators and scholars – must collaborate harmoniously to harness the capabilities of DeFi and blockchain, all while skillfully navigating the attendant challenges. By exercising prudence and diligence, it becomes feasible to unlock the complete potential of these technologies, thereby fostering a more comprehensive, secure, and resilient financial ecosystem that benefits all individuals.

References

1. DeFi and the Future of Money, in: *Advances in web technologies and Engineering book series*, 2023, doi: 10.4018/978-1-6684-6658-2.ch004.
2. Baur, D.G. and Lucey, B.M., Is gold a hedge or a safe haven? An analysis of stocks, bonds and gold. *Financ. Rev.*, *45*, 2, 217–229, 2010.
3. Baur, D.G. and McDermott, T.K., Is gold a safe haven? International evidence. *J. Banking Finance*, *34*, 8, 1886–1898, 2010.
4. Benedetti, H. and Labbé, S., A Closer Look Into Decentralized Finance, in: *The Emerald Handbook on Cryptoassets: Investment Opportunities and Challenges*, pp. 327–340, Emerald Publishing Limited, 2023.
5. Bennett, D., Mekelburg, E., Williams, T.H., BeFi meets DeFi: A behavioral finance approach to decentralized finance asset pricing. *Res. Int. Bus. Finance*, *65*, 101939, 2023.
6. Borisov, S., Defi–potential, advantages and challenges. *Икономически изследвания*, 4, 33–54, 2022.
7. Bouri, E., Lau, C.K.M., Lucey, B., Roubaud, D., Trading volume and the predictability of return and volatility in the cryptocurrency market. *Finance Res. Lett.*, *29*, 340–346, 2019.
8. Bouri, E., Molnár, P., Azzi, G., Roubaud, D., Hagfors, L.I., On the hedge and safe haven properties of Bitcoin: Is it really more than a diversifier? *Finance Res. Lett.*, *20*, 192–198, 2017.
9. Bouri, E., Shahzad, S.J.H., Roubaud, D., Kristoufek, L., Lucey, B., Bitcoin, gold, and commodities as safe havens for stocks: New insight through wavelet analysis. *Q. Rev. Econ. Finance*, *77*, 156–164, 2020.
10. Castonguay, J.J. and Stein Smith, S., Digital assets and blockchain: hackable, fraudulent, or just misunderstood? *Account. Perspect.*, *19*, 4, 363–387, 2020.
11. Catchlove, P., Smart Contracts: A New Era of Contract Use, December 1, 2017. Available at SSRN: https://ssrn.com/abstract=3090226 or http://dx.doi.org/10.2139/ssrn.3090226.
12. Cevik, E.I., Gunay, S., Zafar, M.W., Destek, M.A., Bugan, M.F., Tuna, F., The impact of digital finance on the natural resource market: Evidence from DeFi, oil, and gold. *Resour. Policy*, *79*, 103081, 2022.
13. Chen, Y. and Bellavitis, C., Decentralized finance: Blockchain technology and the quest for an open financial system. Stevens Institute of Technology School of Business Research Paper, 2019.
14. Chen, Y. and Bellavitis, C., Blockchain disruption and decentralized finance: The rise of decentralized business models. *J. Bus. Ventur. Insights*, 13, e00151, 2020.
15. Chopra, M., Mehta, C., Lal, P., Srivastava, A., Does the big boss of coins—Bitcoin—protect a portfolio of new-generation cryptos? Evidence from memecoins, stablecoins, NFTs and DeFi. *China Finance Rev. Int.*, *14*, 3, 480–521, 2024.

16. Corbet, S., Goodell, J.W., Gunay, S., Kaskaloglu, K., Are DeFi tokens a separate asset class from conventional cryptocurrencies? *Ann. Oper. Res., 322*, 2, 609–630, 2023.
17. Reijsbergen, D., Hajek, B., Dinh, T.T.A., Keppo, J., Korth, H.F., Datta, A., CroCoDai: A stablecoin for cross-chain commerce. *Distributed Ledger Technol.: Res. Pract.*, 2024, https://doi.org/10.1145/3702247.
18. Easley, D., O'Hara, M., Basu, S., From mining to markets: The evolution of bitcoin transaction fees. *J. Financ. Econ., 134*, 1, 91–109, 2019.
19. Far, S.B., Rad, A.I., Asaar, M.R., Blockchain and its derived technologies shape the future generation of digital businesses: a focus on decentralized finance and the Metaverse. *Data Sci. Manage., 6*, 3, 183–197, 2023.
20. Gogol, K., Killer, C., Schlosser, M., Bocek, T., Stiller, B., Tessone, C., SoK: Decentralized Finance (DeFi)–Fundamentals, Taxonomy and Risks, 2024, *arXiv preprint arXiv:2404.11281*.
21. Gorton, G.B. and Zhang, J.Y., Taming wildcat stablecoins. *U. Chi. L. Rev., 90*, 909, 2023.
22. Grassi, L., Lanfranchi, D., Faes, A., Renga, F.M., Do we still need financial intermediation? The case of decentralized finance–DeFi. *Qual. Res. Account. Manage., 19*, 3, 323–347, 2022.
23. Grisse, C. and Nitschka, T., On financial risk and the safe haven characteristics of Swiss franc exchange rates. *J. Empirical Finance, 32*, 153–164, 2015.
24. Gubareva, M., Covid-19 and high-yield emerging market bonds: insights for liquidity risk management. *Risk Manage., 23*, 3, 193–212, 2021.
25. Gudgeon, L., Werner, S., Perez, D., Knottenbelt, W.J., Defi protocols for loanable funds: Interest rates, liquidity and market efficiency, in: *Proceedings of the 2nd ACM Conference on Advances in Financial Technologies*, 2020, October, pp. 92–112.
26. Lehdonvirta, V. and Ali, R., Governance and regulation. Distributed ledger technology: beyond blockchain, UK Government Office for Science, London, pp. 40–45, 2016.
27. Li, J., Baldimtsi, F., Brandao, J.P., Kugler, M., Hulays, R., Showers, E., Chang, J., Measuring illicit activity in defi: The case of ethereum, in: *Financial Cryptography and Data Security. FC 2021 International Workshops: CoDecFin, DeFi, VOTING, and WTSC, Virtual Event, March 5, 2021, Revised Selected Papers 25*, Springer Berlin Heidelberg, pp. 197–203, 2021.
28. Li, W., Bu, J., Li, X., Peng, H., Niu, Y., Zhang, Y., A survey of DeFi security: Challenges and opportunities. *J. King Saud Univ.-Comput. Inf. Sci., 34*, 10, 10378–10404, 2022.
29. Liu, B., Szalachowski, P., Zhou, J., A first look into defi oracles, in: *2021 IEEE International Conference on Decentralized Applications and Infrastructures (DAPPS)*, 2021, August, IEEE, pp. 39–48.
30. Lyons, R.K. and Viswanath-Natraj, G., What Keeps Stablecoins Stable? 2020.
31. Makarov, I. and Schoar, A., Cryptocurrencies and decentralized finance (DeFi). *Brook. Pap. Econ. Act., 2022*, 1, 141–215, 2022.

32. Mehta, K. and Sharma, R., Contrarian and momentum investment strategies: Evidence from indian stock market. *Int. J. Appl. Bus. Econ. Res.*, *15*, 9, 107–118, 2017.
33. Mehta, K. and Sharma, R., Unraveling Quantum Complexity: A Fuzzy AHP Approach to Understanding Software Industry Challenges, in: *Deep Learning Tools for Predicting Stock Market Movements*, pp. 39–60, 2024.
34. Mehta, K., Sharma, R., Vyas, V., A quantile regression approach to study the impact of aluminium prices on manufacturing sector of India during COVID era. *Mater. Today: Proc.*, *65*, 3506–3511, 2022.
35. Mehta, K., Sharma, R., Vyas, V., Kuckreja, J.S., Exit strategy decision by venture capital firms in India using fuzzy AHP. *J. Entrep. Emerg. Econ.*, *14*, 4, 643–669, 2022.
36. Murray, A., Kuban, S., Josefy, M., Anderson, J., Contracting in the smart era: The implications of blockchain and decentralized autonomous organizations for contracting and corporate governance. *Acad. Manag. Perspect.*, *35*, 4, 622–641, 2021.
37. Piñeiro-Chousa, J., López-Cabarcos, M.A., Caby, J., Šević, A., The influence of investor sentiment on the green bond market. *Technol. Forecast. Soc. Change*, *162*, 120351, 2021.
38. Piñeiro-Chousa, J., López-Cabarcos, M.A., Sevic, A., González-López, I., A preliminary assessment of the performance of DeFi cryptocurrencies in relation to other financial assets, volatility, and user-generated content. *Technol. Forecast. Soc. Change*, *181*, 121740, 2022.
39. Piñeiro-Chousa, J., Šević, A., González-López, I., Impact of social metrics in decentralized finance. *J. Bus. Res.*, *158*, 113673, 2023.
40. Popescu, A.D., Decentralized finance (defi)–the lego of finance. *Soc. Sci. Educ. Res. Rev.*, *7*, 1, 321–349, 2020.
41. Qin, K., Zhou, L., Livshits, B., Gervais, A., Attacking the defi ecosystem with flash loans for fun and profit, in: *International conference on financial cryptography and data security*, Springer, Berlin, Heidelberg, pp. 3–32, 2021.
42. Salami, I., Challenges and approaches to regulating decentralized finance. 425–429, 2021.
43. Salmon, J., Building the ecosystem. *Int'l. Fin. L. Rev.*, *37*, 39, 2018.
44. Schär, F., Decentralized finance: On blockchain-and smart contract-based financial markets, FRB of St. Louis Review, 2021.
45. Shah, K., Lathiya, D., Lukhi, N., Parmar, K., Sanghvi, H., A systematic review of decentralized finance protocols. *Int. J. Intell. Netw.*, 4, 171–181, 2023.
46. Sharma, R. and Mehta, K., Credit risk and bank specific factors: an empirical study using panel GMM. *Int. J. Econ. Bus. Res.*, *27*, 2, 294–309, 2024.
47. Sharma, R. and Mehta, K. (Eds.), *Deep Learning Tools for Predicting Stock Market Movements*, John Wiley & Sons, 2024.
48. Sharma, R., Mehta, K., Chugh, A., Using analytic hierarchy process to determine forex risk hedging strategies of SMEs. *AIP Conf. Proc.*, AIP Publishing, 2916, 1, 2023, December.

49. Sharma, R., Mehta, K., Rana, R., Cryptocurrency adoption behaviour of millennial investors in India, in: *Perspectives on Blockchain Technology and Responsible Investing*, pp. 135–158, IGI Global, 2023.
50. Sherimon, P.C., Sherimon, V., Thomas, J., Jaimon, K., A Blockchain Framework for Investment Authorities to Manage Assets and Funds, in: *International Conference on Big Data Innovation for Sustainable Cognitive Computing*, 2022, December, Springer Nature Switzerland, Cham, pp. 217–226.
51. Şoiman, F., Dumas, G., Jimenez-Garces, S., The return of (I) DeFiX, 2022, *arXiv preprint arXiv:2204.00251*.
52. Tian, J., Wang, K., Chen, Y., Johansson, B., From IT deployment capabilities to competitive advantage: An exploratory study in China. *Inf. Syst. Front.*, *12*, 239–255, 2010.
53. Toufaily, E., Zalan, T., Dhaou, S.B., A framework of blockchain technology adoption: An investigation of challenges and expected value. *Inf. Manage.*, *58*, 3, 103444, 2021.
54. Urquhart, A. and Zhang, H., Is Bitcoin a hedge or safe haven for currencies? An intraday analysis. *Int. Rev. Financ. Anal.*, *63*, 49–57, 2019.
55. Vyas, V., Mehta, K., Sharma, R., Investigating socially responsible investing behaviour of Indian investors using structural equation modelling. *J. Sustain. Finance Invest.*, *12*, 2, 570–592, 2022.
56. Vyas, V., Mehta, K., Sharma, R., Are bitcoin prices isolated or co-integrated? *Int. J. Bus. Globalisation*, *35*, 1–2, 5–19, 2023.
57. Wang, D., Wu, S., Lin, Z., Wu, L., Yuan, X., Zhou, Y., Ren, K., Towards a first step to understand flash loan and its applications in defi ecosystem, in: *Proceedings of the Ninth International Workshop on Security in Blockchain and Cloud Computing*, 2021, May, pp. 23–28.
58. West, K., Where is Blockchain? Jurisdictional Issues That May Affect Distributed Ledgers, 2018.
59. Wronka, C., Financial crime in the decentralized finance ecosystem: new challenges for compliance. *J. Financ. Crime*, *30*, 1, 97–113, 2023.
60. Yousaf, I. and Yarovaya, L., Spillovers between the Islamic gold-backed cryptocurrencies and equity markets during the COVID-19: A sectorial analysis. *Pac.-Basin Finance J.*, *71*, 101705, 2022.
61. Yousaf, I., Nekhili, R., Gubareva, M., Linkages between DeFi assets and conventional currencies: Evidence from the COVID-19 pandemic. *Int. Rev. Financ. Anal.*, *81*, 102082, 2022.
62. Zetzsche, D.A., Arner, D.W., Buckley, R.P., Decentralized finance. *J. Financ. Regul.*, *6*, 2, 172–203, 2020.
63. Zhang, Y., Chan, S., Chu, J., Liao, X., Helu, M., Stylized Facts of Decentralized Finance (DeFi), in: *Artificial Intelligence and Beyond for Finance*, pp. 289–314, 2024.
64. Androulaki, E., Karame, G.O., Roeschlin, M., Scherer, T., Capkun, S., Evaluating user privacy in bitcoin. In Financial Cryptography and Data Security: *17th International Conference, FC 2013*, Springer Berlin Heidelberg, Okinawa, Japan, revised selected papers 17 pp. 34–51, April 1-5 2013.

9

DeFi-Powered Marketing: Unleashing the Prowess of Decentralized Finance for Revolutionary Customer Experiences

Roop Kamal

University School of Business, Chandigarh University, Mohali, Punjab, India

Abstract

The chapter "The DeFi-Powered Marketing: Unleashing the Prowess of Decentralized Finance for Revolutionary Customer Experiences" explores the creative blending of decentralized finance (DeFi) concepts with marketing tactics to change customer experiences. With the emergence of DeFi, the financial landscape is undergoing a profound change, and marketing experts are investigating cutting-edge strategies to engage clients and foster brand loyalty. The notion of DeFi and its disruptive effects on conventional financial systems are introduced at the beginning of the chapter. It emphasizes the value of applying DeFi ideas to marketing and paves the way for an investigation of its revolutionary potential. Loyalty programs and tokenized incentives are the main topics of the first segment. Marketing firms can thank clients for their enthusiastic support of their brands by issuing branded tokens or working with already-running DeFi projects. A seamless loyalty ecosystem is created *via* tokenized rewards, fostering closer relationships between consumers and brands. The power of decentralized advertising networks is then examined in detail, made possible by DeFi's smart contracts. Direct communication between advertisers and publishers encourages openness in the advertising process by removing middlemen. In marketing initiatives, this decentralized strategy promotes accountability and trust. The revolutionary potential of smart contract-driven campaigns is explored in the third section. These self-executing agreements streamline campaign efficiency, automate incentive distributions, and maintain campaign openness. The benefits of adopting smart contracts to simplify marketing procedures are emphasized in this chapter. In the section that follows, community finance and crowdfunding projects

Email: Roopsandhu901@gmail.com

Renuka Sharma, Kiran Mehta, Vishal Vyas and Vinod Kumar Shukla (eds.) Decentralized Finance and Blockchain: A Game Changing Duo, (193–224) © 2025 Scrivener Publishing LLC

are covered. Decentralized finance enables marketing companies to interact with their communities directly, promoting democratic decision-making and project crowdfunding. This inclusive strategy improves consumer loyalty and strengthens brand-customer interactions. In the section that follows, data ownership and privacy in the digital era are discussed. Marketing firms can provide personalized experiences while guaranteeing that clients keep control over their data by utilizing DeFi's blockchain-based data storage and identity verification, which increases trust and happiness. The final portion examines the difficulties and dangers of DeFi-powered marketing. Marketing professionals are urged to embrace informed decision-making and risk mitigation techniques as regulatory compliance, smart contract vulnerabilities, and security issues are addressed. The chapter concludes by highlighting the revolutionary potential of marketing that is powered by DeFi to redefine customer experiences. Marketing experts may develop customer-focused campaigns and encourage brand loyalty by utilizing tokenized incentives, decentralized advertising, smart contracts, community funding, and better data ownership. The chapter places emphasis on the necessity of taking a cautious yet proactive strategy to overcome obstacles and make use of DeFi's revolutionary potential for transforming marketing techniques for the digital age.

***Keywords*:** Decentralized financing, DeFi in marketing, tokenized incentives, loyalty programs

9.1 Introduction to DeFi

Decentralized finance (DeFi) is a revolutionary approach to finance that makes use of blockchain technology to provide a permission-free, decentralized environment for financial services. It denotes a fundamental transition away from the established, centralized financial systems, such banks and intermediaries, and towards a more open, democratic financial infrastructure. The financial environment is exposed to various types of risks [7, 8, 12, 39]. Decentralized finance is the collective name for a series of platforms and applications built on the blockchain with the goal of replicating and enhancing existing traditional financial services like lending, borrowing, trading, and asset management without the use of conventional middlemen like banks or brokerage houses. Instead, DeFi uses decentralized networks and smart contracts to streamline and automate financial operations [12, 31]. Blockchain technology is the foundation of the innovative financial ecosystem known as DeFi, which aims to democratize and decentralize conventional financial services. Decentralized finance functions without the use of middlemen like banks or centralized authority, in contrast to conventional systems [9, 16]. Instead, it uses self-executing code agreements known as smart contracts to automate and enforce financial

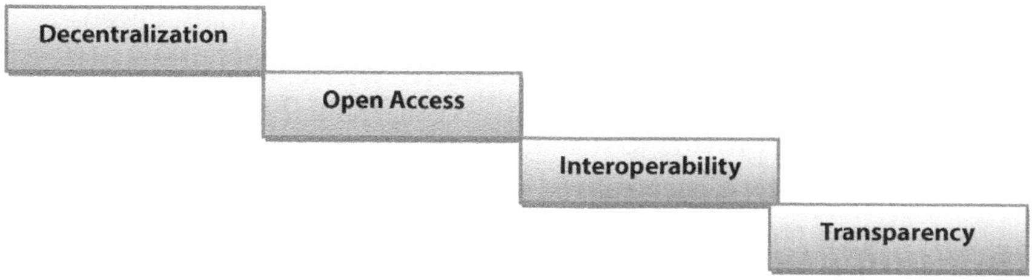

Figure 9.1 Principles of decentralized finance.

agreements. Decentralized exchanges (DEXs), lending, borrowing, trading, yield farming, and other services are all available on DeFi platforms [7, 11]. The researchers have examined cryptocurrency behavior as there is an increased interest from investors in this digital financial instrument [24, 26, 37]. Digital wallets and cryptocurrency can be used to engage with DeFi applications, providing global and round-the-clock accessibility (see Figure 9.1).

9.1.1 Key Principles of DeFi

1. **Decentralization:** Decentralized blockchain networks, like Ethereum, where there is no central authority, are used by DeFi platforms. As a result, security and transparency are improved, and intermediaries are no longer necessary.
2. **Open access:** Most DeFi services are accessible to anyone with an internet connection and a compatible wallet. It is more inclusive because there are no regional or account limits.
3. **Interoperability:** Decentralized finance protocols are built to be compatible, enabling multiple apps to work together without any issues and building a strong, linked ecosystem.
4. **Transparency:** On DeFi platforms, transactions and smart contract code are frequently visible to the public and auditable, fostering user confidence.

9.1.2 Decentralized Finance in Various Sectors

1. **Finance and banking:** Without involving banks as middlemen, DeFi platforms offer substitutes for conventional banking services like savings accounts, loans, and borrowing. Users can obtain loans without a credit check by pledging their assets as security in a smart contract.

2. **Insurance:** Through peer-to-peer risk-sharing pools, decentralized insurance solutions are provided by DeFi protocols. Users can access coverage without relying on conventional insurance providers.
3. **Real estate:** Decentralized finance makes fractional ownership of real estate possible, opening the market to new types of investors. On DEXs, ownership is represented by property tokens.
4. **Energy and sustainability:** Decentralized investment and trading in sustainable efforts are made possible by DeFi projects that investigate tokenizing carbon credits and renewable energy assets. Decentralized finance can be used by energy-sharing companies and smart grids to distribute and compensate energy effectively.
5. **Education and credential verification:** Using blockchain technology, DeFi can assist in securing and validating academic credentials. Users do not need to rely on centralized authorities to present their credentials.
6. **Healthcare and pharma:** By utilizing blockchain for patient information and research data, DeFi can increase data security and interoperability in the healthcare industry. Administrative costs can be decreased using tokenized healthcare payment and insurance solutions.
7. **Marketing:** Decentralized finance can enhance the marketing industry in several ways, including decentralized advertising and tokenized incentives and rewards. Through DeFi-powered marketplaces, tokenized content and intellectual property assist advertisers in keeping tabs on their creative and audience engagement (see Figure 9.2) [21].

9.2 Traditional Financial Systems

Traditional financial systems are the well-established, highly centralized, and frequently highly regulated systems that have long served as the foundation of the global financial industry. These systems' reliance on physical infrastructure, the use of intermediaries, and regulatory control are their defining characteristics [14, 24, 30]. The established structure that has supported the world's financial industry for many years is represented by the traditional financial system. A centralized system made up of banks,

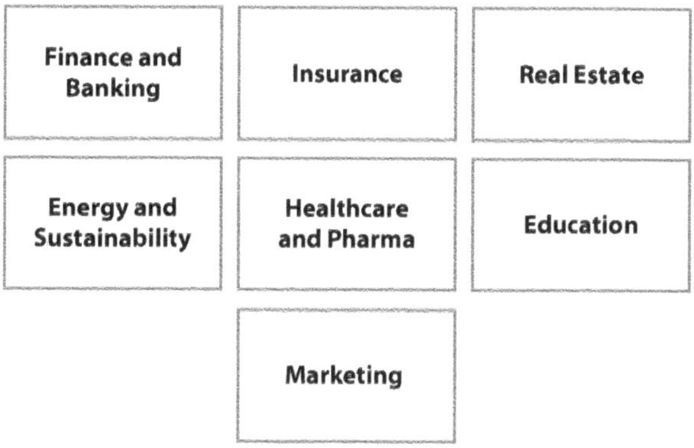

Figure 9.2 Various sectors using the concept of decentralized finance.

financial institutions, and regulatory agencies defines it. These organizations function as middlemen in a range of financial activities, such as lending, borrowing, investing, and payment processing. A significant role in managing the money supply and establishing monetary policy is played by central banks, such the Federal Reserve in the United States. Exchanges for securities, such as the New York Stock Exchange (NYSE), make it easier to trade securities issued by corporations that are publicly traded. Fiat currencies, which are government-issued currencies unrelated to physical assets like gold, are the foundation of traditional finance. This system is based on a network of physical infrastructure, including trading floors, clearinghouses, and bank offices [4, 14, 20]. A complex system of rules and monitoring organizations that promote financial stability, safeguard investors, and uphold market integrity oversee it. Traditional finance has contributed to financial transactions' stability and confidence, but it is also accompanied by restrictions like geographical boundaries, intermediaries' fees, and a lack of access for marginalized groups [16, 30]. Emerging financial technologies such as cryptocurrency and DeFi coexist with it, challenging existing traditions by providing more inventive, accessible, and decentralized financial solutions.

9.2.1 Components of Traditional Financial Systems

1. **Financial institutions:** Traditional financial systems are fundamentally composed of commercial banks, investment banks, and central banks. Commercial banks offer services like accepting deposits, lending money, and processing

payments. Investment banks undertake tasks like assisting mergers and acquisitions and underwriting securities. The money supply is controlled by central banks, which also monitor monetary policy.

2. **Stock exchanges:** Well-established stock exchanges are a part of traditional financial systems where publicly listed corporations issue and trade their shares. The NYSE and the London Stock Exchange (LSE) are two examples.
3. **Regulatory authorities:** To monitor and enact laws governing financial institutions and markets, governments set up regulatory bodies. These authorities work to maintain the integrity of financial systems, safeguard investors, and guarantee stability. The European Central Bank and the U.S. Securities and Exchange Commission are two examples.
4. **Physical infrastructure:** Traditional financial systems are supported by physical infrastructure including bank branches, trading floors at stock exchanges, and settlement hubs. Transactions are frequently performed using outdated technologies, which could cause delays and incur expensive costs.
5. **Fiat currency:** Fiat money, which is created by governments and central banks, is the foundation of conventional financial systems. These currencies' values are determined by government edict rather than by tangible assets like gold.
6. **Intermediaries:** In traditional financial systems, transactions are facilitated and validated by intermediaries like banks, brokers, and clearinghouses. These middlemen offer security and trust in financial transactions, but they can also increase complexity and cost.

9.2.2 Decentralized Finance in Traditional Financial Systems

Decentralized finance can expand financial inclusion, lower transaction costs, and offer financial services to the unbanked and under banked [21]. Additionally, it presents the idea of "programmable money," which enables developers to build cutting-edge financial services and products on open-source platforms. Decentralized finance does face several difficulties, such as scalability problems, security hazards, and legal worries [17]. Despite these obstacles, the disruptive force of DeFi is altering the financial environment and posing a threat to the supremacy of conventional financial institutions. Traditional financial systems could undergo major changes due to DeFi, which has the potential to be disruptive in a number of important ways:

1. **Removal of middlemen:** Decentralized finance applications are based on blockchain technology, which permits peer-to-peer trades and smart contracts. Decentralized finance lowers costs and lowers counterparty risk by doing away with the need for intermediaries like banks, brokers, and clearinghouses.
2. **Universal accessibility:** Decentralized finance is available to everyone with an internet connection and a digital wallet, bringing financial services to those who might not have access to conventional banks in underserved areas. This inclusivity is especially advantageous when it comes to international remittances and financial inclusion.
3. **Constant availability:** Transactions and settlements are delayed by the limitations of traditional financial systems, which include business hours and weekends. Decentralized finance is available around the clock, allowing users to transact and access financial services whenever they choose, increasing efficiency and cutting down on waiting times.
4. **Automatable currency:** Decentralized finance makes use of smart contracts, self-executing contracts with pre-established rules. By automating financial procedures like lending, borrowing, and trading, this programmability reduces the need for manual intervention and streamline operations.
5. **Asset tokenization:** Traditional assets like equities, commodities, and real estate can be tokenized and represented on blockchains. This makes it possible for assets to be owned in fractions, to be liquid, and to be more easily transferred, possibly upending established markets and lowering entry requirements for investors.
6. **Decentralized exchanges:** Decentralized finance systems provide DEXs, which let users trade cryptocurrencies without using centralized exchanges. They give users more control over their assets and lessen the chance of exchange hacks or outages.

9.3 Decentralized Finance in Marketing

Decentralized finance, which ushers in a new era of financial independence and inclusivity, is completely altering the marketing scene [5, 7, 12, 14]. Businesses in traditional marketing frequently rely on middlemen to handle transactions and manage finances, such as banks and payment processors. Decentralized finance, on the other hand, uses smart contracts and blockchain technology to provide a decentralized ecosystem where marketers may directly access financial services without middlemen [16, 18]. Marketers are empowered by this financial paradigm shift since it gives them unheard-of control over their financial activities. Peer-to-peer transactions, access to liquidity pools or loans, and earning interest in assets are all possible in a decentralized and open ecosystem. The borderless nature of DeFi also enables companies to access worldwide markets, connecting clients and partners globally without being constrained by conventional banking institutions. Additionally, DeFi introduces tokenization, allowing business owners to tokenize their goods, services, or resources and sell them on decentralized marketplaces [19, 21, 31]. This creates new potential for creative marketing that can encourage consumer participation and brand loyalty [15, 17]. Examples include reward programs, decentralized affiliate marketing, and loyalty programs based on digital tokens. It is important to understand that there are risks associated with DeFi marketing, though. Due to their decentralized structure, DeFi platforms are not subject to the same regulatory scrutiny as conventional financial institutions, which leaves them open to market volatility and smart contract vulnerabilities [26, 34]. Marketers must exercise caution when navigating this dynamic environment and make sure they are well-versed in the threats posed by technology.

In the current dynamic corporate environment, applying DeFi principles to marketing has many benefits. Here are some key reasons:

9.3.1 Importance of Decentralized Finance in Marketing

1. **Augmented transparency:** Decentralized finance uses blockchain technology, which guarantees data immutability and transparency. Customers will have more faith in the veracity of company statements and actions if this transparency is extended to marketing initiatives. Additionally, it can aid in resolving issues with deceptive marketing techniques and fraudulent advertising.

2. **Confidence and reliability:** Decentralized finance's lack of reliability can be used to increase trust in marketing. Marketing contracts can be automated, ensuring that both sides keep their promises. This lowers the possibility of disagreements and raises the legitimacy of marketing campaigns.
3. **Eliminate mediators:** Decentralized finance renders financial transactions without the need for intermediaries. In a similar vein, incorporating DeFi into marketing might lessen the dependency on middlemen in advertising and client relations. Cost savings and more direct interactions with clients may result from this.
4. **Transnational reach:** Decentralized finance is not limited by geographical borders. Businesses can increase their market reach abroad without the need for complicated cross-border finance arrangements by implementing DeFi principles. For businesses wanting to enter overseas markets, this is very beneficial.
5. **Customization:** Marketing campaigns can be made extremely personalized thanks to smart contracts. Brands may create more effective marketing campaigns by using data stored on the blockchain to customize their messages and product offerings to specific customer preferences.
6. **Incentivization and commitment:** Decentralized finance presents the idea of tokenization, which may be utilized to reward patron loyalty and participation. With tokenized rewards, brands can design loyalty programs that motivate consumers to engage with their products more frequently and enthusiastically.
7. **Data safety:** By improving data security, blockchain technology lowers the possibility of data breaches and privacy violations in marketing. Customers may be more likely to contribute information for individualized marketing efforts if they feel more certain that their data is managed securely.
8. **Innovation:** Decentralized finance is a hub for innovation, with fresh ideas and initiatives developing on a regular basis. Integrating DeFi principles into marketing can help organizations take advantage of cutting-edge ideas and technologies while also offering them a competitive edge.
9. **Price efficacy:** Decentralized finance can lower the cost of financial transactions, and it can do the same for several marketing procedures. Automation of payments, awards,

and settlement is a part of this, and it can lower administrative costs. Several techniques can be used to investigate the price movement of various financial instruments [5, 14, 26, 38].

10. **Customer-centric strategy:** By offering customers more control over their data and how they interact with brands, DeFi can empower customers. Customer happiness and brand perception can both be enhanced by this customer-centric strategy.

Decentralized finance marketing is the process of drawing attention to any DeFi project that someone introduces to the blockchain community. In this situation, DeFi projects are all financial systems that run on smart contract-based apps [16]. Although the original platform that made it possible to create DeFi applications was Bitcoin, the ecosystem of Ethereum is currently far more well-known. Marketing is one of the many areas where DeFi receives a lot of attention and implementation [22]. The term "DeFi" in marketing refers to the enhancing and streamlining of marketing activities through the use decentralized financial tools, platforms, and blockchain technology [20].

9.3.2 Impact of Decentralized Finance in Marketing

The world of marketing is undergoing a significant upheaval thanks to DeFi. Decentralized finance has launched a whole new financial infrastructure that is changing the way companies market and sell their goods and services by utilizing blockchain technology and smart contracts [27, 33]. The democratization of finance is one of DeFi's most important effects on marketing. Companies can readily access crowdfunding and decentralized loans through DeFi platforms, enabling them to finance marketing campaigns or product launches without using conventional middlemen [14, 18, 22]. Since token holders frequently end up being brand ambassadors, this democratization not only expands access to capital but also encourages community engagement. Additionally, the borderlessness of DeFi has allowed advertisers to reach a global audience without being constrained by conventional financial systems [9, 19, 23]. It has also cleared the path for cutting-edge marketing techniques that encourage client participation and loyalty, like decentralized affiliate networks and token-based awards [22]. A new degree of trust and responsibility is also provided by DeFi's visible and irreversible ledger, which aids marketers in establishing credibility with their audience.

DeFi in Marketing

- Tokenized Incentives
- Localised Advertising
- Micro transactions and Content Monetization
- Decentralised Authentication and Data Ownership
- Smart Contracts as a Framework for Branding Deals
- Crowdfunding and fundraising
- Cross-Border Settlements
- Distribution Chain Disclosure

1. **Tokenized incentives:** Decentralized finance enables companies to design their own tokens as rewards for clients, affiliates, and influencers. Within a particular ecosystem, these tokens can be used for payment, rewards, and loyalty schemes. This could promote more brand loyalty and customer involvement.
2. **Localized advertisement:** Decentralized finance systems can provide decentralized advertising networks that let advertisers communicate with publishers and content producers directly, cutting out the need for middlemen. This can lower advertising expenses and increase supply chain transparency for advertising.
3. **Microtransactions and content monetization:** Decentralized finance supports micropayments, which makes it simpler for customers to pay modest sums for premium goods and services. Content producers may be able to lessen their reliance on conventional advertising income methods by more effectively monetizing their work.
4. **Decentralized authentication and data ownership:** Decentralized finance enables consumers to have more control over their online identities and personal data. Users can opt to give their data to marketers in exchange for gifts or other forms of payment, promoting more open and moral data practices.
5. **Smart contracts as a framework for branding deals:** Automated, trustless agreements between marketers, advertisers, and influencers are made possible by smart contracts on blockchain platforms like Ethereum. Smart contracts can be used to encode payment conditions, performance

measures, and other contract terms to lower the likelihood of disagreements.

6. **Crowdfunding and fundraising:** Decentralized finance platforms provide decentralized crowdfunding tools including security token offerings and initial coin offerings. These techniques can be used by marketers to raise money for new initiatives or marketing campaigns.
7. **Cross-border settlements:** Due to DeFi's lack of national boundaries, it is simpler for marketers to carry out cross-border business, pay foreign affiliates, and broaden their clientele internationally.
8. **Distribution chain disclosure:** Decentralized finance can be used to trace and verify product origins and authenticity, which can be a potent marketing tool, in sectors where supply chain transparency is essential, such as food and luxury goods.

Decentralized finance is ready to revolutionize the marketing industry by providing fresh approaches to tried-and-true problems. The possibilities range from decentralized advertising networks that eliminate middlemen to tokenized incentives that increase client engagement and loyalty. Content producers can diversify their sources of income through the integration of micropayments and content monetization through DeFi, while users are given more control over their data through decentralized identification solutions [2, 20]. Marketing agreements are made even more streamlined by smart contracts, which lower the chance of disagreements. Although careful consideration of legal and security considerations is crucial in efficiently utilizing this developing technology, DeFi gives intriguing prospects for marketers to construct more transparent, effective, and customer-centric campaigns.

9.4 Tokenized Incentives and Loyalty Programs

Decentralized finance technology-powered tokenized rewards and loyalty programs offer a revolutionary way to increase consumer engagement and brand loyalty in marketing. Businesses can design their own tokens to represent value inside their ecosystems by utilizing blockchain technologies [26, 32]. These tokens take the place of conventional points or discounts as the main component of loyalty programs. These tokens are given to customers in exchange for a variety of transactions, including purchases, recommendations, and participation on social media. Since the tokens are safely kept in digital wallets, transactions are transparent and unchangeable [22]. Customers can then exchange these tokens for a variety of benefits, enhancing the loyalty program's sense of gamification and customization.

Decentralized finance-based loyalty programs are notable for their interoperability, which enables tokens to be used across various platforms and ecosystems, increasing their overall worth. Decentralized finance loyalty programs also help companies create strong brand communities because they encourage customers to become token holders and brand evangelists in addition to consumers. These programs appeal to contemporary marketers because of their affordability, worldwide reach, and data insights they produce [19, 32].

In addition, client contacts gain a new degree of openness and trust thanks to DeFi-powered loyalty programs. Automating the delivery of rewards and customizing incentives depending on user choices and behavior are both possible with smart contracts. Customer loyalty and satisfaction are increased by this personalized approach. Overall, these initiatives provide organizations with a creative and effective approach to increase consumer interaction, foster brand loyalty, and leverage blockchain and DeFi technology in today's fiercely competitive marketing environment.

Customer engagement and brand loyalty could be revolutionized by tokenized incentives and loyalty programs with the use of DeFi in marketing.

9.4.1 Functions of Tokenized Incentives and Loyalty Programs

1. **Creation of tokens:** Utility tokens are a type of token that may be created by a company or brand on a blockchain platform. These tokens, which can be readily distributed and tracked on the blockchain, serve as a representation of value inside the ecosystem of the brand.
2. **Recognizing customer interaction:** Brands may use their native tokens to reward customers for different types of interactions in place of traditional loyalty programs that award points or discounts. This can be done through shopping, recommending others, writing reviews, or using social media.
3. **Token redemption:** Customers amass these tokens over time, which they can keep in their electronic wallets. They may then exchange these tokens for a variety of benefits, like savings, special access to goods or events, or even goods. The addition of a gamification element to loyalty programs

increases user engagement. Tokens can be redeemed for actual advantages.

4. **Interoperability:** In some instances, these loyalty tokens might be tradable or able to communicate with other DeFi platforms or tokens, enabling users to use them in various ecosystems. Customers benefit from increased value, which promotes token retention.
5. **Privacy and integrity:** Blockchain technology guarantees the transactions and the issuance of tokens is transparent. Customers may check the value of their tokens and their balances, which increases customer confidence in the reward program. The immutability of blockchain records also shields users from fraud and unauthorized adjustments.
6. **Customization:** Smart contracts can be used by DeFi-powered loyalty programs to tailor rewards depending on unique customer behavior and preferences. This degree of personalization can increase client loyalty and happiness.
7. **Community development:** As customers possess and use loyalty tokens, they join a wider group of brand devotees. Increased engagement and advocacy may result from this sense of community and shared interest.

Decentralized finance's capabilities are generally used in marketing to build more engaging, transparent, and effective ways to reward and keep customers through tokenized incentives and loyalty programs [14]. In an increasingly digital and competitive market, these programs can improve brand loyalty and brand-customer interactions. Marketing firms wanting to increase client involvement and brand loyalty may find success by issuing branded tokens or partnering with current DeFi ventures [20]. Marketing firms can then use the advantages of DeFi technology to develop cutting-edge loyalty and incentive schemes.

9.4.2 Importance of Tokenized Incentives and Loyalty Programs

1. **Labelled tokens:** On a blockchain platform, marketing firms can build their own utility tokens, often known as branded tokens. These tokens, which reflect value within the ecosystem of the agency, can be used to reward a range of

client behaviors, including sharing content, recommending friends, and offering feedback.

2. **Affiliation with DeFi projects:** Marketing firms can also work with DeFi projects that already exist and provide token-based incentive schemes. The agency's marketing initiatives may be combined with various DeFi platforms as part of this collaboration, enabling users to get tokens by engaging in DeFi tasks like yield farming or liquidity provision.
3. **Reward schemes for participation:** Clients can get these branded tokens by actively interacting with the brand, whether by taking part in marketing initiatives, attending events, or posting material on social media. These tokens can be utilized within the ecosystem of the agency or traded for a variety of benefits and kept in digital wallets.
4. **Expanded involvement:** Branded tokens and DeFi partnerships gamify client engagement to a new level. Customers are not just inert consumers; they are also active contributors who get paid for what they contribute. Customers may become more involved and more vocal as they work to accumulate more tokens.
5. **Community development:** Branded tokens and DeFi partnerships encourage the development of a committed and active community around the agency's brand. Customers transition from being merely consumers to token holders, creating a sense of community and shared interest.
6. **Cost-efficiency:** Since DeFi-based incentive programs do not require traditional loyalty program providers and have lower administrative costs, they can be cost-effective for marketing agencies.
7. **Global reach:** Programs powered by DeFi are not constrained by territorial boundaries, enabling marketing agencies to interact with a global clientele, which is very helpful for digital marketing efforts.

Marketing companies may take advantage of the promise of blockchain technology to build more transparent, interesting, and effective loyalty and reward programs by incorporating branded tokens and DeFi collaborations into their campaigns [15, 19, 30]. With the help of this strategy, agencies may promote brand loyalty, build stronger customer-brand interactions, and stay on the cutting edge of marketing innovation [22, 36].

A seamless and dynamic loyalty ecosystem that goes beyond traditional loyalty programs is facilitated by tokenized incentives. Brands can encourage and reward customer interaction in a more open and flexible way by utilizing blockchain technology and DeFi concepts [16, 35]. These incentives, which are sometimes portrayed as digital tokens, have intrinsic worth within the ecosystem of the brand and are obtained through a variety of customer activities like purchases, recommendations, or active involvement in marketing efforts. The power of tokenized rewards to promote stronger relationships between customers and companies is what makes them particularly impactful. Customers participate actively in the brand's community in addition to accumulating tokens [7, 23]. These tokens' gamification element encourages users to actively interact with the business and compete for prizes, which promotes brand advocacy and increases customer loyalty. The adoption of blockchain technology also guarantees the security and transparency of award programs [22, 30]. Customers' token balances and transactions may be easily verified, fostering a sense of dependability. The blockchain's unchangeable records prevent fraud, further boosting the trustworthiness of the loyalty ecosystem [16, 34].

Tokenized rewards also enable customized experiences *via* smart contracts. Customers might feel valued and understood when brands customize rewards based on their unique tastes and behaviors [23, 32]. This personalization not only boosts consumer pleasure but also strengthens their emotional bond with the business.

Tokenized rewards essentially transform the transactional aspect of conventional loyalty programs into a loyalty ecosystem. They encourage stronger connections, trust, and brand advocacy by converting consumers into engaged stakeholders. This cutting-edge strategy is at the forefront of contemporary marketing and provides a potent instrument for businesses to create enduring and significant connections with their consumers.

9.5 Decentralized Advertising Networks Due to Decentralized Finance

Decentralized advertising is a revolutionary method of digital marketing that transforms the way adverts are produced, delivered, and consumed. It does this by utilizing blockchain technology and smart contracts. Ad agencies, ad networks, and data brokers are all eliminated in this ground-breaking paradigm, enabling marketers and content producers to communicate directly with their target consumers [21]. Blockchain guarantees ad data's transparency and immutability, fostering honesty and confidence in the advertising process. Smart contracts that verify ad views and user interactions reduce ad fraud, a serious issue in traditional advertising. Decentralized advertising also gives users more control over their data, allowing them to share it on their own terms and fostering privacy and openness. By promoting microtargeting and personalization, this strategy respects user preferences while producing ads that are more relevant and interesting. Smart contracts also automate payments, ensuring that publishers and content providers receive appropriate recompense [14, 27]. With its cost-effectiveness, transparency, and user-centricity, decentralized advertising is ready to upend the current state of digital marketing. This will ultimately change how brands interact with their audiences online.

It is impossible to overstate the influence of decentralized advertising networks, which are supported by the DeFi ecosystem's use of smart contracts. These networks mark a paradigm shift in the field of digital advertising and provide a wealth of beneficial changes. These networks do away with the need for middlemen by using smart contracts, ushering in a new era of cost effectiveness and transparency. Direct communication between publishers and advertisers lowers costs and reduces the dangers of ad fraud. Smart contracts encrypt contract conditions and carry out transactions automatically, bringing transparency and confidence to every step of the advertising process.

Additionally, by dramatically lowering the likelihood of fraudulent impressions and click fraud, these networks solve the ongoing problem of ad fraud. Advertisers may be sure that their budgets are used wisely with smart contracts validating ad views and user interactions. By seamlessly integrating adverts into content, this technology also provides a solution to the proliferation of ad blockers, benefiting both users and marketers.

Decentralized ad networks enable a higher level of micro-targeting and personalization. Advertisers may accurately target their audience using consent-based data exchange on the blockchain, producing more pertinent and interesting adverts while upholding user privacy. In addition, smart contracts streamline payment distribution, guaranteeing publishers and content creators prompt payment and eradicating payment conflicts that plague the sector [20, 30].

These networks present a special chance for advertisers to reach a worldwide audience while meaningfully engaging consumers because of their accessibility on a global scale and the potential for tokenized incentives [17, 25]. These networks promote a more engaging and gratifying ad experience by compensating users for their time and data. Essentially, the potential of decentralized advertising networks, supported by DeFi's smart contracts, promises to transform the advertising sector by making it more effective, transparent, and user-centric, ultimately bringing about benefits for all parties involved.

9.5.1 Challenges and Advantages of Decentralized Advertising Networks

1. **Elimination of middlemen:** Traditional digital advertising frequently uses middlemen, such as ad networks, data brokers, and advertising agencies. By eliminating these middlemen, decentralized advertising networks driven by smart contracts enable direct communication between advertisers and publishers and content producers. As a result, expenses are decreased, ad fraud is reduced, and ad placement transparency is increased.
2. **Increased transparency and trust:** Smart contracts make sure that advertising deal terms are recorded on the blockchain and are carried out automatically when circumstances are met. As a result of their ability to independently check transactions and campaign performance indicators, marketers, publishers, and consumers are more likely to have faith in one another.
3. **Fraud prevention:** Fraud in the advertising sector, particularly click fraud and fraudulent impressions, is a big threat. By automating the verification of ad views and user interactions, smart contracts can reduce fraud by making it far more difficult for fraudulent behaviors to go undetected.
4. **Less ad blocking:** By integrating advertisements more seamlessly into content, viewers are less likely to use ad-blocking software. This helps customers have better online experiences while also helping advertisers reach a larger audience.
5. **Micro-targeting and customization:** Smart contracts make it possible to gather and securely share user data with their express permission. This makes it possible to target advertising more precisely, which might increase their relevancy and lessen users' ad fatigue.
6. **Cost efficiency:** Inefficient payments and disputed payments are frequent problems in conventional advertising. By automating payment distribution based on predetermined criteria, smart contracts make sure that publishers and content producers get paid promptly and fairly for their work.

7. **Incentives for high-quality content:** Smart contracts can be created to pay publishers and content producers according to the popularity and effectiveness of their work. This encourages the creation of interesting, high-quality content, which is advantageous to both consumers and advertisers.
8. **Algorithmic advertising:** Smart contracts enable programmatic advertising, which optimizes ad placement based on data and performance indicators, by automating the purchasing and selling of advertising space in real-time.
9. **Tokenization and rewards:** Some decentralized ad networks employ tokens as a form of payment for user interaction with advertisements or data submission. For consumers, this may result in a more interesting and satisfying ad experience.

Decentralized marketing strategies are an effective catalyst for promoting trust and accountability across the marketing ecosystem [32]. This cutting-edge strategy adds a new degree of openness, verifiability, and fairness to marketing practices by utilizing blockchain technology and smart contracts. Blockchain's immutable ledger makes sure that all campaign information and activities are recorded in an open manner, lowering the possibility of fraudulent or dishonest acts and giving stakeholders a way to independently confirm the authenticity of data [1, 23]. Due to their self-executing nature, smart contracts simplify campaign procedures and enforce agreements, removing conflicts and fostering trust between all participants. Additionally, consumers have more control over their interactions and data, which encourages responsible data management and more moral marketing practices. In the end, a decentralized marketing strategy transforms the marketing environment by aligning it with values of openness, justice, and customer empowerment [28]. It also improves responsibility and trust [13, 27].

A decentralized approach fosters trust and accountability in marketing campaigns by introducing transparency, fairness, and verifiability into every aspect of the marketing process in the following ways:

1. **Visibility:** All actions and transactions within a marketing campaign are recorded on an immutable ledger thanks to blockchain technology, which is at the heart of decentralized methods. This transparency lowers the danger of dishonest or deceptive practices by enabling stakeholders, such as marketers, customers, and regulators, to independently check the validity of data and actions.

2. **Smart contracts:** These self-executing contracts with established rules automate many facets of marketing campaigns. These agreements guarantee that all parties involved perform their obligations, resolving conflicts and fostering confidence among interested parties.
3. **Information processing:** Decentralized systems allow for more careful and open handling of client data. The way and when customers share their data with marketers is more in their hands. Customers feel more in control as a result, and their trust in the ethical use of their data grows.
4. **The elimination of intermediaries:** Marketing campaigns require fewer intermediaries thanks to decentralized technologies. This not only lowers expenses but also lessens the chance of conflicts of interest that could damage trust.
5. **Auditable data:** Decentralized marketing campaigns' metrics and performance information are recorded on the blockchain, creating an auditable trail of the campaigns' success. Because both marketers and publishers can independently evaluate the veracity of metrics, this verifiability fosters confidence between them.
6. **Accountability:** More responsibility is attached to decentralized marketing campaigns. As agreed-upon terms and conditions are enforced by smart contracts, marketers and advertising can be held directly accountable for their conduct.
7. **Client empowerment:** It is a result of decentralization, which gives customers authority over how they interact with marketers. They can control how their information is used and have confidence that their preferences will be honored, resulting in a fruitful and moral marketing partnership.

By utilizing blockchain technology and smart contracts to establish a transparent, equitable, and verifiable environment, a decentralized approach in marketing campaigns fosters trust and accountability [14, 26]. In addition to helping marketers by lowering fraud and disputes, this also improves the whole customer experience by empowering people and protecting their privacy and data. Since trust is essential to effective marketing, the decentralized strategy is set to become more and more important as the market develops.

9.6 Groundbreaking Potential of Smart Contract-Driven Campaigns

A revolutionary age for the marketing sector is ushered in by the unprecedented potential of smart contract-driven campaigns, strengthened by the principles of DeFi. These initiatives, supported by blockchain technology, provide unmatched automation and efficiency, improving marketing procedures and cutting expenses [13, 19]. The integration of DeFi ensures quick and affordable transactions, doing away with the need for middlemen and the lag times associated with conventional financial systems. Furthermore, by combining smart contracts with DeFi principles, campaign data, activities, and payments gain a new degree of verifiability and trust and become impervious to tampering. This promotes confidence among all stakeholders while also reducing fraud [17, 27]. Consumers also gain from having more control over their data and interactions, and cutting-edge incentive structures made possible by DeFi tokenization result in more interesting and rewarding ad experiences. Essentially, DeFi ecosystem smart contract-driven campaigns are ready to change marketing by boosting efficiency, transparency, and fairness, and they promise a future where trust and innovation rule supreme in the marketing scene.

By bringing efficiency, transparency, and justice into marketing, smart contract-driven campaigns and DeFi principles are revolutionizing the industry [21]. The total user experience is improved because of this synergy, which also helps advertisers, publishers, and the marketing ecosystem. Smart contract-driven campaigns within the DeFi landscape are ready to reshape industry norms and practices as the marketing sector continues to develop.

9.6.1 Advantages of using Smart Contracts to Streamline Marketing Processes

1. **Robotics:** Smart contracts automate a number of marketing operations, including content delivery, ad placement, and payment processing. As a result, less manual intervention is required, reducing errors and improving operational effectiveness.
2. **Reliability and privacy:** The cryptographic security provided by blockchain guarantees that marketing data and transactions are shielded from unauthorized access and manipulation. This improves the general safety and reliability of marketing procedures.

3. **Decreased scam:** Ad fraud, such as click fraud impressions, which is a common worry in the advertising industry, is reduced through automated verification of ad views, user interactions, and payment milestones.
4. **Quicker settlements:** Smart contracts make it possible for payments to be settled more quickly and accurately. Advertisers can make sure that publishers and content producers receive fast and equitable payment in accordance with predetermined standards.
5. **Increased responsibility:** Smart contracts enforce the terms and conditions that have been agreed upon, ensuring that each party to a marketing campaign keeps their end of the bargain. The reliability of marketing agreements is strengthened by this responsibility.
6. **Configuration:** By customizing content and rewards based on unique client behaviors and preferences, smart contracts enable highly personalized marketing campaigns. The user experience and conversion rates are improved by this level of personalization.
7. **Improved user experience:** Smart contract automation enhances the entire user experience. Smoother interactions between customers and brands are possible because two factors, which are quicker payment processing and more pertinent content.
8. **Innovation:** Smart contracts open the door to creative incentive systems that let companies pay customers for desired user behaviors like clicking on adverts or giving feedback. As a result, advertisements may become more interesting and satisfying.

There are several benefits to using smart contracts to expedite marketing procedures, and these benefits are fundamentally changing the marketing environment [6, 19]. These automated, self-executing agreements lower the need for human interaction and eliminate mistakes while drastically reducing operational expenses, enabling organizations to use their resources more wisely. Blockchain technology's inherent openness fosters trust among stakeholders and encourages accountability and verifiability in marketing efforts. By automating verification procedures, smart contracts fight ad fraud and ensure that advertisers receive what they pay for [16, 23].

The user experience is improved by quicker settlements and personalized campaigns, and worldwide reach is made possible by the removal of territorial restrictions. Auditable indicators give a clear picture of campaign performance, promoting remuneration equity. In the end, the revolutionary potential of smart contract-driven marketing procedures ushers in a time when successful campaigns prioritize effectiveness, security, and trust.

9.7 Community Funding and Crowdfunding Initiatives in Marketing

Modern marketing methods have changed because of community fundraising and crowdfunding initiatives [29]. These strategies encourage strong and long-lasting relationships with a brand's audience in addition to offering financial assistance for marketing initiatives. Businesses can foster a sense of ownership and loyalty among their supporters by involving the community directly in the funding process. Crowdfunding also offers a crucial method of market validation by demonstrating a high level of interest and demand for a brand's products [1, 21, 30]. Additionally, it provides opportunities for crowdsourcing ideas, market research, and product pre-sales, allowing marketing strategies to become more data-driven and client-focused [4, 6, 19]. Additionally, crowdfunding's intrinsic openness and trust foster long-lasting ties with the community, and the content and narrative efforts connected to these campaigns can be used for bigger marketing campaigns. In essence, community fundraising and crowdfunding aim to create a passionate and active community around a brand, enhancing marketing initiatives in the process.

9.7.1 Impact of Community Funding and Crowdfunding on Marketing

1. **Project financing:** A lot of marketing campaigns and initiatives need a lot of money. Platforms for crowd fundraising, like Kickstarter and Indiegogo, allow companies to solicit money directly from their communities and interested parties. This makes it possible to implement innovative marketing strategies, product introductions, or events that would not otherwise be financially feasible.

2. **Audience interaction:** Active community interaction is necessary for successful crowdfunding projects. These campaigns are used by marketers to generate interest in their projects as well as money. A participating community in the funding process helps increase supporters' sense of loyalty and ownership.
3. **Marketplace validation:** One way to validate the market is through crowdfunding. A marketing campaign or product proposal may be considered to have a strong market demand if it attracts a lot of attention and money on a crowdfunding website. This confirmation can be used to support further marketing initiatives.
4. **Merchandise pre-sales:** Giving backers special benefits or early access to things is a common aspect of crowdfunding. By using this strategy, firms can create pre-sales and learn more about consumer preferences, which can help them design marketing plans and new product ideas.
5. **Crowd-sourced concepts:** By involving the public in the idea-generating process, marketing strategies can be improved. Platforms for crowdsourcing can be used to engage the community in the marketing process by asking for suggestions, criticism, and creative contributions.
6. **Developing brand advocacy:** Supporters of a successful crowdsourcing project may become brand evangelists. These backers are invested in the project's success and can be effective ambassadors for it on social media and through word-of-mouth, expanding the reach of marketing initiatives.
7. **Integrity and trust:** Successful crowdfunding projects must be transparent about their objectives, their progress, and their plans for using the donations. This dedication to openness can foster community trust, which is an important asset in marketing.
8. **Market analysis:** Crowdfunding campaigns offer a venue for gathering important market analysis data. Marketing tactics and customer personas can be influenced by campaign interactions and backer demographics.
9. **Content development:** Effective storytelling and content development are frequently used in crowdfunding efforts. The campaign's lifespan and impact can be increased by using this content in other marketing initiatives including social media campaigns, blog entries, and videos.

10. **Community development:** Community fundraising and crowdfunding programs encourage the development of a passionate following for a product or project. Through continued interaction and feedback from this community, marketing may become more client-focused.

Initiatives for community and crowdfunding have become crucial marketing tools since they present distinctive chances for finance, audience involvement, market validation, and brand promotion [16]. These initiatives can greatly boost a company's success and its capacity to build closer ties with its audience when they are skillfully included in marketing plans.

9.8 Decentralized Finance's Blockchain in Marketing

Decentralized finance's blockchain-based identity verification and data storage will be integrated into the marketing industry, ushering in a new era of data protection, trust, and personalized engagement [9, 17, 23]. Businesses may protect sensitive client information by offering a secure and impenetrable data storage solution, fostering confidence in a time when data breaches are common. Additionally, this technology gives users more power by enabling them to agree to data sharing, which is in line with developing privacy legislation [10]. Just a few of the practical advantages that can boost marketing effectiveness and ROI include accurate client profiles, decreased fraud, and the capacity to conduct highly personalized marketing campaigns. Marketing interactions become frictionless and user-centric with improved customer onboarding and cross-platform consistency, further boosting brand loyalty [4]. In the end, blockchain-based identity verification has the potential to revolutionize the marketing industry by increasing transparency, lowering costs, and enabling businesses to reach a worldwide audience while promoting ethical and responsible data practices.

9.8.1 Impact of Decentralized Finance's Blockchain in Marketing

1. **Improved confidentiality of information:** Decentralized finance's blockchain technology provides an extremely safe and unhackable data storage option. This guarantees the safety of sensitive information from breaches and unauthorized access, creating trust between businesses and their

consumers in the marketing sector, where client data is priceless.

2. **User security and assent:** Users have more control over their personal data thanks to blockchain-based identity verification. They have control over when and how their information is shared, giving advertisers clear permission to access particular data points. This displays dedication to safe data processing and is consistent with evolving privacy rules like the General Data Protection Regulation (GDPR).
3. **Precise client profiles:** By minimizing the chance of data inconsistencies and duplicate records, blockchain-based identity verification can produce more accurate client profiles. This guarantees that marketing initiatives are directed at the appropriate audience, improving campaign effectiveness and efficiency.
4. **Lessened fraud:** Blockchain-based identity verification helps to reduce fraud in marketing initiatives. By confirming that users are who they say they are, it lowers the possibility of bogus accounts, fraudulent clicks, and other dishonest tactics that might waste advertising dollars.
5. **Tailored marketing:** Marketers may deliver more individualized and pertinent marketing initiatives with the use of verified and trustworthy client data. Higher consumer engagement and conversion rates result from this, which ultimately improves return on marketing investment.
6. **Simplified client onboarding:** Blockchain-based identity verification streamlines and expedites the client onboarding process in industries like financial services and e-commerce. Because of the decreased friction in the customer journey, conversion rates are increased, and user experiences are enhanced.
7. **Consistency across platforms:** Blockchain-based identity verification helps ensure user identities are consistent across many platforms and services. This makes it possible for customers to interact with different marketing touchpoints in a seamless manner, resulting in a consistent and unified brand experience.

9.8.2 Challenges of Decentralized Finance-Powered Marketing

Decentralized finance-powered marketing has fascinating prospects, but it also carries a fair share of risks and difficulties [3]. For successful and ethical marketing campaigns in this quickly changing industry, businesses must carefully analyze the regulatory environment, traverse the complexities of DeFi, and avoid financial and security risks.

1. **Regulatory ambiguity:** The DeFi regulatory landscape is still developing, and marketing efforts in this area may come under scrutiny. Businesses may face difficulties and risks when navigating the complicated and frequently opaque regulatory environment, which could result in legal problems or compliance violations.
2. **Variability and risk:** Decentralized finance systems frequently use tokens and cryptocurrencies, which are recognized for their price volatility. If token values change substantially, marketing initiatives that rely on these assets may be at serious financial risk.
3. **Digital contract bugs:** Smart contracts, which DeFi mainly relies on, are not impervious to coding faults or vulnerabilities. Smart contracts that have exploitable defects run the risk of causing financial losses or security lapses, which could be bad for a company's reputation.
4. **Illegal activities and frauds:** Because DeFi is decentralized, it may be a haven for schemes and fraudulent projects. To prevent being linked to shady practices, marketers must use caution when endorsing or collaborating with DeFi enterprises.
5. **Intricacy:** Decentralized finance marketing initiatives can include intricate technical components that might be difficult for non-technical marketers to comprehend and properly manage. Complexity can result in poor management and errors.
6. **A lack of client education:** The typical consumer may find it challenging to understand how DeFi works. Customers' education about DeFi may require investment in marketing activities, which can be time and resource-consuming.
7. **Privacy issues:** Decentralized finance platforms might ask for more personal information from consumers than conventional financial services, which could cause privacy issues. To prevent criticism, marketers must handle customer data sensibly.
8. **Rapid technological development:** Decentralized finance is a field that is constantly changing, with new initiatives

and technology appearing all the time. It can be difficult and time-consuming to keep up with these changes and adjust marketing strategies.

9. **The opponent risk:** Interaction with different parties, including liquidity providers and DEXs, is frequent on DeFi platforms. Marketing initiatives and partnerships may be impacted by the risk of counterparty default or platform vulnerabilities.
10. **Marketplace saturation:** As DeFi develops popularity, the market is being flooded with initiatives and campaigns of a similar nature. It might be difficult to stand out in a crowded area, and rivalry can be ferocious.
11. **Liquidity pitfalls:** Decentralized finance liquidity pools may encounter abrupt fluctuations in liquidity, which could affect marketing efforts that use these pools for token swaps or reward distribution.

9.9 Regulatory Compliance in Decentralized Finance-Powered Marketing

Regulatory compliance is a crucial factor to consider when using DeFi-powered marketing because these platforms' decentralized nature might present special difficulties in adhering to legal and regulatory obligations [36]. When addressing legal compliance in DeFi-powered marketing, the following important factors should be taken into account:

1. **Know Your Customer (KYC) and anti-money laundering (AML) regulations:** Decentralized finance marketing platforms could be governed by KYC and AML laws, depending on your jurisdiction. To ensure that your marketing campaigns do not aid in money laundering or other illicit actions, implement strict KYC and AML standards.
2. **Investments rules:** You must abide by securities rules and regulations if your DeFi marketing strategy involves promoting or selling tokens that are regarded as securities. Consult legal counsel to ascertain whether your campaign complies with these rules and then take the necessary steps to do so. Investors always look for various investment strategies to earn abnormal returns [14].

3. **Consumer protection:** Ensure that the laws governing consumer protection are followed in your marketing initiatives. Users should get clear and accurate information regarding the advantages and risks of engaging in DeFi activities, and dishonest or misleading tactics should be avoided.
4. **Taxes and revenues:** Be aware of the tax repercussions of your DeFi marketing efforts, particularly how cryptocurrencies and tokens are taxed. Observe local tax regulations and record earnings and transactions as necessary.
5. **Data security:** User data is frequently collected and handled in DeFi marketing efforts. Respect user privacy and data rights by adhering to data privacy laws, such as the GDPR in the European Union.
6. **Adherence to DeFi protocols:** Ensure that the governance and rules of the DeFi protocols you utilize are adhered to in your marketing efforts. Financial losses and reputational harm may occur from breaking protocol norms.
7. **Transparency and disclosure:** Keep your marketing communications transparent. Clearly state any relationships, affiliations, or financial stakes you may have in the DeFi initiatives or coins you are endorsing.
8. **Smart contract inspections:** If your marketing strategy makes use of smart contracts, think about conducting security audits to find and fix any flaws that can result in legal trouble or monetary losses.
9. **Legal assistance:** To negotiate the complicated regulatory environment, consult with legal counsel with knowledge of Bitcoin, blockchain technology, and DeFi rules. You can arrange your marketing strategies to comply with applicable legislation with the help of legal counsel.
10. **Constant monitoring:** Laws governing the DeFi industry are always evolving. To preserve compliance, keep up with changing legislation and adjust your marketing tactics as necessary.
11. **International factors:** Decentralized finance marketing frequently crosses international borders. Recognize and abide by the legal requirements of the nations where your business operates, or your target market is located.
12. **Risk evaluation:** Perform a thorough risk analysis of your DeFi marketing initiatives to spot any compliance concerns and put risk reduction plans in place.

9.10 Conclusion

A completely new frontier in customer interaction and business expansion is DeFi-powered marketing. Companies can seize a multitude of chances to re-imagine client experiences by utilizing the possibilities of decentralized financing. The advantages are clear, ranging from improved financial inclusion to increased security, increased effectiveness, and creative loyalty programs. Decentralized finance encourages trust, transparency, and customization in marketing initiatives in addition to streamlining operations. To truly embrace the transformative potential of DeFi in defining the future of marketing, however, organizations must successfully traverse the difficulties of this changing landscape, such as regulatory constraints and technological complexities. The effective adoption and integration of DeFi will enable businesses to not only meet but also surpass the constantly changing expectations of their clients, paving the way for a new era of decentralized, customer-focused marketing.

References

1. Aquilina, M., Frost, J., Schrimpf, A., Decentralised Finance (DeFi): A Functional Approach, January 16, 2023, Available at SSRN: https://ssrn.com/abstract=4325095 or http://dx.doi.org/10.2139/ssrn.4325095.
2. Aramonte, S., Doerr, S., Huang, W., Schrimpf, A., DeFi lending: intermediation without information?, Bank for International Settlements, June 14, 2022.
3. Aramonte, S., Huang, W., Schrimpf, A., DeFi risks and the decentralisation illusion. *BIS Quarterly Review*, p. 6, 2021 Dec 6.
4. Arslanian, H., Decentralised Finance (DeFi), in: *The Book of Crypto: The Complete Guide to Understanding Bitcoin, Cryptocurrencies and Digital Assets*, pp. 291–313, Springer International Publishing, Cham, 2022.
5. Auer, R., Frost, J., Pastor, J.M.V., Miners as intermediaries: extractable value and market manipulation in crypto and DeFi (No. 58), Bank for International Settlements, 2022.
6. Barbereau, T., Smethurst, R., Papageorgiou, O., Sedlmeir, J., Fridgen, G., Decentralised Finance's Unregulated Governance: Minority Rule in the Digital Wild West. *Technol. Soc.*, 73, 1–17, 2022, Available at SSRN 4001891.
7. Maia, G.C. and Vieira dos Santos, J., MiCA and DeFi ('Proposal for a Regulation on Market in Crypto-Assets' and'Decentralised Finance'). *Forthcoming article in" Blockchain and the law: dynamics and dogmatism, current and future*, 2021.
8. Carapella, F. and Swem, N., Decentralized Finance (Defi): Transformative Potential & Associated Risks, 2022.

9. Chu, J., Chan, S., Zhang, Y., An analysis of the return–volume relationship in decentralised finance (DeFi). *Int. Rev. Econ. Finance*, *85*, 236–254, 2023.
10. Szrajber, B., Alon, I. and Levy, S., Systematic Analysis of Decentralized Finance. *J. Glob. Inf. Manag.*, 33, 1, 1–29, 2025.
11. Cong, L.W., Tang, K., Wang, Y., Zhao, X., Inclusion and democratization through web3 and defi? initial evidence from the ethereum ecosystem (No. w30949), National Bureau of Economic Research, 2023.
12. Doerr, J.F., Kosse, A., Khan, A., Lewrick, U., Mojon, B., Nolens, B., Rice, T., DeFi risks and the decentralisation illusion. *BIS Quarterly Review*, p. 21, 2021.
13. Dos Santos, S., Singh, J., Thulasiram, R.K., Kamali, S., Sirico, L., Loud, L., A new era of blockchain-powered decentralized finance (DeFi)-a review, in: *2022 IEEE 46th Annual Computers, Software, and Applications Conference (COMPSAC)*, IEEE, pp. 1286–1292, 2022.
14. Eikmanns, B.C., Mehrwald, P., Sandner, P.G., Welpe, I.M., Decentralised finance platform ecosystems: conceptualisation and outlook. *Technol. Anal. Strateg. Manag.*, 37, 4, 1–13, 2023.
15. Etzel, M.J., Walker, B.J., Stanton, W.J., *Marketing*, McGraw-Hill/Irwin, USA, 2001.
16. Harvey, C.R., Ramachandran, A., Santoro, J., *DeFi and the Future of Finance*, John Wiley & Sons, USA, 2021.
17. Hoshi, T. and Patrick, H.T. (Eds.), *Crisis and change in the Japanese financial system*, vol. 12, Springer Science & Business Media, Germany, 2000.
18. Kotler, P., Burton, S., Deans, K., Brown, L., Armstrong, G., *Marketing*, Pearson Higher Education AU, Australia, 2015.
19. Lamb, C.W., Hair, J.F., McDaniel, C., *Marketing*, Cengage Learning, USA, 2012.
20. Makarov, I. and Schoar, A., Cryptocurrencies and decentralized finance (DeFi) (No. w30006), National Bureau of Economic Research, 2022.
21. Meegan, X., Identifying key non-financial risks in decentralised finance on ethereum blockchain, MIP Politecnico di Milano, 2020.
22. Meegan, X. and Koens, T., Lessons learned from decentralised finance (DeFi), ING, 2021, URL:https://new.ingwb.com/binaries/content/assets/insights/themes/distributed-ledger technology/defi_white_paper_v2. 0. Pdf.
23. Mehta, K. and Sharma, R., Contrarian and momentum investment strategies: Evidence from Indian stock market. *Int. J. Appl. Bus. Econ. Res.*, 15, 2, 87–98, 2017.
24. Mehta, K. and Sharma, R., Unraveling quantum complexity: A fuzzy AHP approach to understanding software industry challenges, in: *Deep Learning Tools for Predicting Stock Market Movements*, pp. 39–60, p. complexity, 2024.
25. Mehta, K., Sharma, R., Vyas, V., A quantile regression approach to study the impact of aluminium prices on manufacturing sector of India during COVID era. *Mater. Today Proc.*, 65, 7, 3506–3511, 2022.

26. Mehta, K., Sharma, R., Vyas, V., Kuckreja, J.S., Exit strategy decision by venture capital firms in India using fuzzy AHP. *J. Entrep. Emerg. Econ.*, 14, 4, 643–669, 2022.
27. Miller, T., Cao, S., Foth, M., Boyen, X., Powell, W., An asset-backed decentralised finance instrument for food supply chains–A case study from the livestock export industry. *Comput. Ind.*, *147*, 103863, 2023.
28. Morgan, N.A., Whitler, K.A., Feng, H., Chari, S., Research in marketing strategy. *J. Acad. Marketing Sci.*, *47*, 4–29, 2019.
29. Ozili, P.K., Decentralised finance and cryptocurrency activity in Africa, in: *The New Digital Era: Digitalisation, Emerging Risks and Opportunities*, pp. 3–11, Emerald Publishing Limited, UK, 2022.
30. Rossi, E., Modularizing Decentralised Finance: The Defi Layered Stack Revisited, 2023, Available at SSRN 4365222. Yavin, O. and Reardon, A.J., What digital banks can learn from decentralised finance. *J. Digital Banking*, 5, 3, 255–263, 2021.
31. Salami, I., Decentralised Finance: The Case for a Holistic Approach to Regulating the Crypto Industry. *J. Int. Banking Fin. L.*, 35, 7, 496–499, 2020.
32. Sharma, R. and Mehta, K., Credit risk and bank specific factors: An empirical study using panel GMM. *Int. J. Econ. Bus. Res.*, 27, 2, 294–309, 2024.
33. Sharma, R. and Mehta, K., *Deep Learning Tools for Predicting Stock Market Movements*, John Wiley & Sons, USA, 2024.
34. Sharma, R., Mehta, K., Chugh, A., Using Analytic Hierarchy Process to determine forex risk hedging strategies of SMEs. *AIP Conf. Proc.*, 2916, 1, 120008, 2023.
35. Sharma, R., Mehta, K., Rana, R., Cryptocurrency adoption behaviour of millennial investors in India, in: *Perspectives on Blockchain Technology and Responsible Investing*, pp. 135–158, 2023.
36. Srokosz, W. and Kopciaski, T., Legal and economic analysis of the cryptocurrencies impact on the financial system stability. *J. Teach. Educ.*, 4, 2, 619–627, 2015.
37. Vyas, V., Mehta, K., Sharma, R., Investigating socially responsible investing behaviour of Indian investors using structural equation modelling. *J. Sustain. Financ. Invest.*, 12, 1, 1–23, 2020.
38. Vyas, V., Mehta, K., Sharma, R., Are bitcoin prices isolated or co-integrated? *Int. J. Bus. Glob.*, 35, 1–2, 5–19, 2023.
39. Xu, J. and Vadgama, N., From banks to DeFi: the evolution of the lending market, in: *Enabling the Internet of Value: How Blockchain Connects Global Businesses*, pp. 53–66, 2022.

10

The Finance Face-Off: Decentralized Finance and Centralized Finance Explained

Gitika Arora[1]* and C. A. Nitin Arora[2]

[1]*Chitkara Business School, Chitkara University, Punjab, India*
[2]*Nitin Surbhi & Company, Jalandhar, Punjab, India*

Abstract
With the advancement of technology, the emergence of two financial models, centralized finance (CeFi) and decentralized finance (DeFi) had made the transformational shift in the financial landscape. The study has analyzed and compared the two financial models (CeFi and DeFi). The research has explained the concepts, characteristics, advantages, and disadvantages of both models, emphasizing their main distinctions. The findings of the study are supported by the prominent DeFi and CeFi platform case study. The study has found that CeFi provides security and a high support to users due to its regulatory adherence, whereas DeFi delivers innovation, transparency, and more inclusiveness. The study suggests the synthesis of both financial models to maximise the financial prosperity of the economy.

Keywords: Decentralized finance (DeFi), centralized finance (CeFi), Binance, Uniswap, Ethereum

10.1 Introduction

Finance is the field that encompasses the activities of generating, managing and investing the funds [12]. Rooted in the ancient practice of barter of goods and assets, finance evolved to the creation of banking system in early Mesopotamian and Roman cultures [10, 13]. Gradually, finance has grown into various areas like personal, public finance and corporate finance, as well as into specialized domains like financial planning, asset

**Corresponding author*: gitika.arora@chitkara.edu.in

Renuka Sharma, Kiran Mehta, Vishal Vyas and Vinod Kumar Shukla (eds.) Decentralized Finance and Blockchain: A Game Changing Duo, (225–238) © 2025 Scrivener Publishing LLC

management, and investment banking. The whole financial system contributes to the overall economic growth by enabling the flow of capital in an economy by channelizing the resources in a productive manner [10, 12]. With the advancement of technology, many innovations are being witnessed in the field of finance like decentralized finance (DeFi) and digital currencies [10]. The advent of centralized finance (CeFi) and DeFi leads to the revolutionary shift in the financial paradigm. Both are two different approaches with their own characteristics and implications in the financial system [13]. Centralized finance refers to the financial service that is centrally controlled and regulated to provide custody, manage assets, and ensure compliance [15, 18]. Centralized finance is considered difficult to understand by the non-experts as it involves a lot of rules and regulations [13]. However, DeFi leverages blockchain to provide transparent, permissionless financial services through smart contracts without the involvement of any intermediaries [4]. While CeFi provides the security and trust to the users, DeFi provides autonomy, transparency, and global access to financial services. This chapter analyzed the concept of DeFi and CeFi in detail by explaining the characteristics, advantages, disadvantages and differences between both the concepts supported by a case study. At last, implications and recommendations are given.

On the reviewing the literature on DeFi and CeFi, the research objective of this chapter is to study and compare DeFi and CeFi using a case study to understand their benefits and challenges.

10.2 Centralized Finance

10.2.1 Overview and Characteristics of Centralized Finance

Centralized finance is a financial system that uses centralized entities to manage transactions, decisions, and services. In CeFi, all funds and transactions are controlled by a centralized governing body [10, 13]. While providing the highest level of security for finances and transactions, governments can also use its central system to restrict citizens' access to payment systems, freeze accounts, and remove funds [10]. To administer their user accounts and carry out transactions, it depends on reliable intermediaries, or custodians [10, 13]. Centralized finance platforms charge transaction fees for depositing funds and withdrawal thereof. These platforms allow to buy and sell cryptocurrencies using fiat currency (American Dollar, Euros) [13].

10.2.2 Key Players in Centralized Finance

Centralized finance involves well-structured financial institutions and cryptocurrency exchanges (CEXs). Major players involve a central authority that manages and controls the transactions and services offered by traditional banks. Cryptocurrency exchanges are centralized entities that allow users to buy, sell, and hold decentralized assets like crypto and non-fungible tokens. Popular CEXs include Coinbase, Binance, and Kraken [10]. Coinbase is the CEX that provides the platform to buy, sell, and trade cryptocurrency. Binance is the order book-based CEX for trading in cryptocurrencies [11, 17]. Various banks and financial institutions such as Goldman Sachs and J. P. Morgan are developing platforms for trading in cryptocurrencies [6].

10.2.3 Advantages of Centralized Finance

Safety and security: Centralized finance platforms are safe and secure since extra security measures and strict regulations are being implemented. Examples are Know Your Customer (KYC) and anti-money laundering (AML) procedures, which aid in minimizing fraud and illegal activities. This framework builds the confidence and trust of customers to trade in the cryptocurrency market as they feel comfortable with the strict regulatory environment [10, 13].

Fiat-to-crypto: Centralized finance offers a platform where large sums of fiat money can be quickly converted by users into cryptocurrency assets, which enhances liquidity and gives dealers healthy profit margins. This provides a user-friendly interface that makes it easily accessible for users new to the crypto space or who are less tech-savvy [16].

Customer service: Various cryptocurrency exchanges provide customer support 24/7 to help them resolve their problems [7, 13].

Cross-chain support: Centralized finance offers cross-chain trading methods for a range of cryptocurrency tokens. It helps users to buy, sell, and trade assets across different networks easily. This makes it convenient for CeFi users to access trade assets through single interfaces without the requirement of managing multiple wallets [14].

Margin trading: Users can also trade with margin accounts on certain CeFi exchanges, where a percentage of the value is loaned to them with interest. It offers users more liquidity and accessibility to a larger lending pool, making it convenient to borrow at comparatively less rates [13].

10.2.4 Disadvantages of Centralized Finance

Third-party control: Since money is kept outside of user custody, governments can utilize their central system to control citizens' finances by withdrawing money, freezing accounts, and blocking access to payment systems [10].
Accounting: Centralized finance handles accounting and reconciliation; it is not supported by code in a smart contract like in DeFi [16].
No privacy and anonymity: In CeFi transactions, user identity is clear and known, and hence a person's anonymity cannot be maintained [7, 13].

10.3 Decentralized Finance

10.3.1 Overview and Characteristics of Decentralized Finance

Decentralized finance is an emerging ecosystem within the world of blockchain technology. It covers a set of financial platforms and applications that make it easier to trade and transfer financial assets without the need for reliable intermediaries. It is a branch of blockchain technology that focuses on offering financial services and solutions based on ledgers with smart contract functionality [7, 10, 13]. One of the key benefits of DeFi is that it facilitates the democratization of finance [10]. Decentralized finance uses smart contracts, which are self-executing programs that autonomously enforce the terms of the agreement between the two parties, to eliminate the need for intermediaries. This network is incredibly creative and inventive. Because it uses a decentralized, public ledger, anybody can see how much money is being transferred, where it is going, and how it is being used. No matter where they live or their financial situation, anyone with an internet connection can use it. It is an innovative method of obtaining financial services that eliminates conventional banks and financial organizations [3, 7, 19].

10.3.2 Key Players in Decentralized Finance

Decentralized finance involves various key players in the form of projects, platforms, and protocols that together form an efficient financial landscape. Notable examples are Aave, Uniswap, Compound, and MakerDAO. Uniswap is centrally regulated and works on the automated market maker (AMM) mechanism where users are allowed to swap their cryptocurrencies. Further, Aave is the lending platform where borrowers lend and borrow cryptocurrencies. Compound and MakerDAO also play key role in the DeFi ecosystem [7, 11].

10.3.3 Advantages of Decentralized Finance

Users control: Decentralized finance gives its consumers immediate management over their assets, regardless of the time. Waiting for banking institutions to open is not necessary. Decentralized finance is available 24/7. All you require is internet connectivity [13].

Transparency: All transactions are on a public ledger, and all are recorded on the blockchain. Hence, it facilitates transparency in transactions, and all credit goes to open-source technology. The capacity to communicate trust in new DeFi systems is made possible by this transparency. This lessens the possibility of corruption and fraud [7, 9, 13].

Less transaction costs: Since there is no involvement of intermediaries such as banks and brokers, there is low buy-and-sell transaction costs [9].

Anonymous: In DeFi, wallet ownership is anonymous, but transactions are transparent and traceable [7, 13].

Democratization of finance: The democratization of finance is one of the main advantages. Decentralized finance eliminates geographical restrictions and discriminatory tactics frequently found in traditional banking systems by enabling anybody to access financial services and products *via* an internet connection [10].

10.3.4 Disadvantages of Decentralized Finance

High level of technical expertise: One of the primary drawbacks is the high degree of technical proficiency needed to implement DeFi practices. For novices and others who are less tech-savvy, the complexity of blockchain technology, smart contracts, and cryptocurrencies might be intimidating [8, 10].

High-risk involvement: The huge number of potential risks that come with DeFi is another significant drawback. These consist of hacking threats, smart contract malfunctions, and market volatility. Furthermore, the DeFi industry usually lacks the insurance and consumer protection measures that regular banking systems provide. Users are therefore required to assume the entire risk of their investments [10].

Scalability issues: The usability and popularity of DeFi applications may be limited by slow transaction rates during busy hours. Transactions *via* blockchain take long to complete. Blockchain technology is still unable to process enough transactions per second to surpass centralized finance [10].

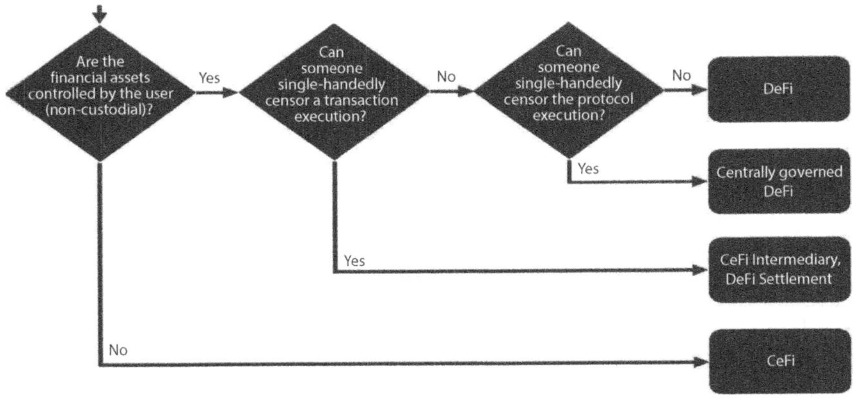

Figure 10.1 The difference between CeFi and Defi [13].

Regulatory challenges: Uncertainties in laws and regulations present a significant obstacle. Many jurisdictions lack clear regulatory frameworks for DeFi because it is a new idea. This may result in ambiguities in the law and possible conflicts [10, 13].

The key difference between CeFi and DeFi is mentioned in Figure 10.1, which is given above [13]. The present study has explained the differences based on the review of literature as mentioned below.

10.4 Difference Between Centralized Finance and Decentralized Finance

Based on the above discussion and the review of literature, the key distinction between CeFi and DeFi is explained as follows:

Central backing authority
The foundation of a centralized financial system is a centralized institution, in which the government supports the value of money. Conversely, permissionless DeFi allows financial assets to be traded and transferred without the need for any reliable intermediaries [7, 10, 13].

Non-stop market hours
In the case of CeFi, there are fixed hours of banking and other financial institutions that are dealing with financial instruments (there is a need to wait for banks to open). It is uncommon for CeFi markets to function

without interruptions. On the other hand, DeFi markets are open around-the-clock. Decentralized finance, therefore, has no pre- or post-market trading time. It gives its users direct control over their assets at any moment of day [13].

Atomicity in transactions

Atomicity in finance refers to a transaction that either fails collectively or performs fully in all its operations. This programmable atomic property: meaning thereby to treat a series of transactions as a single atomic unit is absent in almost all CeFi Transactions. This feature can be incorporated in CeFi transactions with legal agreements. However, multiple financial operations can be combined through sequential actions in DeFi transactions [13].

Execution orders in transactions

Centralized finance's centralized regulatory organizations enforce stringent guidelines for financial institutions and services for the enforcement of transaction ordering. On the other hand, users usually disclose the transactions that are intended to be carried out *via* permissionless DeFi transactions. Because of a lack of centralized entity transactions execution order, all transactions are vulnerable to attacks which is very commonly called as transaction malleability nowadays [13].

Transactions cost

In CeFi, financial institutions usually offer services and various transactions for no costs as generally mandated by the centralized authority to provide free services. However, transaction fees in DeFi transactions are generally essential for prevention of spam and other attacks [13].

Custody and control

Since users are in possession of their private keys, DeFi grants them complete control over their money. However, in CeFi, users usually entrust third parties with the custody and management of their assets [7, 13].

Censoring transactions

In CeFi, an entity must comply with KYC/AML regulations and has the authority to independently censor or interfere in a financial transaction. But in DeFi, miners cannot filter a transaction's execution because they lack the authority to add a transaction to the blockchain [7, 13].

Lending and borrowing

Centralized financial transactions do not involve the idea of a lending pool; instead, the lender extends credit to the borrower. Lending and borrowing, however, take place in the so-called lending pools in DeFi transactions [13]. Essentially, a lending pool is a smart contract that aggregates the assets of both lenders and borrowers. Usually, a lender deposits cryptocurrency into a lending pool to make it accessible for borrowing. Thus, the borrower promises collateral to the lending pool and borrows from it. An important element in this case is that when the lending pool lends out the collateral from borrowers, the borrower also instantly becomes the lender. Traditional CeFi rules, such as bank deposit protection, do not cover assets deposited by users in lending pools [7].

Transparency

Centralized finance always requires complying with KYC requirements. But in DeFI, there are large percentages of anonymity in applications and transactions. In CeFi, user identity is clear, but third parties cannot see transactions. In DeFi, wallet ownership is anonymous, but transactions are transparent and traceable [7, 10, 13].

Security

There is more security in the case of CeFi, whereas in the case of DeFi, less security exists [13].

Fiat currency

Centralized finance platforms make it easier to exchange fiat currency, which is government-issued money like the U.S. dollar. DeFi does not offer fiat-to-cryptocurrency exchange [16].

Accounting

In CeFi, accounting and reconciliation are handled by centralised authority, while in DeFi, these tasks are enabled *via* code in a smart contract. Decentralized finance is a peer-to-peer approach to cryptocurrency transactions, where individuals control their private keys and use smart contracts to execute transactions [16]. Table 10.1 highlights the differences between CeFi and DeFi, which have already been explained in detail in the preceding sections of this chapter.

Table 10.1 The differences between CeFi and DeFi.

Basis of difference	CeFi	DeFi
Central backing authority	Yes	No
Non-stop market hours	No	Yes
Atomicity in transactions	No	Yes
Execution order in transactions	Yes	No
Transaction cost	No	Yes
Custody and control of users over assets	No	Yes
Censoring transactions	Yes	No
Lending and borrowing – an existence of a lending pool	No	Yes
Transparency	No	Yes
Security	More	Less
Fiat currency exchange	Yes	No
Accounting	By centralized authority	By code in smart contract

Source: Authors.

10.5 Case Study Analysis

Based on the above discussion, a case study analysis is performed to support the difference as explained above. Here, the case study of centralized exchange (Binance) and decentralized exchange (Uniswap) is performed to have more practical clarity among both financial models.

10.5.1 Case Study of Uniswap–Decentralized Exchange

10.5.1.1 Overview and Characteristics of Uniswap

Uniswap is the DEX that worked without intermediaries on the Ethereum blockchain. Ethereum-based tokens are traded on the Uniswap. It is based on the feature of AMM, where the mathematical calculations are performed to determine the token prices [22]. There is no requirement of identification of users, i.e. KYC in case of Uniswap. Further, the users are considered as liquidity providers, which support the more efficient market [20].

10.5.1.2 Advantages of Uniswap

Uniswap users do not require the KYC protocol. It is a permissionless platform. Further, it is transparent as the transaction can be seen on the blockchain. Moreover, it provides opportunities of earning to the users in proportion to the quantity of trade in the pool made [20, 22].

10.5.1.3 Disadvantages of Uniswap

In Uniswap, there can be chances of risk in smart contract. However, liquidity providers can also face the risk of temporary losses due to a fluctuation in prices in the liquidity pool. Further, the gas price of Ethereum is comparatively higher as it is not centrally regulated. The gas price is the fee required to perform transactions on various networks, needed especially to maintain security of transactions. It is denoted in Gwei. The gas price of Ethereum is shown in Figure 10.2 below, which reflects the gas price in Gwei over a period of time. Ethereum is the blockchain required to use Uniswap [11].

10.5.2 Case Study on Centralized Finance–Binance

10.5.2.1 Overview and Characteristics of Binance

The world's largest order book-based centralized exchange is Binance. It started in June 2017 and provides a wide range of products like futures,

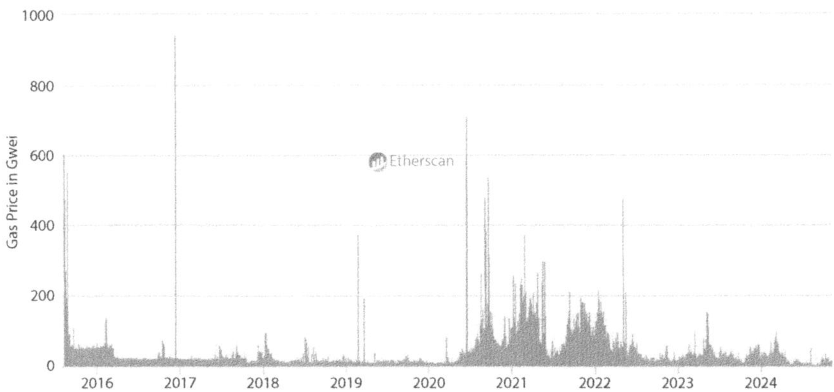

Figure 10.2 Average gas price of Ethereum. Source: https://etherscan.io/chart/gasprice retrieved on November 07, 2024.

savings, spot trading, and lending, making it resourceful for various user requirements. Various DeFi projects are also being supported by the blockchain system of Binance. It is the platform that provides various channels for earning passive income to users who are staking, saving, and earning interest on deposits [7, 11].

10.5.2.2 Advantages of Binance

Binance has made it easy for the beginner to buy the cryptocurrencies as it allows them to use fiat currency, making it simpler for them [11]. Further, the gas price of Binance Smart Chain (BSC) is comparatively lower than Ethereum as it is centrally regulated. BSC is a platform required to use the Binance ecosystem. Figure 10.3 below shows the average gas price of BSC over the period of time.

10.5.2.3 Disadvantages of Binance

The transactions of users of Binance are centrally regulated, hence no control over the personal assets. Further, the situation of idle time occurs in Binance as both the parties must wait for the right price. Lastly, users find it less trustworthy, being non-transparent in nature [11].

The case study explains that both DeFi and CeFi financial models have their unique features as per the requirement of the user. The DeFi platforms like Uniswap have their own traits like being transparent, user-friendly, permissionless, autonomous, and innovative but have high gas

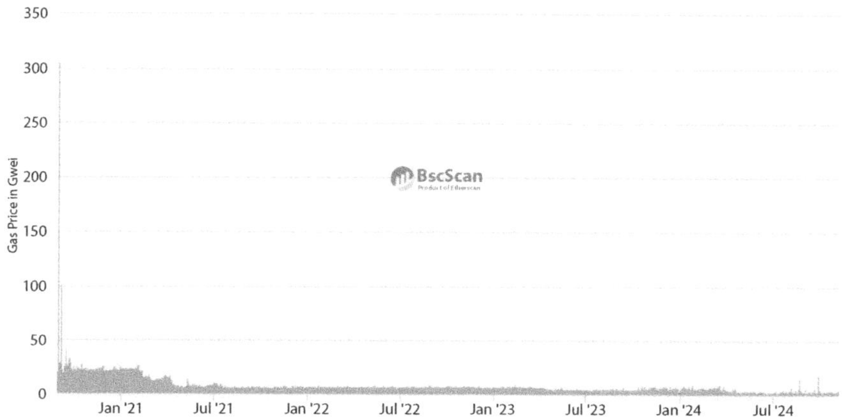

Figure 10.3 Average gas price of Binance. Source: https://bscscan.com/chart/gasprice retrieved on November 07, 2024.

prices, smart contract risk, and issues of regulatory adherence. On the other hand, Binance being centrally regulated has features like security, and high customer support, but at the same time have issues of idle time and asset control.

10.6 Conclusion and Recommendations

The finance face-off has provided the insight about two financial models – DeFi and CeFi. Centralized finance is centrally regulated, having customer support and low fees, and DeFi is transparent and has a potential of high yield, but there is the requirement of a well-defined framework to differentiate both financial models [13]. Though the advent of DeFi leads to the transformational or significant change in the whole financial system, the concern of achieving scale and adherence to regulations are required to be kept in mind by policymakers [2]. The policymakers should focus on developing ways to use the potentials of DeFi and overcome its challenge to have a more efficient financial system. The study recommends to create the balance between regulatory adherence and innovation to ensure consumer protection and security [2, 5]. Further, DeFi is facing the issue of scalability, security, and regulatory compliance that can be tackled by having a proper regulatory framework, protocols for security, and financial literacy of consumers [1]. However, to overcome the limitations of financial technology, a human-centric approach is required. Moreover, human-values need to be deeply rooted in the governance of both financial models to ensure financial prosperity [21]. The study suggests the synthesis of both financial models to maximize the financial prosperity of the economy.

References

1. Adisa, O., Obi, O., Adelekan, O., Awonuga, K., Asuzu, O., Ndubuisi, N., Ilugbusi, B., Decentralized Finance (DEFI) in the U. S. economy: A review: Assessing the rise, challenges, and implications of blockchain-driven financial systems. *World J. Adv. Res. Rev.*, *21*, 1, 2313–2328, 2024, https://doi.org/10.30574/wjarr.2024.21.1.0321.
2. Ahmed, A.A.A., The Rise of DeFi: Transforming Traditional Finance with Blockchain Innovation, 2024, https://doi.org/10.20944/preprints202402.0738.v1.
3. Ahmed, S., Rise of Decentralised Finance | Reimagining Financial Regulation. *Indian J. Law Technol.*, 18, 1, 1–32, 2022, 10.55496/GBYY2818.

4. Ahuja, R. and Khandelwal, J., Challenges, Opportunities and Risk Analysis of Adoption of Decentralized Finance Applications. *ICTACT J. Soft Comput.*, *14*, 1, 3114–3129, 2023, https://doi.org/10.21917/ijsc.2023.0438.
5. Asl, M.G. and Ben Jabeur, S., Tail connectedness of DeFi and CeFi with accessible banking pillars: Unveiling novel insights through wavelet and quantile cross-spectral coherence analyses. *Int. Rev. Financ. Anal.*, *95*, 103424, 2024, https://doi.org/10.1016/j.irfa.2024.103424.
6. Bilgin, E., From Skepticism to Integration: The Banking Sector's Evolving Relationship with Cryptocurrency and Blockchain Technology. *J. Econ.*, *12*, 1, 1–8, 2024.
7. Borisov, S., DeFi – Potential, Advantages and Challenges. *Econ. Stud. (Ikonom. Izsled.)*, 31, 4, 33–54, 2022.
8. Fliche, O., Uri, J., Vileyn, M., Hub, F.I., Decentralised'or 'disintermediated'finance: what regulatory response? ACPR/Banque de France Discussion Paper, April, 2023, https://acpr. banque-france. fr/sites/default/files/medias/documents/20230403_decentralised_disintermediated_finance_en. pdf.
9. John, F., Yadav, K., Soni, M., Decentralized Finance: A Review of the Current Landscape and Future Opportunities. *Int. J. Res. Appl. Sci. Eng. Technol.*, *11*, 4, 3231–3236, 2023, https://doi.org/10.22214/ijraset.2023.50743.
10. Nath, K., CeFi, Fintech and DeFi–Understanding the Benefits, Limitations and Challenges. *Authorea Preprints*, 2023, https://doi.org/10.36227/techrxiv.22274371.v1.
11. Pandey, D., Decentralized Exchanges: A Qualitative Comparison Against Centralized Exchanges, Master's thesis, NTNU, 2022.
12. Pandey, I.M., *Financial Management*, 11th ed, Vikas Publishing House, India, 2015.
13. Qin, K., Zhou, L., Afonin, Y., Lazzaretti, L., Gervais, A., CeFi vs. DeFi–Comparing Centralized to Decentralized Finance, 2021, *arXiv preprint arXiv:2106.08157*, https://doi.org/10.48550/arXiv.2106.08157.
14. Schuler, K., Cloots, A.S., Schär, F., On DeFi and On-Chain CeFi: How (Not) to Regulate Decentralized Finance. *J. Financ. Regul.*, 10, 2, 213–242, 2024, https://doi.org/10.1093/jfr/fjad014.
15. Soni, H., The Interplay of DeFi and CeFi: Analyzing Decentralized Finance through the Lens of the Shiva Milk Story and the Ramayana Metaphor. *Sci. J. Metaverse Blockchain Technol.*, *2*, 2, 162–166, 2024, https://doi.org/10.36676/sjmbt.v2.i2.46.
16. Techtarget.com., Techtarget-Decentralized finance vs. centralized finance: What's the difference? [online], 2023, Available at https://www.techtarget.com/whatis/feature/Decentralized-finance-vs-centralized-finance-Whats-the-difference [Accessed 01 November, 2024].
17. Tripathi, B. and Sharma, R.K., Cryptocurrency Exchanges and Traditional Markets: A Multi-algorithm Liquidity Comparison Using Multi-criteria Decision Analysis. *Comput. Econ.*, 65, 5, 1–29, 2024. 10.1007/s10614-24-10655-9.

18. Wieandt, A. and Heppding, L., Centralized and decentralized finance: Coexistence or convergence?, in: *The Fintech Disruption: How Financial Innovation Is Transforming the Banking Industry*, pp. 11–51, Springer International Publishing, Cham, 2023, https://doi.org/10.1007/978-3-031-23069-1_2.
19. Xu, R., Zhu, J., Yang, L., Lu, Y., Xu, L.D., Decentralized finance (DeFi): a paradigm shift in the Fintech. *Enterp. Inf. Syst.*, *18*, 9, 1170–1209, 2024, https://doi.org/10.1080/17517575.2024.2397630.
20. Lo, Y. and Medda, F., Uniswap and the rise of the decentralized exchange, Munich Personal Repec Archive, 2022, https://mpra.ub.uni-muenchen.de/103925/.
21. Zhang, L., The future of finance: Synthesizing cefi and defi for the benefit of all, in: *Financial Literacy in Today's Global Market*. Poland: IntechOpen, 2023, https://doi.org/10.5772/intechopen.1003042.
22. Zhang, Y., Chen, X., Park, D., Formal specification of constant product (xy=k) market maker model and implementation. *White paper*, 2018.

11

An Empirical Study of Environmentally Efficient Precursors of Green Foreign Direct Investment to Achieve Sustainable Development

Manoj Mishra[1] and Shefali Saluja[2*]

[1]Faculty of Management, Marwadi University, Rajkot, Gujarat, India
[2]Chitkara Business School, Chitkara University, Rajpura, Punjab, India

Abstract

The present study attempts to identify environmentally efficient precursors to attract green foreign direct investment (FDI) to the country. It also attempts to study the impact of these identified precursors on green FDI and sustainable development. Foreign direct investment in renewable energy has been considered as green FDI. This aspect is related to the 7th Sustainable Development Goal (SDG). The 7th SDG, "Affordable and Clean Energy," has been considered to achieve sustainable development. The present study has been using stakeholders' perspectives regarding environmental efficiency to attract green FDI. Administrative personnel of major agencies and institutions of Ministry of New and Renewable energy (MNRE) are the stakeholders of this study. Firstly, factor analysis has been applied to identify antecedents to attract Green FDI. Further, environmentally efficient precursors have been identified. Environmental efficiency has been measured through three aspects namely, climate change mitigation, reduction of air pollution, and the preservation of the ecosystem. The results of a factor analysis revealed that there are five environmentally efficient precursors to attract green FDI, namely, the political environment, market potential, availability of natural resources, government support, and emission policy. Furthermore, a hypothesis has been created to study the impact of these identified precursors on green FDI and sustainable development. A structural equation modeling (SEM) technique has been applied to study the impact of identified environmentally efficient precursors on green

**Corresponding author*: shefali.saluja@chitkara.edu.in

Renuka Sharma, Kiran Mehta, Vishal Vyas and Vinod Kumar Shukla (eds.) Decentralized Finance and Blockchain: A Game Changing Duo, (239–270) © 2025 Scrivener Publishing LLC

FDI and sustainable development. The results of SEM revealed that the political environment, availability of natural resources, government support, and emission policy have a significant impact on green FDI. It is also revealed that the availability of natural resources, government support, and emission policy have a significant impact on sustainable development. Furthermore, the study revealed that green FDI also has a significant impact on sustainable development while considering environmentally efficient precursors. The present study is only limited to environmentally efficient precursors. It can further be extended to economically efficient precursors.

Keywords: Green foreign direct investment, environmentally efficient precursors, sustainable development

11.1 Introduction

In the past few years, there has been a significant depletion of natural resources and environmental degradation, necessitating immediate action to address climate change. Several global issues are motivating governments, organizations, and individuals to investigate environmentally responsible and sustainable energy alternatives to regulate greenhouse gas emissions (GHG). Renewable energy has emerged as a promising solution among these alternatives, with the potential to mitigate the adverse effects of traditional energy sources and promote the 7th Sustainable Development Goal (SDG) of "Affordable and Clean Energy." The country benefits from foreign direct investment (FDI) in two ways: it contributes to the economic growth, development, and expansion of the renewable energy sector. In addition to providing capital, it also enables the transmission of technology, organizational and managerial practices, and skills, as well as access to international markets. As a policy priority, most countries are endeavoring to establish a climate that is conducive to the attraction of FDI. Foreign direct investment regimes are being actively liberalized by countries, in addition to reducing the restrictions on their entrance [1]. Foreign direct investment is an important source where foreign techniques and know-how can be used in the host country. Funds may be invested to take control of other companies or to increase existing businesses in the host country. A host country refers to the country in which funds or technology is to be employed (OECD, 1996). Thus, FDI refers to the investment of funds, technology transfer, knowledge and know-how, which are employed by one country into another country. Funds are invested in the country where a good return on investment is expected. An investment made by an individual residing outside of India through capital instruments is referred to as FDI.

It may be in an unlisted Indian company or in 10 percent or more of the post-issue paid-up equity capital on a fully diluted basis of a listed Indian company. In developing countries, FDI is one of the primary sources of economic growth. To attract FDI in renewable energy, developing countries have implemented a variety of strategies, including policies that are in accordance with environmental regulations. There are two aspects of FDI; it is the pollution haven hypothesis (PHH) and pollution halo hypothesis (PHIH). According to the PHH, FDI may raise carbon emissions, whereas the PHIH assumes that they cause emissions to decrease.

By attracting FDI, developing countries acquire a comparative advantage in polluting products and industries. Despite the fact that industrialized countries are at the forefront of climate action, they remain the most polluting countries. Developed nations may opt to relocate their polluting businesses to comply with their climate objectives and circumvent more stringent environmental regulations. The PHH is the term used to describe this phenomenon of the FDI–environment nexus. The FDI–environment nexus is a study that examines the environmental consequences of FDI in the countries that receive it. Diverse discoveries regarding this phenomenon exist. Some studies have reported a pollutant effect of FDI, while others suggest that FDI may reduce pollution by facilitating the transmission of more efficient and clean energy processes, which can reduce energy consumption [7]. This is called the PHIH. Furthermore, carbon dioxide (CO_2) is a major pollutant in the environment. It is emitted from energy sources. Carbon dioxide is highly emitted from non-renewable energy sources. India has a high potential for renewable energy sources, and it can fulfill energy needs, as well as protect the environment from CO_2 emission and GHG. The research report of the Indian Brand Equity Foundation (IBEF, 2019) also revealed that India is ranked 5th in the largest installed capacity of renewable energy in the world. Furthermore, India is 5th in the largest installed capacity of solar power in the world (investindia.gov.in). Therefore, FDI can be attracted as there are growth prospects for renewable energy in India. There are two definitions of green FDI i.e., FDI in environmental goods and services, and FDI in environmental damage mitigation processes [21]. Therefore, FDI is favorable for the environment and can be considered green. Thus, FDI in renewable energy is considered as Green FDI. Foreign direct investment in the renewable energy sector amounts to nearly 2.226 percent of total FDI in India (Factsheets of RBI, March 2023). The study conducted by Invest India in 2019 revealed that up to 100 percent of FDI is allowed through the automatic route for renewable energy generation and distribution projects by following the provisions of The Electricity Act, 2003.

11.2 Review of Literature

11.2.1 Green FDI

In 2010, the United Nations Conference on Trade and Development (UNCTAD) defined green FDI as the transfer of technologies, practices, or products from multinational corporations (MNCs) to destination countries through equity (FDI) and non-equity investments, such that the related activities generate significantly lower GHG emissions [11]. Green FDI is defined as "the transfer of technologies, practices, or products by multinational enterprises (MNEs) to host countries in a manner that ensures their own and related operations generate lower GHG emissions than those that would be generated in the industry under business-as-usual circumstances [41]. Green FDI has the capacity to ensure the economic and environmental development of any nation. As a result, green FDI is a beneficial economic and environmental outcome of FDI. Achieving ecological growth is advantageous for the nation. Environmental conservation is a component of economic development that is referred to as "Green Growth." Since 2003, there has been a rise in green FDI in renewable energy sources, such as solar, wind, hydroelectric, geothermal, and biomass energy, as a consequence of international efforts to reduce GHG emissions [39, 41]. Green FDI may facilitate sustainable development. It is essential for the country's development because it creates employment opportunities and promotes the development of human capital, which in turn may increase the standard of living. In addition to creating direct and indirect employment opportunities in sectors that are resource-efficient and low-carbon, FDI also has a beneficial effect on the host economy, which is referred to as "green jobs." Additionally, the acquisition of knowledge is a contributing factor to the creation of employment opportunities through FDI [3]. When formulating policies, it is possible to consider a variety of determinants of green FDI, such as economic determinants, market creation policies, promotion, and facilitation [24]. Green FDI is essential for the development of the energy sector, as it entails the transfer of capital, technology, and expertise from the home nation to the recipient country [3]. Moreover, green FDI has a positive impact on employment, local air pollution, and CO_2 reduction [15, 18, 29, 32].

11.2.2 Conceptual Framework of Antecedents to Attract Green FDI

After a rigorous review of the literature, some important antecedents have been used for the study purpose. The feed-in tariff (FIT) ensures the fixed payment to renewable energy producers for what they deliver to the grid. The FIT-related policies regulate and stabilize the price of renewable energy [34]. Producers get a remuneration according to the production of clean energy by following this mechanism. The FIT has a significant and positive association with attracting FDI in renewable energy or green FDI [43]. According to previous research, it has a significantly positive impact on numerous patent activities, especially in solar power [10]. Moreover, the transparency, low administrative barriers, and guaranteed consistent policy execution are crucial for a favorable environment. Policymakers should implement proper incentive policies to attract green FDI [28]. A stable and transparent regulatory environment is crucial to attract Green FDI. The variation in access to finance is considered an important institutional factor [14]. Well-established financial institutions can easily provide loans or other financial facilities. It can enhance the mobilization and allocation of resources [9, 33]. Various incentives related to renewable energy can attract financially attractive investments into the country, and it also can encourage foreign investors to participate in the sustainable projects of the country. Previous studies stated the significantly positive impact on renewable energy projects, particularly solar energy [27]. The previous study disclosed that emission trading schemes and renewable energy consumption positively affects renewable energy investment, especially in the wind energy sector [43]. The previous literature also revealed that institutions for renewable energy play a crucial role in attracting FDI [6]. Adeniyi *et al.* (2015) [36] studied the impact of financial development on economic growth. The study revealed that financial development has a statistically significant impact on economic growth. Gross domestic production (GDP) provides information about the size and performance of the economy in the country [12]. Economic growth required a huge influx of funds, and this requirement can be fulfilled by FDI in Asian regions [45]. An investigation was done on Chinese managers' perceptions about FDI in the renewable energy sector in Germany [42]. They found that the continuity and consistency of rules, policies, and processes in the regulatory dimension play a crucial role in attracting green FDI. The decision of FDI in the developing market is mostly affected by the initial market entry in business (Nicoletti *et al.*, 2005). Subsequently, the simplicity of entry into the business should be prioritized. Additionally, trade openness is another factor that has the potential to either attract or deter FDI. Foreign direct investment is positively correlated with trade openness, as demonstrated by numerous studies [2]. Additionally, developing countries experience elevated levels of political uncertainty in comparison to less developed nations as a result of political instability, corruption, conflicts, and unforeseen policy modifications [26]. The majority of multinational corporations refrain from engaging in FDI in countries that pose significant political risks [19]. The growth of the renewable energy sector in India can be facilitated by a variety of mergers and acquisitions (M&A) transactions, which may also serve to attract green FDI. Additionally, these mergers and acquisitions can facilitate the preservation of partnerships with foreign nations. Furthermore, the location of renewable energy projects can be determined by promotion and facilitation policies, particularly when they are implemented in conjunction with market creation policies [24]. Additionally, foreign investment in sustainable initiatives may be attracted by a lower labor cost. The appreciation of the host country's currency results in a decrease in FDI, while the depreciation of the host country's currency leads to an increase [20]. To attract wind and solar projects to the country, it is crucial to consider the exchange rate volatility, access to land, an efficient bureaucracy, and numerous industry-specific factors, such as priority grid access and FIT [26]. A country may also be encouraged to attract Green FDI due to favorable policies regarding the export of renewable energy. A country enjoys a competitive advantage due to the profusion of specific renewable energy sources. Consequently, the availability of sunlight, wind, bio-power, hydropower, ocean-energy, and geo-thermal heat is a critical factor in the attraction of green FDI. A previous study indicated that a comprehensive development plan for renewable energy initiatives is necessary to attract green FDI into a country (Mehbub *et al.*, 2022). Furthermore, the consumption of renewable energy is augmented by the investment in infrastructure for renewable energy. The reduction of environmental degradation is directly correlated with it [7]. The renewable energy certificate mechanism is designed to encourage the use of renewable energy and to simplify the process of complying with renewable purchase obligations (RPO). Solar and wind power generation in China is effectively promoted by RPO and renewable energy policy reforms [17]. Consequently, the attraction of green FDI is also significantly influenced by the implementation of suitable legal provisions for renewable energy certificates. The government's initiative to promote renewable energy to mitigate GHG emissions may also serve as an incentive for green FDI. Additionally, the public's endorsement of fossil fuels may serve as an inhibitor to greenfield investments in renewable energy [30]. Consequently, a sufficient understanding of renewable energy can contribute to the increase in its consumption and can also help to mitigate environmental degradation. Green FDI may be attracted to stringent environmental regulations. Additionally, subsidies for fossil fuels may result in an increase in carbon emissions, which could potentially compromise the quality of the environment, as seen in Indonesia. Individual countries are encouraged to strive to mitigate climate change by maintaining high environmental quality through carbon neutrality, as stipulated by the United Nations' SDGs [39]. Revenue certainty can be achieved in the long term through the use of power purchase agreements (PPAs) or RPOs. Investors may also be attracted to the renewable energy sector by well-designed and transparent market mechanisms that guarantee a stable and predictable market. The country's commitment to sustainable development is demonstrated by its efforts to regulate the temperature up to 1.5°C above pre-industrial levels. Consequently, this can also entice green FDI. Many laws and regulations are included in environmental legislation to regulate the interaction between humans and the naural world, thereby preventing the escalation of environmental threats. The renewable energy sector has no adverse effects on the environment to meet energy demands. In addition, subsidies, particularly in the renewable energy sector, continue to be a critical component of the green FDI attraction process. Additionally, climate policies can significantly influence the appeal of green investment [4]. The development of renewable energy is significantly influenced by land [22]. The most significant impediment to the advancement of solar power in India is land acquisition (World Bank, 2007). Draft Electricity Rules, 2021; decentralized solar power; shift towards non-conventional energy; green cities; developing renewable energy; and hybrid projects are some strategies that can be implemented to increase renewable energy. Consequently, the country must have the necessary rules and regulations to regulate renewable energy initiatives, which will contribute to both economic and environmental growth, as a result of government engagement.

11.3 Research Methodology

The present section explains the detailed methodology used for the study. It deals with the objectives, universe of the present study, sample size, sampling techniques, research tools used for the data collection purpose, data resources, and statistical tools applied for the analysis of the data.

11.3.1 Objectives of the Study

The present research emphasizes the identification of antecedents to attract green FDI. Furthermore, it will identify the Environmentally efficient antecedents of the country to encourage green FDI. Moreover, the impact of these identified environmentally efficient antecedents on green FDI and sustainable development will be studied. Lastly, the impact of green FDI on sustainable development will be studied.

11.3.2 Universe and Population of the Study

There are five agencies and institutions in India that deals with renewable energy. These five agencies and institutions are targeted as the universe of the study. The population covered only administrative personnel such as top management, middle management, and lower management.

11.3.3 Sample and Response Rate of the Study

Barclay *et al.* [8] were the first to propose the 10-times formula subsequently incorporated in the partial least squares structural equation modeling (PLS-SEM) has become a standard approach for analyzing complex interrelationships between observed and latent variables. The 10-times rule was articulated for determining an appropriate sample size [37, 44]. The sample size must be 10 times the number of statements in the questionnaire. The questionnaire contained 70 statements, which resulted in a sample size of 700. The research instrument was distributed to 700 respondents, of whom only 647 responded and 38 were not fully completed. Consequently, the analysis is based on a sample size of 700. This investigation implemented a straightforward random sampling methodology. Each sampling unit of a population has an equal probability of being included in the sample in simple random sampling. As a result, each potential sample has an equal likelihood of being chosen. By identifying and addressing prospective issues at the outset of the research process, a pilot study can contribute to the enhancement of the quality of primary research. Data has been collected from 75 respondents for the pilot survey. The Cronbach's alpha test was employed to evaluate the reliability and validity of the research schedule. Then, the research schedule was finalized for the entire sample. The study's response rate is 87 percent, calculated as (609/700*100).

11.3.4 Sources of Data Collection

For the collection of primary data, a well-structured research schedule was designed. The research schedule was prepared by selecting the appropriate variables from the extensive review of the literature.

The scale used in the study consists of five points in the Likert scale to collect responses from the respondents [31]. The survey includes a sample size of 609. These stakeholders are affiliated with agencies and institutions that are part of the MNRE. The Indian Renewable Energy Development Agency, National Institute of Solar Energy, National Institute of Wind Energy, SSS National Institute of Renewable Energy, and Solar Energy Corporation of India are agencies and institutes in question. As stakeholders for data acquisition in this investigation, the administration departments of agencies and institutions were selected. The respondents' names were withheld to protect the privacy and sensitivity of their personal information. The questionnaire is organized into the subsequent sections. Section I of the questionnaire comprises inquiries regarding the respondents' demographic profiles. Section II of the questionnaire includes inquiries regarding the antecedents necessary to entice green FDI to achieve sustainable development. Section III of the questionnaire comprises inquiries regarding the influence of green FDI and sustainable development. Section IV of the questionnaire includes inquiries regarding the environmental efficiency aspect due to green FDI.

11.3.5 Statistical Techniques Used in the Study

The Statistical Package for Social Sciences (SPSS 21) was employed to conduct descriptive and factor analysis. SmartPLS was subsequently implemented to analyze the data in accordance with the structural and measurement models. To achieve the study's objectives, SPSS, and SmartPLS were implemented to analyze the data. The subsequent statistical methodologies were implemented. A recommended two-step approach was employed to analyze the PLS results [4], namely, the testing of the hypotheses/structural model (inner model), and the evaluation of the outer model or measurement model (reliability and validity of the measurement model). The PLS-SEM analysis evaluates structural models and measurement models. The measurement model establishes the reliability and validity of the constructs. The structural model determines the importance of the hypothesized relationships. Various hypotheses were proposed to achieve the study's objective.

11.4 Data Analysis and Interpretation

11.4.1 To Identify Antecedents in Attracting Green FDI into the Country

In this section, a suggested two-step approach is used to analyze the PLS results that have been employed [4]. The demographic profile of the respondents indicates that the majority of them are from the National Institute of Solar Energy (32.51), National Institute of Wind Energy (30.04), Solar Energy Corporation of India (20.68), The Indian Renewable Energy Development Agency (15.46), and SSS National Institute of Renewable Energy (1.31). The study also found that 67.7 percent of respondents are male, and 32.3 percent respondents are female. It also revealed that majority of the respondents' educational qualification is of graduation level (65.02); 40.23 percent of respondents have four to six years of educational experience; and the majority of respondents' annual income level is less than Rs. 5,00,000 annually.

Factor loading: Factor loading refers to the correlation between an item and a factor. Factor loading can range from -1 to +1, with higher absolute values indicating a higher correlation of the item with the underlying factor. Table 11.1 revealed that there are 12 factors for these variables, and these are named as presented in the table. All items in the study had factors loading greater than the recommended value of 0.50 except for five items, namely, V22, V25, V41, V42, and V51. Hence, only five items are deleted due to a low factor loading. The Cronbach's Alpha ranges from 0.624 to 0.91.

The overall assessment of the criteria for the model fit is acceptable as presented in Table 11.2. Furthermore, the validity of the scale is measured with the help of the following measures, namely, construct validity, convergent validity, and discriminant validity. According to Fornell and Larcker (1981), under the construct validity, even if the average variance extracted (AVE) is less than 0.5 but the composite reliability (CR) is greater than 0.6, the convergent validity of the construct is adequate as presented in Table 11.3.

Therefore, the study identified 12 factors based on the exploratory factor analysis, namely, the availability of natural resources (NR), environment policy (ENP), renewable energy (RE), political environment (PE), government support (GS), economic performance (ECP), emission policy (EMP), investment freedom (IF), market potential (MP), country measures (CM), labor environment (LE), and financial environment (FE).

Table 11.1 The factor loadings and naming of factors.

	Factor loading	Cronbach alpha	Factor name		Statement
V34	0.819	0.842	Availability of Natural Resources	NR1	Availability of Ocean energy
V31	0.793			NR2	Availability of Wind for wind energy
V33	0.781			NR3	Availability of Hydro power
V35	0.754			NR4	Availability of Geo-thermal heat
V30	0.667			NR5	Availability of Sunlight
V32	0.63			NR6	Availability of Bio-power
V45	0.86	0.859	Environment Policy	ENP1	1.5 Degree Temperature Condition
V43	0.839			ENP2	Removal of subsidy on Fossil fuel
V44	0.829			ENP3	Power Purchase Agreement
V50	0.768			ENP4	Supportive Environmental policies for pollution
V38	0.797	0.784	Renewable Energy Specific	RE1	Infrastructure for Renewable Energy
V39	0.785			RE2	Legal provisions for Renewable Energy Certificates
V37	0.771			RE3	Renewable Purchase Standards
V47	0.658			RE4	Subsidy on installation cost of Renewable Energy
V36	0.549			RE5	Development Plan
V1	0.848	0.841	Political Environment	PE1	Clear and Consistent Policies
V19	0.834			PE2	Public Investment (Govt. funds for Renewable energy projects)
V13	0.781			PE3	Legal Framework
V10	0.772			PE4	Political Risk
V53	0.895	0.91	Government Support	GS1	Government engagement for environment
V52	0.882			GS2	Supportive land acquisition laws
V46	0.849			GS3	Environment Legislation

(Continued)

Table 11.1 The factor loadings and naming of factors. (*Continued*)

	Factor loading	Cronbach alpha	Factor name		Statement
V6	0.862	0.77	Economic Performance	ECP1	Institutional quality
V8	0.763			ECP2	Gross Domestic Production (GDP)
V7	0.72			ECP3	Financial development
V5	0.68			ECP4	Emission Trading Schemes (ETS)
V40	0.908	0.865	Emission Policy	EMP1	Target for GHG emission
V49	0.869			EMP2	Net Zero Emission Policy of the country
V48	0.85			EMP3	Carbon tax
V11	0.821	0.767	Investment Freedom	IF1	Ease of Entry in host country
V12	0.82			IF2	Trade openness
V17	0.75			IF3	Local country requirements
V14	0.66			IF4	Merger and Acquisition Policies
V15	0.844	0.722	Market Potential	MP1	Larger market size
V18	0.755			MP2	Scope for diversification
V16	0.689			MP3	Product potential to cover Market
V9	0.674			MP4	Growth prospects of Investment
V26	0.816	0.738	Country Measures	CM1	Weaker (depreciation) currency
V27	0.811			CM2	Volatility in Exchange rate
V28	0.682			CM3	Counterparty Risk
V29	0.631			CM4	Flexibility in Policies
V21	0.891	0.725	Labor Environment	LE1	Skilled and qualified workforce
V24	0.802			LE2	Access to training and development programs
V23	0.606			LE3	Appropriate Wage rate
V20	0.573			LE4	Favorable labor laws
V3	0.808	0.624	Financial Environment	FE1	Easy access to Local finance
V4	0.723			FE2	Tax incentives
V2	0.69			FE3	Feed in Tariff

Source: Compiled from SPSS.

Table 11.2 Model fit indices.

Fit indices	Recommended value	Value
CMIN/df	<5 (Hair, Black, Anderson & Tatham, 1998)	1645.635/1011 = 1.628
P value		0.000
RMSEA	<0.08 (Hair, Black, Anderson & Tatham, 1998)	0.032
CFI	>0.9 (Hair, Black, Anderson & Tatham, 1998)	0.943
GFI	>0.9 (Hair, Black, Anderson & Tatham, 1998)	0.901
AGFI	>0.8	0.885
TLI	>0.9 (Hair, Black, Anderson & Tatham, 1998)	0.937

Source: Compiled results from AMOS.

11.4.2 To Identify Environmentally Efficient Antecedents

The structural equation modeling (SEM) technique has been used to identify these antecedents. The following hypotheses have been formulated:

H_1: The 'political environment' has a significant positive impact on environmental efficiency.
H_2: The 'investment freedom' has a significant positive impact on environmental efficiency.
H_3: The 'economic performance' has a significant positive impact on environmental efficiency.
H_4: The 'country measures' has a significant positive impact on environmental efficiency.
H_5: The 'market potential' has a significant positive impact on environmental efficiency.

Table 11.3 Discriminant validity according to Fornell and Larcker.

CR	AVE	Factors	PE	FE	ECP	MP	IF	LE	CM	NR	RE	EMP	ENP	GS
0.884	0.655	**PE**	*0.809*											
0.785	0.5506	**FE**	0.07	*0.742*										
0.844	0.5765	**ECP**	0.2	0.08	*0.76*									
0.831	0.553	**MP**	0.13	0.03	0.13	*0.743*								
0.849	0.586	**IF**	0.07	0.08	0.01	-0.04	*0.766*							
0.815	0.533	**LE**	0.19	0.1	0.11	0.21	-0.01	*0.73*						
0.827	0.547	**CM**	0.06	0.07	0.09	0.14	-0.02	0.23	*0.739*					
0.88	0.553	**NR**	0.06	0.09	0.02	0.08	0.05	0.03	-0.09	*0.74*				
0.839	0.51	**RE**	0.09	-0.1	-0	0.09	0.01	0.01	-0.06	0.18	*0.718*			
0.908	0.7674	**EMP**	0.06	-0.01	0	0.09	-0.04	0.17	0.08	0.11	0.04	*0.876*		
0.895	0.681	**ENP**	0.03	-0.01	-0.1	0.08	-0.05	0.05	0.01	0.04	0.29	0.01	*0.825*	
0.908	0.766	**GS**	0.05	-0.04	0.06	0.07	-0.03	-0.01	0.02	0.11	0.51	0.01	0.2	*0.875*

Source: Compiled from SmartPLS.

H_6: The 'labor environment' has a significant positive impact on environmental efficiency.
H_7: The 'financial environment' has a significant positive impact on environmental efficiency.
H_8: The 'availability of natural resources' has a significant positive impact on environmental efficiency.
H_9: The 'renewable energy specific' has a significant positive impact on environmental efficiency.
H_{10}: The 'government support' has a significant positive impact on environmental efficiency.
H_{11}: The 'emission policy' has a significant positive impact on environmental efficiency.
H_{12}: The 'environment policy' has a significant positive impact on environmental efficiency.

11.4.2.1 Measurement Model

The quality of constructs is assessed based on the measurement model. This evaluation starts with the evaluation of factor loading, which is followed by establishing reliability and validity.

The factor loadings of all items of economic efficiency and environmental efficiency are greater than the recommended value of 0.40. Therefore, no item has been deleted. The study can proceed toward naming the factors. All the factors are named, and information is revealed in Table 11.4.

Table 11.4 The naming of factors for environmental efficiency.

V. no.	Factor loading	Factor name	Item code	Statement
V72	.820	Environment Efficiency (ENEFF)	ENEF2	The environmental efficiency of the country helps reduce air pollution.
V73	.793		ENEF3	It also helps in the preservation of the ecosystem.
V71	.778		ENEF1	The environmental efficiency of the country helps in climate change mitigation.

Source: Compiled from SPSS.

In compliance with the guidelines [5], the scale comprises all items with peripheral loadings of 0.70 or higher. Items with outer loads less than 0.70 are examined. Certain items, such as RE2, RE4, and CM3, are eliminated to increase the value of AVE. The study includes certain outer loadings that are less than 0.7, as their removal does not lead to an increase in the AVE value.

Multicollinearity indicator: The multicollinearity of indicators is assessed using the variance inflation factor (VIF) statistic (Kock, 2015). Multicollinearity is not a significant issue when the VIF value is less than 5 [23]. Table 11.6 displays the VIF values for the indicators in the study, and it is clear that the VIF for each indicator is below the recommended value. The VIF of each indicator is less than 5. As a result, collinearity does not influence the investigation's indicators. The CR should surpass 0.7 [23]. Table 11.5 contains the CR and Cronbach's alpha results. The CR statistics ranged from 0.793 to 0.943. Construct validity is established when discriminant validity and convergent validity are present (Krabbe, P.F.M, 2017). Convergent validity refers to the degree to which multiple attempts to quantify the same concept are consistent. The convergent validity results are because all constructs have a value greater than 0.50, as indicated by the AVE statistics in the current investigation. Consequently, convergent validity is not a matter of concern. Furthermore, in 1981, Fornell and Larcker introduced a criterion for assessing the discriminant validity of constructs in a measurement model. The reliability and validity of Table 11.5 are demonstrated in accordance with the requirements of Fornell and Larcker. This investigation illustrates that the construct exhibits a more robust correlation with itself than with any other construct. The CR statistics ranged from 0.793 to 0.943, while the Cronbach's Alpha ranged from 0.624 to 0.91. The AVE statistics suggest that all constructs are greater than 0.50, as indicated by the convergent validity results of the current study. Consequently, convergent validity is not a matter of concern.

According to the Fornell and Larcker (1981) criterion, discriminant validity is established when the square root of AVE for a construct is greater than its correlation with all other constructs. This study presents that the construct has greater correlation to its own than to other constructs as presented in Table 11.6.

Table 11.5 The reliability and validity for $E_C EA$ and $E_N EA$.

Cronbach alpha	CR	AVE		CM	ECP	ENEF	ENP	EMP	FE	GS	IF	LE	MP	NR	PE	RE
0.738	0.833	0.557	**CM**	*0.746*												
0.77	0.801	0.512	**ECP**	0.065	*0.716*											
0.766	0.865	0.681	**ENEF**	0.035	0.075	*0.825*										
0.859	0.886	0.662	**ENP**	0.01	0.078	0.024	*0.814*									
0.865	0.915	0.783	**EMP**	0.079	0.009	0.122	0.005	*0.885*								
0.624	0.8	0.572	**FE**	0.072	0.076	0.069	0.002	0.006	*0.756*							
0.91	0.943	0.846	**GS**	0.019	0.013	0.108	0.204	0.009	0.039	0.92						
0.767	0.833	0.558	**IF**	0.026	0.039	0.008	0.058	0.038	0.079	0.028	*0.747*					
0.725	0.828	0.616	**LE**	0.209	0.066	0.07	0.053	0.185	0.089	0.032	0.004	*0.785*				
0.722	0.793	0.573	**MP**	0.155	0.148	0.158	0.037	0.099	0.057	0.113	0.003	0.198	*0.757*			
0.842	0.883	0.56	**NR**	0.089	0.029	0.462	0.056	0.117	0.089	0.101	0.056	0.046	0.151	*0.749*		
0.841	0.869	0.63	**PE**	0.077	0.142	0.039	0.055	0.069	0.089	0.069	0.029	0.22	0.162	0.045	*0.794*	
0.784	0.854	0.664	**RE**	0.046	0.013	0.096	0.283	0.058	0.082	0.585	0.014	0.01	0.15	0.198	0.079	*0.815*

Source: Compiled from SmartPLS.

Table 11.6 R^2, Q^2, and a significance of paths.

	R^2	Q^2
ENEF	0.246	0.204

Source: Compiled from SmartPLS.

Table 11.7 Path coefficient.

	Original sample (O)	Sample mean (M)	Standard deviation (STDEV)	T statistics (|O/STDEV|)	P values	
CM -> ENEF	0.049	0.051	0.042	1.181	0.119	
ECP -> ENEF	0.059	0.047	0.06	0.972	0.166	
ENP -> ENEF	-0.003	-0.006	0.043	0.071	0.472	
EMP -> ENEF	**0.061**	**0.061**	**0.036**	**1.707**	**0.044**	**Accepted**
FE -> ENEF	0.025	0.032	0.042	0.594	0.276	
GS -> ENEF	**0.089**	**0.08**	**0.043**	**2.068**	**0.019**	**Accepted**
IF -> ENEF	-0.028	-0.027	0.051	0.553	0.29	
LE -> ENEF	0.032	0.028	0.06	0.534	0.297	
MP -> ENEF	**0.073**	**0.079**	**0.043**	**1.697**	**0.045**	**Accepted**
NR -> ENEF	**0.449**	**0.444**	**0.036**	**12.49**	**0**	**Accepted**
PE -> ENEF	**0.098**	**-0.093**	**0.05**	**1.956**	**0.025**	**Accepted**
RE -> ENEF	0.047	-0.032	0.043	1.101	0.135	

Source: Compiled from SmartPLS.

11.4.2.2 Structural Model

The structural model in SEM is usually represented as a path diagram. The structural model can be assessed based on the R^2, Q^2 and significance of paths.

The efficacy of each structural path is determined by the R^2 value of the dependent variables, which establishes the model's goodness (Penalver *et al.*, 2018). The R^2 values for endogenous latent variables are evaluated as follows: 0.26 (considerable), 0.13 (moderate), and 0.02 (weak) [13]. The predictive capability of the model is demonstrated in Table 11.6. Additionally, the predictive relevance of the endogenous constructs is established by Q2. The predictive relevance of the model is demonstrated by the fact that the value of Q2 exceeds the threshold value of 0. The findings indicate that the constructs' predictions are significant.

As revealed by Table 11.7, there are five environmentally efficient antecedents namely, political environment, market potential, availability of natural resources, government support, and emission policy.

11.4.3 Impact of Environmentally Efficient Antecedents on Green FDI and Sustainable Development

The study revealed five environmentally efficient antecedents to attract green FDI. Therefore, the present section has been attempted to study the impact of these antecedents on green FDI and sustainable development. The following are hypotheses to study the impact of Environmentally efficient antecedents on green FDI and sustainable development.

H_{13}: The 'political environment' has a significant positive impact on green FDI.
H_{14}: The 'market potential' has a significant positive impact on green FDI.
H_{15}: The 'availability of natural resources' has a significant positive impact on green FDI.
H_{16}: The 'government support' has a significant positive impact on green FDI.
H_{17}: The 'emission policy' has a significant positive impact on green FDI.
H_{18}: The 'political environment' has a significant positive impact on sustainable development.
H_{19}: The 'market potential' has a significant positive impact on sustainable development.
H_{20}: The 'availability of natural resources' has a significant positive impact on sustainable development.

H_{21}: The 'government support' has a significant positive impact on sustainable development.
H_{22}: The 'emission policy' has a significant positive impact on sustainable development.
H_{23}: The 'green FDI' has a significant positive impact on sustainable development from an environment perspective.

11.4.3.1 Measurement Model

The quality of constructs is assessed on the basis of the measurement model. This evaluation starts with the evaluation of factor loading, which is followed by establishing reliability and validity.

The factor loadings of all items of green FDI and sustainable development are greater than the recommended value of 0.40 except for three items. Therefore, the three items, which are V61, V62, and V63 were deleted due to lower factor loading (Table 11.8).

11.4.3.1.1 Outer Loadings to Study the Impact of ENEA

According to Fornell and Larcker (1981) recommendations, all items with outer loadings ≥ 0.70 are considered in the scale [5]. Items with outer loadings less than 0.70 are analyzed.

Table 11.9 presented outer loadings of constructs. Some items are deleted to increase the value of the AVE, such as PE4 and MP4. Some outer loadings are less than 0.7, and these are considered for the study because their deletion does not lead to an increase in AVE value.

11.4.3.1.2 Indicator Multicollinearity

The VIF statistics are used to assess multicollinearity of indicators. According to, multicollinearity is not a serious issue if the VIF value is less than 5. Table 11.10 presents the VIF values for the indicators in the study, and it is revealed that the VIF for each indicator is less than the recommended value.

11.4.3.1.3 Reliability and Validity Analysis

Reliability is the extent to which a measuring instrument is consistent and stable. The fundamental attribute of reliability is repeatability. Repeated administration of an instrument will yield identical outcomes. The following are the two most frequently used methods for determining reliability. These are Cronbach alpha and CR. The Cronbach alpha and CR parameters should exceed 0.6 and 0.7, respectively. Table 11.11 contains CR and Cronbach alpha

Table 11.8 Naming of dependent variables.

V. no.	Factor loading	Factor name	Item code	Statement
V56	.807	Green FDI (GFDI)	GFDI3	Green FDI can promote access to research and development.
V60	.725		GFDI7	Green FDI can help to achieve net zero emission.
V59	.720		GFDI6	Green FDI can stimulate exports of the country.
V55	.720		GFDI2	Green FDI may help generate employment opportunities.
V57	.714		GFDI4	Green FDI may help enhance international cooperation to provide clean energy.
V58	.708		GFDI5	Green FDI may help the government to frame and implement policies to enhance green FDI.
V54	.659	Green FDI (GFDI)	GFDI1	Green FDI can bring new ideas for renewable energy sector.
V65	.845	Sustainable Development (SD)	SD2	It may increase the usage of clean cooking fuel for household.
V66	.826		SD3	Reduced dependence on imported oil may help to achieve sustainable development.
V64	.774		SD1	It may help to increase the access of electricity for household.
V67	.714		SD4	It may help increase the share of renewable energy in total energy consumption.

Source: Compiled from SPSS 21.

Table 11.9 Outer loadings to study the impact of $E_N EA$.

	EMP	**GFDI**	**GS**	**MP**	**NR**	**PE**	**SD**
EP1	0.946						
EP2	0.868						
EP3	0.843						
GFDI1		0.673					
GFDI2		0.710					
GFDI3		0.802					
GFDI4		0.739					
GFDI5		0.710					
GFDI6		0.725					
GFDI7		0.738					
GS1			0.955				
GS2			0.923				
GS3			0.876				
MP1				0.586			
MP2				0.981			
MP3				0.626			
NR1					0.761		
NR2					0.773		
NR3					0.815		
NR4					0.743		
NR5					0.651		
NR6					0.725		
PE1						0.591	
PE2						0.856	

(Continued)

Table 11.9 Outer loadings to study the impact of $E_N EA$. (*Continued*)

	EMP	GFDI	GS	MP	NR	PE	SD
PE3						0.911	
SD1							0.743
SD2							0.810
SD3							0.844
SD4							0.816

Source: Compiled from SmartPLS.

Table 11.10 Variance inflation factor for impact of $E_N EA$.

	VIF		VIF		VIF
EMP1	3.052	GS1	3.611	NR5	1.358
EMP2	2.22	GS2	3.188	NR6	1.765
EMP3	2.115	GS3	2.693	PE1	1.999
GDF11	1.669	MP1	1.386	PE2	2.041
GDF12	2.048	MP2	1.486	PE3	1.716
GDF13	2.256	MP3	1.399	SD1	1.589
GDF14	1.757	NR1	2.038	SD2	1.939
GDF15	1.679	NR2	1.787	SD3	2.003
GDF16	1.804	NR3	2.302	SD4	1.589
GDF17	1.759	NR4	1.457		

Source: Compiled from SmartPLS.

results. The Cronbach's alpha ranged from 0.722 to 0.91, while the CR statistics ranged from 0.787 to 0.942. In the context of PLS-SEM, construct validity is established when there is convergent validity and discriminant validity (Krabbe, 2017). Convergent validity refers to the degree to which multiple attempts to quantify the same concept are consistent. Convergent validity is

Table 11.11 Reliability and validity for impact of ENEA.

Cronbach alpha	**CR**	**AVE**		**EMP**	**GFD1**	**GS**	**MP**	**NR**	**PE**	**SD**
0.865	0.917	0.786	**EMP**	*0.887*						
0.853	0.888	0.532	**GFDI**	0.305	*0.729*					
0.91	0.942	0.844	**GS**	0.007	0.042	*0.919*				
0.722	0.787	0.566	**MP**	0.11	0.064	0.112	*0.752*			
0.842	0.883	0.557	**NR**	0.109	0.153	0.105	0.151	*0.746*		
0.828	0.836	0.637	**PE**	0.072	0.042	0.05	0.111	0.096	*0.798*	
0.82	0.88	0.647	**SD**	0.2	0.282	0.044	0.076	0.1	-0.033	*0.804*

Source: Compiled from SmartPLS.

established when the AVE surpasses 0.50 [25]. The AVE statistics suggest that all constructs are greater than 0.50, as indicated by the convergent validity results of the current study. Consequently, convergent validity is not a matter of concern. Table 11.11 displayed the AVE value for each construct. In 1981, Fornell and Larcker introduced a criterion for assessing the discriminant validity of constructs in a measurement model. The discriminant validity is the degree to which two theoretically distinct constructs are empirically distinct. In other words, it indicates whether the constructs' measures are not excessively correlated and can be distinguished from one another.

Table 11.11 presented the discriminant validity for economic efficiency. Given by Fornell and Larcker (1981), the discriminant validity is established when the square root of AVE for a construct is than its correlation with all other constructs. This study presents that the construct has a greater correlation with its own than with other constructs.

11.4.3.2 Structural Model (Path Model)

The structural model can be assessed by examining the R^2, Q2, and significance of trajectories. The coefficient of determination (R^2) is employed to assess the model's explanatory power [40]. The coefficient of determination (R^2) as a metric that spans from 0 to 1, with a higher value indicates a greater explanatory power [23]. The acceptability of these values is contingent upon the discipline, and as a result, values as low as 0.10 can also be considered adequate [38]. The model's quality is determined by the R^2

value of the dependent variables, which is the intensity of each structural path [35]. The R^2 values are evaluated for endogenous latent variables as follows: 0.26 (considerable), 0.13 (moderate), and 0.02 (weak) [13]. The values for R^2 were presented in Table 11.12. The valuation of the predictive accuracy of the model is the consequent recommended course of action [40]. The Q2 value can be employed to investigate it [16]. The Q2 value establishes the prognostic relevance of endogenous variables in the model. The model's predictive relevance is illustrated by exceeding the threshold value of 0 by the value of Q2 [16]. The model's predictive capability was demonstrated in Table 11.12.

Table 11.12 R^2 & Q^2 for the impact of E_NEA.

	R^2	Q^2
GFDI	0.108	0.089
SD	0.103	0.025

Source: Compiled from SmartPLS.

Table 11.13 Structural model assessment for impact of E_NEA.

	Original sample (O)	Sample mean (M)	Standard deviation (STDEV)	T statistics (|O/STDEV|)	P values	
EMP -> GFDI	**0.29**	**0.292**	**0.039**	**7.368**	**0.000**	A
GFDI -> SD	**0.473**	**0.424**	**0.216**	**2.196**	**0.014**	A
NR -> GFDI	**0.116**	**0.124**	**0.04**	**2.896**	**0.002**	A
EMP -> SD	**0.122**	**0.122**	**0.045**	**2.722**	**0.003**	A
PE -> SD	0.032	0.015	0.069	0.463	0.322	
NR -> SD	**0.214**	**0.217**	**0.084**	**2.557**	**0.005**	A
MP -> SD	0.045	0.042	0.055	0.808	0.21	
GS -> SD	**0.149**	**0.154**	**0.025**	**5.934**	**0.000**	A
GS -> GFDI	**0.266**	**0.28**	**0.039**	**6.863**	**0.000**	A
MP -> GFDI	0.011	0.016	0.048	0.223	0.412	
PE -> GFDI	**0.241**	**0.238**	**0.119**	**2.025**	**0.021**	A

Source: Compiled from SmartPLS.

PathCoefficients:

The evaluation of the degree of correlation between endogenous and exogenous variables is facilitated by the values of path coefficients. The hypothesized relationships between various constructs are represented by the standardized values of path coefficients, which range from -1 to +1. The path coefficient values that are closer to zero (0) indicate weaker relationships, while those that are closer to -1 indicate powerful negative relationships. Values that are closer to +1 indicate positive relationships. Additionally, significance levels, t-statistics, and the value of path coefficients are examined in conjunction. Table 11.13 displays the path coefficient values for hypothesis testing.

11.5 Results and Conclusion

H_{13} evaluates whether there is a significant positive impact of 'political environment' on green FDI as per Table 11.14. The results revealed that political environment has significant positive impact on green FDI (beta = 0.214; t = 2.025; and p = 0.021). Hence, H_{13} is supported. The bureaucratic hurdles can be reduced through a transparent and streamlined regulatory framework. Supportive, clear, and consistent policies of renewable energy development can attract green FDI by ensuring predictable environment growth. H_{14} evaluates whether there is a significant positive impact of 'market potential' on green FDI. The results revealed that market potential has no significant positive impact on green FDI (beta = 0.011; t = 0.223; and p = 0.412). Hence, H_{14} is not supported. H_{15} evaluates whether there is a significant positive impact of 'availability of natural resources' on green FDI. The results revealed that availability of natural resources has a significant positive impact on green FDI (beta = 0.116; t = 2.896; and p = 0.002). Hence, H_{15} is supported. The study found the significant positive impact of 'availability of natural resources' on environment efficiency. The abundant renewable energy resources play an important role in encouraging Green FDI. Countries with great potential for specific renewable energy technologies have a competitive advantage in attracting investments in these sectors. The presence of ample solar radiation, wind speeds, or hydroelectric potential, encourages the development of solar power plants, wind farms, or hydroelectric facilities, respectively, leading to an improved environmental efficiency. H_{16} evaluates whether there is a significant positive impact of 'government support' on green FDI. The results revealed that government support has a significant positive impact on Green FDI (beta = 0.266; t = 6.863; and p = 0.000). Hence, H_{16} was supported. Government support for research and development (R&D) in renewable energy technologies promotes innovation and technological

Table 11.14 Results on the impact of environmentally efficient antecedents.

Hypotheses	P value	Result
H_{13}: The 'political environment' has a significant positive impact on green FDI.	**0.021**	**Accepted**
H_{14}: The 'market potential' has a significant positive impact on green FDI.	0.412	
H_{15}: The 'availability of natural resources' has a significant positive impact on green FDI.	**0.002**	**Accepted**
H_{16}: The 'government support' has a significant positive impact on green FDI.	**0.000**	**Accepted**
H_{17}: The 'emission policy' has a significant positive impact on green FDI.	**0.000**	**Accepted**
H_{18}: The 'political environment' has a significant positive impact on sustainable development.	0.322	
H_{19}: The 'market potential' has a significant positive impact on sustainable development.	0.21	
H_{20}: The 'availability of natural resources' has a significant positive impact on sustainable development.	**0.005**	**Accepted**
H_{21}: The 'government support' has a significant positive impact on sustainable development.	**0.000**	**Accepted**
H_{22}: The 'emission policy' has a significant positive impact on sustainable development.	**0.003**	**Accepted**
H_{23}: The 'green FDI' has a significant positive impact on sustainable development from an environmental perspective.	**0.014**	**Accepted**

Source: Presentation of results.

advancements. H_{17} evaluates whether there is a significant positive impact of 'emission policy' on green FDI. The results revealed that emission policies have a significant positive impact on green FDI (beta = 0.29; t = 7.368; and p = 0.000). Hence, H_{17} is supported. Emission policies may establish regulatory frameworks and environmental standards that govern the energy sector. It may include limits of carbon emission and requirements for cleaner technologies. The government may encourage adoption of renewable energy technologies by providing incentives, and it may also discourage investments in high-emission fossil fuel-based projects by enforcing strict emission standards. The enforcement of strict environmental standards may help to attract green FDI as the country offers a more favorable business environment for renewable energy investments. Furthermore, emission policies can create market access opportunities for renewable energy by introducing renewable energy certificates or green power procurement mechanisms. These opportunities encourage the development of renewable energy projects and increase their market demand, attracting green FDI from companies looking to participate in green energy markets and fulfill their sustainability commitments. H_{18} evaluates whether there is significant positive impact of 'political environment' on sustainable development. The results revealed that the political environment has no significant positive impact on sustainable development (beta = 0.032; t = 0.463; and p = 0.322). Therefore, H_{18} is not supported. H_{19} evaluates whether there is a significant positive impact of 'market potential' on sustainable development. The results revealed that market potential has no significant positive impact on sustainable development (beta = 0.045; t = 0.808; and p = 0.21). Therefore, H_{19} is not supported. H_{20} evaluates whether there is a significant positive impact of 'availability of natural resources' on sustainable development. The results revealed that availability of natural resources has a significant positive impact on sustainable development (beta = 0.214; t = 2.557; and p = 0.005). Therefore, H_{20} is supported. Since renewable energy sources are green energy sources, they assist to meet energy needs sustainably. Therefore, the availability of renewable energy resources is crucial to achieve 7th SDG and by transitioning into a low-carbon future. H_{21} evaluates whether there is a significant positive impact of 'Government Support' on Sustainable Development. The results revealed that government support has a significant positive impact on sustainable development (beta = 0.149; t = 5.934; and p = 0.000). Therefore, H_{21} is supported. The government can offer financial incentives, grants, subsidies, tax breaks, and loans to foster private and public investments in sustainable energy infrastructure. Financial resources can be mobilized to support renewable energy projects, energy-efficient technologies, and energy access initiatives by establishing favorable investment climates and leveraging public funds. Governments may also promote research and development activities to foster innovation and advancements in clean energy technologies so that the share of renewable energy can be increased. H_{22} evaluates whether there is a significant positive impact of 'emission policy' on sustainable development. The results revealed that emission policies have a significant positive impact on sustainable development (beta = 0.122; t = 2.722; and p = 0.003).

Hence, H_{22} is supported. Emission policies have a significant positive impact on the 7th SDG, which aims to ensure access to affordable and clean energy for all. Emission policies often emphasize energy efficiency improvements to increase renewable energy consumption. By implementing and enforcing emission policies, government may enhance energy productivity, lower emissions, and improve energy access for all. H_{23} evaluates whether there is a significant positive impact of 'green FDI' on sustainable development from environment perspective. The results revealed that green FDI has a significant positive impact on sustainable development (beta = 0.473; t = 2.196; and p = 0.014). Therefore, H_{23} is supported. Green FDI plays an important role in the development of renewable energy technologies. Foreign investors may contribute to expand sustainable energy sources by investing in renewable energy projects of the country. Renewable energy projects assist in reducing reliance on fossil fuels, which in turn decreases GHG and mitigates the impact of climate change. Therefore, green FDI may be helpful to increase the accessibility of electricity for households by increasing the share of renewable energy. It may also help improve the environmental efficiency of the country.

References

1. A Global Survey. Tax Incentives and Foreign Direct Investment. *United Nations Conference on Trade And Development Geneva*, ASIT Advisory Studies No. 16, 2006.
2. Aqeel, A., Nishat, M., Bilquees, F., The determinants of foreign direct investment in Pakistan. *Pak. Dev. Rev.*, 43, 4, 651–664, 2004, http:// www.jstor.org/stable/41261019.
3. Abe, M., Branchoux, C.L.M., Kim, J., Renewable Energy Sector in Emerging Asia: Development and Policies. TIID Working Paper No. 01/17, ESCAP Trade, Investment and Innovation Division, Bangkok, 2017.
4. Anderson, and Gerbing, D.W., An Updated Paradigm for Scale Development Incorporating Unidimensionality and its Assessment. *J. Travel Res.*, 10, 2, 12–29, 1988.
5. Bagozzi, R.P., Yi, Y., Phillips, L.W., Assessing construct validity in organizational research. *Adm. Sci. Q.*, 36, 3, 421–458, 1991.
6. Baklouti, N. and Boujelbene, Y., Impact of institutional quality on the attractiveness of foreign direct investment. *J. Behav. Econ. Finance Entrepreneurship Account. Transp.*, *2*, 4, 89–93, 2014.
7. Balsalobre-Lorente, D., Gokmenoglu, K.K., Taspinar, N., Cantos-Cantos, J.M., An approach to the pollution haven and pollution halo hypotheses in MINT countries. *Environ. Sci. Pollut. Res.*, *26*, 23010–23026, 2019.

8. Barclay, D., Thompson, R., Higgins, C., The Partial Least Squares (PLS) Approach to Causal Modeling: Personal Computer Use as an Illustration. *Technol. Stud.*, 2, 2, 285–309, 1995.
9. Beck, T., Demirguc-Kunt, A., Levine, R., Maksimovic, V., Financial Structure and Economic Development: Firm, Industry, and Country Evidence, in: *Financial Structure and Economic Growth*, Policy Research Working Paper; No. 2423, World Bank, Washington, DC, 2000, https://openknowledge.worldbank.org /handle/10986/19809.
10. Böhringer, C., Cuntz, A., Harhoff, D., Asane-Otoo, E., The Impact of the German Feed-In Tariff Scheme on Innovation: Evidence Based on Patent Filings in Renewable Energy Technologies. *Energy Econ.*, 67, 545–553, 2017, doi: 10. 1016/j.eneco.2017.09.001.
11. Buntaine, M.T. and Pizer, W.A., Encouraging clean energy investment in developing countries: What role for aid? *Clim. Policy*, 15, 5, 543–564, 2015, doi: 10.1080/14693062.2014.953903.
12. Callen, T., What is gross domestic product. *Finance Dev.*, *45*, 4, 48–49, 2008.
13. Cohen, J., *Statistical power analysis for the behavioural sciences*, 2nd edn, Lawrence Erlbaum Associates, New York. NY, 1988.
14. Contractor, F.J., Nuruzzaman, N., Dangol, R., Raghunath, S., How FDI inflows to emerging markets are influenced by country regulatory factors: An exploratory study. *J. Int. Manag.*, 27, 1, 100834, 2021.
15. Djellouli, N., Abdelli, L., Elheddad, M., *et al.*, The effects of nonrenewable energy, renewable energy, economic growth, and foreign direct investment on the sustainability of African countries. *Renew. Energy*, 183, 676–686, 2022, https://doi.org/10.1016/ j.renene.2021.10.066.
16. Dolce, P., Esposito Vinzi, V., Lauro, C., Predictive path modeling through PLS and other component-based approaches: methodological issues and performance evaluation, in: *Partial Least Squares Path Modeling*, H. Latan and R. Noonan (Eds.), pp. 153–172, 2017.
17. Dong, F. and Shi, L., Regional Differences Study of Renewable Energy Performance: A Case of Wind Power in China. *J. Clean. Prod.*, 490–500, 2019, doi: 10.1016/j.jclepro.2019.06.098.
18. Dvořák, P., Martinát, S., der Horst, D.V., *et al.*, Renewable energy investment and job creation; a cross-sectoral assessment for the Czech Republic with reference to EU benchmarks. *Renew. Sustain. Energy Rev.*, 69, 360–368, 2017, https://doi.org/10.1016/j.rser. 2016.11.158.
19. Edwards, S., Capital Flows, Foreign Direct Investment, and Debt-equity Swaps in Developing Countries, No. w3497, National Bureau of Economic Research, Massachusetts, USA, 1990.
20. Froot, K.A. and Stein, J.C., Exchange rates and foreign direct investment: an imperfect capital markets approach. *Q. J. Econ.*, 106, 4, 1191–1217, 1991, https://doi.org/ 10.2307/2937961.
21. Golub, K. and Yeres, Defining and Measuring Green FDI: An Exploratory Review of Existing Work and Evidence. *OECD Working Papers on*

International Investment, 2011/02, OECD Publishing, Paris, 2011, http://dx.doi.org/10.1787/ 5kg58j1cvcvk-en.
22. Guest editorial, Renewable energy policies in the European Union. *Energy Policy*, 34, 251–255, 2006, doi: 10.1016/j.enpol.2004.08.032.
23. Hair Jr., J.F., Hult, G.T.M., Ringle, C.M., Sarstedt, M., *A primer on partial least squares structural equation modeling (PLS-SEM)*, Sage Publications, USA, 2021.
24. Hanni, M.S., van Giffen, T., Kramer, R.M., Krüger, R., Mirza, H., Foreign direct investment in renewable energy: Trends drivers and determinants. *Transnational Corporations*, 20, 2, 29–65, 2011, doi: 10.18356/673b9e6f-en.
25. Henseler, J., Ringle, C.M., Sinkovics, R.R., The use of partial least squares path modeling in international marketing, in: *New challenges to international marketing*, vol. 20, pp. 277–319, Emerald Group Publishing Limited, USA, 2009.
26. Keeley, A.R., Investors' Perspective on Location Determinants of Foreign Direct Investment in Renewable Energy, Kyoto University, Japan, 2018.
27. Khan, H., Khan, I., Kim Oanh, L.T., Lin, Z., The Dynamic Interrelationship of Environmental Factors and Foreign Direct Investment: Dynamic Panel Data Analysis and New Evidence from the Globe. *Math. Probl. Eng.*, 2020, https://doi.org/10.1155/2020/2812489.
28. Kilicarslan, Z., The Relationship between Foreign Direct Investment and Renewable Energy Production: Evidence from Brazil, Russia, India, China, South Africa and Turkey. *Int. J. Energy Econ. Policy*, 9, 4, 291–297, 2019, Retrieved from https://www.econjournals.com/index.php/ijeep/article/view/7879.
29. Kim, K., Park, H., Kim, H., Real options analysis for renewable energy investment decisions in developing countries. *Renew. Sustain. Energy Rev.*, 75, 918–926, 2017, https://doi.org/10.1016/j.rser. 2016.11.073.
30. Knutsson, P. and Flores, P.I., Trends, investor types and drivers of renewable energy FDI. OECD Working Papers on International Investment, 2022, https://dx.doi.org/10.1787/4390289d-en.
31. Likert, R., A Technique for the Measurement of Attitudes. *Arch. Psychol.*, 140, 5–55, 1932.
32. Mahesh, A. and Shoba Jasmin, K.S., Role of renewable energy investment in India: an alternative to CO_2 mitigation. *Renew. Sustain. Energy Rev.*, 26, 414–424, 2013, https://doi.org/10.1016/j.rser. 2013.05.069.
33. McKinnon, R.I., *Money and Capital in Economic Development*, Brookings Institution, Washington, DC, 1973.
34. Mohsin, M., Ullah, H., Iqbal, N., Iqbal, W., Taghizadeh-Hesary, F., How External Debt Led to Economic Growth in South Asia: A Policy Perspective Analysis from Quantile Regression. *Econ. Anal. Policy*, 72, 423–437, 2021, doi: 10.1016/J. EAP.2021.09.012.
35. Peñalver, B.A.J., Bernal Conesa, J.A., De Nieves Nieto, C., Analysis of corporate social responsibility in Spanish agribusiness and its influence on

innovation and performance. *Corp. Soc. Responsib. Environ. Manag.*, 25, 2, 182–193, 2017, https://doi.org/10.1002/csr.1448.
36. Pradhan, R.P., Mak, B.A., Neville, R.N., Insurance Development and the Finance-Growth Nexus: Evidence from 34 OECD Countries. *J. Multinatl. Financ. Manag.*, 31, 1–22, 2015.
37. Raaij, E.M.V. and Schepers, J.J.L., The acceptance and use of a virtual learning environment in China. *Comput. Educ.*, 50, 3, 838–852, 2008.
38. Raithel, S., Sarstedt, M., Scharf, S., Schwaiger, M., On the value relevance of customer satisfaction. Multiple drivers and multiple markets. *J. Acad. Mark. Sci.*, 40, 4, 509–525, 2012.
39. Sasana, H. and Ghozali, I., The Impact of Fossil and Renewable Energy Consumption on the Economic Growth in Brazil, Russia, India, China and South Africa. *Int. J. Energy Econ. Policy*, 7, 3, 194–200, 2017.
40. Shmueli, G. and Koppius, O.R., Predictive analytics in information systems research. *MIS Q.*, 35, 3, 553–572, 2011.
41. UNCTAD, The least developed countries report 2017: Transformational energy access, United Nations, Geneva, 2017.
42. Vaccarini, K., Spigarelli, F., Tavoletti, E., Lattemann, C., Chinese FDI and psychic distance perceptions on regulations in the German renewable energy sector, in: *Cultural Distance in International Ventures*, pp. 103–134, Palgrave Macmillan, USA, 2017, https://doi.org/ 10.1007/978-3-319-62193-7_5.
43. Wall, R., Grafakos, S., Gianoli, A., Stavropoulos, S., Which Policy Instruments Attract Foreign Direct Investments in Renewable Energy? *Clim. Policy*, 19, 59–72, 2019, doi: 10.1080/14693062.2018.1467826.
44. Wasko, M.M. and Faraj, S., Why Should I Share? Examining Social Capital and Knowledge Contribution in Electronic Networks of Practice. *MIS Q.*, 29, 1, 35–57, 2005.
45. Zhao, C. and Du, J., Causality between FDI and economic growth in China. *Chin. Econ.*, 40, 6, 68–82, 2007.

12

AI and Blockchain in Healthcare: A Systematic Literature Review through Network Analysis

Payal Bassi[1]*, Cheenu Goel[1] and Pankaj Kathuria[2]

[1]*Chitkara Business School, Chitkara University, Rajpura, Punjab, India*
[2]*University School of Business, Chandigarh University, Punjab, India*

Abstract

Artificial intelligence (AI) and blockchain continuously spur innovation in all sectors of the economy and have emerged as a much-required practice of the business world. The healthcare sector attained a dynamic transformation with the appropriate usage of AI and blockchain in their daily operations. Advancements like AI and technology related to blockchain in healthcare have enabled practitioners to detect and diagnose medical conditions at a much earlier stage. It is undeniable that the assimilation of the internet and technology has reshaped the healthcare sector efficiently and in an organized way. Thus, it has piqued the interest of researchers, academicians, and practitioners in this enticeful business domain. In this chapter, the relevant papers published in the Scopus database in the last decade and then further inclusion and exclusion criteria were applied along with the selected keywords to fetch the accurate sample chosen for the study. The data was reviewed and projected with the help of network diagrams for providing details into the keyword co-occurrence, most influential journals contributing to the chosen area undertaken in the present study, and bibliographic coupling related to authors and countries could be examined. Further, the local and global impact of journals and sources, conceptual structure, and countries of corresponding authors were analyzed.

Keywords: Artificial intelligence, blockchain, artificial applications, healthcare, electronic healthcare records, systematic literature review

**Corresponding author*: payalbassi@gmail.com

Renuka Sharma, Kiran Mehta, Vishal Vyas and Vinod Kumar Shukla (eds.) Decentralized Finance and Blockchain: A Game Changing Duo, (271–294) © 2025 Scrivener Publishing LLC

12.1 Introduction

The healthcare industry has grown multifold and is allowing patients and medical representatives all across the world to collaborate, analyze, and diagnose the medical situation of the patient. This is possible with the assimilation of technology in building-secured knowledge repositories. This is an era where every business irrespective of its size is adopting digitalization of all its tasks not only to record the transactions forever, but also to frame structured systems where the data could be recorded systematically and can be assessed at any point in time. Despite several developments taking place in the digital world, the assimilation of artificial intelligence (AI) and blockchain has revolutionized the healthcare industry and its convergence has added value to every business. Technology has extended a handholding for medical experts who can treat infectious diseases and save lives of patients. Also, AI is enabling medical representatives to detect problems at a nascent phase and give accurate results (Shinde *et al.*, 2022) [1].

Artificial intelligence has reshaped the way the healthcare industry used to work and has reduced the time and cost involved in the treatment. It can generate accurate results and can even diagnose the disease and give programmed enabled solutions, which require human intelligence. Artificial intelligence algorithms are assisting practitioners from the medical industry to diagnose and analyze the medical images retrieved from X-rays, MRIs, CT scans, Fibro scans, etc. accurately and in much less time. Artificial intelligence further enables practitioners to examine drug details and their potential benefits and side effects. It can also determine treatment responses, schedule appointments, disperse timely aid to patients in remote areas, and safeguard sensitive medical information of patients.

Blockchain has emerged as a disruptive technology and has led to an outbreak in a traditional business practice where third-party verification was required, as blockchain procures the details of each transaction made online. Further, any tampering of data cannot be done as an alarming signal will be sent to all members engaged in the contract, and any changes to be made are subject to every party's consent (Smit *et al.*, 2016 [2]; Abboushi, 2017 [3]; Extance, 2015 [4]; and Nowinski and Kozma, 2017 [5]). Blockchain is digital and decentralized. It is a distributed ledger that stores the record of each exchange at every step, thus ensuring digital security (Treiblmaier, H., 2018) [6]. Blockchain ensures transparency and immutability in blocks (Greenspan, 2015a [7]; Christidis and Devetsikiotis, 2016 [8]). Blockchain maintains digital security and the privacy of the patients' health, thus fostering interoperability. The amalgamation of AI and blockchain has the potential to change the way the healthcare industry was operating till date as it provides medical assistance to each individual, even those residing in remote locations. It also enables medical practitioners to collaborate and devise effective treatments, keep patients informed on who is assessing their digital records and for what purpose.

12.2 Review of Literature

Technological upgradation has the primary motive of easing tasks of human beings and innovations in the last decade and ensures reduced time and complexity, ensuring smooth conduction of events. One such technological disruption is AI, which has the potential to automate the tasks, requiring minimum human intelligence (Anantrasirichai *et al.*, 2021) [9]. It has fostered security, trust, the ability to collect real time data, forecast trends and shifts toward the automation of numerous tasks (Aruna S., 2023) [10]. Artificial intelligence is the key driving force of industries in the wave of industry 4.0 and has changed the regular and older process of work (Goodell *et al.*, 2021 [11]; Lim, 2020 [12]; Zhang *et al.*, 2021 [13]).

Technology related to blockchain has remarkably enhanced services offered by telehealth and telemedicine. It has further boosted the industry by offering transparent, traceable, decentralized, tamper-proof, trustworthy, dependable, and secure healthcare services (Ahmad *et al.*, 2021 [14]). Potential difficulties and challenges were gauged in the field of teleconsultation, remote health services, and digital healthcare with the usage of blockchain technology (Hussien *et al.*, 2021) [15]. Blockchain facilitates healthcare workers to properly track medical testing kits and record the details of doctors along with their qualifications and areas of expertise when treating patients in remote areas. The healthcare sector highly benefits in the usage of blockchain technology as the data can be secured and managed effectively by assuring privacy (Farouk *et al.*, 2020) [16].

The encryption in blockchain technology seems to be transparent, safe, and impervious to hackers as it is decentralized and thus leads to a reduction in intermediary fees, (Narikimilli *et al.*, 2020) [17]. The study mentions an extensive analysis of the prevalent concerns faced by the healthcare industry today and proposes a few cutting-edge applications of blockchain technology in the field of healthcare, including the federated blockchain, smart contract-based health care intelligent claim processing and precertification, a body-worn fitness device integration, and health surveillance. The paper investigated the ability of blockchain technology to enhance the data safety, confidentiality, and accessibility of medical repository.

The role of distributed ledger technology is inspected in transforming the medical management industry and topics related to safety, accessibility, and clinical data management are addressed (Metler, M., 2016) [18]. The paper examines the impact of technology on data sharing and maintaining e-health records. The development of efficacious electronic healthcare record authorization techniques required to provide assured client recognition, collaboration, and consent by the introduction of blockchain technology and smart contracts (Sookhak *et al.*, 2020) [19]. Adhering to the stringent regulatory obligations of the Health Insurance Portability and Accountability Act of 1996, blockchain applications in the medical business need strong safety and confidentiality mechanisms for high-level verification, congruence, and electronic health record (Hussien *et al.*, 2019) [20].

The prominent features of blockchain technology along with the origin/source of data, transparency, validation of various transactions taking place in several blocks, immutability and validation of data by all the stakeholders along with confidential and accurate data management of patient, track, and progress of the disease, record keeping and application of data analytics and predicting the speed of progress are highly favorable in the clinical trials in the healthcare industry, (Omar *et al.*, 2021) [21]. Blockchain is the latest disruption that eliminates intermediate concerns by using a concurrence method and the concept of digitally decentralized ledger technologies. Blockchain technology can allow various healthcare stakeholders to exchange ingress to the data repositories without breaching the safety and information safeguarding by enabling to track the origin of the data and any modifications made (Singh Y. *et al.*, 2023) [22].

The application of machine learning algorithms and big data constructs was examined in the patient care sector and the innovation of digital ledger was analyzed to ensure protection and confidentiality of the entire patient data among different doctors/medical specialists engaged in the process of treatment (Manogaran G. and Lopez, D., 2017) [23]. Several research are focusing on advocating the assimilation of the distributed database and its positive impact on the treatment of the patients, creating e-healthcare records of all patients and thus facilitating and easing communication among healthcare representatives by ensuring privacy and keeping the patient informed about the information being shared. The efficiency and effectiveness of blockchain technology were highlighted in maintaining and safeguarding the data in the healthcare industry. It assures the safety and security of data while exchanging medical data (Shi, 2020 [24]; Yue *et al.*, 2016 [25]; and Kuo *et al.*, 2017 [26]). In the paper "Towards secure and privacy-preserving data sharing in e-health systems via consortium blockchain," the technology was used to ensure secrecy and privacy of data in digital repositories (Zhang A. and Lin X., 2018) [27].

12.3 Research Methodology

Healthcare is a vast sector, and numerous publications related to different aspects of healthcare have already taken place in a large number of knowledge repositories. To reach to the accurate sample of the selected papers that would suffice the research questions; papers published at the final publication stage from the Scopus database were considered. The papers were retrieved, keeping in consideration the final string as mentioned in Table 12.1. The sample was narrowed down in the light of eligibility criteria in the form of PRISMA model as shown in Figure 12.1. Thus, the final sample of 249 papers were finalized and considered for the study.

The string was finalized after analyzing various keywords appropriate for the literature search, but the researchers were not able to fetch appropriate results. After applying several keywords, the final string was finalized as mentioned in Table 12.1.

Table 12.1 The final string.

Database	Final string
Scopus	"Artificial Intelligence" and "blockchain" and "Healthcare"

Source: Author's compilation.

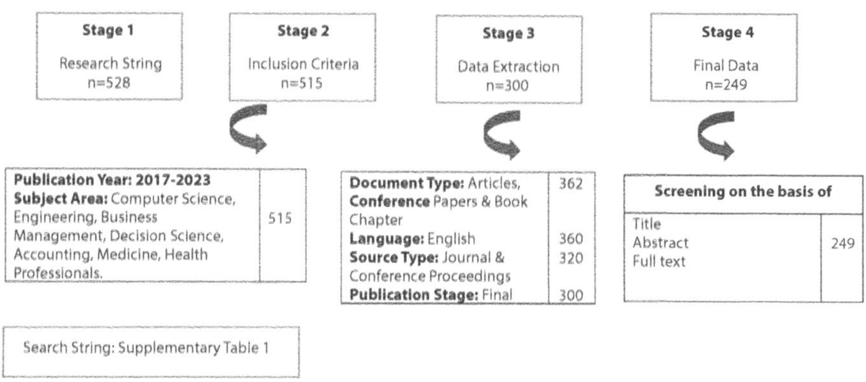

Figure 12.1 PRISMA model. Source: Author's compilation.

12.4 Data and Network Analysis

The analysis was done with the help of a bibliometric analysis using R, and the network analysis was performed in the help of VOSviewer.

12.4.1 Depictive Analysis

12.4.1.1 Substantive Information

Table 12.2 demonstrates the meaningful information related to the sample extracted from the Scopus database. It is evident that during the time span of 2018 until 2023, a total of 300 documents from 232 sources got published about the selected keywords. Out of a total of 1117 authors, 19 authors have authored individual research documents while the rest has collaborated among other authors of the related domain. The sample comprises 30.67% of international co-authorship and a contribution of co-authorship per document is 4.06.

Table 12.2 A detailed description of a retrieved sample.

Illustration	**Results**
Relevant information of data	
Time Period	2018:2023
Sources (Articles, Journals, Books, etc.)	232
Research Documents	300
Annual Growth Rate %	57.05
Average Age of document	2.34
Citations per doc (Average)	14.75
References	14230
Document contents	
Keywords Plus (ID)	1586
Author's Keywords (DE)	807

(*Continued*)

Table 12.2 A detailed description of a retrieved sample. (*Continued*)

Illustration	Results
Authors	
Authors	1117
Authors of single-authored docs	19
Authors collaboration	
Single-authored docs	19
Co-Authors per Doc	4.06
International co-authorships %	30.67

Source: Author's compilation.

12.4.1.2 *Year-Wise Publication*

Figure 12.2 represents the data related to the number of documents published during the last decade, i.e. 2012–2023. The analysis revealed that there was no document related to the string that got published during years 2012–2016. Thus, the graph mentions the detail from 2017 onwards; it is further synthesized that in the year 2022, there were maximum publications in the field of AI and blockchain in healthcare (n=169).

Figure 12.2 Publications by year. Source: Author's compilation.

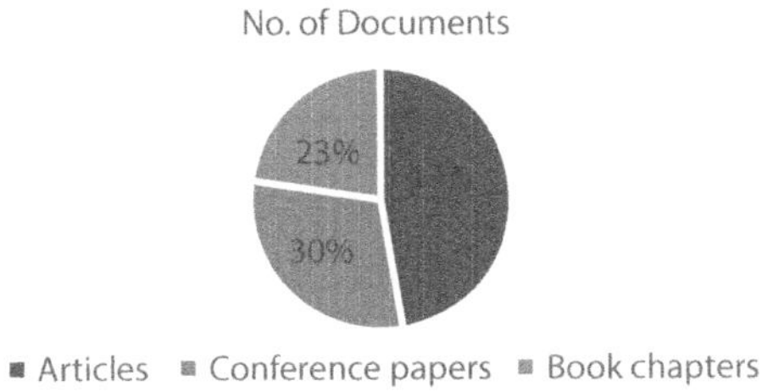

Figure 12.3 Publications by type. Source: Author's compilation.

12.4.1.3 Publications by Type

Figure 12.3 mentions publication based on their type. The data was retrieved by applying the inclusion and exclusion criteria of articles, conference papers, and book chapters. It can be inferred from the data that the sample comprises 142 articles, 90 conference papers, and 68 book chapters.

12.4.1.4 Publications by Source

Figure 12.4 mentions the information of research articles published in various sources during the recent five years. The IEEE Access, IEEE Internet of Things Journal, ACM International Conference Proceeding Series,

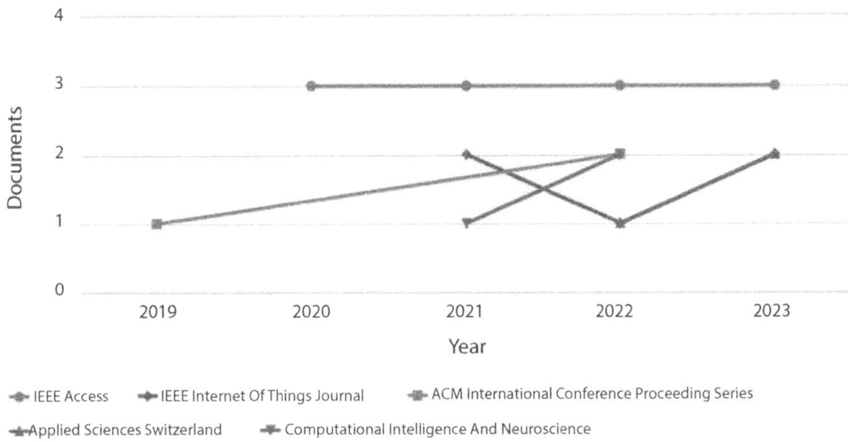

Figure 12.4 Publications by source. Source: Author's compilation.

Applied Sciences and Computational Intelligence, and Neuroscience are among the top sources considering research related to AI and blockchain in Healthcare. The IEEE Access is consistent with the number of publications since 2020. Table 12.3 mentions the contribution of influential sources related to the publication of articles in the recent decade along with the total citation score and h-index of those sources. The H-index has been calculated from SCImago Journal & Country Rank (SJCR), and the citation score of journals is derived from the data collected from the database of Scopus.

Table 12.3 The contribution of 10 most influential sources.

Sources	Articles	Total citation	h-index
IEEE Access	12	1022	8
IEEE Internet of Things Journal	6	221	5
Computational Intelligence and Neuroscience	5	74	3
IEEE Journal of Biomedical and Health Informatics	3	47	3
International Conference on Advanced Communication Technology, Icact	3	120	3
Blockchain Applications for Healthcare Informatics: Beyond 5G	3	15	2
Computers, Materials and Continua	3	21	2
Conference Proceedings - IEEE Southeastcon	3	10	2
Electronics (Switzerland)	3	38	2
Handbook of Research on Blockchain Technology	3	21	2

Source: Author's compilation.

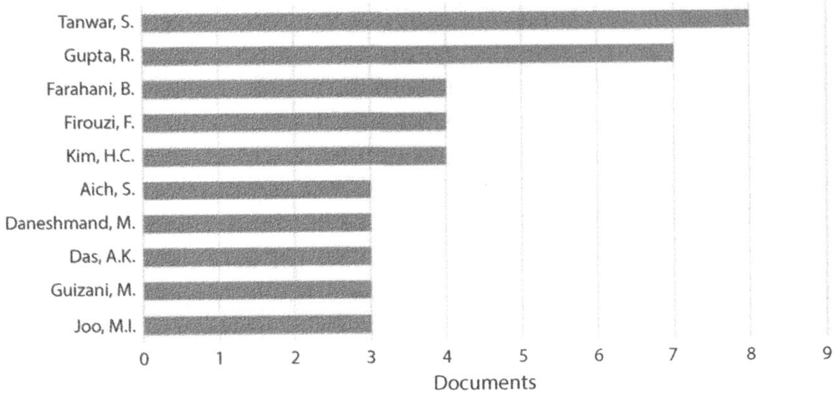

Figure 12.5 Publications by authors. Source: Author's compilation.

12.4.2 Bibliometric Analysis

12.4.2.1 Publications Based on Documents by Author

Figure 12.5 mentions the number of documents published by various authors in the said domain; the data is extracted post-comparison of document counts for up to 15 authors. Tanwar, S. has published maximum (n = 8) articles in the Scopus database; followed by Gupta, R., who has published second highest number of articles (n = 7); while Joo, M. I. has published only three articles until the 25th September 2023.

12.4.2.2 Authors' Productivity Overtime

Tanwar S. tops the list and published one article in 2020 and received six total citations in the same year of publication. In year 2021, three Scopus indexed articles got registered to his credit with the total annual citation of 30.5, which was the maximum number of citations received for his published work while the total citation for his three research documents decreed up to 11 citations. The darker shade of the dots represents the maximum number of articles and citations received during a particular year of the related author, as shown in Figure 12.6.

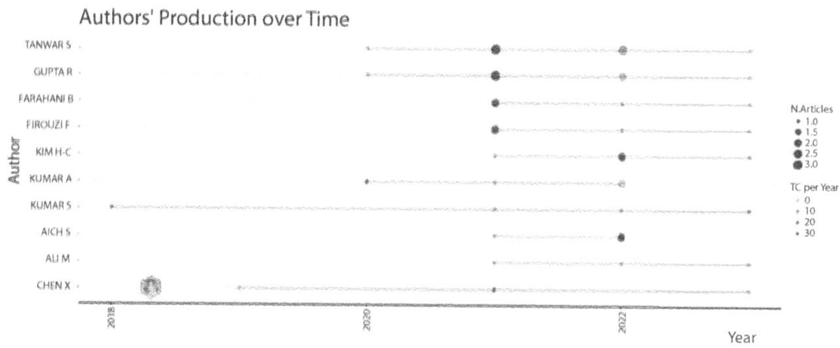

Figure 12.6 Publications of authors over time. Source: Author's compilation.

12.4.2.3 Local Impact of Authors

Table 12.4 mentions the data related to the authors' impact in the selected domain of keywords for the present study. Tanwar S. has the maximum local impact since he published his first research work (2020) on AI and blockchain in healthcare. His h_index is the highest (n=6) among others in the list of top 10 authors with local impact. He had a total citation of 185 for his eight documents, which were published in the database of Scopus. Gupta R. emerged second place with a total citation of 165 for his seven documents published from 2020 with an h_index of 5.

Table 12.4 Authors' local impact.

Author	h_index	g_index	m_index	TC	NP	PY_start
Tanwar S.	6	8	1.2	185	8	2020
Gupta R.	5	7	1	165	7	2020
Farahani B.	4	4	1	149	4	2021
Firouzi F.	4	4	1	149	4	2021
Kim H-C.	4	4	1	136	4	2021
Kumar S.	4	4	0.571	172	4	2018
Aich S.	3	3	0.75	120	3	2021
Ali M.	3	3	0.75	55	3	2021
Daneshmand M.	3	3	0.75	80	3	2021
Guizani M.	3	3	0.6	748	3	2020

Source: Author's compilation.

12.4.2.4 Local Impact of Sources

The top 10 journals/sources that published works related to AI and blockchain in healthcare are reflected in Table 12.5. It further demonstrates the total number of citations and publications of each author along with their h-index, g-index, and m-index. The IEEE Access research document earned maximum citations for its 12 publications that got published in the recent decade. The h_index of IEEE Access reached up to 8 until the time data was extracted from the Scopus database; followed by the IEEE Internet of Things Journal (h-index of 5), and the IEEE Journal of Biomedical and Health Informatics (h-index of 3).

Table 12.5 Source local impact.

Source	h_index	g_index	m_index	TC	NP	PY_start
IEEE Access	8	12	1.6	1022	12	2020
IEEE Internet of Things Journal	5	5	1.25	221	5	2021
Computational Intelligence and Neuroscience	3	3	0.75	74	3	2021
IEEE Journal of Biomedical and Health Informatics	3	3	1	47	3	2022
International Conference on Advanced Communication Technology, Icact	3	3	0.75	120	3	2021
Blockchain Applications for Healthcare Informatics: Beyond 5G	2	3	0.667	15	6	2022
Computers, Materials and Continua	2	3	0.5	21	3	2021
Conference Proceedings - IEEE Southeastcon	2	2	0.333	10	2	2019
Electronics (Switzerland)	2	3	0.4	38	3	2020
Handbook of Research on Blockchain Technology	2	2	0.4	21	2	2020

Source: Author's compilation.

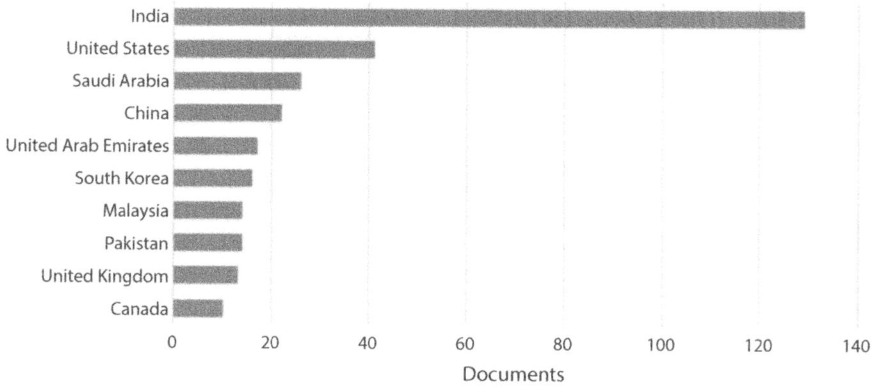

Figure 12.7 Publications based on countries. Source: Author's compilation.

12.4.3 Scientific Production of Countries

12.4.3.1 Publication Based on Countries

Figure 12.7 reveals the data of publications based on the authors' country of origins and the country where these research has taken place. Authors from India majorly contribute in the present research area; followed by authors from United States and Saudi Arabia.

12.4.3.2 Country-Wise Scientific Production of Research Documents

Figure 12.8 presents the visualization of a country's scientific production for the application of AI and blockchain in healthcare. India produced the

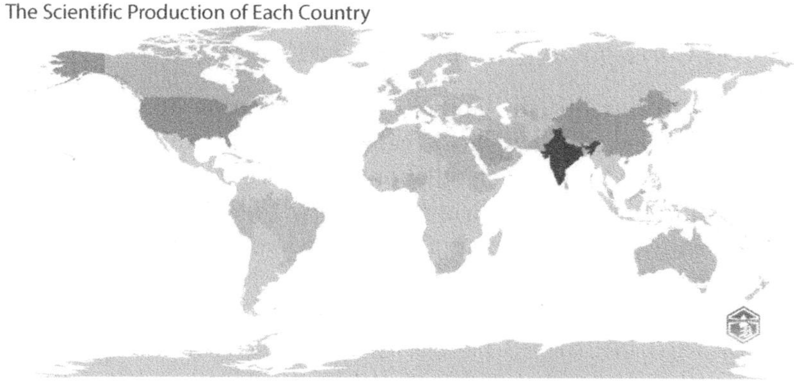

Figure 12.8 The scientific production of each country. Source: Author's compilation.

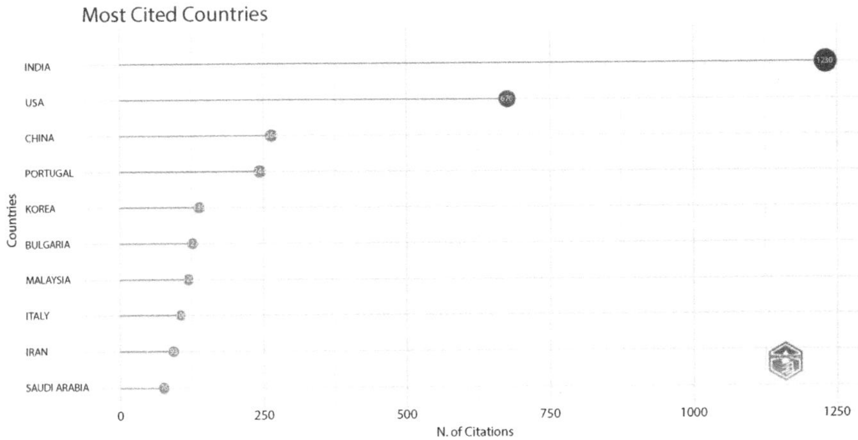

Figure 12.9 Most cited countries. Source: Author's compilation.

largest number of documents in this area with n=406; followed by USA with 134 documents and China with 95 research documents. The darker shade represents the maximum number of research documents in the selected domain. Countries like Austria, Denmark, Euthopia, New Zealand, and Switzerland are at a very nascent stage and have just got just one research document published in the domain of AI and blockchain in the field of healthcare during the recent decade in the database of Scopus.

The top 10 most cited countries in the field of AI and blockchain in healthcare with respect to their publications can be seen in Figure 12.9. India has received maximum citations (n=1230) for its 406 research documents; followed by USA, which received 676 research publications for 134 documents, and China with 264 citations for 95 research documents.

12.4.3.3 Corresponding Author's Countries

Figure 12.10 describes the author-wise distribution of corresponding authors in the field of AI and blockchain in healthcare. Indian corresponding authors topped this list of collaborations with foreign authors in single and multiple country publications (MCPs); followed by China and the USA. Germany and Morocco are the countries with a single country publication, while Hong Kong and Iran have MCPs.

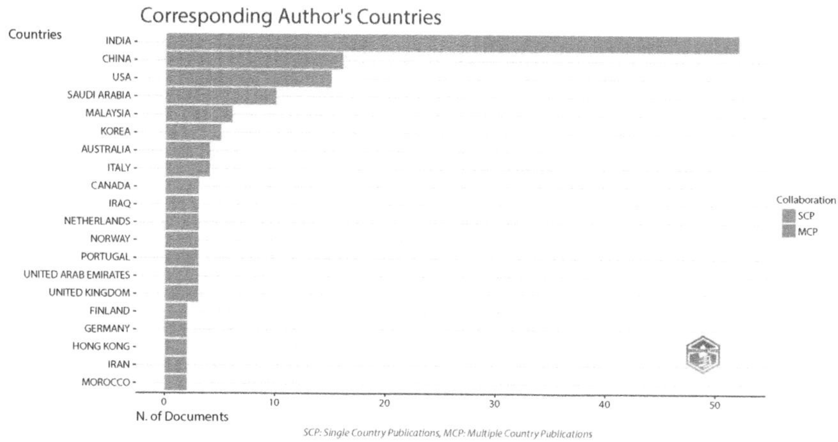

Figure 12.10 The countries of corresponding authors. Source: Author's compilations.

12.4.3.4 Top 10 Most Contributing Organizations

The list of the top 10 contributing organizations relevant to the selected keywords is retrieved from the database generated from Scopus and presented in Table 12.6. Nirma University from India has produced 19 articles,

Table 12.6 Analysis of top contributing organizations.

Affiliation	Country	Articles
Nirma University	India	19
Huazhong University of Science and Technology	China	16
Inje University	South Korea	13
University of Johannesburg	South Africa	10
University of Mons	Belgium	8
Chusj—Centro Hospitalar E Universitário De São João	Portugal	7
Maastricht University	Netherlands	7
Qilu University of Technology	China	7
Galgotias University	India	6
Johns Hopkins University At Eastern	America	6

Source: Author's compilation.

followed by Huazhong University of Science and Technology from China and Inje University from South Korea with a research contribution of 16 and 13 research articles, respectively.

12.4.3.5 Keyword Analysis

Figure 12.11 mentions the visualization of the top 50 keyword categories in conceptual structure maps using a factorial analysis through the multidimensional scaling (MDS) method, thus representing keywords in five clusters. The first cluster comprises 23 keywords, such as blockchain, artificial intelligence, healthcare, digital storage, diagnosis, network system, 5g mobile communication systems, hospital data processing, and other related keywords. The second cluster has 17 keywords, thus mentioning the related search in machine learning, deep learning, edge computing, medical computing, and learning algorithms. The third cluster depicts keywords related to humans and data privacy; followed by three keywords in each of the fourth and fifth clusters. Figure 12.12 represents the dendrogram of factorial analysis, and the height of each cluster reflects the relationship between various keywords hierarchically and their grouping in the current scenario.

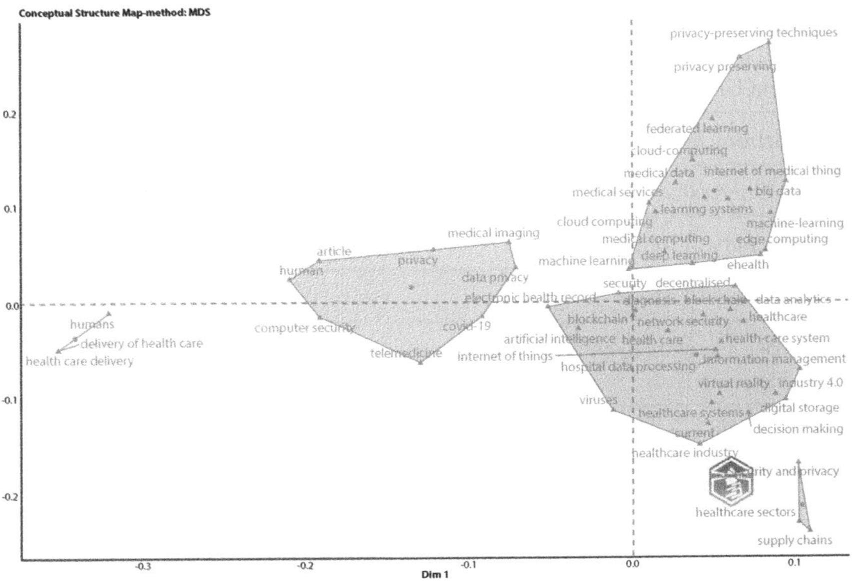

Figure 12.11 A conceptual structure map through the MDS. Source: Author's compilation.

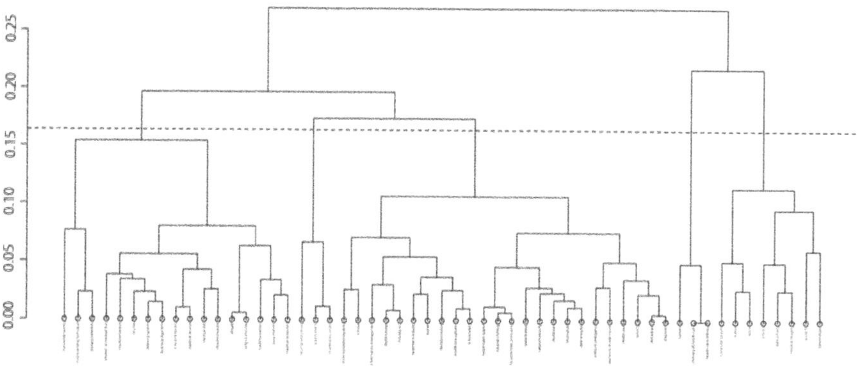

Figure 12.12 The dendrogram of factorial analysis. Source: Author's compilation.

12.4.3.6 Network Analysis

12.4.3.6.1 Co-Occurrence of Author Keywords

Figure 12.13 demonstrates the co-occurrence of author keywords for the 249 papers considered for the present chapter. The network is generated with the help of co-occurrence and author keywords in a full counting method. There is a minimum of 5 occurrences per keyword. As a result, 33 keywords were selected, where blockchain emerged as the most occurring keyword with a total link strength of 305, and e-health emerged five times with a total link strength of 23.

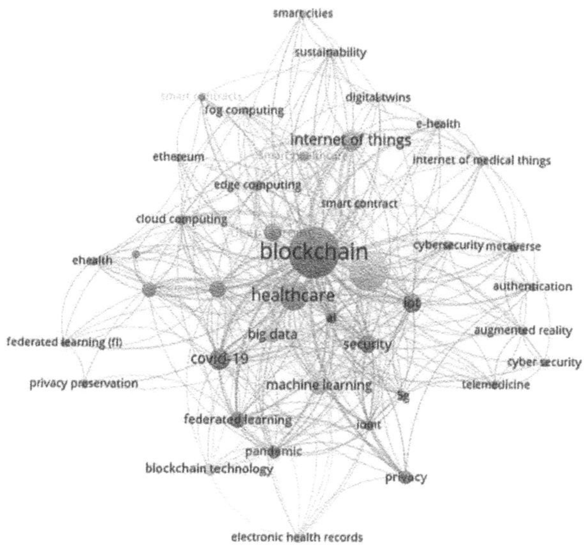

Figure 12.13 Co-occurrence of author keywords. Source: Author's compilation.

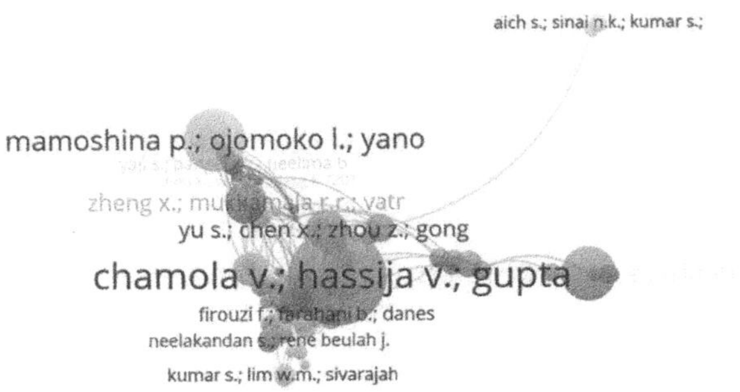

Figure 12.14 Bibliographic coupling of documents Source: Author's compilation.

12.4.3.7 Bibliographic Coupling of Documents

The network visualization of bibliographic coupling with documents on a full counting method is a minimum of two documents as shown in Figure 12.14. The largest connected items consist of 74 items, while 131 items in the sample were disconnected. The documents by Mamoshinna P., Ozomoko I., Yanovich Y., and Ostrovski were the most cited documents (n = 291) with total link strength of 13; followed by Kumar A., Krishnamurthi R., Nayyar A., and Sharma K. with 134 citations and total link strength of 12; and Zheng X., Mukkamala R.R., Vatrapu R., Ordieres-Mere with 129 citations and total link strength of 17 emerged as the three top most cited documents.

12.4.3.8 Bibliographic Coupling of Authors

Figure 12.15 mentions different authors who have collaborated in the domain of AI and blockchain concerning the healthcare sector. Out of 247 authors, 159 met the minimum threshold. The network was derived with six items, three clusters, eight links, and total link strength of 18, the largest set of 92 connected items. These 92 items were derived from the network diagram with 13 clusters, 245 links, and a total link strength of 310.

12.4.3.9 Bibliographic Coupling of Countries

The network diagram for the bibliographic coupling of countries with a fractional counting method is obtained in Figure 12.16. The network was restricted to a minimum of five documents per country, thus resulting in 14 countries. The threshold contains 66 countries with 15 items clustered in four clusters. It further represents 14 items in four clusters with 85 links and a total link strength of 5,784. India emerged as the country with maximum citations of 1520 for 114 documents: followed by the United States with 725 citations and a total link strength of 1653 for 32 documents. The United Kingdom comes in next with 493 citations for nine documents and a total link strength of 878.

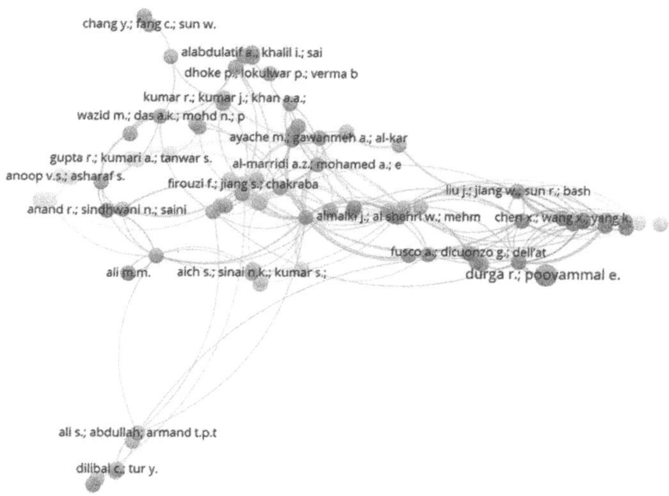

Figure 12.15 Bibliographic coupling of authors. Source: Author's compilation.

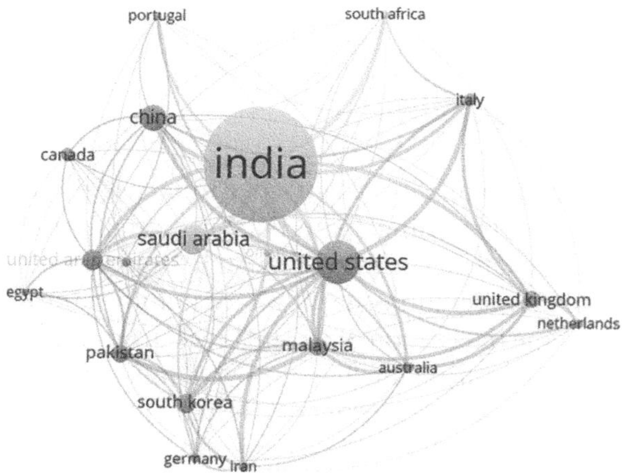

Figure 12.16 Bibliographic coupling of countries. Source: Author's compilation.

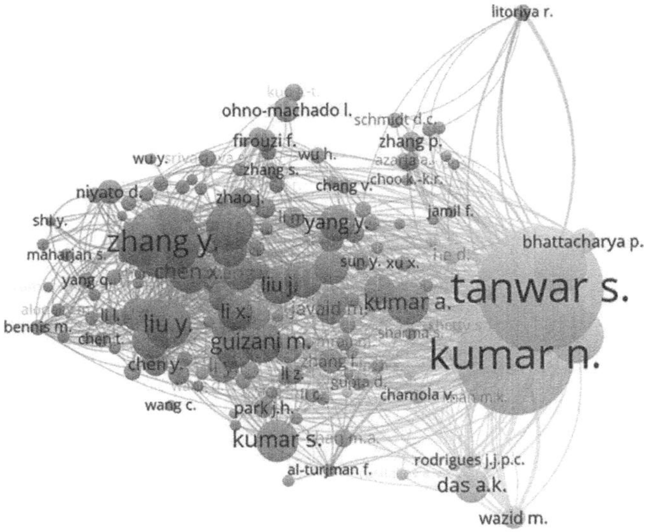

Figure 12.17 Co-citation with cited authors. Source: Author's compilation.

12.4.3.10 Co-Citation with Cited Authors

Figure 12.17 reflects the information of co-citation with cited authors whose documents have been published in the Scopus database. Research authored by Tanwar S. is the most cited work (n = 184) with a total link strength of 7,727; followed by Kumar N. whose work is the second most cited for the period considered with 11 citations and a total ink strength of 7,101, and Gupta R. is the third most cited author with 86 citations and a total link strength of 4,073.

12.5 Conclusion

Artificial intelligence and Blockchain hold immense promise in revolutionizing healthcare, providing more personalized, secure, and efficient services. However, challenges such as regulatory frameworks, standardization, and ethical considerations need to be carefully addressed for widespread adoption. The integration of AI and blockchain can further enhance healthcare systems. Artificial intelligence algorithms can operate on health data stored in a blockchain, ensuring privacy and security. Blockchain can provide a transparent and traceable record of AI model training and validation, ensuring trustworthiness. In the present study, IEEE Access, IEEE Internet of Things Journal, ACM International Conference Proceeding

Series, Applied Sciences and Computational Intelligence and Neuroscience are among the top sources considering research related to AI and blockchain in healthcare. It is evident that the documents by Mamoshinna P., Ozomoko I., Yanovich Y., and Ostrovski were the most cited documents; followed by Kumar A., Krishnamurthi R., Nayyar A., Sharma K., and Zheng X. Documents from Mukkamala R.R., Vatrapu R., and Ordieres–Mere have emerged as the top three most cited papers. Research authored by Tanwar S. is the most cited work; followed by Kumar N. and Gupta R. Further, India emerged as the country with maximum citation, followed by the United States and the United Kingdom. Blockchain is one of the most effective technological disruptions that have spurred innovation and freedom to share data among medical practitioners. The healthcare sector highly benefits from better information security management using blockchain technology, which would allow healthcare data to be shared and analyzed while maintaining its confidentiality and privacy. The present chapter will contribute to the existing literature of knowledge and will also provide input for policymakers and medical practitioners who are analyzing the application of blockchain in the medical stream.

Review of research documents related to AI in blockchain has gained popularity in the recent past, and a lot of focus is being laid toward its application. The extensive literature was analyzed with the help of a bibliometric analysis, which enabled the further exploration of gaps that exist in published literature. Firstly, researchers must emphasize more on privacy preservation, medical imaging, and ethical considerations while generating health records, wearable devices, chronic diseases, and framing patient-centric remote monitoring. Further, authors must focus on MCPs so that the same benefits can be received with the adoption of AI and blockchain. This can enhance the confidentiality of patients and facilitate effective and generative AI applications in healthcare.

References

1. Shinde, R., Patil, S., Kotecha, K., Potdar, V., Selvachandran, G., Abraham, A., Securing AI-based healthcare systems using blockchain technology: A state-of-the-art systematic literature review and future research directions. *Computer Science > Cryptography and Security*, 2022, arXiv preprint, https://doi.org/10.48550/arXiv.2206.04793.
2. Smit, R., Patil, S., Kotecha, K., Potdar, V., Selvachandran, G., Abraham, A., Cigarettes, dollars and bitcoins: An essay on the ontology of money. *J. Institut. Econom.*, *12*, 2, 327–347, 2016, https://doi.org/10.1017/S1744137415000405.

3. Abboushi, S., Global virtual currency: A brief overview. *J. Appl. Bus. Econ., 19*, 6, 10–18, 2017, http://www.na-businesspress.com/JABE/AbboushiS_19_6_.pdf.
4. Extance, A., The future of cryptocurrencies: Bitcoin and beyond. *Nature, 526*, 7571, 21–23, 2015, https://www.nature.com/articles/526021a#citeas.
5. Nowiński, W. and Kozma, M., How can blockchain technology disrupt existing business models? *Entrep. Bus. Econ. Rev., 5*, 3, 173–188, 2017, https://doi.org/10.15678/EBER.2017.050309.
6. Treiblmaier, H., The impact of the blockchain on the supply chain: A theory-based research framework and a call for action. *Supply Chain Manag. Int. J., 23*, 6, 545–559, 2018, https://www.emerald.com/insight/content/doi/10.1108/scm-01-2018-0029/full/html.
7. Greenspan, G., Ending the Bitcoin vs. blockchain debate, 2015a, Retrieved from http://www.multichain.com/blog/2015/07/bitcoin-vs-blockchain-debate.
8. Christidis, K. and Devetsikiotis, M., Blockchains and Smart Contracts for the Internet of Things. *IEEE Access*, 4, 2292–2303, 2016, doi: 10.1109/ACCESS.2016.2566339.
9. Anantrasirichai, N. and Bull, D., Artificial intelligence in the creative industries: A review. *Artif. Intell. Rev.*, 55, 589–656, 2022, https://doi.org/10.1007/s10462-021-10039-7.
10. Aruna, S., Mohana Priya, S., Reshmeetha, K., Salai Sudhayini, E., Ajay Narayanan, A., Blockchain Integration with Artificial Intelligence and Internet of Things Technologies. *2023 7th International Conference on Intelligent Computing and Control Systems (ICICCS)*, pp. 688–694, 2023, https://www.semanticscholar.org/paper/Blockchain-Integration-with-Artificial-Intelligence-Aruna-Priya/e3e9573f99a65a11e1a0d788af10f60b98bac2ef.
11. Goodell, *et al.*, Artificial intelligence and machine learning in finance: Identifying foundations, themes, and research clusters from bibliometric analysis. *J. Behav. Exp. Finance*, 32, 2021, Article 100577, https://doi.org/10.1016/j.jbef.2021.100577.
12. Kuo, T.T., Kim, H.E., & Ohno-Machado, L., Blockchain distributed ledger technologies for biomedical and health care applications. *Journal of the American Medical Informatics Association (JAMIA)*, 24, 6, , 1211–1220, 2017.
13. Zhang, C., Chen, Y., Chen, H., Chong, D., Industry 4.0 and its Implementation: a Review. *Inf. Syst. Front.*, 26, 1773–1783, 2021, 10.1007/s10796-021-10153-5.
14. Ahmad, R.W., Salah, K., Jayaraman, R., Yaqoob, I., Ellahham, S., Omar, M., The role of blockchain technology in telehealth and telemedicine. *Int. J. Med. Inf.*, 148, 104399, 2021, doi: 10.1016/j.ijmedinf.2021.104399. Epub 2021 Jan 28. PMID: 33540131; PMCID: PMC7842132.
15. Hussien, H.M., Yasin, S.M., Udzir, N.I., Ninggal, M., Salman, S., Blockchain technology in the healthcare industry: Trends and opportunities. *J. Ind. Inf. Integr.*, 22, 2021, Article 100217, doi:10.1016/j.jii.2021.100217.

16. Farouk, A., Alahmadi, A., Ghose, S., Mashatan, A, Blockchain platform for industrial healthcare: Vision and future opportunities. *Comput. Commun.*, 154, 223–235, 2020. https://doi.org/10.1016/j.comcom.2020.02.058.
17. Narikimilli, N., Kumar, A., Antu, A.D., Xie, B., Blockchain Applications in Healthcare – A Review and Future Perspective, 2020, 10.1007/978-3-030-59638-5_14.
18. Mettler, M., Blockchain technology in healthcare: The revolution starts here. *2016 IEEE 18th International Conference on e-Health Networking, Applications and Services (Healthcom)*, Munich, Germany, pp. 1–3, 2016, doi: 10.1109/HealthCom.2016.7749510.
19. Sookhak, M., Jabbarpour, M., Safa, N., Yu, F., Blockchain and smart contract for access control in healthcare: A survey, issues and challenges, and open issues. *J. Network Comput. Appl.*, 178, 102950, 2020, 10.1016/j.jnca.2020.102950.
20. Hussien, H.M., Yasin, S.M., Udzir, S.N.I., Zaidan, A.A., Zaidan, B.B., A Systematic Review for Enabling of Develop a Blockchain technology in Healthcare Application: Taxonomy, Sustainability Analysis, Motivations, Challenges, Recommendations and Future Direction. *J. Med. Syst.*, 43, 10, 320, 2019, Doi: 10.1007/s10916-019-1445-8. PMID: 31522262.
21. Omar, I.A., Jayaraman, R., Salah, K., Yaqoob, I., Ellahham, S., Applications of Blockchain Technology in Clinical Trials: Review and Open Challenges. *Arabian J. Sci. Eng., 46*, 4, 3001–3015, 2021, https://doi.org/10.1007/s13369-020-04989-3.
22. Singh, Y., Jabbar, M.A., Kumar Shandilya, S., Vovk, O., Hnatiuk, Y., Exploring applications of blockchain in healthcare: road map and future directions. *Front. Public Health*, 11, 1229386, 2023, doi: 10.3389/fpubh.2023.1229386.
23. Manogaran, G. and Lopez, D., A survey of big data architectures and machine learning algorithms in healthcare. *Int. J. Biomed. Eng. Technol.*, 25, 182, 2017, 10.1504/IJBET.2017.087722.
24. Shi, S., He, D., Li, L., Kumar, N., Khan, M.K., Choo, K.R., Applications of blockchain in ensuring the security and privacy of electronic health record systems: A survey. *Comput. Secur.*, 97, 101966, 2020 Oct, doi: 10.1016/j.cose.2020.101966. Epub 2020 Jul 15. PMID: 32834254; PMCID: PMC7362828.
25. Yue, X., Wang, H., Jin, D., *et al.*, Healthcare Data Gateways: Found Healthcare Intelligence on Blockchain with Novel Privacy Risk Control. *J. Med. Syst.*, 40, 218, 2016, https://doi.org/10.1007/s10916-016-0574-6.
26. Kuo, T.T., Kim, H.E., Ohno-Machado, L., Blockchain distributed ledger technologies for biomedical and health care applications. *J. Am. Med. Inf. Assoc.*, 24, 6, 1211–1220, 2017, https://doi.org/10.1093/jamia/ocx068.
27. Zhang, A. and Lin, X., Towards Secure and Privacy-Preserving Data Sharing in e-Health Systems via Consortium Blockchain. *J. Med. Syst.*, 42, 140, 2018, https://doi.org/10.1007/s10916-018-0995-5.

Index

Printed and bound by CPI Group (UK) Ltd, Croydon, CR0 4YY

17/09/2026

14964261-0003